ANIMAL, VEGETAL, MARGINAL

GERMAN JEWISH CULTURES

Editorial Board:

Matthew Handelman, *Michigan State University*
Iris Idelson-Shein, *Ben-Gurion University of the Negev*
Samuel Spinner, *Johns Hopkins University*
Joshua Teplitsky, *University of Pennsylvania*
Kerry Wallach, *Gettysburg College*

Sponsored by the Leo Baeck Institute London

ANIMAL, VEGETAL, MARGINAL

THE **GERMAN LITERARY GROTESQUE** FROM **PANIZZA** TO **KAFKA**

JOELA JACOBS

INDIANA UNIVERSITY PRESS

This book is a publication of

Indiana University Press
Office of Scholarly Publishing
Herman B Wells Library 350
1320 East 10th Street
Bloomington, Indiana 47405 USA

iupress.org

© 2025 by Joela Jacobs

All rights reserved
No part of this book may be reproduced or utilized in any form or by any means, electronic or mechanical, including photocopying and recording, or by any information storage and retrieval system, without permission in writing from the publisher.
The paper used in this publication meets the minimum requirements of the American National Standard for Information Sciences—Permanence of Paper for Printed Library Materials, ANSI Z39.48-1992.

Manufactured in the United States of America

First Printing 2025

Library of Congress Cataloging-in-Publication Data

Names: Jacobs, Joela, author.
Title: Animal, vegetal, marginal : the German literary grotesque from Panizza to Kafka / Joela Jacobs.
Description: Bloomington, Indiana : Indiana University Press, 2025. | Includes bibliographical references and index.
Identifiers: LCCN 2024045271 (print) | LCCN 2024045272 (ebook) | ISBN 9780253071972 (hardback) | ISBN 9780253071989 (paperback) | ISBN 9780253072009 (ebook)
Subjects: LCSH: German literature—20th century—History and criticism. | Grotesque in literature. | Plants in literature. | Animals in literature. | Jews in literature. | LCGFT: Literary criticism.
Classification: LCC PT405 .J328 2025 (print) | LCC PT405 (ebook) | DDC 838/.9120915—dc23/eng/20241022
LC record available at https://lccn.loc.gov/2024045271
LC ebook record available at https://lccn.loc.gov/2024045272

CONTENTS

Acknowledgments vii

Introduction 1

SECTION 1: The Grotesque: A Censored Literary Genre and Its Authors

1. Characteristics of *die Groteske* 13
2. *Grotesken* in a Nexus of Censorship 19
3. A Literary Network of the Marginalized 23

SECTION 2: The Vegetal: Panizza, Ewers, and Turn-of-the-Century Censorship

4. The Crime in Tavistock Square 37
5. The Petition 66
6. Why Plants? 77

SECTION 3: The Animal: Panizza, Kafka, and the Modernist Crisis of the Self

7. From the Diary of a Dog 87
8. Investigations/Researches of a Dog 109
9. Why Dogs? 117

SECTION 4: The Human: Panizza, Friedlaender, and the Rise of Fascism

10. The Operated Jew 127
11. The Operated Goy 147
12. Why Humans? 168

Conclusion 172

Notes 177
Bibliography 225
Index 255

ACKNOWLEDGMENTS

This book has been a long time in the making. Based on research that began in 2011 under the guidance of Christopher J. Wild, Eric Santner, David E. Wellbery, and Mark Payne at the University of Chicago's Department of Germanic Studies, with support of the Franke Institute of the Humanities, many of its ideas have benefited from conversations, feedback, and other projects since. Some of these endeavors have revolved around the same primary texts or authors, and I am grateful for the ways in which the editors and reviewers of subsequent articles (referenced in my notes throughout the book) have expanded my thinking and writing about these materials. I have been able to pursue this work with the support of institutions like the University of Arizona, particularly its Department of German Studies in the College of Humanities as well as my other affiliated homes at the Arizona Institute for Resilience: Solutions for the Environment and Society, the Department of Gender and Women's Studies, the Arizona Center for Judaic Studies, and the Graduate Interdisciplinary Program on Social, Cultural, and Critical Theory. A shout-out to the many colleagues across campus who shared their experiences and advice; those who facilitated professional development opportunities, workshops, and learning communities; and the librarians and university staff members whose knowledge makes it all work. My particular gratitude goes to my departmental colleagues Chantelle Warner, Janice McGregor, David Gramling, Obenewaa Oduro-Opuni, and my head Barbara Kosta for their work toward a shared vision and their feminist friendship. Many undergraduate and graduate students have inspired me over the years, particularly my former PhD students Lydia Heiß, Sina Meißgeier, Thomas Benjamin Fuhr, and Christina Becher, now colleagues who make me proud.

Archives like the Monacensia in Munich; professional associations like the German Studies Association, Coalition of Women in German (now known as Coalition for Feminist German Studies), American Comparative Literature Association, Society for Literature, Science, and the Arts, Association for the Study of Literature and Environment; and cocreated scholarly communities like the UChicago Animal Studies Workshop, the Cultural and Literary Animal Studies Netzwerk, the 3G DFG-Netzwerk, the Literary and Cultural Plant Studies Network, and the Diversity, Decolonization, and the German Curriculum collective, especially its accountability and write-on-site groups, have given me much-needed space for productive encounters, drafty experimentation, and time with collaborative colleagues over the years. Among the latter, a particular thanks goes to my coconspirators, co-organizers, and ultimately coeditors of various projects, Isabel Kranz, Solvejg Nitzke, Agnes Malinowska, Nike Thurn, and Luisa Banki, and to Peter D. G. Brown and Jay Geller for invaluable advice on our shared subject matter. The most impactful community for this project was certainly my "book group," grown out of the lifeline that was the UChicago "dissertation writing group": Hannah Vandegrift Eldridge, Sunny Yudkoff, Matthew Handelman, Tatyana Gershkovich, and Peter Erickson in the early days. Your poignant and constructive advice has made this book what it is, your patient rereading and willingness to show up for one another have kept me going, and your example showed me that it could be done. In getting this project to the finish line, I am particularly grateful for the support of my editors at Indiana University Press, the editorial team of the "German Jewish Cultures" series, and my anonymous peer reviewers for their immense investment in this book. Their insightful feedback has strengthened the project at every turn, and any lingering mistakes are my own.

I am thankful for friendships kept up over years and miles with Maraike Bethmann, Marius Maximus, Annekathrin Bieling, Laura Schüller, Constance Sommerey, Barbara Laubach, and Lydia Chemali, and for forming new ones with colleagues like Nicole Coleman, Jamele Watkins, and Ina Linge. From being in the same classroom to voice messages across time zones, Tine Knopp has anchored my old roots and Katharine Mershon my new ones, as family. My parents, Gerd and Irene Zeller; my brother,

Benjamin, with Sumithra Zeller and their children, Taliah and Elijah; my sister, Tabea Fina, and her daughter, Sarah; my in-laws, William and the much-missed Audrey Jacobs; my sister-in-law, Amy, with Mike Kennedy and their kids, Michael, Ayla, and Sofia; and my extended family: your support and love has been sustaining and kept me grounded. My husband, Philip, and our furry companions, Tiffany, Max, Sammy, and Charlie—you have my heart. Thank you for giving some of your time with me to this book.

ANIMAL, VEGETAL, MARGINAL

Introduction

Masturbating plants, dogs undertaking research, Nazis converting to Judaism—these are just some of the scenarios of the provocative Germanophone genre of the modernist literary grotesque or *die Groteske* (*Grotesken* in the plural) at the center of this book. This censored and forgotten short prose form uses literary strategies such as exaggeration, defamiliarization, and ambiguity to elicit a reaction oscillating between horror and laughter for the purpose of social criticism. From the perspective of plants, animals, and marginalized human figures, *Grotesken* play in a satirical way with the norms and limitations of being human and of being accepted as such by society. Their particular humor and (bio)political critiques made these narratives wildly successful around 1900, but these characteristics also led to their censorship, marginalization, and subsequent descent into popular and academic oblivion. Yet in many ways, the texts could not be more relevant today, as they respond to one of the big questions of their time that continues to reverberate in our own: What does it mean to be human?

The turn of the twentieth century was a period of artistic and scientific experiments, fueled by doubts and discoveries that drew many previous certainties about humankind and the world into question. In his introductory lectures on psychoanalysis, Sigmund Freud described this modern moment as a crisis and placed it within a history of turning points that fundamentally altered the way humankind conceived of itself and its position in the world:

> Humanity, in the course of time, has had to endure from the hands of science two great outrages against its naive self-love. The first was when humanity discovered that our earth was not the center of the universe, but only a tiny

speck in a world-system hardly conceivable in its magnitude. This is associated in our minds with the name "Copernicus," although Alexandrian science had taught much the same thing. The second occurred when biological research robbed man of his apparent superiority under special creation, and rebuked him with his descent from the animal kingdom, and his ineradicable animal nature. This re-valuation, under the influence of Charles Darwin, Wallace and their predecessors, was not accomplished without the most violent opposition of their contemporaries. But the third and most irritating insult is flung at the human mania of greatness by present-day psychological research, which wants to prove to the "I" that it is not even master in its own home, but is dependent upon the most scanty information concerning all that goes on unconsciously in its psychic life.[1]

These three attacks on human exceptionalism had decentered the earth with Copernicus, dethroned Man with Darwin, and deposed autonomous rational subjectivity with Freud. Each of these moments destabilized the traditional Adamic paradigm of Man created in the image of God, in which all others, such as women and animals, played supporting roles to fulfill his needs. Without the certainty of Man's mastery over all of creation, his superior place in the world was threatened, which required a reassessment of the self and the other that took shape in a variety of ways in philosophy, the arts, and natural sciences around 1900. The quest for a *neuer Mensch* (New Human) was rampant in numerous intellectual arenas of the time, some of which intended to broaden, while others meant to shore up the paradigm of Man.[2] The prevalence of the question shows in concepts as different as Friedrich Nietzsche's formulation of the *Übermensch*, the feminist New Woman, and eugenic ideas of the *Untermensch* (subhuman). As the understanding of the human as Man (or, in today's terms, a white, Western, Christian, heterosexual, able-bodied, neurotypical, educated, middle-/upper-class, cis male) increasingly conflicted with the much more pluralistic reality of the human, various movements—for instance, those fighting for Jewish civil rights, women's suffrage, and colonial independence—actively sought to shift the exclusionary power structures and the limited notion of the human that underpinned societal belonging and participation.

Grotesken turn to perspectives outside of the traditional archetype of Man to broaden its narrow normative confines and undermine its assumed exceptionalism, often in satirical ways. By drawing on the viewpoint of plants, animals, and marginalized human figures who are not granted equal human rights or respect, the stories shine a critical light on society and its criteria of belonging. Readers of *Grotesken* and this book will encounter, for instance, priests who prohibit botany instruction in schools for fear that pupils might learn about same-sex or nonmonogamous erotic pleasures from bees and flowers; dogs that taxonomize humankind and use philosophical logic to determine that Man is the lowest of all creatures; and Weimar Nazis converting to Judaism through a set of complicated physical operations, thus commenting on the contemporary "Jewish Question." While these figures poke holes in the notion of Man's superiority by ridiculing his behaviors and limitations, they simultaneously draw out similarities—in some *Grotesken* between the concerns of individuals with different marginalized identities and in others between the treatment of human and nonhuman life. Those proximities show the lingering impact of the second "outrage" Freud described—the response to Darwin's description of evolutionary developments—which had revealed kinship relations and cross-species parallels between plants, animals, and human beings. As a result, the relationship of Man to any "others," be they animal or vegetal, female or nonwhite, had to be reconsidered, since the perceived difference had served to define Man and his powerful place in the world for so long. If Man was no longer to be conceived of as "that which is not animal," an entirely new approach to the human self-conception and indeed a redefinition of all life forms was required.[3]

Grotesken approach this challenge by giving a voice to those traditionally considered or historically rendered voiceless. When plants, animals, and marginalized human figures speak or express themselves in these narratives, they reinforce the third "outrage" in Freud's history of crises—namely, Man's loss of certainty in his own autonomous rational subjectivity. Reason has traditionally been bound up with language, and these characteristics had been virtually synonymous with Man, perhaps most strongly since the enlightenment, whose impactful ideas justified excluding women and people of color from the formulation of human rights by considering them irrational and closer to mute beasts and "nature."[4] Yet just as psychoanalysis cast doubt on the paradigm of reason around 1900, modernist art also underwent a crisis of confidence in language at the time. The so-called *Sprachkrise* (language crisis) entailed the realization that language appeared unfit to express one's thoughts and describe the world accurately, anticipated by Nietzsche's claims for the metaphorical nature of all language and fully expressed in Hugo von Hofmannsthal's famous "Chandos Letter" from 1902, whose speaker writes, "I have completely lost the ability to think or speak coherently about anything at all."⁵ Unable to put anything into meaningful words (except, ironically, the contents of his eloquent letter, which exemplifies the artistic inspiration and search for new poetic language that this crisis also entailed), the writer is no longer in control of language or thought. Embroiled in such fundamental skepticism regarding both reason and language, Man in modernity has lost hold of the notions that had constituted his sense of self and superiority.

Responding to these points of disorientation, *Grotesken* give a voice to plants, animals, and marginalized human figures, or if they do not speak for themselves in these narratives, their bodies become a central site of negotiating human language and expression. The texts' criticisms target society's norms and institutions, which are often exemplified by representatives of the church and state, or members of social and intellectual elites—all of them typical embodiments of Man. In the confrontation of their normative perspectives with nonhuman and marginalized bodies, *Grotesken* expose the structures of biopolitical regulation enacted by governmental institutions with the support of science, law, and social conventions. When the narratives shift focus from bodies to the realm of the mind, their nonhuman and marginalized human perspectives undermine the hegemonic paradigms of reason and language by pointing to the regulation of thought: the restriction of free expression through the vast apparatus of contemporary censorship and concurrent practices of institutionalizing those who think differently with the help of psychiatric and penal codes. In addition, they turn to philosophical concepts from ontology and epistemology to interrogate human certainties about the self and other. By presenting Man not as the superior rational being or Western society as "the pinnacle of civilization," and instead pointing to a past and present full of human failures and abuses that are propped up by racial, gendered, and ableist physiognomic pseudoscience in conjunction with religious and political discrimination, the nonhuman and marginalized human perspectives of these texts expose the exclusionary structures of their contemporaneous society and its understanding of humanity.

Because of these criticisms, *Grotesken* were both very popular and heavily censored in their heyday from the 1890s to the eve of the Second World War, and their censorship is part of why this genre is practically unknown today. As section 1 of this book will explicate in more detail, most authors who took to writing *Grotesken* were silenced, and in this context marginalized and themselves excluded from the status of Man to varying degrees: for the pioneer of this short prose form, Oskar Panizza, censorship turned into prison sentences, institutionalization, and exile before the twentieth century even began, and the books of all other authors in this monograph ended on the pyres of the Nazis. Despite censorship and its repercussions, many authors adapted the principles of the genre in distinct ways during the first decades of the twentieth century and created a complex and popular body of work. With a combined corpus of several hundred *Grotesken*, the four most important and productive practitioners span the virtually unknown and the world famous by today's standards: following Panizza, early film director and bestselling author Hanns Heinz Ewers capitalized on sensationalist shock value before the First World War, while the philosopher Salomo Friedlaender subsequently created intellectual wordplay for the Weimar cabaret and radio. Ultimately, *die Groteske* transformed into its most renowned shape in Franz Kafka's oeuvre, which shifts the common perception of this author as a literary outsider by recontextualizing him within a literary network.[6]

Kafka's reputation as a dark and serious writer has left little room for the comedy he is known to have seen in his own works.[7] One of *die Groteske*'s central features is a mode of satire that elicits laughter: the texts exaggerate societal normativity to grotesque extremes that render it momentarily funny, or ludicrously absurd, yet they do so with topics of such gravity—for instance, antisemitism—that the laughter turns into horrified shock upon the realization of what is at stake. *Das Lachen bleibt einem im Halse stecken* (laughter gets stuck in one's throat), as a German expression has it. The shocking effect is especially dominant today, as hindsight allows us to see the historical outcomes of ideas such as the Aryan "superhuman" that relied on the existence of the notion of the "subhuman," which these narratives criticize with discerning foresight. By redefining Man even more narrowly as Aryan and violently dehumanizing everyone else, the Holocaust's mass application of mechanisms of exclusion gave the comedic satire of *Grotesken* a bitter taste after 1945. Indeed, the impact of Nazi ideology fundamentally altered the way *Grotesken* were understood and received, further contributing to the disappearance of these texts, traditions, and literary networks from public and scholarly awareness. The humorous exaggerations of the genre had been supplanted by the experience of the atrocities of the Shoah and the war, which exceeded the texts' biopolitical imagination. Gershom Scholem witnessed this effect and, in 1975, wrote about it in his memories of

Walter Benjamin in a way that is central to the understanding of *Grotesken* in this book:

> Ich verdanke ihm unter anderem die Bekanntschaft mit den Grotesken – einer nach Hitler unmöglich gewordenen und heute kaum mehr zugänglichen Literatur-Form – von Mynona [Friedlaender], vor allem mit dem Band *Rosa die schöne Schutzmannsfrau*, einem unübertroffenen Werk dieser Gattung, über das ich damals vor Lachen fast vom Stuhl fiel und das ich heute nur noch mit völliger Gleichgültigkeit wiederlesen kann.

> Among the things I owe to Benjamin is my acquaintance with the grotesque tales (a literary form that became impossible after Hitler and is virtually inaccessible today) of Mynona [Friedlaender], particularly the volume entitled *Rosa die schöne Schutzmannsfrau* [Rosa the beautiful policeman's wife], an unsurpassed work in this genre that almost knocked me off my chair with laughter at the time; unfortunately, I can read it today only with utter indifference.[8]

The comedy of *Grotesken* now belongs to a distinct era and requires contextualization and close reading to be made accessible in order to understand the critical potential and impact of these narratives. In doing so, this monograph excavates a forgotten piece of literary and cultural history leading up to the Nazi regime, and it is the first book-length study to map the genre's strategies of biopolitical critique and track its development over time with the help of detailed textual analyses.

Section 1 of this book situates *die Groteske* as a modernist literary genre in the context of grotesque aesthetics writ large and maps its characteristics. The genre's specific approach to narration, institutionalization, language, and sexuality sets up the close readings of *Grotesken* in the subsequent parts, which focus on vegetal (section 2), animal (section 3), and marginalized human figures (section 4), respectively. To illustrate how different texts in the *Grotesken* tradition reworked their concern about the status of the human over the course of fifty years, each of these sections pairs an in-depth analysis of a pioneering narrative by Panizza with that of one of the writers who followed in his wake: first Ewers with a focus on plants and sexuality, then Kafka with a modernist crisis of the self that is narrated by dogs, and last Friedlaender's appeal against antisemitism in the discussion of what it means to be human on the eve of the Third Reich. These four authors are not commonly read side by side, which is why the next section also provides some literary-historical and sociopolitical context to show what connected and differentiated them. In particular, the experience of *Grotesken* writers was shaped by censorship, which conflated authors with their texts and critical causes, so that individuals suffered the consequences of the regulation of language in an embodied way. In many ways, the writers' choice of literary form and the genre's strategies themselves can therefore not be disentangled from their biopolitical effects. The genre of *die Groteske* thus crystallizes discursive patterns among a network of authors who contested the hegemonic normativity that would ultimately bring devastation from Germany into the world.

SECTION 1

THE GROTESQUE

A Censored Literary Genre and Its Authors

The first three years of the 1890s saw the publication of the majority of Oskar Panizza's short prose, which laid the foundation for the genre of *die Groteske* (*Grotesken* in the plural) that was actively produced in significant numbers until the late 1930s.[1] These literary "grotesques" share many characteristics of "the grotesque" writ large (*das Groteske*, without a plural)—a broader aesthetic phenomenon in literature and the arts. Germanist Wolfgang Kayser defines the grotesque in this general sense in his canonical study on *das Groteske* as a motif or style that originated in the visual arts and tends to resurface as a literary strategy in times of conflict and change, especially during renaissance, romanticism, and modernism. Such grotesque aesthetics characteristically oscillate between comedic-burlesque caricature and monstrous, nightmarish horror, which is also true for the genre of *die Groteske* at the center of this book. Toying with the expectations of the audience and crossing the borders of "good taste" and societal consensus, grotesque art elicits laughter that is stifled by shock when the comedic suddenly exposes its horrifying underbelly. Its dark side suggests the possibility that the world is in fact as nightmarish as it is depicted, which explains the preference for this style in times of crisis.

Die Groteske differentiates itself from the broader aesthetic phenomenon of the grotesque (*das Groteske*) by virtue of being a specific type of literary text—a microgenre. I use this term in the sense of *kleine Formen* (small forms), which designate subgroupings within the traditional, broad generic parameters of prose, lyric, and dramatic that are also literally "small"—that is, short, which *Grotesken* tend to be.² Small forms emerged in the late nineteenth century with the proliferation of newspapers and stylize themselves as addressing, then and now, audiences with limited focus—be it due to media or time constraints, or an emerging need for variety and entertainment. In the context of the emergence of mass media in the early twentieth century, *Grotesken* were particularly popular in the burgeoning cabarets and on the radio. The genre's choice of name, *die Groteske*, shows its purposeful participation in the stylistic tradition of the grotesque writ large (*das Groteske*), and it is part of a general modernist preoccupation with grotesque aesthetics that expressed itself not only in the development of this short prose form but also in the visual arts, poetry, drama, novels, and film.³ Indeed, a 1925 account of expressionist literature calls *die Groteske* "a favorite form [*Lieblingsform*] of the time."⁴

Grotesken draw on a specific set of influences from the aesthetic history of the grotesque writ large—namely, the literary topoi and themes of the romantics, especially E. T. A. Hoffmann and Edgar Allan Poe. Several *Grotesken* volumes under discussion in this book are explicitly dedicated to one of these two authors, with manifold references to their oeuvre, and their narrative short prose form follows in the generic footsteps of Hoffmann's novellas and Poe's short stories.⁵ Hoffmann's penchant for investing nonhuman figures with typically human features reappears throughout the genre, and Poe's innovation of having his characters investigate incidents that break natural laws is also a central strategy of many *Grotesken*. Yet unlike the ultimate explanation of the fantastic in Hoffmann's tales or the resolution of the mystery in Poe's detective stories, *Grotesken* often conclude without any clarification. Instead, they thrive on alienating readers and produce— despite a fair amount of programmatic laughter—varying degrees of terrified confusion. As the editor's foreword to the 1914 *Buch der Grotesken* puts it, "*Die Groteske* is therefore like life itself: deceptive, unpredictable, excitable and devious, before long corralling strange things, while ripping apart harmonious matters, confusing appearance and reality, a quarter truth, three quarters hallucination."⁶

The emphasis on horror and gothic darkness is particularly true of *Grotesken* written before the First World War, while the Weimar Republic saw a shift toward the comedic in the genre.⁷ Just as the experience of the

Holocaust and Second World War would foreclose the humorous reception of these texts altogether, the First World War's realization of some previously only imagined horrors so close to home changed the tastes of German audiences. The unstable interwar period with its emphasis on new forms of entertainment liked to package its criticisms in satirical humor. Salomo Friedlaender, whose witty *Grotesken* excel at humorous wordplay and were particularly successful in the Weimar cabaret, theorized widely about the world-changing function of laughter.[8] His *Grotesken* were meant to be read aloud to audiences (as he did on the radio), providing a space for criticism of a social and political reality that was unraveling in unprecedented ways. This performative aspect and its emphasis on laughter is characteristic of many *Grotesken*, which abound with direct speech and descriptive detail that is sometimes reminiscent of stage directions and enacts additional meaning—perfectly suited for the cabaret. Friedlaender is the only writer of *Grotesken* to provide something like a definition of the genre, which describes *die Groteske*'s function as upsetting everyone's inherent bourgeois sensibilities by exaggerating reality to such a degree that it causes change. In Friedlaender's own words, which are central to the understanding of the genre in this book, the creator of *Grotesken*

> ärgert und chockiert den fast unausrottbaren Philister in uns, der sich, aus Vergesslichkeit, mitten in der Karikatur des echten Lebens ahnungslos wohlfühlt, dadurch, dass er die Karikatur bis in das Groteske eben übertreibt, solange, bis es gelingt, ihn aus dem nur gewähnten Paradies seiner Gewöhnlichkeiten zu vertreiben.[9]

> angers and shocks the nearly ineradicable philistine in us—who, out of forgetfulness, naively feels good in the midst of the caricature of genuine life—by exaggerating the caricature to the point of being grotesque, until it succeeds in driving him [the philistine] out of the merely imagined paradise of his customs.

By including himself in this characterization of everyone's "inner philistine," who has grown too comfortable with the horrors of the world, Friedlaender drives home the urgency of facing the illusions that allow us to ignore the abysses of our reality—a sentiment that has not lost any of its relevance today.[10]

Aside from Friedlaender's essay, there has been little detailed or extended theorization of *die Groteske* as a literary genre.[11] One of the reasons is inherent in the text form itself: since the most central feature of these narratives is their critique of rules and norms, fitting *Grotesken* into the confines of a formal definition runs counter to what the authors aimed to achieve with their radical kind of writing. The genre's mission of challenging "the merely imagined paradise of the philistine's customs," according to Friedlaender's definition, included the upheaval of literary and linguistic conventions, as, for instance, Panizza's purposefully idiosyncratic spelling habits underscore.[12] As these narratives resist the confines of the literary canon, this book is not intent on developing a traditional genre definition either; instead, it distills the shared aesthetic strategies and biopolitical critiques of a distinct historical moment by close reading *Grotesken*. Despite variation among the authors, the discourse in documents of the time shows that there is an awareness and understanding of *die Groteske* as a genre, within which the authors inscribed themselves to varying degrees, even if its form was not precisely defined. In lieu of such a set of fixed formal rules, one might think that the moniker *Groteske* attached to a text might suffice in identifying the corpus of the genre, but in the spirit of the developing form, the label is not always a reliable indicator either. Texts were sometimes called a *Groteske* or a *groteske Erzählung* (grotesque narrative) by the authors themselves, by other authors, or by the press, and sometimes not at all.[13] And while many texts that are explicitly labeled *Grotesken* are short prose narratives, there is also modernist poetry and several never-staged short plays or one-acters with this moniker. These variations emphasize the emerging genre's penchant for experimentation and defiance of rules, and they also confirm certain overarching patterns, including close ties to theater and cabaret, and brevity as a persistent formal feature.[14] In order to get a better sense of how the genre was understood at the time, the first chapter of this section develops four additional characteristics that are common among *Grotesken* but have not yet been described elsewhere. These four features also show the ways in which the development of *die Groteske* as a text type was actively shaped by literary censorship, to which chapter 2 turns in more detail.

ONE

Characteristics of *die Groteske*

The following four characteristics of *Grotesken* supplement the description on the previous pages, which has defined the genre as a short prose form with romantic roots and ties to the performative, whose effect oscillates between horror and laughter, and, as we will see in more detail in what follows, usually contains sociopolitical criticism by giving a voice to nonhuman and marginalized human perspectives. The four additional attributes of this chapter, whose nuances will emerge more fully in the close readings of the selected *Grotesken* in the next sections of this book and which take on varying shapes across authors and texts as the genre develops, are: (1) the genre's approach to narration, (2) the connection it makes between institutions and institutionalization, (3) its ambiguous and defamiliarizing language, and (4) its recourse to bodies, with a particular focus on sexuality.

Narration

Opposite their nonhuman or marginalized human protagonists, *Grotesken* tend to feature at least one figure embodying Man and representing an institution, such as the church, university, police, court, hospital, or military. This figure frequently leads the reader through the story, often from the narrative position.[1] These typically male, bourgeois narrators/protagonists are presented as figures of trust for the reader because of their status as educated, responsible representatives of institutional authority; yet as the stories unfold, their displays of what seemed to be common sense go awry in the face of a grotesque encounter, and the reader must acknowledge that the control and authority of these "philistines," to recall Friedlaender's words, are illusory. The reader finds that they have trusted flawed and limited figures who are caught up in the story world of the text. In other cases, the reader is confronted with such a distanced narrative voice that its matter-of-factual response to grotesque events becomes alienating. Across these variations, narrators cease to provide orientation, and the most unsettling form of narration is one that does not seem to register a grotesque event as unusual at all, which is famously symptomatic of Kafka's storytelling.[2] The trust traditionally given to priests, physicians, and policemen is shattered in the course of the narratives when these figures are exposed as unreliable and flawed. Close reading reveals that the reliability of the narrating persona has been subverted from the beginning and that the reader has been led astray by these authority figures from the onset. Going beyond the popular literary convention of the unreliable narrator, this systematic and specific strategy prompts the reader to question why they assumed that these authority figures were trustworthy or represented common sense, and it introduces a pointed criticism about the unreliability of the powerful institutions regulating society. This discovery simultaneously inverts the roles of the subject and object of the story, as the seemingly reliable sources are suddenly in need of a closer examination. The reader must reassess the status of the nonhuman or marginalized human voice or presence in the text, all of which is bound to change the interpretation of the grotesque encounter or event around which the story is organized. *Die Groteske*'s approach to narration criticizes the norms and laws regulating the world (which often produce scenarios that are akin to what we have come to describe as Kafkaesque), and it leaves the reader with an inability to trust any of the available voices.

Institutionalization

The reader's loss of trust in (the representatives of) institutions usually goes along with a reassessment of the grotesque circumstances presented by these narrators/protagonists. Who or what can be trusted, and what is considered the norm or grotesque is often negotiated via the other protagonists and the idea of "madness" in *Grotesken*. This "madness" (*Wahnsinn*) is cast as a general sense of delusion or illusion and does not usually correspond to any diagnosable mental illnesses or conditions in the texts.[3] Rather, it shows up, explicitly or implicitly, as a term that describes another protagonist's diverging response to or perception of the world (such as taking a grotesque event seriously, or taking on a nonhuman or marginalized perspective) that deviates from that of the authority figure. As an aberration from the socially and legally encoded norms that the policemen, physicians, or priests represent, "madness" is typically "institutionalized" in the texts in one of two ways, which marks the second characteristic of the genre: "madness" is either excised from society by institutionalizing (i.e., sending to an "insane asylum") those protagonists who do not conform; or, perhaps more surprisingly, it becomes part of one of the institutions regulating society (i.e., is institutionalized in the sense of "made normative") when it is accepted as a new standard by one of its authority-wielding representatives so that order can be restored. What is more, *Grotesken* suggest that these two modes of institutionalization are not that different from each other, proposing that "madness" has become the norm and that the everyday world is delusional, with grotesque effects (again akin to the Kafkaesque). Together with the nonconforming protagonist who ends up in the asylum, the reader gets caught up in this "mad" reality, in which the stability of norms and the meaning of concepts that are used to ensure social order, such as "sane" and "insane," have become unsettled. The grotesque writ large (i.e., *das Groteske*) is generally associated with the disorienting experience that the "world is a madhouse," yet while "madness" as a deviation from the norm is coded negatively in this tradition, in line with how the representatives of institutions would see it, *Grotesken* redefine "madness" as positive for the nonhuman and marginalized human figures.[4] *Grotesken* do not present aberrations from the norm as signs of chaos and "madness"; rather, they see the ordered world as grotesque and uncover the "madness" that masquerades as the rule of law. Ironically, this makes the so-called insane asylum a space that assembles and allows for the grotesque and for alternative thinking. Together with the specter of "madness," the asylum therefore figures prominently in many *Grotesken*.[5] As "madness" becomes the norm, the texts showcase the relativity of norms themselves. With the loss of guidance by the authority figures that tried to determine the narrative, the reader is prompted to read between the lines and make up their own mind regarding the criticisms of normativity that *Grotesken* present.

Language

As norms are under scrutiny in the first two characteristics of the genre (narration and institutionalization), laws and rules also come undone in its third, the ambiguous and defamiliarizing language of *Grotesken*. Language is the place where the authoritative narrative voice or the protagonist's account of events is undermined, often by the voices or described behavior of the traditionally mute, nonhuman and silenced, marginalized human figures. With the discovery of the unreliability of the authority figure and the presentation of grotesque events surrounding these "others," the reader is left unsure about who can be trusted or what exactly is happening, and the context of modernism's language skepticism in the *Sprachkrise* (described in the introduction) adds an additional dimension of unsettling insecurity on the level of form. Drawing every word and its potential meanings into doubt, the ambiguity of language is on vivid and experimental display in *Grotesken*. Yet the authors address the language crisis not with the poetic *l'art pour l'art* approach of their modernist peers; rather, their literary mastery is on display in everyday language that is nonetheless full of multiple meanings and additional layers of references. Kafka's seemingly simple word choices have famously given way to endless interpretations; Friedlaender's stories are full of witty wordplay on the surface, while their additional philosophical subtext requires added analysis; Ewers's words managed to shock audiences to the point of fainting; and Panizza's use of multiple languages, phonetic spelling, and neologisms bespeak his urge to find new means of expression that could both depict and expose the institutional(ized) workings of this world—despite or perhaps precisely because of the repercussions of censorship, which further complicated the writing of *Grotesken*. By constraining freedom of speech, both censorship and the language crisis unleashed an experimental use of language and creative processes that established entirely novel forms of expression. Language limitation turned into expressive abundance, even excess—a phenomenon we find not just in modernism but also as an attribute of grotesque aesthetics writ large.[6] Yet unlike the metalinguistic forms of expression of contemporaneous silent film and Dada, or the focus on high-brow poetic language in modernist poetry and novels, *Grotesken* anchor their polysemicity in everyday language and focus on communication. By highlighting the linguistic ambiguity of the mundane, the potential of everyday conversations for misunderstandings, *Grotesken* amplify their horrific-comedic effect, since they defamiliarize the familiar to ensure that the reader recognizes themselves and contemporary society in the genre's criticisms.

Sexuality

In many *Grotesken*, the conceptualization of language is closely connected to the genre's fourth characteristic, the way the texts present bodies, frequently with a focus on sexuality. As a social taboo and one of the central targets of censorship, which mainly pursued offenses like blasphemy, lèse-majesté, and what was called "crimes against morality," sexuality functions as an inherently subversive element in the texts. Exposing this taboo with its constraints and double standards seems to be of particular concern to many authors of *Grotesken*, who are writing in the context of the emerging disciplines of sexology and psychology, including the psychoanalytic engagement with human sexuality.[7] The censoring of sexuality in literature not only reflects the normative social and moral understanding of what is considered appropriate at a given time but also mirrors the laws that govern actual (i.e., nonfictional) sexual acts. These biopolitical laws and norms entail the regulation of health, bodies, reproduction, and sexual taboos. Around 1900, both literary and sexual prohibitions were controlled by the same governmental institution—the police—and thus followed the same set of rules, which made it as punishable under the law to write or speak publicly about forms of sexuality that were illegal or even just considered amoral as to engage in such sex acts.[8] This rendered the censoring of sexuality in the language of literary works and the regulation of physical behavior in society two sides of the same biopolitical coin. In his formulation of the "repressive hypothesis," Michel Foucault explains the historical importance of censoring sexuality from public discourse and suggests that the regulation of physical acts was of lesser significance. He states, "As if in order to gain mastery over it [sexuality] in reality, it had first been necessary to subjugate it at the level of language, control its free circulation in speech, expunge it from the things that were said, and extinguish the words that rendered it too visibly present."[9] This form of biopolitics demonstrates an entanglement of sexuality with language that the *Grotesken* make apparent when the institutions in charge of biopolitical control, through their representative authority figures in the texts, are forced to articulate their own prohibitions, which leads them to speak about acts they censor in other people's words and lives. Foucault makes clear that "more important was the multiplication of discourses concerning sex in the field of exercise of power itself: and institutional incitement to speak about it, and to do so more and more."[10] Pointing to this catch-22 of multiplying language about sexuality by those who are prohibiting language about sexuality, *Grotesken* satirize and undermine the attempted repression of erotic language and thought in literature and beyond, while suggesting the reexamination of contemporary sexual standards and laws. One of the main preoccupations of these regulations is the definition of morally acceptable sexual behavior as acts aimed at reproduction rather than pleasure—a goal that the stories continuously undercut with their recourse to masturbation, fetishism, sex work, and same-sex encounters. This priority of pleasure over reproduction applies both to the sexual acts the authors chose to present and the way they present them: rather than clearly describing procreative acts, the texts revel in linguistic excesses that makes the erotic pleasures that are described appear ambiguous and suggestive. In the context of the modernist language crisis, overlapping notions of failed linguistic and sexual reproduction instead make room for aesthetic and erotic pleasure in the texts. Foucault locates discourses about pleasure in the realm of psychiatry—that is, the institutional space of the asylum.[11] This brings together all four characteristics of *Grotesken* and shows the genre's approach to social critique: the narrative figures representing institutions "institutionalize" aberrations from the norm (conceived of as "madness" and appearing often in the form of nonhuman and marginalized human protagonists or perspectives), which corresponds to the censorship of language/discourse and the biopolitical regulation of bodies/sexuality. This societal process of regulation, the *Grotesken* suggest, is what is actually grotesque, instead of the aberration from the norm, as it first seemed through the eyes of the authority figures. Since the sexuality of *Grotesken* takes place entirely in the literary sphere, its biopolitical regulation took the form of censorship, which is in many ways constitutive of the genre, as the next chapter will explain.

TWO

Grotesken in a Nexus of Censorship

As the discussion of the four characteristics of *Grotesken*—narration, institutionalization, language, and sexuality—has suggested to some extent already, the history of the genre is dominated by its complex interrelationship with censorship, which shaped the texts as much as the lives of their authors. Since *Grotesken* provocatively criticize the norms and behaviors of government, church, and society, they regularly incited censorship charges of lèse-majesté, blasphemy, and crimes against morality. These charges resulted in the prohibition and destruction of texts as well as in fees, prison sentences, and ultimately dispossession and exile, which were consequences not only for authors but often also for publishing personnel under Wilhelmine and Weimar law (though restrictions gradually loosened over time).[1] Dictated by the need to hold a person accountable in court, the legal structures of censorship conflated people with texts, which made the writing of censored texts a form of activism, whether intentional or not. The equal measures censorship applied to forbidden acts and forbidden thought furthered the complex interrelation between fiction and sociopolitical reality in the case of *Grotesken*. Censorship forced the authors to develop creative strategies of circumvention, such as the defamiliarization, exaggeration, and ambiguous wordplay that became characteristic of the genre. The limitation of art therefore also prompted artistic innovation, and the aesthetics of *Grotesken* as a genre that centered on social criticism was hence decisively shaped by censorship—as were the lives of its authors.

For modernist contemporaries, censorship's particular distaste for the grotesque was an established fact. In a review of a new volume of Friedlaender's

Grotesken in 1920, Walter Mehring writes sarcastically, "Grotesque literature has always found a warm welcome [*herzlichen Anklang*] here, whether the authors starved to death (Scheerbart) or ended in prison (Panizza)."[2] Oskar Panizza can, in fact, be considered a test case in negotiating literary censorship: his pioneering writings often went too far or did not veil the targets of their criticism well enough, which led to arrests and the most infamous censorship scandal in the history of the Wilhelmine Empire in 1895. He was sent to prison for a year, the longest censorship sentence under Wilhelm II, due to charges of blasphemy against his play *Das Liebeskonzil* (*The Love Council*, 1894).[3]

Panizza's name became synonymous with censorship, and his contemporaries looked at his deliberate provocation of censorship authorities as a measure to determine how far they could go in their own writing. In 1930, decades after Kaiser Wilhelm's rule and Panizza's infamy, Walter Benjamin asserted that Panizza would have fared much the same in the Weimar Republic:

> At the moment, Panizza's name and oeuvre are in the same state that began for Hoffmann in the middle of the previous century and lasted to the turn of the century. He is as unknown as he is infamous. Yet while the memory of Hoffmann, even though it had ceased in Germany, never ceased to be celebrated in France, such satisfaction is not to be expected for Panizza. It causes the most unimaginable difficulties even just to assemble his writings in near-completion in Germany. Though there has existed a Panizza Society since last year, it has not found the means and ways to reprint his most important writings. And that is because of many reasons, of which possibly the most important one is that these writings would end up being prosecuted, just like 35 years ago.[4]

Several instances of censorship of Hanns Heinz Ewers's provocative work during the 1920s support Benjamin's claim about continued prosecution, whereas Salomo Friedlaender was careful to keep his satire veiled enough to escape the censoring eye.[5] Yet only three years after Benjamin's statement, Friedlaender's works were censored too, as the Nazis declared the majority of *Grotesken* "degenerate art," and some of the most important voices of this generation of writers and critics were exiled and silenced.[6] Panizza, Ewers, Friedlaender, and Kafka fulfill several criteria that incurred the immediate prohibition of their writings by the Nazis: two of them were Jewish; most of them had been ascribed anarchist, pacifist, or left-leaning politics; and all of them wrote in experimental, modernist, and critical ways. Despite his early membership in the Nazi Party, Ewers's name was on the 1933 list of forbidden authors, and Kafka's writings were some of the first to be burned.[7] Friedlaender fled to Paris in the same year, where he lived in exile, sick and impoverished, until his death thirteen years later. Panizza is ironically the only author whose name is not found on the list of books forbidden by the Nazis, but, as Benjamin's statement indicates, this is only because his writing had been censored and destroyed to the extent that it was already unavailable and increasingly unknown at this point.[8]

Censorship effects also contributed to the *Grotesken* genre's rapid descent into oblivion after 1945. The death of an entire generation of authors, publishers, and readers in the years around the war, the loss of a vibrant cabaret culture, and the disappearance of some of its institutional targets had wiped out the genre's network of production, distribution, and reception.[9] This included the destruction of the lives or livelihoods of its many German Jewish authors, readers, publishers, and supporters—ranging from Friedlaender and Benjamin to Kurt Tucholsky and Emil Tuchmann, just to name a few of the most prolific ones—who seemed to be especially drawn to the genre and its depiction of the world as grotesquely malfunctioning during the 1920s and 1930s. Attempts to reinvigorate *die Groteske* failed, since its humor felt out of place and had become "inaccessible after Hitler," as Scholem put it in 1975.[10] A 1965 review of Friedlaender's *Grotesken* anticipates Scholem's verdict about the genre that once "made him nearly fall off his chair with laughter": "The stale itching powder [*das Juckpulver aus der Retorte*] of the Scheerbart-generation does not make us laugh anymore after the rough jokes on the political stage of our country."[11] Today, modernist authors of *Grotesken* are either not well-known (such as Wolfgang Goetz, Wieland Herzfelde, Manfred Kyber, Artur Landsberger, Hans Reimann, Richard Rieß, and Hermann Harry Schmitz) or are better known for their other literary works, as in the case of Tucholsky and Otto Julius Bierbaum.[12]

Beyond censorship, the grotesque writ large and the genre in particular are characterized by marginalization in additional ways.[13] As the subsequent sections of this book analyze with detailed specificity, *die Groteske* presents the perspectives of those who were denied their humanity by society and did not experience equality before the law, from same-sex couples to German Jews. Writing critically and often provocatively about these concerns led to various forms of persecution and sociopolitical pressure for the authors too, which the next chapter outlines to illustrate censorship's conflation of writer and text while highlighting some of the commonalities and differences between the four authors' critical agendas. As a genre that uses everyday language for its satire of social and political concerns, while pursuing similar goals of entertainment (or at least laughter) as cabaret and mass media like film, *Grotesken* have also been marginalized as so-called lowbrow literature, or *Trivialliteratur*—an effect the authors felt during their lifetimes and that persists in both publishing and research contexts into the present.[14] While Kafka's oeuvre would surely be excluded from this verdict today, Gilles Deleuze and Félix Guattari have characterized his writing as "minor literature"—a controversial idea relating to marginalization that rests on Kafka's subversion of the "major" language German from within and, at least in this respect, resonates with the often multilingual language play of other authors in this study that is characteristic of *die Groteske*.[15] Yet just as marginalization and censorship are constitutive elements of *die Groteske*, they are also one of its measures of success: the reception in its own time shows that the genre's criticisms mattered enough to be pursued by those in power (thus corroborating the genre's description and critique of how these institutions operated), and today, the texts provide us with a sense of popular everyday concerns of the time and show the humorous side of a historical period that is often interpreted only through the lens of its devastating aftermath. Since *Grotesken* are grounded in an experience of the world as grotesquely malfunctioning, writing them is a form of sociopolitical activism against these failures of the system, which is why the critical impetus of the genre is inextricably linked to the authors' convictions vis-à-vis contemporary politics and their own biopolitical experiences with retribution, suppression, and persecution. The following pages therefore briefly outline relevant aspects of the lives of the central authors in this book within their historical context. This distills some of the ideological convictions that shaped their *Grotesken* and shows how the authors did or did not embody them themselves, while bringing out both differences and commonalities within this group. In other words, the next chapter sketches out the connecting threads that hold together a previously unrecognized literary network of seemingly disparate—and in the case of Kafka, also presumably isolated—writers, while highlighting the varying paths *Grotesken* took as the genre developed over time.

THREE

A Literary Network of the Marginalized

The four main authors in this study—Panizza, Ewers, Friedlaender, and Kafka—are not usually read side by side, and accordingly, many connections between their lives and writing have gone unnoticed. The historical and scholarly marginalization of most of these writers goes along with the incomplete picture of the genre of *die Groteske*. One of the links between them is consequently an element that others attributed to their person because of their writing: the genre's critical and irreverent approach to social, literary, and linguistic norms was frequently interpreted as an indicator of anarchism—one of the great specters of the late nineteenth and early twentieth century. During that time, anarchists carried out several violent attacks on government officials, including German Kaiser Wilhelm I, in the belief that so-called *Propaganda der Tat* (propaganda of the deed) would "wake up" society.[1] The 1890s, the decade in which *Grotesken* production began, saw a series of bombings, and prominent political figures such as the presidents of France (Sadi Carnot in 1894) and the US (McKinley in 1901) as well as Empress Elisabeth of Austria (1898) were assassinated by anarchists. These notorious events equated anarchism with terrorism in the minds of many, and they resulted in the persecution of anyone who seemed to sympathize with its ideas, including many people involved in the writing and publication of *Grotesken*. Around the First World War, anarchists played major roles in various revolutionary movements such as in the Russian Revolution of 1917 and in Germany, where Kaiser Wilhelm II and the monarchs of his territories, like King Ludwig III of Bavaria, were ousted in the so-called November Revolution between 1918 and 1919. All around the country, from Friedlaender's Berlin to Ewers's Düsseldorf, violent struggles between various political factions ensued, and a little further east, Kafka's Prague declared independence from the splintering Austro-Hungarian Empire to become the capital of Czechoslovakia in 1918. In Panizza's Munich, the short-lived *Münchner Räterepublik* (Bavarian Soviet Republic) of 1919 foreshadowed the Weimar Republic's political instability, and Hitler's failed 1923 "Beer Hall Putsch" became a marker of the rise of fascist ideology. Yet while hindsight often makes the development from the *Kaiserreich* via the Weimar Republic to the Third Reich appear seemingly inevitable, the *Grotesken*'s contemporaneous criticisms bring into focus the messy complexity and political plurality of the period.

Though none of the four authors was a self-declared anarchist nor engaged in political violence, many of their criticisms overlap with ideas from the anarchist milieu, albeit in quite different ways and at different times and places for each. Panizza's open criticism of Kaiser Wilhelm II was one of the main reasons for his repeated run-ins with censorship authorities, and accusations of anarchism were most pronounced in his case.[2] Panizza, Ewers, and Friedlaender also shared an interest in the atheist and nihilist thought of the philosopher, journalist, and early anarchist Max Stirner (1806–1856) that resurfaces in their writing.[3] Stirner's "ethical egoism," which Nietzsche (1844–1900) would later develop in a similar vein, accepted neither religious nor political authority and moreover rejected any authority within the self that would suppress its own desires, such as Freud would capture in his concept of the ego.[4] Instead, Stirner postulated that moral values were subjective and thus propagated an extreme individualism (one of several subgroupings of anarchist ideology today), which was, however, interpreted very differently by the various *Grotesken* authors. Yet the fact that they all turned to Stirner's ideas is not surprising, particularly because he grappled with the question of the human, as *Grotesken* do. He developed one of the ideas of the New Human that would become so prevalent at the time, also called *der Eigner* (ego, in a pre-Freudian sense), whom he defined as self-creating and fundamentally free. This freedom entailed the abolition of all governmental institutions, and instead of these structures, Stirner suggested that New Humans would form communities according to self-interest. German anarchists around 1900 were steeped in Stirner's ideas, and many of the most important thinkers of his own time, such as Karl Marx, Friedrich Engels, and Ludwig Feuerbach, engaged with his theories in a variety of ways. However, the Prussian censors of the mid-nineteenth century ensured that Stirner's legacy, particularly his magnum opus *Der Einzige und sein Eigentum* (*The Ego and Its Own*, 1845), would be as marginalized as *Grotesken* and the majority of their authors.[5] Today, almost all of Stirner's papers are lost; a biography from 1898 remains the standard reference work for his life and works; and except for a posthumous caricature by Engels, there is no extant image of him.[6] This structure of marginalization of a once popular writer whose ideas were suppressed by censorship is repeated in several of the lives of the authors of *Grotesken*, as the following pages of this chapter show, particularly in the case of the pioneer Panizza, whose texts are the springboard of every subsequent section of this book.

Panizza

Oskar Panizza (1853–1921) was a trained psychiatrist and multifaceted author, who faced persecution for his provocative writing about sexuality and disease as well as his pointed criticism of the Wilhelmine Empire and the Catholic Church throughout his life.[7] He knowingly took profound risks by writing against a policed societal consensus that ultimately put his entire existence at stake, as he was incarcerated, dispossessed, and exiled. His *Grotesken* engage with complex topics such as race, gender, antisemitism, nationalism, capitalism, militarism, and colonial as well as religious zeal. They usually feature a figure at the margins of society and irreverently criticize contemporary institutions, norms, and morals. In his *Grotesken*, readers encounter many unexpected scenarios, such as a factory that produces humans, the man in the moon who steals cheese from the Dutch to feed his thirty children, and a Native American chieftain orchestrating the suicide of his people.[8] Writing in all major genres, Panizza was originally part of the lively bohemian scene of the *Münchner Moderne* (Munich Modernism), but as his texts caused progressively bigger scandals and the repercussions reached new heights with his one-year censorship prison sentence, the disillusioned and increasingly isolated author wrote a scathing *Abschied von München* (Farewell to Munich, 1897), gave up his German citizenship, and took up residence in Zurich.[9] In 1898, he was unexpectedly expelled from Switzerland, which he attributed to sanctions against anarchist intellectuals in the aftermath of the assassination of Empress Elisabeth of Austria, "Sisi," in Geneva.[10] A postcard he sent details his situation, and the original also showcases his multilingual use of German, French, and Latin as well as his typical idiosyncratic spelling:

> Me voilà! Expulsé, persecuté, chassé! –
> Der Fall Lucheni [Elisabeth's anarchist assassin] hat die Diplomaten aller Länder zur Verzweiflung gebracht. Plözlich hat man entdekt, daß ich Anarchist bin: Anarchist des Gedankens. Denn die Mädchenaffäre in Zürich (Mit-in-die-Wohnung-nehmen einer Prostituirten) ist ja doch nur Vorwand. Der 'große Kanton' – sagte mir ein Schweizer – d.i. Deutschland – hat dem kleinen Kanton einen Befehl erteilt. Trozdem hat man sich gescheut, mich offen als Anarchisten zu deklariren. Exempla trahunt. Was wird noch aus mir werden? Jetzt hoke ich mit 10 000 Bänden in Paris. Dazu 1 Büffet, ein Schreibtisch, ein Bett! – [. . .] Vive l'Allemagne!
> Ihr Pzza.[11]

> [French:] Here I am! Expelled, persecuted, hunted!—
> [German:] The Lucheni case [Elisabeth's anarchist assassin] has driven the diplomats of all countries to despair. Suddenly, one has discovered that I am an anarchist: an anarchist of thought. For the affair with the girl in Zurich (into-the-apartment-taking of a prostitute) is only a pretext after all. The "big canton"—a Swiss man said to me—i.e., Germany—has given the small canton an order. Nonetheless, one did not dare declare me an anarchist openly. [Latin:] Examples compel. [German:] What will become of me? I am now squatting in Paris with 10,000 volumes. In addition, one sideboard, a desk, a bed!—[. . .] [French:] Long live Germany!
> [German:] Your Pzza.

Panizza and his thoroughly read, large library subsequently moved to Paris until the threat of dispossession in the shape of an international warrant for his arrest forced him to return to Munich to face charges of lèse-majesté prompted by an 1899 poem cycle (*Parisjana*) that criticized Kaiser Wilhelm II.[12]

Panizza's quick descent into oblivion during his own lifetime surprised many of his contemporaries, which demonstrates both the scope of the immediate impact of his work and the swift destruction of his infamy through censorship. His contemporaries confirmed, "We knew his writings almost without exception; they enthralled us to the same degree as they alienated us."[13] Walter Benjamin valued him as "a heretical icon painter [*häretischer Heiligenbildmaler*]"; Kurt Tucholsky was convinced that Panizza was "the most impudent and audacious, the most brilliant and revolutionary prophet of his country [...]. One, compared to whom Heine could be called a flat lemonade [*matte Zitronenlimonade*]"; and even the aged Theodor Fontane said that "he either deserves the stake or a monument."[14] The provocative nature of his work brought about both his fame and his demise. In 1893, Otto Julius Bierbaum, a fellow author of the Munich Moderns, had seen promise precisely in the provocative potential of the emerging writer:

> I have no doubt that he will soon belong to the most discussed modernist [*den besprochensten modernen*] authors in Germany—but also one of the most infamous. For: he lacks the fig leaf that we are supposed to cover ourselves with. And: he doesn't cover his loud *mouth* either. And: he has a *wicked* mouth [*Denn: er mangelt des Feigenblattes, das wir haben sollen. Und: er nimmt sich auch vors* Maul *kein Blatt. Und: er hat ein* böses *Maul*].[15]

Judging from the scholarship of the past century, Bierbaum could not have been more wrong about Panizza's reception, as censorship led to a persistent dearth of editions, resulting in few academic studies.[16]

Panizza's texts and their treatment suggest that he was "too modern" for his time, and the renewed censorship of his *Liebeskonzil* play in 1994, a century after the original trial for blasphemy, indicates that this is still the case.[17] Yet Bierbaum's statement was comically prophetic in another way: Panizza quite literally lacked the required "fig leaf" when he sought to be committed to a mental institution by roaming the streets without pants in 1904.[18] This deliberate decision to be institutionalized was the radical culmination of Panizza's thought as expressed in his writing, and it resonates with the many fictional institutionalizations in his *Grotesken*.[19] In a biographical twist that appears almost stylized, the psychiatrist Panizza, who trained in an asylum after his medical degree, had provided his own diagnosis already in 1898: called *Psichopatia criminalis* in reference to Richard von Krafft-Ebing's *Psychopathia sexualis* (1886), it has been described as a "political brain disease."[20] In Panizza's own words, it is the malaise of critical thinking, "das innere freche Denken" (the internal impudent thinking) medicalized as the *"mania anti-gouvernementalis,"* that kept him locked away for the last sixteen years of his life.[21] Panizza suffered from auditory hallucinations around the time of his institutionalization. He had been afraid of a hereditary psychological illness all his life, but the increasing and acute persecution he suffered at the time likely had a hand in these acoustic manifestations of paranoia.[22] Yet what he considered the safe haven of the asylum became a prison once more when his family had him declared legally incompetent.[23] In an act of self-censorship that is summed up in the title of one of his last poems, "lived in vain," Panizza subsequently ceased writing and only spoke French, the language of his exile and his Huguenot ancestors, for the remaining years of his life in the asylum—a final act of defiance against Germany's censorship of free expression.[24]

Ewers

Like Panizza's, the writing of the oft-arrested Hanns Heinz Ewers (1871–1943) provoked the ire of the authorities and the public, mostly because his depictions of sexuality were considered near-pornographic and the violence in his texts made his audience faint on occasion.[25] Yet the same factors also rendered his texts best-selling successes, since themes such as vampirism, femmes fatales, and religious mass hysteria hit a nerve in prewar Germany. Ewers was influenced early on by Stirner's antimoralist thought, and his multifaceted biography reads as a tale of contradictions: a dueling fraternity brother from an artistic family—nicknamed *Pistolenhans* (Pistol Hans)—and a law student in the Rhineland, he publicly took a stand against the law on the occasion of Oscar Wilde's sentencing.[26] His advocacy for gay rights was not limited to this headline-making case, which coincidentally happened in the same year as Panizza's big censorship trial. He also published in Germany's first journal for gay men, named *Der Eigene* (1896–1932) in reference to Stirner, which was censored for its erotic and anarchist content.[27] With his first wife, he spent a lot of time in the *Lebensreform* (Life Reform) paradise Capri, which was a place of sexual and political freedom.[28] His fascination with spirituality, from occultism to voodoo, and his penchant for drugs fueled his literary fantasies.[29] He first became famous for his satirical texts through his work for the Berlin cabaret *Überbrettl* in 1900 and afterward took to roaming the world as a travel correspondent, which brought his racism to light.[30] As one of the early film pioneers, he produced *Der Student von Prag* (*The Student of Prague*, 1913), which is considered the first German art film and is saturated with grotesque elements.[31] His activities as an editor with the Georg Müller publishing house put *Grotesken* into circulation, and in this context, he also managed to reprint the majority of Panizza's early short prose in the book series *Galerie der Phantasten* (Gallery of the Fantastic) in 1914.[32]

At the beginning of the First World War, Ewers found himself in the US and put his writing in the service of German propaganda efforts until the US entered the war and he was interned.[33] His wartime stay deflated his literary career and damaged his reputation severely, and upon his return to Germany in 1920, the disillusioned writer had trouble finding his place in the Weimar Republic.[34] After a meeting with Hitler in 1931, he joined the Nazi Party.[35] Yet the Nazis met him with opposition from the beginning for two reasons: the scandalous reputation of his writing and lifestyle, and what they considered "pro-Jewish" sentiments manifesting in Ewers's admiration for Walther Rathenau and texts like "Der Jude ein Pionier des Deutschtums" (The Jew a pioneer of Germanness, 1905).[36] As part of the early Nazi propaganda machine, he wrote the *Horst Wessel* book and film script, which was ironically also the first of his works to be prohibited by the Nazis.[37] Ewers's name is said to have been on the assassination list for the so-called *Röhm-Putsch* in 1934, and in the same year, he was confronted with a general publication prohibition and attempts to dispossess him.[38] After the Nazis passed the Nuremberg Laws in 1935, Ewers helped Jewish friends secure visas to other countries, and his letters and manuscripts in the years until his death in 1943 apply his satirical skills to the Nazis and wartime life.[39] His nickname *Alraune im Braunhemd* (Mandrake in the Brown Shirt)—a combination of his most successful novel and the Nazi *Sturmabteilung* (SA) uniform—aptly sums up the many contradictions of a life between best-selling expressionist success as a globe-trotting, drug-fueled proponent of sexual freedom (with a tendency for slasher aesthetics) and participation in Nazi propaganda.[40]

Friedlaender/Mynona

The Jewish philosopher and physician Salomo Friedlaender (1871–1946) and his writing could not be more different from his contemporary Ewers (whom he actively disliked and occasionally satirized in his *Grotesken*), yet these two disparate authors made the genre a staple of modernist literary consumption.[41] Under the pseudonym Mynona (*anonym*/ous spelled in reverse), Friedlaender published what is the largest number of *Grotesken* by one author.[42] Unlike Ewers, he was able to translate the genre success of the generally more gruesome prewar *Grotesken* into the Weimar 1920s through an emphasis on wit, laughter, and wordplay. Instead of a focus on horror and blood, he imbued his *Grotesken* with—no less provocative—philosophical depth and a linguistic, performative comedy, which already a 1914 review in the influential journal *Jugend* called a vast improvement over Ewers's *Grotesken*, who appears as H. H. E. in the text:

> What is new about the *Grotesken*: their scaffolding is the *word*. The *word* becomes quirk [*wird zur Schrulle*], wittily bunched together [*komisch zusammengeknäult*], and, escaping from the tangled snarl [*dem krausen Gewirr entwichen*], is suddenly again another thing, a creature of the author, which stands steadfast in the oddly bright light of intellectuality. This is an unheard-of enhancement, compared to all *Grotesken* so far. No longer hero and situation (oh! H. H. E.), but the word!⁴³

Despite the linguistic and philosophical complexity of his wordplay that often requires close reading to untangle, Friedlaender—who called himself "a synthesis of Kant and Clown"—and other artists performed his *Grotesken* successfully in cabarets and on the radio.⁴⁴

Friedlaender was actively involved in the philosophical and literary debates of his time in Berlin, and his *Grotesken* express his sociopolitical critique of the increasing militarism and nationalism of the Weimar Republic as well as his interest in the developments surrounding the human psyche.⁴⁵ His philosophical texts, which negotiate Kantian ideas in the school of Ernst Marcus and show his engagement with Schopenhauer, were widely received and spurred debates within his illustrious circle of friends, including Martin Buber, Karl Kraus, Alfred Kubin, Gustav Landauer, Else Lasker-Schüler, and many more.⁴⁶ Friedlaender also founded the *Stirner-Bund* (Stirner Society) and a journal called *Der Einzige* (The Only One/The Ego, 1919–1925), a reference to Stirner's most important work.⁴⁷ In Friedlaender's own philosophical magnum opus, *Schöpferische Indifferenz* (Creative indifference, 1918), Kant meets Stirner and Nietzsche in the idea of one's own divine creative power (*Schöpferkraft*) that is suppressed by an egotistic self (*Ich*).⁴⁸ In-dividuality, to Friedlaender, is freedom from the power of this *Ich*.⁴⁹ However, much unlike Ewers, he saw his writing tasked with a didactic obligation—one that he increasingly put in the service of pacifism.⁵⁰ The Friedlaender *Groteske* discussed most in depth in this book provides an incisive, deliberate mirror perspective to one of Panizza's by commenting critically on contemporary antisemitic currents, the acute awareness of which led him and his family to flee the country as early as 1933. Increasingly impoverished and physically weakened, Friedlaender continued to write about the power of laughter as a means of resistance against the Nazis in exile in Paris, where he died in 1946.

Kafka

Like his writing, Franz Kafka's life (1883–1924) has been studied in depth, and the trouble with his profession, family, women, and health are therefore well-known. As a Jewish German-language writer in Prague and a creative spirit bogged down by institutional regulation in his day job as an insurance claim adjuster, Kafka shared the outside perspective onto society and its institutionalized norms as well as the sense of isolation that characterize particularly the later decades of Panizza's, Ewers's, and Friedlaender's lives. Kafka's final wish to have Max Brod burn all his papers has become infamous, and it is usually attributed to a range of personal and artistic concerns. Read in conjunction with the stifling administration and random acts of governance in his texts, this wish can also be understood as a kind of self-censorship that is in line with the distant, neutral voice of his narrators. Does that make Kafka an apolitical writer, or rather one who perfected the art of defamiliarization that requires his readers to read between the lines? Politically, Kafka has been situated in the left-leaning and even anarchist camp, but approaching Kafka's politics is a difficult endeavor, which Bill Dodd exemplifies well with one of Kafka's diary references to a representative of existentialist anarchism:

> Another diary entry, from the previous year: "Don't forget Kropotkin!" (15.x.13; *D1*: 330) has attracted relatively little critical attention even though Max Brod recalls that the memoirs of this nineteenth-century Russian anarchist were amongst Kafka's favorite books. Where it has been commented on it has often been played down. Here, too, the elliptical form of the diary entry itself does not help us make up our minds. What are we to read into these words: an intellectual or emotional commitment, a special indebtedness—or simply a note on an overdue library book?[51]

As there is little guidance throughout Kafka's fragmentary writing, both in the literary works and the diary, the reader is indeed forced to make up their own mind—be it about Kafka's politics or the interpretation of his works. Yet reading Kafka comes with an undeniable sense of alienation from a world in which the law and social norms make no sense. Instead, a dysfunctional and inhumane machinery of sociopolitical institutions invariably crushes the individual. In the absence of overarching values and acceptable authorities, the reader can only draw on individual moral values—a task in line with the genre of *die Groteske* and Stirner's philosophy, whether it is understood as an invitation to anarchist, free thought, as by

Ewers and Panizza, or interpreted as a moral obligation, as by Friedlaender. While these individual ideological convictions, contemporary sociopolitical developments, and the systematic marginalization through censorship shaped the literary history of *Grotesken* from the 1890s to the eve of the Second World War, the genre's specific criticisms and literary characteristics are best explored by closely reading the narratives themselves, which the subsequent three sections of this book perform exemplarily with a focus on the perspectives of their animal, vegetal, and marginalized human figures.

SECTION 2

THE VEGETAL
Panizza, Ewers, and Turn-of-the-Century Censorship

The first section of this book introduced the genre of the literary *Groteske*, which is a censored and marginalized Germanophone short prose form of the late nineteenth and early twentieth century that criticizes society's norms from the perspective of nonhumans and those not accepted as human. In this context, chapter 1 developed four genre characteristics, which this section of the book will elucidate by turning to two *Grotesken* about plants. As a brief reminder, these four characteristics are (1) seemingly trustworthy narrators representing institutions like the church or state, who are exposed as unreliable and flawed when they attempt to enforce society's normative order; (2) an association of "madness," as defined in the previous section, with the nonhuman or marginalized human perspectives that leads to the institutionalization of those who do not conform to social norms; (3) the genre's play with ambiguous and defamiliarizing language, through which it addresses both its censorship by the authorities and the artistic concerns of the contemporaneous *Sprachkrise* in the literature around 1900; and (4) the focus on bodies and specifically sexuality as a site of biopolitical regulation that takes the shape of institutionalization and censorship, which conflates textual and actual acts. The *Grotesken* in this section not only share a focus on plants but, as some of the earliest texts discussed in this book, also illustrate these original genre parameters most aptly.

By analyzing two *Grotesken* in depth, this section shows how the genre channels its criticisms through the lens of its nonhuman figures, in this case plants, whose sexual reproduction was censored in both school curricula and literature around 1900. Satirizing attempts to curtail reproductive knowledge that can be observed in nature, Oskar Panizza's "Das Verbrechen in Tavistock-Square" (The crime in Tavistock Square, 1891) and Hanns Heinz Ewers's "Die Petition" (The petition, 1904) demonstrate that plants were the focus of an intense anxiety about sexuality, pleasure, and reproduction at the time.[1] The two *Grotesken* displace specific issues of normative morality, such as sexual pleasure, onto plants to counter, circumvent, or challenge a societal consensus that is policed by church and state. In the narratives, representatives of these institutions discover and describe satirically overdrawn sexual plant behaviors to report these transgressions. The reporting priest and policeman are consequently institutionalized or designated for the so-called insane asylum because they reproduced prohibited sexual knowledge and behavior in language. As the previous section has indicated and this one will expand further, *Grotesken* and their authors experienced censorship and its marginalizing consequences, including institutionalization just like these figures, making censorship a constitutive element of the genre. The narratives in this section expose both the workings of censorship mechanisms and contemporary anxieties surrounding nature, which arose against the backdrop of the vegetal aesthetics of art nouveau, back-to-nature movements, and scientific findings such as Darwin's that challenged Man's position at the apex of creation. The close readings of the two *Grotesken* in this section show that this combination of aesthetic and scientific concerns—negotiated by religious, moral, social, and political considerations—contributes to the uncertainty about what it means to be human in the time around 1900, which is one of the central concerns of the genre of *die Groteske*.

Oskar Panizza's "Das Verbrechen in Tavistock-Square" led to the author's first arrest for crimes against morality, anticipating the infamous censorship scandal that his play *Das Liebeskonzil* would cause just a few years later.[2] In the Wilhelmine Empire, the police was in charge of the punishment of both deeds and discourses of a sexual nature, and Panizza's *Groteske* ridicules this institution's inability to respond adequately to either, so as to criticize the inept literary censorship apparatus. In the narrative, a young policeman tries to report an unsettling discovery but has trouble putting it into words, until he finally bursts out in an elaborate description that is typical of the text and the genre of the *Groteske*:

SECTION 2: THE VEGETAL

Es waren Berührungen, *Sir* – rief der Polizist und holte tief Athem, – wie sie vor Gott und der Welt nicht erlaubt sind, es waren Liebkosungen, Entblößungen, Entleerungen, es war ein Gekicher, ein Schleifen, ein Von-sich-Geben, ein Umranken, eine Art Küssen. . . . ein Küssen, *Sir* – . . . [. . .] *Sir* – schrie und schluchzte der junge, fanatische Polizist, – die Rosen und Magnolen im *Tavistock Parc* trieben S e l b s t - B e f l e c k u n g, – es war veritable P f l a n z e n - O n a n i e! (VTS, 117)

There was touching, *Sir*,—the policeman said and took a deep breath,—as it is not allowed in the face of God and the world, there was fondling, denuding, discharging, there was giggling, grinding, emitting, entwining, a kind of kissing. . . . kissing, *Sir*,— . . . [. . .] *Sir*,—the young fanatical policeman cried out and sobbed,—the roses and magnolias in *Tavistock Park* were practicing s e l f - m a c u l a t i o n,—it was veritable p l a n t - o n a n i s m!

I will return to this key passage later to unpack in detail what the discovery of masturbating plants might mean, but for now, it serves to present the argument that this section makes about the text's relationship with language and censorship: because the police is tasked with censoring erotic language, they are themselves unable to describe the crimes in question; and when one of them eventually has to report erotic transgressions—like the young policeman at the center of Panizza's story—his speech is self-censored or arrested by hesitation, which stretches over several pages. These interruptions are visible in the many dashes, ellipses, and emphases in the text, which are part of Panizza's purposefully idiosyncratic spelling and punctuation that are preserved according to the original here. After the policeman-turned-perpetrator finally bursts out with his candid verdict of "p l a n t - o n a n i s m," he is institutionalized for the crime of speaking about sexuality (which appears to be just as transgressive as engaging in the act itself), so order can be reestablished. As the previous section introduced, Foucault argues that institutions geared toward silencing discourses of sexuality were in fact constantly reproducing them, an institutionalized catch-22 that Panizza's text locates within literary censorship, which undermined its own bans by having to define and describe the transgression in the first place.[3] Therefore, the consequence of censorship is the production of more language, which is directly reflected in the genre of *die Groteske*. Limiting language inadvertently prompts an abundance of creative expression and ambiguity of meaning on the level of the text, as the reporting policeman haltingly tries to find ways to describe—and even reenact—the crime without using offending language. This resonates with the contemporaneous *Sprachkrise*, in which authors doubted the ability of language to depict the world accurately. Yet *Grotesken* revel in linguistic ambiguity rather than despairing over it and do so frequently in everyday language, with real-life targets of criticism, rather than turning to the stylized poetic expression that became many a skeptic's refuge. Ultimately, as this section of the book will show, Panizza's *Groteske* makes the police and the reader complicit in the ongoing linguistic reproduction of the erotic act of the plants by engaging them in the aesthetic pleasure of interpretation. Since this is the first *Groteske* analyzed in this book and it demonstrates the characteristics of the genre so well, the text will be discussed at some more length than others, both to revel in the aesthetic pleasure of interpretation as intended and to unfold how these kinds of narratives work.

The second *Groteske* in this section, Hanns Heinz Ewers's "Petition," addresses similar problems of vegetal eroticism thirteen years later. The narrative centers on a petition, written by a young priest who seeks to ban botanical instruction from schools. He is convinced that learning about plant reproduction is traumatizing students and will lead them to a life of "sexual degeneracy." At the time of the text's publication, the biological sciences were in fact almost entirely banned from German secondary education, and Ewers's narrative thus not only criticizes this bizarre censorship reality but also reproduces the forbidden knowledge to undermine its ban. As a result, the priest faces one of two possible outcomes at the end of the text: either he will be institutionalized in an asylum like the young policeman in Panizza's text, or he will advance to the position of minister of education—suggesting that "madmen" are in charge of enforcing the norms of state institutions and that the norms are themselves "mad." Ewers knew Panizza's text and republished it in 1914. The similarities between the two satirical narratives demonstrate not only that there was a shared sense of the genre of *die Groteske* at the time but also that censorship played a central role for its form and content. Additionally, the two texts showcase the persistence of anxieties about vegetal eroticism around 1900 that were part of negotiating the question of what it means to be human. This section of the book will follow the chronology of the two narratives and engage first in depth with Panizza's, then more briefly with Ewers's *Groteske*. The analysis begins by contextualizing Panizza's narrative further in censorship history since these processes are integral to understanding the genre and the criticisms of both texts.

FOUR

The Crime in Tavistock Square

"Das Verbrechen in Tavistock-Square," one of Panizza's earliest pieces of published prose, was censored for *Verbrechen wider die Sittlichkeit* (crimes against morality) in 1891.[1] The alleged offense resonates with the story's title and moreover corresponds with what the narrative describes as a "Verbrechen wider die Natur" (VTS, 115). A "crime against nature" is a legal term for "unnatural" (*widernatürliche*) sexual behaviors, historically applied to acts ranging from anal sex to bestiality and from pedophilia to oral sex, which the police uses in reference to the masturbating plants in the text.[2] As a result of these linguistic convergences, Panizza's *Groteske* and the ensuing arrest appear almost like a calculated act of performance art about censorship, since the alleged crimes within the highly performative text and the author's experiences reflect on each other. Panizza's eagerness to provoke an official reaction had been noted as early as 1894 by a fellow satirical author, Karl Kraus, who said that Panizza was "one of the most pugnacious fighting cocks [*abenteuerlichsten Kampfhähne*], who apparently wants to be confiscated [*der geradeaus auf das Confisciert-werden auszugehen scheint*]."[3]

Panizza achieved this "goal" of being confiscated not only because of the sexual content of "Das Verbrechen in Tavistock-Square" but also due to the text's satire of the police, the agents in charge of literary censorship. The premise of the text ensures a focus on the police and their behavior: a German law student comes to England to study the justice system and observes a London police squadron for that purpose. He describes his experiences in a first-person narrative that mainly focuses on two figures: the police chief of the station and Jonathan, or Johny, a young subordinate. The deeply religious chief is obsessed with the control of sexuality and declares, "Wir müssen die *'lust'*, den bestialischen Componenten aus dem Zeugungs-Akt entfernen, ohne die Fortpflanzung selbst zu stören" (VTS, 111; we must remove '*lust*,' the bestial component, from the act of procreation, without disrupting reproduction itself). Using the English term *lust* and the German equivalent *Wollust* makes clear that he considers sexual desire and pleasure a deadly sin. Via the term *bestial*, the chief associates "lust" with animals and nature, introducing plants subtly through the term *Fortpflanzung* (reproduction), which contains the word *Pflanze* (plant). With the connotation of bestiality, he simultaneously defines lust as a "crime against nature." This sets up the discovery of the scandalous crime in the story's title, which is observed only by Jonathan and reported to the chief after the fact in direct speech. It takes four of the text's nine pages for Jonathan to overcome his halting hesitation and for his suggestive description to culminate in the verdict of "veritable p l a n t - o n a n i s m!" The police chief breaks down in response to this news, but the narrator reports hearing ten years later that the chief advanced to the position of chief justice, whereas Jonathan is sent to an asylum. As the story develops, it becomes clear that Johny is actually, or perhaps also, exposing the masturbating habits of his colleagues, which additionally calls up a subtext of same-sex desire, but the text resists being "resolved" through a neat allegorical transfer of human sexuality onto flowers.

To write about sexuality under the conditions of literary censorship and simultaneously showcase this constraint, Panizza transfers nonnormative sexual behaviors from humans to plants and moves the startling discovery of masturbating flowers to another country. The early 1890s marked the beginning of an intensive study of human sexuality—a development that the psychiatrist Panizza followed closely and took up in many of his texts.[4] Mostly marked as "perversions," practices like autoeroticism and homosexuality (the latter was often said to be the former's consequence) were officially named and analyzed for the first time by researchers like Havelock Ellis.[5] As such, they gradually became topics of debate, spurred by publications such as Richard von Krafft-Ebing's study *Psychopathia sexualis* (1886) and Sigmund Freud's work, later systematically laid out in his *Drei Abhandlungen zur Sexualtheorie* (1905).[6] "Proper" sexual behaviors were limited to marriage with the goal of reproduction, and the appropriate place to talk about pleasure, which was considered perverted, was in psychiatry, pointing us to Jonathan's fate.[7] Pleasure-focused activities appear threatening in this context because they involve desire that is uncontrollable and challenge a societal consensus about sexual norms that is biopolitically policed by institutions such as the church or state.

The "crime" of the plants and the chief's damnation of "lust" indicate that sexual activity is considered aberrant as soon as it involves nonreproductive acts for pleasure's sake. Ascribing desire and pleasure (let alone the self necessary for self-pleasure) to flowers—the reproductive organs of plants—places them in the realm of human morality rather than in the category of the botanical. As it removes the perception of human control over nature, it also subverts the pleasure humans tend to take in fragrant, colorful blossoms. Yet flowers "spill seed" as part of their reproductive process. In the text, the random distribution of pollen ("plant sperm") by uncontrollable natural forces such as the wind is recast as masturbation within the framework of human sexuality.[8] By turning pollination into masturbation, the text undoes the supposed divides between sexual reproduction and pleasure, between humans and plants, and between natural behavior and "crimes against nature." Together, these category transgressions threaten the societal code of morality and "the order of things" upheld by governing institutions. In "Das Verbrechen in Tavistock-Square," Panizza critiques these mechanisms and the insecurities surrounding them, and he ridicules the social and biopolitical attempts of controlling sexuality as well as the censorship of sexual content in literature.

Censorship Law

To understand the strategies at work in Panizza's *Groteske* fully, it is necessary to explain the censorship law of the time and the involvement of the police in a little more detail. Though the preventive censorship (*Vorzensur*) of manuscripts had been abolished in Panizza's day, and the 1849 constitution granted freedom of speech and the press, a copy of every published work still had to be presented to the local police in a retroactive procedure called *Nachzensur*.[9] This development simply shifted the censorship process from before to after publication and from centralized prohibition to local law. Due to each German state's varying regulations and in the absence of explicit laws about literature, offenses in the realm of fiction were assessed like transgressions in "real life" according to Criminal Code paragraphs concerning crimes against morality, blasphemy, and lèse-majesté.[10] Because published texts could no longer be amended if they were found to violate these paragraphs, *Nachzensur* exacerbated the likelihood of their prohibition. If found guilty of such charges, texts would be confiscated, destroyed, and permanently prohibited, and authors, publishers, and other people involved in the production would be fined or sentenced to prison time.

At the time, the police was a vaguely defined, small task force that underwent no specific or consistent training to discover equally ill-defined literary transgressions. Instead, those attempting to enforce the law consulted large volumes of *Policeywissenschaft* (police science) for all unclear cases. Containing collections of various public policy documents, these volumes required study and interpretation themselves. So, to judge whether the reading and interpretation of certain texts was dangerous, the police first had to read and interpret other texts. The outcomes were inconsistent rulings that created uncertainty about what constituted a criminal offense at any given place or time—both among police and writers. Since the texts under *Nachzensur* had usually not been distributed yet, there were no readers other than the police to accuse these manuscripts of violating the law, thereby implicating the police in the offense through the act of reading unlawful materials and making them skewed literary critics. In the absence of genuine complaints, policemen also acted as plaintiffs in the censorship trials—such as in the case of Panizza's *Liebeskonzil*. Taking on all these roles simultaneously, the police as literary censorship agency collapsed the separation of powers. By the turn of the century, a new law attempted to clarify and tighten the haphazard hodgepodge of partly unconstitutional censorship ordinances, though with limited success: *Lex Heinze*, named after a Berlin procurer who killed a sex worker, made solicitation a criminal offense, but it also censored the "public display of immorality" in artworks, literature, and theater—and it threatened offenders with prison sentences. Alongside conservative states that wanted to retain their own legal powers, artists and liberal intellectuals protested the vague and far-reaching paragraph extensively, pointing to all the canonical artworks threatened by it. The art and theater paragraph was removed from *Lex Heinze* almost immediately after its introduction in 1900, which left only explicitly pornographic writing and images to the prosecution.[11] The outbreak of the First World War ultimately ended the debates about a unified German censorship legislation of the arts in the Wilhelmine Empire.

Panizza's "Verbrechen in Tavistock-Square" was published in 1891 and was subject to *Nachzensur*. Unsurprisingly, it was censored immediately, despite using typical strategies to avoid censorship by moving the plot to a different time and place. Even if the narrative is supposedly about the English police force of ten years prior, Kaiser Wilhelm II and the English royals were so closely related that it undermines the distancing effect. In addition, the Metropolitan Police Act of 1829 had established the first modern police force in London, which served as a model for other countries, including Germany. Invoking this connection, the narrator of the story is a guest of the *"metropolitan police-station"* (VTS, 109). The German text is full of English expressions like this to authenticate the setting. In England, the narrator is told, "ich weiß, daß Sie als Deutscher vor allem nach Bildung streben" (VTS, 109; I know that you, as a German, strive most of all for learning), seemingly alluding to the theoretical reputation of German *Policeywissenschaft*. The sentence about *Bildung* (learning, formation) evokes German enlightenment ideas and literary traditions like the *Bildungsroman*, but it also satirizes an obsession with the theoretical and the written word. The text claims that the "niedere Gerichts-Praxis" (VTS, 109; lower practices of justice) can only be acquired in England, while Wilhelmine Germany seems to have a thought police, which mostly operates in theory. This not only portrays the German police as inept in practical matters but also alludes to the policing of thoughts and writing—that is, censorship. This subtle introduction of the topic early in the story makes way for the narrative's engagement with censorship throughout. To set up the discovery of the unusual plant crime at the center of the text, the next part of this chapter first outlines what constitutes regular police practice and ordinary crimes to the personnel of the story; then it introduces the two protagonists in more detail by contextualizing their relationships to religious morality and contemporary science in order to elucidate the depiction of sexuality and the persecution of pleasure.

Policemen and Their Crimes

Panizza's narrator admits early on that "die englische Gerichtsbarkeit [. . .] nach vierzehn Tagen mich nicht mehr interessierte, als die Gerichtsbarkeit irgend eines anderen Landes" (VTS, 110; after fourteen days, the English jurisdiction [. . .] did not interest me any more than the jurisdiction of any other country). Instead, he studies "den englischen Charakter" (VTS, 110; the English character) and entertains long discussions about religion, morality, and natural science with his host. The practice of law and examples of criminal cases thus seem to be of less importance than initially signaled, and the narrator only presents one case other than the masturbating plants. That makes the narrative more about the behavior of the policemen than crime, and it shifts the narrator's study from policy to a kind of anthropology that creates space for the possibility of police wrongdoing and a satirical depiction of their missteps. This shifting focus is explained when the narrator finds the law to be not a fixed and sacrosanct entity but consisting mainly of the "originellen Entscheidungen, die mein Chef oft entgegen der allgemeinen Meinung und den Vorschriften der Gesetz-Bücher zu treffen sich erlaubte" (VTS, 112–13; original decisions against the general opinion and the rules of the law books that the chief allowed himself to make). Indeed, police officers on duty divide crimes into minor and major offenses and judge the former immediately themselves. Similar to German censorship law, no separation of powers is upheld for minor crimes, and individual opinion becomes indistinguishable from law. Only major crimes lead to formal court proceedings.

To exemplify this police practice, the text presents a minor offense with the trope of someone stealing bread because he was hungry. Hailing from London's *"Mincing Lane"* (VTS, 111), the bread thief represents the lower-class poor and is shown mercy because his crime was about survival.[12] "Wer nur einen Leib Brod gestohlen hatte, ging straflos aus, wofern er nur arm war" (VTS, 111; Who had only stolen a loaf of bread, was left unpunished, if only he was poor). The spelling of the stolen loaf of bread as *Leib* (body) instead of *Laib* (loaf) invokes the Eucharist, endowing physical nourishment with additional spiritual capacity. The chief, who has strong Christian convictions, believes in human betterment, as the thief "muß doch leben und essen, weil er sonst nicht denken kann; und um besser zu werden, muß er doch zunächst vorzüglich denken!" (VTS, 111–12; must live and eat because he cannot think otherwise; and to become better, he must first of all think excellently!). Therefore, the chief not only grants amnesty but also gives the thief money and congratulates him on choosing the finest bakery. While this charitable attitude seems philanthropic and reformative, the pardon is also a demonstration of power. On the foundation of a class-based social and economic hierarchy that ensures dependence, the chief creates an expectation for law-abiding behavior without undoing the unjust conditions that have led to the crime. Instead of ensuring livable wages for the thief to be able to "think and better himself," the latter is set up to fail as soon as the money runs out, and he will be judged much more harshly as a repeat offender.

The chief plays God regularly, deciding to damn or redeem transgressors according to his own convictions. The narrator legitimizes this power by describing the chief's unfailing talent for identifying the (un)deserving and eliciting confessions from them: "Und nicht selten hatte ich Gelegenheit, über den feinen Instinkt und den großen Scharfsinn des *Mr. Thomacksin* zu staunen, der namentlich verstockte und sich auf's Läugnen verlegende Missethäter mit einer ganz bestimmten, nie fehlenden, sicheren Methode zu entwaffnen verstand" (VTS, 113; And not infrequently had I the opportunity to marvel at the fine instinct and the great acumen of *Mr. Thomacksin*, who knew to disarm especially obdurate delinquents, who resorted to denial, with a very specific, never failing, certain method). The chief's endeavor to discern what is denied resonates with the goals of literary censorship to find illegitimate ideas hidden in texts—whether they are there or not. Yet the power differential makes it impossible to say whether these "criminals" might not just have been worn down by the interrogation and admitted to something they did not do. After all, they are "disarmed," and since the inquisition is invoked shortly after, the chief's "certain method" might include violence. The behavior of the chief exposes that policing processes consist of subjective and random decisions, and the example of the bread thief, while seemingly merciful, highlights the absolute power of governmental and religious institutions. As the separation of powers appears nonexistent for the police and the chief's religious convictions inform his decisions, the text also critiques alliances between church and state, particularly their joint role in German censorship efforts, which Panizza targeted even more explicitly in his other writing. Church and state seem to merge quite literally in the descriptions of the two protagonists, as the next two sections will show. In the following analysis of the chief's and Jonathan's respective physical appearances and belief systems, fears regarding same-sex attraction, gender roles, bachelorhood, and reproduction emerge from the anxiety surrounding the masturbating plants.

The Chief: Executioner, Preacher, Inquisitor, Judge

Granting amnesty is just one page in the police chief's book of random rules. When it comes to crimes against morality, specifically of a sexual nature, the narrator says that the "milde[ ], freundliche[ ] Mann von der größten Herzensgüte [...] ließ [...] die volle Gesetzesstrenge walten, und, ich glaube, er ging sogar über das gesetzlich zulässige Maaß hinaus" (VTS, 111; mild, friendly man of the greatest kindness of heart [...] applied [...] the full severity of the law, and, I believe, he even went beyond the lawfully permissible measure). Because of the sexual nature of their crime, the chief classifies the masturbating plants as major offenders, yet they cannot very well be put on trial or jailed. The chief would not mind a death sentence for them, however, given his goal of eradicating sexual pleasure, and he seems ready to act as executioner himself:

> Die "*lust*", wie er es nannte, war das Ziel seiner Vernichtungspläne. Wenn er das Wort "*lust*" aussprach, gewann sein Gesicht einen unsäglich harten, wilden Ausdruck; mit den grauen erbarmungslosen Augen schaute er wie mit Marbelsteinen zu mir herüber und die geöffneten Lippen zeigten die Härte eines Henkers. (VTS, 111)

> "*Lust*," as he called it, was the target of his eradication plans. When he pronounced the word "*lust*," his face took on an unspeakably hard, wild expression; with gray merciless eyes he looked over to me as if with marble stones and his opened lips displayed the severity of an executioner.

Simultaneously passionate and stone-cold, the chief is clothed "[i]mmer in dem gleichen, alten, abgeschabten schwarzen Rock" (VTS, 110; always in the same old threadbare black gown), so that his dress choice and zealous conduct evoke both the image of a strict executioner and a fervent preacher. These positions ultimately merge in the fanatical "Inquisitor. Und nicht die Strafe eines Menschen zur Besserung war ihm so wichtig als die Analyse der innersten Triebfedern einer Persönlichkeit. [...] Er glaubte an einen fortschreitenden Reinigungs-Prozeß der Menschheit bis zur endlichen Gottähnlichkeit" (VTS, 110–11; inquisitor. And not the punishment of a person for betterment was as important to him as was the analysis of the innermost mainsprings of a personality. [...] He believed in a progressive purification process of humanity to the point of final godlikeness). The roles of the executioner, preacher, and inquisitor appear to be steppingstones on a path toward "höchstmöglicher Gottgleichheit" (VTS, 111; highest possible godlikeness). When he attains "eine höchst einflußreiche und wohl dotirte Ober-Richterstelle" (VTS, 118; a highly influential and well-paid chief justice position) at the end of the story, the reader learns immediately afterward that this changes the chief's physical appearance as well: "Er war auch sehr dick geworden" (VTS, 118; He had also become very fat). Initially, he was described as "ein langer, ausgemergelter Mensch mit glattrasirtem Gesicht, mit dünnem, schnappenden Fisch-Maul, einer langen, großlöchrigen Nase und grau-blauen vigilirenden Augen, die einen heißen, stets paraten Gedankenschatz hinter sich hatten" (VTS, 110; a long, emaciated person with a clean-shaven face, thin snapping fish-mouth, a long, big-nostriled nose and gray-blue vigilant eyes, which had a hot, ever ready treasure trove of thoughts behind them). This contrasting physicality signals complacency, even sinful gluttony, and indicates that officially achieving the powerful position of chief justice was his goal, whose privileges he was arguably already enacting before.

The chief's behavior is based on his religious beliefs: "Er war Swedenborgjaner" (VTS, 110; He was a Swedenborgian). Emmanuel Swedenborg (1688–1772), a Swedish scientist, mystic, and Christian theologian, established the so-called New Church based on visions he had of the spiritual world. His writing centers on the idea of individual responsibility by emphasizing the importance of charity and good deeds in addition to faith to achieve salvation. The chief's charity toward the bread thief and his striving for personal betterment both resonate with the importance of good deeds, while his obsession with the elimination of "lust" grapples with Swedenborg's principle that marriage presents the only legitimate space for sexuality. Swedenborg's publication *Die Wonnen der Weisheit über die eheliche Liebe sowie die Wollüste der Torheit über die buhlerische Liebe* (*Wisdom's Delight in Marriage Love: Followed by Insanity's Pleasure in Promiscuous Love*, 1768) argues that earthly marriages continue to exist in heaven. This explains the chief's fixation on sexuality as a problem because he, like Swedenborg, is a bachelor, which leaves no legitimate space for his own sexuality anywhere but the asylum, as indicated by the *Torheit* (insanity) in Swedenborg's book title. To better humanity, the chief thus hopes to do away with sexual desire altogether, for "wenn ich den Wollust-Faktor aus dem Calcül der Menschen-Erzeugung eliminiren könnte, dann hätten wir gewonnen" (VTS, 111; if I could eliminate the lust-factor from the intentions inherent in the production of humans, we would have won).

As the epigraph of "Das Verbrechen in Tavistock-Square" demonstrates, the chief applies moral concepts to plants in accordance with Swedenborg: "Hüten wir uns, immer nur allein den Menschen schuldig zu finden; überall, in der gesammten Natur, steckt, unter einem feinen Schleier verborgen, die *Sünde*. / *Swedenborg*" (VTS, 190; Beware of always only finding man guilty; everywhere, in all of nature, hidden behind a fine veil, is *sin*. / Swedenborg). The case of the masturbating plants showcases this peculiar application of moral responsibility to nature, which points to the insecurities regarding what it means to be human at the end of the nineteenth century. Major advances in the natural sciences such as Darwinism challenged the Christian idea of Man as creation's crowning glory and emphasized the biological mechanisms of human bodies.[13] The narrative engages with these anxieties through the chief's discussion of religion and science (even mentioning his math and science library; see VTS, 111), particularly his many references to human betterment that suggest evolutionary processes and influences of contemporary Social Darwinism. Darwin's *On the Origin of Species* (1859) describes evolution with the help of plants and animals instead of humans, which somewhat softened the study's conclusions about humankind's own evolutionary origin and development as well as the resulting parallels between species. When considering the British setting of the narrative and the polyglot Panizza's repeated use of English throughout the text, a multilingual hermeneutic layering around the term *origin* emerges that brings together science and religion in the chief's police practice.[14] In addition to referencing Darwin's *Origin of Species*, the chief not only makes "originelle[] Entscheidungen" (VTS, 112; original decisions) when it comes to crimes but is also described as "*Original* im besten *Sinn* des Worts" (VTS, 110, emphasis added; an original in the best sense of the word). The German phrase, moreover, contains the words *Original Sin*, the root of the evil that he is after, and even his name, Mr. Edward Thomacksin, ends in "sin," the target of the eradication strategy that determines his "original decisions."

The chief integrates Darwin's ideas into his religious and moral framework about sinful "lust" with the help of the phallic plant metaphor of the thorn:

> Schneiden Sie sie aus, die Wollust, diesen Dorn, an dem sich Alle blutig ritzen, und Alles wird gut gehen, – rief er mit Emphase aus, und begann ein längeres Capitel aus Darwin zu citiren, wonach eine Funktion, die durch Jahrhunderte langes Gehen-Lassen ungeahnte Dimensionen angenommen, innerhalb weniger Jahrzehnte durch planmäßiges Ersticken ausgerottet werden könne... (VTS, 113)

> Cut it out, the lust, this thorn on which all scratch themselves bloody, and everything will go well,—he called out with emphasis, and began to cite a longer chapter from Darwin according to which a function, which had taken

on unforeseen dimensions because it was left alone for centuries, could be eradicated by way of planned suppression [literally: suffocation] within a few decades...

This likely refers to the first chapter of Darwin's *Origin of Species*, which explains the selective breeding of plants and animals to introduce the theory of evolution. The selection according to a breeder's imagined outcome is supposed to enhance or diminish certain characteristics of a species, just like the chief wants to eradicate "lust" and tries to better both himself and the criminals he encounters. However, evolution in nature does not put a breeder in charge, and the analogy to such a figure describes an act of interference with the factors that actually determine evolution: natural and sexual selection. As police chief, Thomacksin sees himself in the position of a godlike breeder, yet the human legal apparatus functions based on a notion of responsibility that is absent in nature. Only the human concept of morality turns the behavior of the plants into a crime in need of punishment. Swedenborg's religious concepts thus seem to help the chief negotiate the acceptance of Darwinian teachings at the time because they introduce moral guidance and a spiritual goal to the depiction of nature as an uncontrollably reproducing and developing force. The kinship between nonhumans and humans in evolution results in their shared sinfulness, which can be found "in all of nature" according to the Swedenborgian epigraph. Yet the chief's thinking about selective breeding to exterminate sinful "lust" also evokes contemporary notions of eugenics that were closely entangled with the spheres of the police and the asylum through assumptions about poverty, criminality, and disease, and which extend to the police station through the description of Jonathan.

Jonathan: "Better Human Material"

The chief's convictions exert a strong influence on the other protagonist of the story. Jonathan, the young policeman, is described as

> ein feiner, junger, blonder Bursche, von delicatem Aussehen, mit großen leuchtenden Augen, einer mädchenhaften, einschmeichelnden Stimme, weißen, schön gebauten Händen, kurz von jener Sorte Menschen, die sich auf den ersten Anblick als aus besserem Menschenmaterial gebaut erweist, und der auffällig gegen die übrigen Polizisten roheren Schlags abstach. (VTS, 112)

> a fine young blond boy, of delicate appearance, with big shiny eyes, a girly pleasing voice, white beautifully built hands; in short, he was of the type of

people who prove to be made from better human material at first sight, and he contrasted sharply with the other policemen of coarser kind.

Delicate, sensitive, enthusiastic, and artistic, Jonathan is said to be different in a way that designates him as "better human material." This odd materiality introduces a hierarchy that differentiates Jonathan from the "coarser kind" of the other policemen while simultaneously foreshadowing that Jonathan's effeminate masculinity does not correspond to the traditional idea of Man. The language of "kinds of humans" resonates furthermore with the British class system and the chief's ideas about betterment and breeding, and it will introduce a biological as well as literary category, the *Gattung* (genus but also genre). The root of this word connotes biological reproduction and places it in a matrimonial context—such as *begatten* (copulate) and *Gatte/Gattin* (husband/wife). The idea of different kinds of humans thus evokes the notion of a taxonomy, established by Linnaeus's *Systema Naturae* (1735) and *Species Plantarum* (1753) for plants, animals, and minerals, as well as contemporary physiognomic pseudoscience that fueled eugenics and its obsession with hindering or furthering reproduction and the inheritance of certain traits in certain people. Categorizing humans in the same way as plants and animals ultimately calls up Darwinism's social legacy once more while betraying insecurities about Man's waning exceptionalism, which can be redressed, in part, by the idea of evolutionarily hierarchical taxonomies of humans.

The language of human taxonomies and evolution informs not just Jonathan's characterization but also the portrayal of his relationship to the chief:

> Wie ich hörte, hatte *Sir Edward* den jungen Mann aus einer nebensächlichen Lebensstellung veranlaßt, in seinem Sprengel als *policeman* Dienst zu nehmen. Thatsache war, daß mein Chef dienstlich mit Niemanden lieber verkehrte, als mit Jonathan; und daß dieser, dessen Lebens-Gewohnheiten gänzlich von denen der Leute niederer Gattung abwichen, nur dadurch sich bei seinen Kameraden zu halten vermochte, daß er durch seine Fürsprache bei *Sir Edward* diesen manche dienstliche Vortheile und Erleichterungen verschaffte, die sonst sicher ausgeblieben wären. (VTS, 112)

> I heard that *Sir Edward* had arranged for the young man from a marginal position in life to serve as a *policeman* in his parish. Fact was that at work my boss preferred to consort with nobody more than with Jonathan; and that the latter, whose life and habits deviated entirely from those of the lower kind

of people, was only able to get along with his comrades by procuring some
work benefits and mitigations through his advocacy with *Sir Edward*, which
otherwise would have surely not occurred.

Both the chief's favoritism toward Jonathan and class seem to set the two
protagonists hierarchically apart from the other policemen, the "lower kind
[*Gattung*] of people." Throughout the story, the metaphors for the relationship between Jonathan and his superior vary, but they all emphasize the
latter's more dominant and powerful position, which, in turn, affords Jonathan some benefits over others. The chief treats him "mit väterlicher Milde"
(VTS, 115; with fatherly kindness), and to the narrator, Jonathan appears as
his disciple because he shares the latter's opinions unquestioningly: "[S]o
schien es mir, als sei Jonathan nicht nur ein gehorsamer und pflichtgetreuer
Untergebener, sondern hätte auch mit einem gewissen Enthusiasmus die
eigenthümlichen Anschauungen seines Herrn in sich aufgenommen" (VTS,
112; So it seemed to me as if Jonathan was not only an obedient and dutiful subordinate but had also incorporated the peculiar views of his master
[or: lord] with a certain enthusiasm). The analogies of lord and subject,
father and son, teacher and disciple codify the relationship with biblical
connotations but "incorporating" [*in sich aufnehmen*] the chief's opinions,
"consorting [*verkehren*] at work," and a vaguely implied allusion to the close,
potentially homoerotic relationship of the biblical Jonathan with David,
along with the description of Jonathan as having a "girly," "pleasing" voice
and a delicate physique stereotypically suggest a subtext of same-sex desire
that would rival the scandalous crime of the masturbating plants. The fact
that attraction to members of the same sex must remain dormant in this
historical context mirrors the crime of which the plants are accused. Masturbation has also been cast as an outlet for sexual desires that cannot be acted
on with others or openly. These parallels point to problems with finding a
legitimate space for sexuality—be it homo- or heterosexual—that bachelors
like Jonathan, the chief, or Panizza himself faced in late nineteenth-century
society. Because bachelors were not integrated into the "alliance system of
marriage" that offered the only legitimate space for sexuality, they (and their
desire) appeared as uncontrollable and dangerous.[15] In lieu of the institution
of marriage, Jonathan's end in the asylum safeguards society from him as
an unattached, uncontrollable sexual being. Institutionalization successfully excises Jonathan from a social structure that only allows for sexuality
in the conjugal sphere and that ensures mutual dependence through the

result of reproduction—that is, the responsibility for children. The genre's overwhelmingly male point of view, while certainly one of its historical shortcomings, nonetheless mobilizes bachelorhood as a space of radical (and potentially queer) sexuality.[16]

The focus on single, male protagonists in the two *Grotesken* in this section stands out particularly because the narratives engage openly with sexual reproduction and refer to eroticized flowers, blossoms, or nature in general, which are often associated with femininity—even in the grammatical gender of these terms in German (*die Blume/Blüte/Natur*) and particularly in the contemporaneous imagery of art nouveau that frequently showed young women sensually entangled in flowers and vines.[17] The term *Fortpflanzung* (reproduction, or literally, "planting on") also points to the ways in which botany and the study of human sexuality have been intertwined for centuries.[18] In attributing human ideas about gender and sexuality to plants, the *Grotesken* draw on a long history of anxieties about vegetal eroticism that began in the eighteenth century with Linnaeus's famous categorization of plants according to their reproductive organs.[19] Ewers's text, to which I will turn later, even explicitly refers to the twenty-four different classes of plants that emerged from this taxonomy. Linnaeus's sexual system applies binary human concepts of sex and gender to plants, but the proliferating multitude of sex combinations and forms of reproduction found in the natural world undermines normative moral ideas about reproduction. The Linnean classification system shows that it is natural for many plants to have two sexes in the same plant or flower (called bisexual or hermaphroditic plants), to reproduce with themselves, or to be indiscriminately pollinated by anyone and anything passing by. Since Linnaeus compared plants to humans in overt metaphors, such as calling pollination "marriage" and referring to stamen and pistil as women and men in a "bridal chamber," the implications of his work caused outrage and fundamentally altered the way people thought about plants and botany.[20] The discipline became a place to think about sexuality, making it improper for women to engage in the study of plants and resulting in the production of literary texts that imbued the vegetal world with erotic innuendo, such as Erasmus Darwin's poem "The Loves of Plants" (1791).[21] By the time the *Grotesken* pick up this eighteenth-century anxiety one hundred years later, the focus has turned toward a broader range of sexual behaviors and ideas about gender, including masturbation, same-sex desire, and what we would today subsume under various labels for queer identities.²² In the two *Grotesken* about vegetal eroticism, the naturally occurring sexual diversity of plants is used to critique societal norms based on a limited understanding of sexuality that focuses only on (heterosexual, married, monogamous) reproduction and renders pleasure perverted. Turning to the discovery of the masturbating plants in the next part, I will show how Panizza's text reproduces the act through ambiguous language and physical gestures while implicating everyone else in the sexual transgression.

The Crime

Jonathan's attempts to deliver his report about the masturbating plants to the chief takes up most of the text. Agitation about his shocking discovery is palpable in Jonathan's speech: "No *Sir*![ ] – sagte Jonathan in tiefer Erregung, – es hat sich etwas außerordentliches zugetragen! [...] Der Brustton, mit dem der Polizist sprach, und das Fibrirende in seiner Stimme waren Symptome, die einem Menschenkenner, wie meinem Chef, nicht entgingen" (VTS, 114; No *Sir*![ ]—said Jonathan with great excitement,—something extraordinary has happened! [...] The utter conviction with which the policeman spoke and the vibration in his voice were symptoms that did not elude a judge of human nature like the chief). Jonathan's speech shows the symptoms of what Victorian novels call a brain fever, the result of a severe emotional upset, making him appear infected and foreshadowing his containment in the form of institutionalization.²³ He is already figuratively "arrested" by self-imposed, censoring interruptions (frequently rendered as suggestive dashes and dots in the text) that point to the limitation of free speech vis-à-vis censorable acts. Describing the crime verbally will implicate him in the transgression according to censorship laws, and perhaps for this reason, but also because he does not know how to put into words what he has witnessed, he resorts to physical gestures that implicate him even more. He enacts the flailing movements of masturbatory stimulation: "Der Polizist rang im Zwang mit sich selbst" (VTS, 115; The policeman was wrestling with himself compulsively). This gestural reenactment continues throughout the text, as the policemen all face the same conundrum in discussing the crime. Jonathan first begins to talk about what he has seen in the antechamber of the police station, but the other policemen ridicule what they hear, uttering "leises Gemurmel und unterdrücktes Gekicher" (VTS, 114; quiet murmuring and suppressed giggling). The revelation in the antechamber is anticlimactic because it fails to bring across what Jonathan has detected. He keeps trying to explain, however, and continues to build momentum physically.

The chief becomes interested quickly when he sees Jonathan's agitation and hears about another kind of suspicious giggling—coming from plants:

> Es war kein menschliches Gekicher; es war etwas Verdächtiges, und glänzende Stoffe fielen aus den großen Magnolenkelchen zur Erde, und ein unkeuscher Geruch verbreitete sich; ein Blitz, *Sir*, fuhr mir gleich durch den Kopf! [...] – Der Polizist stund fiebernd vor Erregung; seine Augen strahlten; in dem rohen, schwarzen Polizeikittel stund der blonde, zarte Mensch dort wie ein junger Prediger. (VTS, 115)

> It was no human giggling; it was something suspicious, and glossy materials fell from the big magnolia chalices to the ground and an unchaste smell spread; lightning, *Sir*, shot immediately through my head! [...]—The policeman stood feverishly excited; his eyes were beaming; in the rough black police gown the blond tender person stood there like a young preacher.

Jonathan is physically excited, as a state of arousal (*Erregung*) has infected him like a fever. The eyes with which he has witnessed the crime are ablaze. The figure of a policeman once again converges with that of a preacher, both because of the black clothing and the fervor of speech. Jonathan is not struggling for words because he is unsure about what happened or what to think about it; rather, he says, language is at fault: "*Sir*, die englische Sprache ist nicht ausreichend um die Scheußlichkeit zu umfassen!" (VTS, 115; *Sir*, the English language is not enough to contain this abomination!). Language neither contains the right words for the act nor can it contain or control it, which becomes especially clear through the word *umfassen*, which is itself an act of touching or embracing (*anfassen, umarmen*) similar to the entwining of the plants. Because of Jonathan's lack of uncontaminated or appropriate words, which is either a sign of or the performance of his naivete, he reverts to a euphemism that is as telling about his innocence as it is about his colleagues' laughter. He compares what he has seen to "....Bewegungen, wie sie .... Polizisten oft Nachts auf der Pritsche machen...." (VTS, 115; ....movements like .... policemen often make them on their cots at night....), suggesting with elliptical hesitation that he has witnessed other policemen engaging in masturbation. It becomes evident now that the description of both plants and policemen as "giggling" was not coincidental—and the "unchaste smell" surrounding the plants might similarly have accompanied the policemen's nightly movements on their cots.

Jonathan's seemingly innocent observation reveals that his colleagues are engaged in the same criminal behavior as the plants, which makes it difficult for him to distinguish right from wrong, and plants from humans. Yet this aspect of his report has seemingly no consequences in the story, which suggests that the police chief is either the most naive of them all and does not understand the allusion or is implicated himself and therefore chooses to ignore it:

> "Johny, – sagte mein Chef mit väterlicher Milde zu seinem Untergebenen, – Locomotiven machen bestimmte Bewegungen, und Polizisten machen wieder besondere Bewegungen Nachts auf der Pritsche; das Alles ist kein Maaßstab, Du mußt Dich präciser ausdrücken. Was hast Du gesehen?" – "'Sir, – es war zum Grausen; es war ein Verbrechen wider die Natur; '"ich stund wie angewurzelt; ich konnte mir nicht helfen!'" (VTS, 115)
>
> "Johny,—the chief said with fatherly kindness to his subordinate,— locomotives make certain movements and policemen make other movements at night on their cots; all that is no measure, you have to express yourself more precisely. What did you see?"—"'Sir,—it was gruesome; it was a crime against nature; '"I stood rooted to the ground; I couldn't help myself!'"

In the face of discovering "a crime against nature," Jonathan himself stands as if rooted (*wie angewurzelt*), or figuratively arrested like a plant. Once again, the description plays with the indistinguishability of arrester and arrested, of human and plant—all while the chief demands more precise language. By witnessing the crime and having to report it, Jonathan has become implicated, and his physical arousal (*Erregung*) during the report paints him potentially guilty. As he says, "I couldn't help myself!" Could he be reporting his own transgression in the guise of a story about plants?[24]

Jonathan's description of his vegetal rootedness in response to the discovery is one of many instances of the text using physical gestures to express ideas that cannot be spoken about openly: Jonathan's convergence with the accused plants signals both a form of arrest and self-implication, and the masturbatory movements that accompany his initially anticlimactic attempt at reporting extend this idea and will be taken up in the chief's own physical reaction toward the end. These gestures point to the limits of language in the context of the contemporary *Sprachkrise* while making the censorship of language and literature visible as a different kind of linguistic limitation. In its gestural descriptions, the text showcases an expressive creativity that circumvents these limits and satirizes them by entangling those who enact censorship in their own prohibitions. The expression "crime against nature," for instance, exemplifies the paradoxical and ultimately impossible undertaking of censoring language. In this phrase, "nature" does not signify the opposite of culture but is a part of it: "nature" in this sense stands for human morality or supposedly moral behavior, against which the crime of masturbation offends. Yet the plants *are* "nature" (in the sense of landscape or environment) and engaging in a natural process. "Nature" in the second sense, thus, runs counter to "nature" in the first, and what is considered a nonreproductive, pleasure-focused activity (masturbation) is in fact part of a reproductive act for plants (pollination). The paradox of "unnatural nature" therefore showcases the human hubris of applying normative, anthropocentric concepts to others, regardless of fit, and it justifies doing so with an essentializing vocabulary of naturalness and originality. The "crime against nature" itself leads those notions ad absurdum since it features "nature" both as a synonym for morality and as a perpetrator of perversions. The "crime" therefore loses its frame of reference, and by extension, so does the meaning of words like "nature," parsing out the language skepticism of the *Sprachkrise*. These narrative strategies reach their climax when Jonathan's attempts to clarify reveal the criminals to be masturbating plants.

A Climax of Narration

Panizza's *Groteske* performs how censorship restrictions unleash a new experimental and creative wealth of language, and linguistic limitation therefore turns into the abundance of polysemous and defamiliarizing descriptions that are typical for the genre, which allow the texts to show what they cannot say. This is illustrated most clearly in Jonathan's expression, which not only includes self-interruptions visible in frequent dashes and dots but also culminates in a frenzied accumulation of euphemisms and synonyms when he finally finds words for the crime. Each of his halting attempts to clarify the deed of the plants seems to obscure the details of the event even more, and only after the chief loses his patience does Jonathan burst out with an explicit portrayal in the central paragraph of the story:

> ""Es waren Berührungen, *Sir* – rief der Polizist und holte tief Athem, – wie sie vor Gott und der Welt nicht erlaubt sind, es waren Liebkosungen,

Entblößungen, Entleerungen, es war ein Gekicher, ein Schleifen, ein Von-sich-Geben, ein Umranken, eine Art Küssen .... ein Küssen, Sir, – ..."" – "Ja, in drei Teufel's Namen, hast Du denn Niemand gesehen? Zogst Du nicht Deine Blendlaterne heraus?" – ""Sir, es war Niemand da. Die Rosen und Magnolen waren unter sich. Auch waren die Geräusche und Berührungen nicht menschliche"". –"Nicht menschliche?" – frug mein Chef, – "ja, was war es dann?" – ""Sir, – schrie und schluchzte der junge, fanatische Polizist, – die Rosen und Magnolen im *Tavistock Parc* trieben S e l b s t - B e f l e c k u n g, – es war veritable P f l a n z e n - O n a n i e!"" – (VTS, 117)

""There was touching, Sir,—the policeman said and took a deep breath,—as it is not allowed in the face of God and the world, there was fondling, denuding, discharging, there was giggling, grinding, emitting, entwining, a kind of kissing .... kissing, Sir,— ..."" —"But in the name of three devils, didn't you see somebody? Did you not pull out your bull's eye lantern [literally: blinding lantern]?"—""Sir, nobody was there. The roses and magnolias were among themselves. Also, the sounds and touches were not human.""—"Not human?"—asked my boss,—"but what was it then?"—""Sir,—the young fanatical policeman cried out and sobbed,—the roses and magnolias in *Tavistock Park* were practicing s e l f - m a c u l a t i o n,—it was veritable p l a n t - o n a n i s m!""—

The short exchange is full of descriptions that highlight the physical aspects accompanying Jonathan's words—such as breathing in deeply, crying out, and sobbing—and of defamiliarizing descriptions of plants, such as fondling, denuding, grinding, discharging, giggling, and entwining. The intensity of Jonathan's agitation (*Erregung*) that has been building momentum is released in the escalating list of plant behaviors, which briefly hesitates again in a repetition of "kissing, Sir" before culminating in the descriptor of "veritable p l a n t - o n a n i s m!" Pent-up arousal (*Erregung*), built up and halted by the repeated anticlimactic attempts and delays, finally releases the climactic admission of the crime in the form of a cry and is followed by tears, a quasi-orgiastic emission of fluids. The plants are discharging (*Entleerungen*) or ex-pressing and emitting (*Von-sich-Geben*) something too, which has equally sexual and linguistic connotations—yet they almost disappear behind Jonathan's reenacting performance. According to censorship law, what is expressed here is not supposed to be articulated or transmitted to others. Jonathan, however, has been infected and passes on the forbidden content in prohibited language, which turns out to be more important than the sexual act itself.[25] The breach of society's norms is reproduced in bodies and language.

In Jonathan's account, the plants simultaneously break the law and offend his sense of morality, which conflates the two and once again raises questions about the legality of police procedures. By turning to the terms *plant-onanism* (in reference to the biblical Onan who spilled his seed to avoid procreation) and *self-maculation* to describe what he has seen, Jonathan suggests that he is witnessing a sin. God killed Onan for his transgression, and self-maculation is a deed that includes its own punishment in the form of a stigmatizing stain—thus, neither requires any police involvement. In response to the sinful discovery, the usually pious chief forgets about his own morality for a minute and reverses the Holy Trinity by swearing "in the name of three devils." He asks about the *Blendlaterne* (literally a "blinding" lantern, named for the blinds that focus its light), a tool of the trade that seems to signify the moral blinders of the institution of the police rather than shedding light on the situation. Despite the blinding lantern or perhaps because of these blinders, Jonathan cannot see what is happening, and he cannot make an arrest because he is arrested (*angewurzelt*) himself. The institution of the police gets in its own way, even before it becomes entangled in censored language use. Police tools are no match for this crime, which suggests that the police is not equipped to assess sexual and, by extension, literary transgressions.

Despite what could be considered an anthropomorphic description of plant sexuality, Jonathan calls the vegetal "touches and sounds" explicitly *not* human. In response to the chief's question, "Not human? [...] but what was it then?" Jonathan draws on Swedenborgian vocabulary once more, calling the plants "Spitzbuben [...i]m Sinne des Großartig-Unmenschlichen'" (VTS 116; scoundrels in the sense of the grand-inhuman). Rather than nonhuman, they are *Unmenschen*—that is, inhuman. While thus suggesting that they are morally abject, Jonathan also gives them a rather colloquial name for a criminal: *Spitzbuben* (scoundrels). One might even argue that the term is gendered, since it literally translate to "pointy boys," which invokes both the phallic thorns of the roses and the metaphorical usage of *spitz* as "horny." The contrasting grandeur (*Großartig-Unmenschlich*) of their inhumanness would put them in the category of major offenders in terms of police matters, even though "scoundrels" makes their offense sound rather minor. The inhuman is thus a *Gattung* or kind of human beings who are not accepted as human because they supposedly do not take responsibility for their actions. According to Jonathan's choice of words, the masturbating plants are in a similarly confusing state of nonhuman humanity because they are by species nonhuman, yet they commit transgressions according to human morality—which, because they do not accept responsibility or show remorse, would render them criminals of the inhuman kind. This classification seems necessary both to put plants in their place as nonhumans and to legitimize the application of human laws to them as inhumans. The narrative once more reveals an uncertainty about what it means to be human. Now that the crime has been described in explicit language, the chief responds with a performance of his own, but he is unable to apply the law.

The Grand Finale

The chief's response to the discovery of libido in plants is as strong as Jonathan's, and he is initially also at a loss for words and turns to gestures:

> In diesem Moment sprang *Mister Edward Thomacksin*, Vorstand der *police-station of Marylebone-Street*, wie von einer Tarantel gestochen in die Höhe. Einen Augenblick starrte der alte, ausgemergelte Mann, der, wie mir schien, in seinen Erwägungen hinsichtlich der Angaben des jungen Jonathan sich in einer ganz andern Richtung bewegt hatte, mit glasigen Augen den kühnen Polizisten an. Dann, als er sah, daß hier keine Illusion mehr möglich, streckte der verzweifelte Swedenborgjaner krampfhaft die Hände empor und mit einer veränderten heulenden Stimme, wie ich sie niemals von ihm gehört, schrie er zur Decke hinauf:, *"Lord, holy Lord*, wende ab Dein Aug von der Schöpfung! Das scheußlichste Verbrechen haben jetzt die Rosen, die keuschesten Blumen, glücklich den Menschen abgeguckt. Lord, sie warten nicht mehr auf Deine Erlaubnis für den infernalen Akt. Du hast ihnen die Fähigkeit verliehen sich zu vermehren. Aber das genügt ihnen nicht. Sie wollen um jeden Preis sündigen. Lord, schicke eine neue Sündfluth, und verderbe Deine Schöpfung, oder die Welt geht aus ihren Fugen!" – Dann stürzte *Thomacksin*, dessen Gesicht wie Mörtel geworden war, schluchzend zusammen, und mußte fortgetragen werden. – (VTS, 117)

> At this moment, *Mister Edward Thomacksin*, chief of the *police station of Marylebone-Street*, jumped in the air as if stung by an adder. For a moment, the old, emaciated man, who, it seemed to me, had moved in a completely different direction in his deliberations regarding the allegations of young Jonathan, stared with glassy eyes at the daring policeman. Then, when he saw that an illusion was no longer possible in this case, the distraught Swedenborgian raised his hands convulsively and with a changed, wailing

voice, like I had never heard from him, he cried up to the ceiling: "*Lord, holy Lord*, avert Your eye from Your creation! The roses, the chastest flowers, have successfully copied the most abominable crime of humankind. Lord, they no longer wait for Your permission for the infernal act. You have given them the ability to procreate. But that is not enough for them. They want to sin at all costs. Lord, send a new Deluge and ruin Your creation, or the world is going to pieces!"—Then, *Thomacksin*, whose face had become like mortar, collapsed crying and had to be carried away.—

The limitations placed on sexual language seem to require a physical reenactment of the act, just like in Jonathan's case, and the masturbatory arousal, which he built in his many interrupted explanation attempts until the quasi-orgiastic admission, is released a second time in the chief's climactic reaction. The chief jumps up suddenly, halts, raises his hands to the heavens, cries out, and collapses. His loss of control also comes with the discharge of a bodily fluid, his tears. As he is asking God to avert his eyes, the chief's own eyes are described as glassy as that of a corpse and his face as white as mortar. His body is performing *la petite mort*, "the little death" or orgasm. This reenactment of the crime emphasizes that he is part of the corrupted creation from which he asked God to avert his eyes, and since the chief is reintroduced with his full title at the beginning of this paragraph, this equally implicates the institution of the police. The chief does not mention legal transgressions or consequences for the crime and those implicated; his only concern is the sin that appears to have seduced the "chastest flower"— that is, the rose as a symbol of innocence and love. Fulfilling his role as the inquisitor, the chief calls for a second deluge to eradicate this vegetal "lust" according to his principles. His wailing prayer laments the fall of creation, which was brought about by the fruit of the tree of knowledge. Yet ironically, plants were the only living beings that survived the biblical deluge: when Noah sent birds to find out whether land had reemerged, they bring back an olive branch. "Lust" therefore threatens morality—even sanity—but not nature.

After witnessing this breakdown, one might expect to find the chief in a mental institution, but on the contrary: "Nur der arme Jonathan kam in's Irrenhaus" (VTS, 118; Only poor Jonathan was committed to the insane asylum). Institutions that regulate (language containing) sexuality institutionalize those who speak of sexual acts, whether they are literary authors or one of their own, like Jonathan, whose discovery forced him to reproduce the crime in language and gestures. Curiously, neither the plants nor the implicated policemen appear to experience consequences, even though they prompted the prohibited language and presumably committed the act. In the logic of the text, they remain unpunished because they do not share their solitary sexual acts linguistically—unlike Jonathan. His report reproduced sexual behavior in language and disseminated it to the public, as the flowers were "spreading their seed" in the act of reproduction. Because the context of human morality misconstrues this reproductive act as purely pleasure-focused masturbatory behavior, the infectious spread of knowledge must be contained. Yet discourses of sexuality prove uncontainable, and censorship remains caught in a paradoxical conundrum. Drawing on the performativity of the physical reenactments of masturbatory arousal and climax in the text, the next part, which is the last to focus only on "Das Verbrechen," turns to narrative strategies typical for *Grotesken* to show how the story makes the reader complicit in the same process of reproduction and pleasurable interpretation.

Narrative Strategies of the *Groteske*

So far, the close reading of Panizza's text has shown how three of the four typical characteristics of *Grotesken* outlined in chapter 1 can take shape and work in a text: the correlation between governing institutions that enforce society's norms and the involuntary institutionalization of those who do not conform, like Jonathan; the ambiguous language play as a symptom of the *Sprachkrise*; and the focus on bodies and sexuality as sites of the reproduction of society's normativity, which has been particularly evident in the crime's linguistic and gestural reenactment. This final section about Panizza's text further elucidates these points, especially the latter two, and addresses the remaining characteristic of narration: *Grotesken* expose seemingly trustworthy narrators and protagonists who represent societal norms as unreliable and flawed. The performativity of the genre, which has become clear to some extent in this text's use of language and the description of physical gestures, is of particular importance to the narrative position. Examining elements of theatricality and performance in conjunction with the narrative situation will bring out the *Groteske*'s strategies regarding reading and interpretation, or, in other words, the hunt for clues—aspects of detective work that are performed by the police as censors and ultimately also implicate us readers.

There are multiple indicators that "Das Verbrechen in Tavistock-Square" is staging a performance that follows theatrical structures: the narrator remains in the background while providing us with dialogues in direct speech; the entire plot seems to take place in the space of one room, while the crime is introduced in a kind of teichoscopy; stage directions and comical props appear; the action is halted before its climax; and the protagonists' physical performance culminates in scenes that, given the directions, could be reenacted with filmic precision.[26] These traditional theatrical means contrast with Panizza's own provocative dramatic work that led to his imprisonment and the naturalist plays of the time that would later incur the wrath of *Lex Heinze*. Both in terms of theater history and in the context of *die Groteske* with its ties to the cabaret, this deliberate use of a more conventional conception of theater as a narrative strategy appears outdated and insufficient, and by association, this applies to the position of the police it represents. One example for theatrically ridiculing the efficacy of the police is the narrative's emphasis on police tools as mere props in a comedy of errors that underscores a failing strategy of witnessing and reporting crimes. Jonathan's halting report gives ample opportunity for linguistic absurdity, and the detailed narrative descriptions enable physical slapstick, often with a potential for erotic undertones. Particularly its bureaucratic laboriousness resonates with scenes in Kafka's writing. To give an example, a lengthy portion of dialogue addresses the question whether it would have been appropriate for Jonathan to use his police whistle when he discovered the crime. Making comic use of complicated bureaucratic expressions and peppered with an abundance of exclamation marks to indicate the intensity of the exchange, the conversation nonetheless ends quite anticlimactically:

> "Hast Du denn Deine Pfeife nicht gezogen?" – "'*Sir*, – da war nichts zu pfeifen!'" – "Du konntest doch immerhin pfeifen!" – "'*Sir*, – es war kein Fall zum Pfeifen!'" – "Aber bei der Merkwürdigkeit des Vorfalls, wie du sagst, war es doch immer gerathen, durch die Pfeife Deinen Kameraden an der nächsten Ecke wenigstens zu avertiren!" – "'*Sir*, – der Vorfall war so wenig nach der Richtung geeignet, daß er die Möglichkeit der Anwendung der Pfeife direct ausschloß!'" – "Johny, paß auf: Die Geneigtheit des Vorfalls steht doch in keinem Verhältnis zu der Möglichkeit der In-Bewegungsetzung der Pfeife!" – "'Sehr wohl, *Sir*, – die Möglichkeit des Pfeifens war nicht ausgeschlossen; aber ich hielt einerseits den Gegenstand nicht für werthvoll genug, um mir durch die Pfeife materiellen Beistand zu sichern; andererseits ging er doch wieder weit über die Bedeutung des Pfeifens hinaus; mit anderen Worten, er

war *extraordinary*, aber nicht gefahrdrohend; – abgesehen davon wäre mir der Ton beim Versuch in der Kehle stecken geblieben"". – (VTS, 115–16)

"Did you not pull out your whistle?"—""*Sir*,—there was no reason to whistle!""—"But you could have whistled anyway!"—""*Sir*,—it was not a case for whistling!""—"But with the peculiarity of the incident, as you say, it was still advisable to alert your comrade at the next corner with your whistle!"—""*Sir*,—the incident was so unsuitable in that direction that it directly excluded the possibility of the utilization of the whistle!""—"Johny, pay attention: The suitability of the incident is in no relation to the possibility of the actuation of the whistle!"—""Very well, *Sir*,—the possibility of whistling was not excluded; but on the one hand, I did not consider the matter worthwhile enough to ensure material assistance by way of the whistle; on the other hand, it went far beyond the significance of whistling; in other words, it was *extraordinary* but not dangerous;—aside from that, in the attempt, the sound would have gotten stuck in my throat in the attempt.""—

The previously mentioned "blinding" bull's eye lantern (which also appears in VTS, 114 and 117) and the police whistle are tools of the police practice that happens in public, and they amplify physical abilities, such as sight and sound, which represent police actions of witnessing and reporting. The objects are meant to protect both the policeman and, by extension, the law he upholds, but in Jonathan's particular case, these "tools of civilization" fail at domesticating "nature" and comically highlight the police's helplessness when trying to enforce morality. Instead of casting light on the matter or helping him witness the crime, the lantern momentarily blinds Jonathan, and in keeping with his inability to describe the crime in fitting language, he finds the regular response of blowing his whistle inappropriate, since "the sound would have gotten stuck in my throat." The beginning of this book argued that *die Groteske* produces the effect of "laughter getting stuck in one's throat," once the readers or audience realize the darker aspect of its satirical wordplay—a self-censoring response to a grotesque event that is invoked here quite literally. Neither being able to witness nor report the crime properly, the police once again emerges as unable to address transgressions both on the level of the plot and in its role as the censor of texts.[27]

Other theatrical strategies further emphasize the police's inability to read and interpret the situation accurately. In addition to Jonathan's trouble with responding appropriately to the situation, the chief addresses the narrator in the form of three asides that seem to go unnoticed by everyone else: "Wieder

Kopfbewegung von *Sir Edward* zu mir herüber, und die Flüster-Bemerkung: 'Das ist Swedenborg!' – Laut: 'Warum gingst du denn nicht auf die Sache los?'" (VTS, 116; Again head movement from *Sir Edward* to me and the whispered remark: "That is Swedenborg!"—Loudly: "Why did you not have a go at the matter?"). The contrast between whispered explanatory commentary (implying how pleased he is with Jonathan) and the loud, impatient questions (as per the "stage directions") adds the sense of a confidential "behind the scenes" moment that demonstrates just how gravely the chief misreads the situation. Confidently expecting his protégé to deliver a model crime report in front of his guest and delighted by the use of his favored Swedenborgian terminology, the matter of the actual report takes the chief entirely by surprise and shows that he has been misinterpreting and misjudging the situation completely—a fatal flaw for a man whose professional assessment and judgment of people and crimes is supposedly foolproof and quite consequential.

The three theatrical asides highlight the complexity of the narrative situation in this text. The lawyer-in-training who narrates "Das Verbrechen in Tavistock-Square" functions as a witness too, despite or maybe because of his participation as the chief's conversation partner in the story. The overarching strategy of witnessing is made explicit in the repeated emphasis on the eyes of the protagonists, which begins the first time the narrator meets the chief:

> Als ich ihm zum erstenmal meine Aufwartung machte, schaute er mich fast grimmig einige Minuten starr an, und sagte dann lauernden Blicks, zögernd und mit scharfer Betonung: "Ich weiß nicht, ob Ihr Auge, mein junger Freund, genügend reinen Sinn verspricht, um der moralischen Aufgabe, die Ihrer hier wartet, gewachsen zu sein!" (VTS, 110)

> When I first paid my respects to him, he stared at me almost grimly for a few minutes, and then said with a lurking look, hesitant and with sharp emphasis: "I don't know if your eye, my young friend, promises enough pure sense to be up to the moral task that awaits you here!"

Though the reader knows little about him, the narrator nonetheless seems reliable at first and thus appears as if he is up to the task of witnessing (the "moral task that awaits" him) because he is introduced with multiple markers of respectability, such as proof of good education, the right social relations, and polite behavior. The narrators of *Grotesken* are typically educated observers who are confronted with a strange, unusual experience and belong to the institutions under scrutiny, whether as physicians like Panizza himself, academics, or representatives of the law, such as in this case. Yet Jonathan's hesitant report about witnessing the crime raises doubt that a witness's eyes or memory can be trusted, and the trustworthiness of the witnessing narrator has itself been undermined in subtle ways from the start: by the way he describes the protagonists' gestures as reenacting the crime of masturbation, for instance, he implicates himself in the censorship offense through his own suggestive language use.[28]

The narrator's language choices are fundamentally important to the understanding of the reproduction of discourses of sexuality in this text. His role in the plot is obscured by the fact that the protagonists and their unusual experiences, reported mostly in direct speech, take all attention away from him. He seems to go to great lengths to relay the events accurately, but the reader must ultimately realize that there are multiple layers of unreliability: The narrator describes how he witnessed *circa ten years ago* that someone (Jonathan) told someone else (the chief) *in perfectly crafted direct speech* but *in another language* (English instead of the German of the text and the narrator's first language) what he *thought* he glimpsed in the dark of the night. The text's unreliability is effectively underscored on each of these layers, and it culminates in the representation of a simply unbelievable event—the masturbating plants. This realization leaves the reader without a reliable guide through the narrative, and it is simultaneously an indictment of police practices that rely on witness testimony. Ultimately, the reader must make up their own mind about what happened and interpret the narrative based on clues from the text—thus stepping into the shoes of the police. Yet the performative nature of the narrative and the way it draws language into question makes it difficult to rely on anything that is said or done, entangling the reader in the same issues as the policemen in the text.

The story's play with a multiplicity of clues and ambiguous language that is full of arresting interruptions renders Jonathan's trouble with language not a limitation but rather a performance that heightens the aesthetic pleasure of interpretation. Even though it seems as if he is struggling, Jonathan is the star of the text, and his defamiliarized descriptions are both concealing and revealing in a sophisticated textual striptease. Since the chief assumed Jonathan's innocence, his usually avid interpretation skills are led astray, and the reader might have similarly taken Jonathan for naive. Until his big reveal, Jonathan is therefore given opportunity to express himself without being censored by others. Precisely because he censors himself, reveling in defamiliarizing erotic descriptions (as does the narrator) and not "just saying" what he has seen, his interpreters, both the police in the text and the reader, do not realize that they have become complicit not only in the reproduction and spread of his ideas but also in the prohibited pleasure, or "lust," that is the aesthetic pleasure of interpreting ambiguous language. Readers become complicit by reading, just as Jonathan has become complicit by reporting (and the narrator by narrating), and they further reproduce the prohibited knowledge and language through reading. The more it is prohibited, the more it is spread, so censorship and the *Groteske* enable each other in a constitutive relationship. Ultimately, the text seems to outrun habituated reading expectations by constantly evolving further layers of possible interpretation.

Rather than providing answers, then, "Das Verbrechen in Tavistock-Square" raises a host of questions: What did Jonathan see? What does one make of the fact that there are only two kinds of reactions to his story? There are the policemen, who seem to be in utter disbelief, and the chief, who does not seem to doubt Jonathan's report whatsoever. Why is there no further investigation of the plants? Is Jonathan possibly displacing his own sexual desire or behavior onto the plants and therefore feeling the need to confess, repent, and be punished? Is the assumption of Jonathan's guilt the reason for his institutionalization, or does he possibly only repent for witnessing the other policemen masturbate? Do the other policemen then ridicule his report not for its naivete but out of fear of their own detection? Is that why he cannot use his whistle to elicit their support? Or do the plants really masturbate and is Jonathan literally becoming plantlike—*verwurzelt* and *angewurzelt* (rooted and arrested)—because of his discovery of plant sexuality? Like a touch-me-not or shameplant of the genus *Mimosa pudica* (*schamhafte Sinnpflanze, Mimose*), fascinated Jonathan recoils from the shameless sexual acts he has witnessed among plants and men. Or finally, is Jonathan simply lying, "planting evidence" if you will, or *jemanden pflanzen*, which literally translates to "plant someone" and means "to lead someone astray," by creating his own story as an unreliable witness? While not presenting us with one clear interpretation, the array of possibilities in the text is meaningful in itself and highlights the mutability of meaning in the context of the *Sprachkrise*. By reproducing ambiguity and reveling in oversignification rather than lamenting it, the text is a typical *Groteske*, which thrives in hermeneutic diversity and refuses to reveal simple, nonnegotiable conclusions in the face of censorship.

Yet Panizza's story, like other *Grotesken*, conveys a pointed critique, despite its interpretative ambiguity. It criticizes the use of religion for the legitimization of power and control, and it condemns social injustice, poverty, and class hierarchies. It also warns against merging the branches of state powers, just like it cautions against the union of church and state. Furthermore, the narrative lambastes the fact that institutions punish the ones reproducing language about sexuality (both Jonathan and Panizza) while not investigating the possible perpetrators of crimes (most notably those among their own ranks), which is a corrupt practice that ultimately advances those in positions of power, like the promoted chief. Finally, by engaging with Darwin's discoveries within an explicitly Christian worldview, the text raises questions about negotiating science and religion, and what these realms have to say about the place of humankind in the world, especially vis-à-vis other species, such as plants. A little over a decade after Panizza's text, Hanns Heinz Ewers attested to these ongoing concerns and anxieties in a *Groteske* that also uses eroticized vegetal imagery to address the regulation of human sexuality and the censorship of scientific knowledge by state and church.

FIVE

The Petition

Ewers's "Die Petition" (1904) draws on a vegetal imaginary like that of Panizza's story (which he knew) while emulating the genre strategies of *Grotesken* in general and of "Das Verbrechen in Tavistock-Square" in particular. The narrative revolves around twenty-seven-year-old Catholic priest Liborius Dornblüth from Gampelskirchen, a fictional Bavarian village, whose last name connotes the *Dornen* (thorns) and *Blüten* (blossoms) of the rose bushes in Panizza's narrative. It is also only an *Umlaut* away from an injury inflicted by those thorns (from the blossoms in "blüt" to *Blut* or blood), which evokes the suffering of Christ—pierced by a crown of thorns and a spear that is often called a *Dorn*. Just as the police chief had ferociously persecuted "lust"—the phallic thorn "on which all scratch themselves bloody" (VTS, 113)—"[d]er Herr Pfarrer, das stand fest, nahm es ernst mit seinen Pflichten, so blutig ernst, dass seine Vorgesetzten manchmal mit den Köpfen schüttelten" (P, 111; the Herr Reverend, that was clear, took his duties seriously, so bloody seriously that his superiors sometimes shook their heads). Like Panizza's text, Ewers's *Groteske* consists almost entirely of a report (the titular petition) that shows that Dornblüth not only takes his pastoral duties seriously but ultimately takes them too far.

The first sentence of the narrative introduces the celibate protagonist by way of his elderly housekeeper, Frau Obermüller: "Ueber die Haushälterin des Herrn Pfarrers Liborius Dornblüth zu Gampelskirchen hätte auch das allerliberalste Witzblatt keine Scherze machen können" (P, 111; Even the most liberal satirical magazine could not have made jokes about the housekeeper of the Reverend Liborius Dornblüth of Gampelskirchen). Given that the story was originally published in the prominent modernist journal *Jugend*, a liberal magazine with a strong satirical and critical current, this self-referential metacommentary is setting up the reader for the real target of the parody. Under attack is Dornblüth, the priest, who metonymically represents the Catholic Church, which functions, like the police, as a censoring agent in this story. This simultaneously implicit and candid first sentence introduces and draws attention to the main theme of the narrative—illicit sexual conduct—by denying it. Just like censorship inadvertently spreads sexually explicit content by prohibiting it, this first sentence introduces sex by rejecting its possibility. Despite the fact that the typical lewd joke about secret sexual relations between a priest and his housekeeper can supposedly not be made about the almost seventy-year-old woman who takes care of Dornblüth's home, food, and health in a maternal fashion throughout the story, the first sentence references a common conception that expects the need for some kind of sexual outlet in the face of celibacy (or bachelorhood). In this way, the housekeeper's maternal role corresponds to the police chief's fatherly behavior, complete with erotic subtext that is evoked by denying it. By repudiating that priests and elderly women are sexual beings, the sentence is displaying their sexuality and playing with the notion of secrecy and exposure through its implicit language and explicit associations. The phrase insinuates that the suppression of these figures' desires will find other, secret outlets, such as masturbation, thus suggesting that celibacy might be considered moral but not "natural." In only one sentence, the text makes clear that the institution of the Catholic Church is outlawing sexual behavior that is found among their own, just like the police in Panizza's *Groteske*.

Yet Dornblüth's reputation is one of fulfilling his duties to the letter, and his chastity seems therefore indubitable. Almost as zealous as the police chief, he is nonetheless as isolated as Jonathan and takes his work as seriously.

> Der Pfarrer ging auf in seiner Arbeit. Die Seelsorge, die er aufs peinlichste erfüllte, liess ihm, da seine Gemeinde nur klein war, viel freie Zeit, und diese Zeit füllte er teils mit einem angestrengten Studium, teils mit Kranken- und Armenbesuchen aus. Aber obwohl feststand, dass er den ganzen Jahresertrag seines kleinen Vermögens und sicher die Hälfte seiner Pfarrgelder zu wohltätigen Zwecken hergab, obwohl man ihm ansah, dass er sich die Pfennige absparte, um sie den Armen geben zu können, genoss er doch keine rechte Beliebtheit. (P, 111–12)

The priest was completely absorbed in his work. The pastoral care that he performed meticulously left him a lot of free time, since his congregation was only small, and he filled this time partly with strained studies, partly with visits to the sick and poor. Though even it was a fact that he gave the entire annual return of his small fortune and surely half of his allowance to charitable causes, even though one could glean from his appearance that he skimped and saved pennies to give to the poor, he did not quite enjoy any popularity.

Working for clerical publications without pay, his fervor is taken advantage of so much that his housekeeper begins to worry about his health. She "kannte die Herren da oben fast alle persönlich" (P, 113; knew the gentlemen up there almost all personally) and writes a letter to the bishop because of which Dornblüth is tasked with school inspections. This appointment is both a distinction and a way to stop his writing, which resonates with censorship.[1] The inspections endeavor "ihn von der schädlichen Nachtarbeit fern zu halten" (P, 113; to keep him from the damaging night work), which consists of his contributions to clerical publications but also evokes potential masturbatory acts like the policemen committed "on their cots at night." The priest goes about this new task "mit Feuereifer" (P, 114; with ardent, or literally fiery zeal) and "[s]eine Revision wurde bald der Schrecken aller Schullehrer, an keinem Tage konnte man vor seinem Besuche sicher sein" (P, 114; his examination soon became the terror of all schoolteachers, one could be safe from his visit on no day). The teachers who usually give *Zensuren* (grades) are now being *zensiert* (graded or censored).

Dornblüth's almost pathological obsession soon attaches itself to a specific school subject, and one day he comes home extremely upset:

> "Es geht nicht so weiter!" rief er. "Man muss da einschreiten!" [...] "Die Botanik!" schrie er wild. "Die Botanik!" Er besann sich sofort und bereute sein unschickliches Aufbrausen. "Ich bitte Sie inständig, mir zu verzeihen, Frau Obermüller!" sagte er leise. Und ganz, ganz sanft, aber mit einem unglaublichen Hasse im Tonfall fügte er hinzu: "Die Botanik!" (P, 115)

> "It cannot go on like this!" he shouted. "Someone has to intervene!" [...] "Botany!" he yelled wildly. "Botany!" He recollected himself immediately and regretted his unbecoming eruption. "I implore you to forgive me, Frau Obermüller!" he said quietly. And very, very gently, but with an unbelievable hate in his voice, he added: "Botany!"

The priest's otherwise dormant passion erupts for a moment in this display of his excessive hatred of botany (reminding us of the climactic eruptions in Panizza's text), but he censors himself immediately. Nonetheless, the teachers also take note of the priest's new obsession, and one quips that Dornblüth "wünsche mich noch heute für meine Sünden lebendig braten zu lassen!" (P, 116; would like to see me roasted alive for my sins this very day!). In lieu of that option, Dornblüth begins to compile a petition in favor of ending the teaching of all natural sciences—a seemingly bizarre demand that nonetheless corresponds to historical reality: From 1882 to 1908, aspects of biology education were removed from secondary schools in Germany. This happened against the backdrop of the *Kulturkampf* (1872–1878), the "cultural struggle" over control in education between Bismarck-led Prussia and the powerful Catholic Church with its stronghold in Bavaria. The ban was primarily concerned with theories of evolution and an approach to the entire ecological system, while allowing some rudimentary botany and zoology instruction in lower grades. Biologists opposed this prohibition against teaching Charles Darwin's and Ernst Haeckel's work, staging public campaigns that provocatively asked for religious instruction to be outlawed instead.[2] Publications in the realms of popular science and of fiction, like Ewers's *Groteske* about the Bavarian priest, not only satirized this debate but became alternative sites of knowledge reproduction.[3] Ewers's use of basic botanical structures to point to a greater ecological context (from plant reproduction to the sexual and natural selection of evolution) seems to suggest that for censorship to achieve its goals, it would have to prohibit the teaching of rudimentary botany in schools as well. The text thus demonstrates how knowledge that can be witnessed in nature can never be successfully contained. As in Panizza's text, censorship mechanisms appear inherently flawed and doomed to fail, and as the next part of this chapter will show, language play is a central strategy of Ewers's *Groteske* too.

The Language of the Petition

Seven of the narrative's thirteen pages consist of the priest's petition that lends the text its title. As a work of writing, it is very different from Jonathan's halting verbal report, since it is a rather wordy pamphlet about the "Gefährdung der Sittlichkeit" (P, 117; danger to morality), which the teachings of botany pose. This vocabulary is immediately familiar as it recalls Panizza's conviction for *Verbrechen wider die Sittlichkeit* (crimes against morality) and his plants' "crime against nature." Once again, nature is seen as a threat to morality, and a normative human understanding of what is "natural" is introduced. Moreover, one of the first sentences of the pamphlet mentions positively censorship efforts that target sexuality: "[D]ank der segensreichen Initiative der Fraktion des Centrums [werden...] Bücher und Zeitschriften unkeuschen Inhalts [...] nach Möglichkeit von dem Publikum ferngehalten" (P, 117; Thanks to the benedictory initiative of the Centrum faction, books and journals of unchaste content will be kept as far as possible from the public). Not only is this a direct allusion to the introduction of *Lex Heinze*, with which Ewers was well familiar due to his training as a lawyer, it is also another self-referential gesture to the politicized journal culture of the time, as journals like *Jugend*, where the text was first published and which is mentioned in it explicitly, were repeatedly subject to censorship. The Centrum was a Catholic political party with strong support in Bavaria and therefore a major force in the context of the *Kulturkampf*. As a religious political party, it undermines the separation of church and state, which constitutes one of Ewers's criticisms.

Perhaps unsurprisingly, the priest's petition is interspersed with biblical language too, similar to Jonathan's and the police chief's repertoire, and Dornblüth lists many examples for the "wie ein hässlicher Moloch ihr Haupt frech erhebende[ ] Sittenlosigkeit" (P, 117; immorality that raises its head like an ugly Moloch), whose cause he believes to have discovered: "Sie liegt in der S c h u l e und sie heißt B o t a n i k!" (P, 118; It resides in the s c h o o l s and it is called b o t a n y!). He goes on to describe what he has observed during his school inspections, which is the knowledge of the *Bienchen und Blümchen* (literally: little bees and flowers or, more idiomatically but less biologically sound in English, the knowledge of the birds and the bees):

> Unter Anleitung der Lehrer, die darin nur den vorgeschriebenen Unterrichtsbüchern folgen, werden die jungen Seelen genöthigt, das Geschlechtsleben der Pflanze bis in die kleinste Einzelheit zu studieren. Ohne mit der Wimper zu zucken, führt der Lehrer die reinen Gemüter in einen Pfuhl des Lasters, in ein Sodom der unerhörtesten Perversionen. Der ganze Unterricht der Botanik ist nur zugeschnitten auf eine Betrachtung der ekelhaften Ausübung ihrer Geschlechtsfunktionen! Bis in das Kleinste wird den Kindern z. B. der Bau des weiblichen Geschlechtsteiles der Blumen, des sogenannten Stempels, auseinandergesetzt, nicht nur im Bild, sondern gar an den Pflanzen selbst. Sie werden gezwungen, die Narbe, den Griffel, den Fruchtknoten, den Keimmund, den Keimsack zu zeigen. Statt vor Scham in den Boden zu

sinken, setzt ihnen der Lehrer mit zynischer Offenheit auseinander, wie die Pflanzen bald eine Selbstbefruchtung, bald eine Fremdbefruchtung vornehmen. Er erklärt den harmlosen Knaben oder Mädchen haarklein, wie die Blume durch ihre Farbe und ihren Duft die Insekten anlockt, wie diese in die Blume hineinkriechen, um den Honig zu naschen, den ihnen die Blume gewissermassen als Belohnung für ihre kupplerische Tätigkeit bietet. Er setzt ihnen auseinander, wie die Käfer, Bienen, Hummeln, nachdem sie in der einen Blüte sich mit dem männlichen Blütenstaub beschmiert haben, nunmehr in die nächste Blüte fliegen, um dort auf der weiblichen Narbe den ekelhaften Staub wieder abzustreifen und sie so zu befruchten! Wahrlich, in einem Bordelle können nicht widerwärtigere Gespräche gepflogen werden! (P, 118–19)

Under the guidance of the teachers, who are only following the mandatory curriculum of the schoolbooks, the young souls are forced to study the sexual life of plants in the smallest detail. Without batting an eye, the teacher leads the pure minds into a hotbed of sin, to a Sodom of the most egregious perversions. The entire instruction of botany is solely tailored to the observation of the disgusting practice of their [the plants'] sexual functions! For example, the structure of the female genitals of flowers, the so-called pistil, is explained to the children to the smallest detail, not just in a picture, but even on the plants themselves. They [the children] are forced to point out the stigma, the style, the ovary, the micropyle, the ovule. Instead of sinking into the ground with embarrassment, the teacher explains to them with cynical candor how the plants sometimes conduct autogamy [self-fertilization] and sometimes allogamy [cross-fertilization]. He meticulously explains to the innocent boys and girls how the flower attracts insects with its color and scent, how they crawl into the flower to nibble the honey that the flower offers them as a kind of reward for their pandering activity. He explains to them how the bugs, bees, bumblebees, after they have smeared themselves in one blossom with the male pollen, now fly on to the next blossom to wipe off the disgusting powder on the female pistil there and pollinate it this way! Truly, even in a brothel you could not entertain more abominable conversations!

The description infuses plant reproduction with human notions of sexual pleasure, and while Dornblüth identifies this as a traumatic experience for the "young souls," he seems to be the one who is traumatized. The detailed explanation of vegetal reproduction with its "disgusting pollen" and the mechanism of "self-fertilization" makes use of a surprising amount of botanical vocabulary (ranging from pistil and micropyle to auto- and allogamy), and it embeds plant reproduction in a moralized framework, just as in Panizza's *Groteske*. Human sexuality is mapped onto plant sexuality, and this displacement turns nature into a "danger to morality." The report itself is another example of a member of an institution reproducing the language that it is trying to silence. The text suggests that Dornblüth will ultimately be punished by his institution in the same way as Jonathan, precisely because of the reproduction of banned knowledge through his petition.

In his writing, Dornblüth goes on to attack Linnaeus's organization of plants according to their number of male and female sexual organs. This includes polyandria and gynandria—plants with multiple or simultaneously male and female sexual organs. They make the others ironically appear as "die einzigen halbwegs anständigen Pflanzen" (P, 120; the only half decent plants) within Dornblüth's framework of morality. The vegetal challenge to binary human ideas of sex and gender along with their many methods of reproduction seem to trigger the obsession with their sexuality that is central to both Ewers's and Panizza's text. On the next pages of his petition, Dornblüth gives more examples of teaching methods that he thinks traumatize children, such as detailed exams about plant reproduction and a school trip to help with the local chestnut pollination.[4] The smell of chestnut blossoms is commonly associated with that of semen, which Ewers's *Groteske* "Aus dem Tagebuch eines Orangenbaumes" (From the diary of an orange tree, 1907) makes explicit when saying that blooming chestnut trees smell of "ewig siegende[r] Männlichkeit" (156; eternally victorious masculinity). This evokes the "unchaste smell" the plants were emanating in Panizza's narrative. And indeed, the priest asks the church to enforce consequences that sound eerily like the chief's radical wishes for a deluge because of the identical vocabulary of eradication (*Ausrottung*) and lust (*Wollust*):

> Das Beste wäre es ja, alle Pflanzen auf der ganzen Erde auszurotten, diese wollustgierenden, blutschänderischen, perversen Geschöpfe mit Stumpf und Stiel auszurotten. Bittsteller ist sich wohl bewusst, dass wir zurzeit ausserstande sind, dieses Mittel anzuwenden, das eine spätere, reinere und christlichere Generation zweifellos benutzen wird. Aber ein anderes können wir tun, können das schamlose Geschlecht der Pflanzen einfach übersehen: es existiere nicht mehr für einen guten Christen! Und der erste Schritt hierzu ist der: "F o r t   m i t   d e m   B o t a n i k u n t e r r i c h t   a u s   d e n   S c h u l e n !" [...] Möge es die Seelen unserer Kinder, die Zukunft des bayerischen Volkes reinhalten von einer jauchenden Fäulnis, die die Dirne Wissenschaft in einem Jahrhundert des Unglaubens ausgespien hat! (P, 123–24)

The best would be to eradicate all plants on the entire earth, to destroy these lusting, incestuous, perverse creatures root and branch. Petitioner is well aware that we are currently unable to apply this measure, which a later, purer and more Christian generation will undoubtedly use. Yet we can do something else, can simply overlook the shameless genus [*Geschlecht*, also: sex] of plants: May it cease to exist for the good Christian! And the first step toward it is the following: "A w a y w i t h t h e t e a c h i n g o f b o t a n y i n s c h o o l s!" [...] May it keep the souls of our children, the future of the Bavarian people clean from the fermenting putrefaction that the whore named science has spewed out in a century of disbelief!

Short of an eradication of "the shameless genus of plants," which would entail the annihilation of human life, the only escape is ignorance. Not knowing suggests a prelapsarian state, before Original Sin was introduced to humankind by a plant that signified knowledge. (Carnal) knowledge is furthermore a biblical and legal euphemism for sexuality, so knowledge once again emerges as the target of censorship control in more than one way. If this knowledge cannot be contained, however, the speaker must be institutionalized, which is what the next and final part of this chapter addresses.

The Asylum as a Place of Freedom

At the end of Ewers's narrative, the perspective changes. The "Berichterstatter der Petitionskommission" (P, 124; representative of the petition commission) interrupts reading the petition to take a pinch of snuff and invoke a martyr: "'Heiliger Polycarp! [...] der Mann kommt entweder ins Irrenhaus –' Er nieste zweimal heftig. '– – oder –' fuhr er etwas bestimmter fort, 'oder er wird einmal bayrischer Kultusminister'" (P, 124; "Holy Polycarp! [...] the man will either be committed to the insane asylum—" He sneezed twice violently. "— — or—" he continued a little more definitively, "or he will become Bavarian minister of education one day"). The reader learns nothing further about the outcome of the petition or the fate of the passionate priest, but education history accounts for the reintroduction of the censored aspects of the curriculum four years after the narrative was published. The similarities to Panizza's *Groteske* are clear: being a patient in an asylum is paralleled with government positions that have the power to control and determine norms and behavior, such as minister of education or chief justice.[5] Both texts indicate that censorship control, or even the law in general, is "mad" and that the people in power are "madmen." As Albrecht Koschorke has asked about Panizza's oeuvre, "Who is treating whom as mad?"[6] The line between institution and institutionalization blurs, revealing itself as a constructed distinction that can devour those who try to police it. Yet the fate of protagonists who end up in mental institutions also makes it appear as if the paranoia driving the rigorous regulation of censorship has paradoxically come to institutionalize a space for freedom of thought in the asylum—a form of *Narrenfreiheit*, or fool's freedom. As a trained psychiatrist himself, Panizza had been thinking about this sentiment and wrote about it in an early poem. In "Das rothe Haus" (The red house, 1886), he calls mental institutions alluring, safe spaces that provide freedom of thought: "Eine geist'ge Freistatt suchen Sie hier / Für Ihre Ideen und Sparren, / Die sollen Sie haben – die andern schrei'n / 'Wir haben die feinsten Narren!'" (You are looking for an intellectual sanctuary here / For your ideas and follies, / You shall have it—the others shout/ "We have the finest fools!").[7] As the first section of this book detailed, Panizza opted for this *Narrenfreiheit* himself by seeking to be institutionalized in 1904 and spending the last sixteen years of his life in a sanatorium.

Both Ewers's and Panizza's *Grotesken* criticize a reality in which specific kinds of knowledge and language are limited because they are considered dangerous and in need of censorship control. The two narratives suggest that a fear of uncontrollable critical thought plagues institutions like the police, schools, church, and government. Panizza's aforementioned self-diagnosis of *Psichopatia criminalis*, which parodied Richard von Krafft-Ebing's contemporaneous case studies of "sexual aberrance" in *Psychopathia sexualis*, describes the kind of thinking and speaking that would get someone arrested and institutionalized at the time. An extract from Panizza's satirical text emphasizes the importance of the critical potential of literature and illustrates the connection between the suppression of critical thought, language, and institutionalization (while bringing back the anarchist Stirner from section 1):

> Denken ist immer eine schlimme Sache. [...] Soll das so weiter geduldet werden? Sollen wir erlauben, dass Jeder mit seiner respektiven Grösse, Jeder mit seinem bischen in seinem Kopfe steckenden Geistes-Ferment, mit seinem bischen Hirn auftrete, und die Massen vergifte und zum Staats-Ungehorsam erziehe? [...] Heute, wo wir in den prächtigen, parketbelegten Irrenhäusern, in den woligen Badewannen, Mittel besizen, diese turbulenten, germanischen Köpfchen ihr süsses Gedanken-Räuschchen

ausschlafen zu lassen? Heute sollen wir noch Empörung dulden, freche Ideen *Schiller's* und *Stirner's*? Wo wir wissen, dass diese Ideen, auch nur ausgesprochen, in der Versamlung verkündet, auf Papier gedrukt, weiterfressen, länger fressen als der Wurm, der dieses Papier zernagt, und die folgenden Jahrhunderte beeinflussen? [...] Was werden die folgenden Jahrhunderte von uns sagen? Dass wir den bürokratischen Aparat nicht bis zur Zitronenpresse, nicht bis zur Vernichtung aller nicht fürstlich-ortodox-Denkenden ausgenüzt haben?[8]

Thinking is always a terrible thing. [...] Should that be tolerated any longer? Should we allow that everyone with his respective greatness, everyone with his little spiritual ferment, with his bit of brain appear and poison the masses and raise them for civil disobedience? [...] Today, when we have means in the splendid, parquet-lined insane asylums, in the comfortable bathtubs, to let the turbulent little Germanic heads sleep off their sweet little thought-intoxication? Today, we should still bear rebellion, *Schiller's* and *Stirner's* bold ideas? When we know that these ideas, even just said out loud, declared in a congregation, printed on paper, keep on eroding, keep on destroying for longer than the worm that is gnawing away on this paper and will influence the coming centuries? [...] What will the following centuries say about us? That we did not use the bureaucratic apparatus like a lemon squeezer; that we did not capitalize on it for the eradication of all non-princely-orthodox thinking ones?

As the two examples have shown, the power of ideas "said out loud" or "printed on paper" is central to *Grotesken* and their entanglement with censorship and institutionalization. Both texts point to the role of the asylum as a tool of church and state in the biopolitical regulation of nonnormative language and behavior, pathologized as "unnatural" particularly when it comes to sexuality.

Panizza's and Ewers's *Grotesken* nonetheless pursue different purposes and relationships with their respective readers. Panizza's "Verbrechen in Tavistock-Square" declares the label of "madness" a distinction and leads readers of all convictions astray by rendering them complicit, which extends his criticism to everyone. Ewers's "Petition" uses "madness" and the asylum to stigmatize the church and state by association, and therefore develops a stance of superiority and shared criticism of characters and institutions between reader and author. There is no hero in his text, not even an unlikely one like Jonathan, leaving any position of superiority to the author and reader. Ewers's wordplay can often be resolved into its various components and related to specific contexts, whereas Panizza's story leaves many open questions, even after several interpretative attempts. Ewers's *Groteske* targets a very specific audience, confirming a certain view of the political circumstances of his time, whereas Panizza's ultimately raises larger questions about power, language, and institutions—and about plants.

SIX

Why Plants?

The two *Grotesken* in this section show the intricate entanglement of plants with the regulation of sexuality, reproduction, and thought by the church and state of their time. By turning to plants as a vehicle of social critique, *Grotesken* tie into a thriving vegetal imagination around 1900 that considered plants as both subjects of scientific knowledge and objects of aesthetic pleasure. Public knowledge about the natural sciences and especially evolutionary theory was increasing quickly in the late nineteenth century. These ideas went along with a decline in religious belief, which marks what "the German Darwin" Ernst Haeckel, a central figure in *Kulturkampf* debates, called "a second Copernican turn" in the history of Man:

> I am firmly convinced that in future this immense advance in our knowledge will be regarded as the beginning of a new period of the development of Mankind. [...]. Just as the *geocentric conception* of the universe—namely, the false opinion that the earth was the centre of the universe, and that all its other portions revolved round the earth—was overthrown by the system of the universe established by Copernicus and his followers, so the *anthropocentric conception* of the universe—the vain delusion that Man is the centre of terrestrial nature, and that its whole aim is merely to serve him—is overthrown by the application (attempted long since by Lamarck) of the theory of descent to Man. As Copernicus' system of the universe was mechanically established by Newton's theory of gravitation, we see Lamarck's theory of descent attain its causal establishment by Darwin's theory of selection.[1]

The discovery of masturbating plants provocatively satirizes the anxieties produced by a shift away from religiously fueled anthropocentric worldviews due to the equalizing effect of evolutionary processes shared by humans and nonhumans. Simultaneously, the turn of the century saw a rise of nature and plant aesthetics, for instance in art nouveau, which frequently depicted human figures erotically entangled in flowers and vines (for instance, on the cover of the journal *Jugend*, which inspired the German term for art nouveau, *Jugendstil*). To see the centrality of the organic to the arts in the year 1900, one only has to follow Panizza on his visit of the World's Fair in Paris (as A. S. Byatt does in her 2009 historical novel *The Children's Book*), wandering among exhibition booths displaying plant-themed products from the English arts and crafts movement and art nouveau goods.[2] The exhibition's central *Porte Monumentale*, designed by architect René Binet, was inspired by the elaborate depictions of the natural world in Ernst Haeckel's famous *Kunstformen der Natur* (*Art Forms of Nature*, 1899), which inextricably connected scientific knowledge and aesthetic representation.[3]

Against this backdrop, the two *Grotesken* undo the synonymity of the term *vegetality* (being plant) with *vegetativity*, which is usually characterized as a fixed and passive state with specifically asexual connotations (think of the problematic characterization of brain-dead or comatose individuals as "vegetables"—an understanding of plantness as matter without mind).[4] Instead, the texts return to the etymological roots of *vegetability*, which connotes a vigorous and flourishing power of life and animated mobility.[5] The roses, magnolias, and chestnut trees in the two narratives step out of the background and draw attention to their specific vegetal behaviors. The rose's beautiful visual display and fragrant scent, which attract both pollinating insects and human passersby, has come to be associated with representations of "love" in the arts and signals "chastity" to the chief, but it is first and foremost a sexual strategy, as an entire squadron of London police is reminded.[6] Rather than the passive, chaste, "lust"-less behavior that the representatives of church and state expect as "natural" from their subjects and try to reinforce, flowers therefore emerge as a corrupting threat to morality due to their active display of sexuality and pleasurable aesthetic appeal that crosses species boundaries—and they have done so since Linnaeus foregrounded their sexual functions in the eighteenth century, to the priest's chagrin.[7] By blaming plants for "crimes against nature," the two *Grotesken* satirically highlight contemporary anxieties surrounding sexuality, pleasure, and morality as well as a deep-seated insecurity about what it means to be human, since Man can no longer be considered separate from and therefore superior to "nature."

Breaking with the assumed vegetal passivity and expected symbolic functions in *Grotesken* shows that both plants and literature have the power to animate the human imagination in ways that elude control. The ability of the vegetal realm to threaten institutions of authority to the extent that they institutionalize their own makes plants powerful agents and points to the futility of literary censorship to control what people think.[8] The two narratives opt to exaggerate into absurdity the imaginary threat that plants pose to morality in order to reveal the illusion of human control over both nature and the mind. The human imagination, they therefore seem to suggest, cannot be controlled by institutions or even the self, as Freud had famously made clear from a different angle with his recognition of the role of the unconscious—what he considered the third Copernican turn or insult to humankind with which this book began. Instead, the mind is susceptible to a range of influences, among them those of nature and literature, which upsets traditional hierarchies that put Man in charge and raises questions about the human that are taken up by dogs in the *Grotesken* featured in the next section.[9]

SECTION 3

THE ANIMAL

Panizza, Kafka, and the Modernist Crisis of the Self

In a 1926 review of Franz Kafka's novel *Der Prozess* (*The Trial*, 1925), Kurt Tucholsky writes, "Since Oskar Panizza, nothing of such striking force of the imagination [*eindringlicher Kraft der Phantasie*] has been seen. The language is heavy, pure, and except for a few spots worked through wonderfully. Who is speaking? [*Wer spricht?*]."[1] Today, the direction of the comparison seems astonishing, since Kafka's writing has become the benchmark, while his style is simultaneously considered beyond compare. Censorship had made Panizza infamous among his contemporaries, yet five years after his death, by the time of the 1926 review, it had already begun to annihilate his legacy, which Tucholsky fought unsuccessfully by attempting to secure the rights to publish Panizza's collected works. Tucholsky's comparison of Kafka's to Panizza's writing—their shared power of the imagination and distinct language or style—is one of few places in literary history that brings the two authors together. This section of the book extends Tucholsky's commentary and reads Kafka's and Panizza's texts side by side for the first time to show in more detail what their writing has in common. In addition to stylistic and thematic convergences, this entails the shared genre of *die Groteske*. The analysis of the recontextualized narratives in this section therefore provides insights for both Kafka and Panizza scholarship, the understanding of *Grotesken*, and the figure of the canine narrator within literary animal studies.[2]

The texts at the center of this analysis, Oskar Panizza's "Aus dem Tagebuch eines Hundes" (From the diary of a dog, 1892) and Franz Kafka's "Forschungen eines Hundes" ("Investigations" or "Researches of a Dog," 1922/1931), are both told from the perspective of a dog.[3] By virtue of their ability to speak but also because they engage with communication explicitly, these animal narrators raise questions about the limits of language that tie into the concerns of the *Sprachkrise*, as *Grotesken* tend to do. In this context, Tucholsky's question "Who is speaking?" takes on new meaning: On the one hand, it points to sociopolitical questions about who is able to speak and be heard, which resonates with the censorship that accompanied and actively shaped the genre of *die Groteske*, as the previous two sections showed.[4] In the context of literary texts narrated by dogs, it also becomes clear that "anthropocentrism, in the context of which the dog is degraded to a silent being, is a form of censorship."[5] At the same time, the *Sprachkrise* is about a particularly human problem regarding the bounds of subjective expression and the representation of the world in language. A speaking animal, as it occurs in the two texts by Panizza and Kafka, disrupts what is at stake in these questions, including the epistemological and ontological implications of this crisis of subjectivity. Modernist language skepticism often expanded into an epistemological crisis about how humans not only express themselves but also understand one another, relate to others, and gain knowledge about the world, which led to such fundamental concerns as whether the self and a world full of other minds even exist. Having an animal voice such concerns, from which it is typically excluded, exacerbates the underlying questions about the ability to know oneself, others, and the world. This section of the book will show how the two canine narrators in Kafka's and Panizza's *Grotesken* negotiate these interlocking concerns with language and speaking, self and other. The unusual narrative perspective of these texts is key both to understanding better what is at stake in modernist issues of subjectivity and how the genre of *die Groteske* develops over time, as there are thirty years between them.

Unlike Ewers and Friedlaender, neither Panizza nor Kafka explicitly labeled their texts as *Grotesken*, though their work has often been called "grotesque" and occasionally *Grotesken* by others. What makes the two narratives in this section *Grotesken* in the way this book has established are (1) the nonhuman narrative perspective of speaking dogs—a complicated merging of the untrustworthy narrators and nonhuman perspectives of other *Grotesken* that is nonetheless fraught with questions about whose view of the world to trust, precisely because it is presented by an animal; (2) the way in which these narrators deviate from, critique, and satirize the institutionalized conventions and norms of human and canine societies, particularly the rules of communication, which leads to their own isolation; (3) the ambiguous and defamiliarizing language play in response to the *Sprachkrise* that is bound up with these questions of communication; and (4) the way bodies figure into attempts to relate other and self through both communicative and physical acts, which range from sexuality to encounters with death.

In Oskar Panizza's "Aus dem Tagebuch eines Hundes," a dachshund chronicles his observations of city life in a defamiliarizing manner, but his attempts to understand humans, fellow dogs, and the world make him aware of complex problems of perception and language that draw him into his own crisis of language, including epistemological and ontological ramifications.[6] Franz Kafka's "Forschungen eines Hundes" is also about a canine narrator's attempt to study other dogs and the world, but this dog seems to be in an epistemological crisis from the beginning, and his descriptions are often difficult to relate to any familiar frameworks, which leaves unclear whether the story world contains any humans at all. Neither of the texts can be easily summed up with the help of a plot, but both animal narrators reflect on and extend the primarily aesthetic concerns of the *Sprachkrise* to the social sphere by depicting the failure of everyday communication and social interactions. While the ambiguity of language causes communication to fail on the plot level, it is utterly successful on the level of narration, since the deceptively simple language of the equivocal descriptions multiplies their potential meanings. Ambiguity and the upheaval of conventions thrive in *Grotesken*, and the two texts upend notions of the success or failure of language with the help of their narrating dogs.

Panizza's and Kafka's choice of canine narrators goes hand in hand with a heightened interest in animals and their abilities around 1900. Developments in the natural sciences (such as Pavlov's experiments) and entertainment trends (like shows that featured dogs and horses seemingly solving math equations and answering questions) led to increasing animal welfare activism and extended into literary representations.[7] In 1918, Oskar Walzel diagnosed a contemporary surge of literary texts about animals: "Especially characteristic of our newest ones is the keen striving to empathize with the animal and learn about the activities of its soul [*Seelenvorgänge*]."[8] From Mark Twain to Virginia Woolf, canine narrators were particularly popular within the same period as *Grotesken*. These texts have literary predecessors that date back to antiquity in the tradition of what Theodore Ziolkowski has called a "philosophical dog."[9] The most well-known example is Berganza: this dog and his philosophical musings originated with Miguel de Cervantes but were popularized in the German-language canon in the early nineteenth century by E. T. A. Hoffmann, one of Panizza's literary favorites.

The defamiliarizing viewpoint of animals onto society provided by narrating dogs lends itself perfectly to the preoccupation of *Grotesken* with raising questions about societal conventions and norms.[10] By discussing human sexuality through plant reproduction, the previous section has shown that one purpose of such defamiliarization is to attempt avoiding censorship. In situations that bar human protagonists from uttering their point of view freely, plants and animals seem to have greater flexibility. In the texts of this section, the canine narrators' defamiliarized descriptions purposefully destabilize anthropocentric perspectives onto the world, yet like in the previous section, this defamiliarization also serves aesthetic goals. Panizza's dog diary is dedicated to Jonathan Swift, the author of *Gulliver's Travels* (1726) and a master of defamiliarizing language (like his namesake Jonathan in the plant story). Kafka had been impacted deeply by Swift's novel too, which he read in the year before he wrote his own dog story.[11] In the novel's travels, Gulliver describes everyday items as seen through the eyes of, for instance, the tiny people of Lilliput. When they make an inventory of the contents of Gulliver's pockets, his money-purse and handkerchief become comically distorted because their sheer size makes them impossible to relate to any framework in their tiny world. This defamiliarizing strategy is taken up in the two dog texts and raises questions about the reliability of the one describing the world in this way—something typical for Swift's writing and the genre of *die Groteske*.

Yet defamiliarization also becomes a central element of canine narration because the speaking dogs run up against the limits of language and epistemology in an unprecedented way. The specifically modernist dog's-eye view of the two stories introduces a satirical perspective onto human behavior that challenges fundamental abilities such as meaningful communication and social interaction, and the knowledge of the self and the world. The upcoming chapter 7 traces these epistemological and linguistic problems through Panizza's text, from the onset of thought in the first sentences of the dog's diary to his crisis of self and other, which is prompted by central scenes of failed communication that relate to sexuality and death. Chapter 8 highlights comparable moments in Kafka's text that reveal a severely exacerbated crisis of subjectivity, before concluding this section in chapter 9 with an array of answers to the question why these narrators are—of all species—dogs.

SEVEN

From the Diary of a Dog

Neither Kafka's nor Panizza's *Groteske* explains why the dog narrating the story can speak, whether he can write, or to whom he might be addressing his musings.[1] Yet the placement of a nonhuman in the position of the narrator highlights language as the fundamental prerequisite of narration (without teasing apart the relationship between thought and language) and challenges the assumption that language is the defining feature that differentiates humans from animals. Panizza's *Groteske* begins with the dog describing his move from the countryside to the city, and he seems to be uttering some of the very first words of his existence when he says,

> Ich kann sagen, seit gestern fühle ich, daß ich ein Hund bin. Ich denke. Früher tat ich dies Alles unbewußt. Ich sehe, Denken ist eine Arbeit, die oft Schmerz bereitet. Was mich beunruhigt, ist, daß man sie nicht freiwillig verrichtet. Ich bin nicht mehr so glücklich wie früher, aber stolzer. (TH, 55)

> I can say that since yesterday I can feel that I am a dog. I am thinking. In the past I did all this unconsciously. I see that thinking is a labor that often causes pain. What alarms me is that one doesn't do it voluntarily. I am not as happy as before, but prouder.

Notably, this canine variation on the Cartesian *cogito* (I can feel that I am a dog) does not focus on cognitive abilities (i.e., I think, therefore I am a dog) but equates the new experience of self-awareness with feeling instead, as if it were a sensual, physical property. In addition, the sentence right after "I am a dog" could also be translated as "I think" instead of "I am thinking" and therefore read either as a measure of drawing doubt on the previous one (I am a dog, I think.) or as an equation that makes thinking an essential quality of dog existence (I am a dog. I think.). Punctuation and idiomatic usage suggest that these interpretations are secondary layers of meaning, yet the fact that this seemingly simple sentence has more potential meanings than words is characteristic for the play with language and its ambiguity in *Grotesken*. At the same time, an animal that says "I think" contradicts the Cartesian framework, since that takes animals to be bodies without a mind or the capacity to think, so-called animal machines.[2] The text's first words seemingly respond to Tucholsky's question "Who is speaking?" with *ich kann sagen* or "I can say," yet this literalized speech act (which professes the dog's ability to speak) points to the many questions that will arise around this *ich* in the course of the text. Uttered by an animal at the very beginning of a text it is narrating, the sentence *ich denke* therefore introduces the reader to the central topics of the limits of language in the *Sprachkrise*, the epistemological crisis of knowing the self and other, and the ontological problem of what is a human or animal.

While the prominent position of these reflections about feeling, thinking, and speaking at the beginning of the text signals that these concerns are of central significance, they also foreshadow the many communication problems in the narrative. The first sentences circle entirely around the dog's *ich*, and despite apparently speaking the human language, he is unable to communicate with humans in the text. He lives as a pet and describes his detached relationship with his master as one marked by human aggression and canine disdain, without meaningful communication:

> Aus dem letzten Monat finde ich beim Zusammenzählen: 12 Stockhiebe; 25 Fußtritte, 6mal Prügel und Püffe mit der Faust oder Hand; 3mal furchtbaren Durst leiden müssen; 1mal steinharte, abgenagte Knochen; 35mal "Ei di di di di di di das schöne Hunderl!"; ca. 40mal "A dä dä dä dä dä dä das schwarze Dakkerl!". Auf meiner Seite, der Leistungen, stehen: 120 Beleckungen; 370 Beriechungen; 500 Schweifwedeleien, und an die 699 Speichelleckereien. – Ein jeder schlägt sich eben durch, wie er kann! – (TH, 73–74)

> In the last month I count: 12 blows with a stick; 25 kicks with the foot; 6 times beatings and blows with the fist or hand; 3 times having to endure terrible thirst; 1 time bones that were gnawed bare and hard as stone; 35 times "Cootchie-cootchie-coo, such a pretty doggie!"; circa 40 times "Goochie-goochie-goo, little black bow-wow!". The services on my side are: 120 licks;

370 sniffs; 500 tail-wags, and close to 699 times brown-nosing.—Each one finds their way to get by!—

In this rather abusive approach to pet-keeping, meaningless sound components of the baby talk variety indicate that the dachshund's master—perhaps unsurprisingly for an embodiment of Man—does not take his pet to be a reasoning, speaking creature on equal footing. Yet the dog denies his master those qualities as well, and the contrast between the master's ungrammatical pet-directed speech and the canine narrator's own eloquence subverts the infantilization. While the dog admits a level of dependence (e.g., by having to go thirsty), he makes clear that the gestures he offers up are calculated and he is paying a bill with them: they serve as a means to an end and the dog knows exactly what kind of behavior and how much is expected of him within this trade of services. Yet the canine narrator's inability to converse with humans on the same level, even though he is fluent in their language, raises the *Sprachkrise*'s question of how the possession of language matters when it cannot be used to communicate meaningfully.

Hierarchies Turned Upside Down

In his diary, Panizza's dog studies humans beyond his master to categorize them like a new Linnaeus (see TH, 86) and name them akin to Adam in Genesis. Both gestures satirize and undermine two traditional ways of legitimatizing human dominion over animals: on the one hand, the religious idea of a God-given superiority as creation's crowning glory, and on the other, the enlightenment notion of rational authority based on knowledge, scientific observation, and the deductive reasoning of research, which is written into the title of Kafka's "Investigations/Researches of a Dog" and also undertaken by Panizza's dachshund.[3] As indicated in the introduction of this book, there is concern about both of these notions around 1900, as humankind's divinely endowed superiority is called into question by new discoveries in the natural sciences and the infallibility of rational thought is dissected in modern epistemology, psychoanalysis, and language skepticism. Yet Panizza's dachshund initially appears to be untroubled by these problems of perception and observation. He describes humans and his mission in their world as follows:

> Hier die entsetzlichsten Gegensätze; der Eine hüpft, der Andere scharrt; der Eine treibt das Hinterteil hinaus, der Andere die Brust nach vorn; Der wackelt, Jener zirpt; Dieser zeigt fortwährend Zunge und Zähne, Der dort

stiert mit weißen Augäpfeln durch künstlich angeschnallte kleine Guck-Fensterchen. Welcher Wirrwarr! Welche unübersehbare Verschiedenheit! Anfangs wollte ich mich nicht drum kümmern. Doch seh ich, ich muß. Ich muß diese ganze Bagage registrieren, einteilen, schablonieren. Einteilung der Menschenbagage! (TH, 55–56)

Here the most terrible oppositions; one is jumping, the other scratching; one is pushing the hindquarters out, the other the chest; this one jiggles, that one chirps, this one keeps showing tongue and teeth, the one over there is staring with white eyeballs through small, artificially strapped-on peepholes. What a mess! What unmanageable diversity! In the beginning, I did not want to care about it. Yet I see that I must. I must index them, categorize and fit them in a template. Classification of the human brigade!

What sounds like animals, for instance the chirping and showing of teeth, is the beginning of a description of human communication through gestures and sounds. Yet while the phrasing makes humans appear like animals, it does not identify humans as creatures like dogs; instead, it is meant to demonstrate humankind's "unglaublich niedere Stellung in der Tierreihe" (TH, 75; unbelievably low position in the animal kingdom), thus undermining its assumed superiority. Throughout the text, human behavior is described as chaotic and in need of order and classification. In the spirit of both Adam and Linnaeus, the dog feels tasked to organize this perceived mess.

To this end, he creates a neologistic taxonomy of people as *"Beinzeiger und Beinverstecker"* (TH, 60; *leg-showers* [i.e., those who wear pants] and *leg-hiders* [i.e., those who wear skirts]), which corresponds to the typical male and female dress codes of the time, regulating whose bodies and which parts can and cannot be exposed. This differentiation corresponds to Linnaeus's sex-based classification system for plants familiar from the previous section while also evoking his taxonomy of animals, and humankind becomes an object of study this way, which removes any individual differentiation. In the same vein, the text uses no personal names: dogs and humans are referred to by their species category and other external markers, such as their size and the appearance of their clothing or fur. In analogy to the scientific classification of the world undertaken at the time (which recall Linnaeus, Darwin, and Haeckel from the previous section and point to the physiognomic pseudoscience in the next), any individual human qualities become collective traits in the big picture of the human species that is painted by Panizza's dachshund. What remains is *"the* human"—a category that is as generalized as it is incomplete. By inverting the usual human–animal hierarchy and its classification category of "the animal," the dog not only points to the power structures organizing an anthropocentric world but also shows the hubris inherent in the notion of human superiority, as their understanding of other species is exposed as incomplete and flawed.[4] Having an animal treat humans in the way Man usually treats other species highlights how supposedly scientific distinctions are mapped onto beings from the outside and then translated into essentialized differences that render them as "other," with implications about, for instance, race, gender, and ability that mirror speciesist generalizations about animal kinds.

Communicative Encounters

In response to not understanding humans and their interactions, as his earlier descriptions of their communication suggest, Panizza's narrator presents an alternative model of behavior that he considers superior because it is canine. His account of the varied and inconclusive human acts in communicative situations is contrasted with a canine communication model that is not based on language, and it begins to elucidate the epistemological relationship of sensory impressions to the realm of thought and language:

> Sieht man zwei Hunden zu, die sich zufällig treffen und sich gegenseitig ausforschen, in wenigen Minuten ist Alles gethan. Wir wissen, er klagt über Frost, er hungert, er ist geschlagen worden, er hat eine weiche Seele, er ist trotzig, er ist mißtrauisch; der Hauch sagt uns Alles; seine Seele liegt offen vor unserer Nase. Nun betrachte man aber zwei Menschen! Ja, wer das nicht gesehen, dem werde ich kaum einen Begriff geben. Dieser Embarras! Dieser Aufwand von Geräuschen und Bewegungen! [...] Der Frosch, der Spatz, das Eichhorn, die Krähe, der Storch und der Wolf zusammengenommen könnten nicht die Summe jener Laute aufbringen, die die Menschen nötig haben, um sich zu fragen: Wie geht's? Hast Du Hunger? – Ja, ich frage mich oft, ob alle diese Quatsch- und Fistel-Laute etwas zu bedeuten haben; ob diese Race trotz des kolossalen Aufwands schließlich weiß, was der Andere selbst denkt, und was er von ihm denkt! [...] Ob die was von einander wissen? – Von der Beschaffenheit ihrer Seele? – Arme Spezies! – (TH, 62–64)

> When you watch two dogs who meet by chance and explore each other, everything is done in a few minutes. We know that he is complaining about the frost, he is going hungry, he has been beaten, he is defiant, he is suspicious; one whiff tells us everything; his soul lies open before our nose. But

now watch two humans! Indeed, whoever hasn't seen this I can barely give an impression of it. This embarrassment! This effort in sounds and movements! [...] The frog, the sparrow, the squirrel, the crow, the stork and the wolf combined could not produce the sum of the sounds that humans need to ask each other: How are you? Are you hungry?—Indeed, I often ask myself whether all these nonsensical and whimpering sounds mean something; whether despite this colossal effort, this race finally knows what the other thinks by himself, and what he thinks of him! [...] Whether they know something about each other?—Of the composition of their soul?—Poor species!—

This depiction of canine communication emphasizes the efficacy and depth of sensory communication by way of scents, and it relegates vocalizations as well as gestures to a category of secondary, less refined means of expression. Due to the anthropocentric primacy of vision, the sense of smell is often dismissed and associated with animality and sexuality: bad odors denote uncleanliness, disease, and death, and even pleasant scents traditionally connoted perfumed sex workers and vulgar pleasures such as the "unchaste smell" of the masturbating plants in the previous section (aromas, smells, and noses will also return the context of antisemitism in the next section).[5] In the canine encounter, the olfactory is presented as a way of instantly knowing the peculiarities of an individual (i.e., the soul), and it appears superior to an abstract system of signs and gestures that is unable to answer a seemingly simple question like "How are you?"[6] The dog's shift of emphasis from seeing and hearing to smelling thus challenges the foundation of human epistemology, as language and gestures lead humankind into a skeptical crisis, in which the self is unable to know the other. If humans are unable to pose the question "How are you?" and receive a satisfying answer, they are also unable to know themselves. Yet dogs escape this linguistic and epistemological crisis, it seems, through their instinctive attention to the body. They do not become frustrated by attempting to communicate on an abstract level but instead focus their attention on the particularity of another's corporeal presence. Indeed, they seemingly do not separate body and mind, and the *Seele* therefore appears to be a soul in the Aristotelian sense: the form of the living dog, or its dog-ness. In the Aristotelian hierarchy, animals have nutritive and sensitive souls (*anima*) but are not burdened with the rational soul of humans.[7] In the "animal epistemology" of the dachshund, dogs thus can avoid a range of problems faced by humans, though the narrator ultimately does not. Whereas species distinctions often use language as the main reason to place Man in a superior hierarchical position to animals, the canine-centric perspective of Panizza's *Groteske* suggests that language is in fact an obstacle to the perception of the world and the self, which ties into the concerns of the modernist *Sprachkrise*.

Communicative Failure, Eroticized

Whenever Panizza's dachshund describes communicative failures among humans, it appears to be conflated or at least intricately connected with notions of reproduction—both in the linguistic and the sexual sense of the word—a constellation familiar from the plant section. The dog understands himself as a "Geschichtschreiber" (TH, 76) of humanity (i.e., a historian or chronicler but also a storyteller or writer), and he therefore details not only the reproduction of speech but also the reproduction of the species. First, he discovers the "Reproduction oder Wiederholung der Menschenrace durch ein einzelnes Individuum" (TH, 87–88; reproduction or repetition of the human race through a single individual).[8] What sounds impossible or at least like a highly complicated endeavor turns out to be something much more straightforward but extremely suggestive: humans can reproduce themselves by looking in the mirror—something dogs cannot do because they fail to recognize "the other dog" as themselves, though in this case, the illustration accompanying the text does not show a human but an ape-ish devil in front of the glass.[9] This act of reproduction is called "das Geheime Laster" (TH, 90; the Secret Guilty Pleasure), capitalized as if an understood term or euphemism, and thoroughly satirized:

> Dieses gegenseitige Gezwinker und Augenblinzeln, dieses Mundspitzen, diese Begrüßungen und Beglückwünschungen, als sagten sie sich: Wie geht's? Du siehst ja prächtig aus! Wie freut es mich, Dich zu seh'n! Wie Du schön bist! Du Prachtmensch! Du göttergleiches, küssenswertes Wesen! Du bist ein Gott, und Alles Andere ist Schund! (TH, 89)

> This mutual winking and blinking of the eyes, this pursing of lips, these salutations and congratulations, as if they said to each other: How are you? You look simply glorious! How happy I am to see you! How beautiful you are! You splendid human being! You divine, attractive [literally: kiss-worthy] being! You are a god, and everything else is crap!

The narcissistic infatuation of this human figure with its own mirror image suggests autoeroticism (familiar from the plants) as well as human hubris.

He seems to be in love with himself, throwing kisses and praising his own beauty above everything else. The anthropocentric Man who is absorbed in his own mirror image in Panizza's text calls himself "a god" (instead of a being created in God's mirror image or acknowledging his devilish, animal exterior); yet hearing about this rather ridiculous scene from the observing dog instantly satirizes and subverts this superior position (even literally, if you will, at least in English, through the anadrome god/dog). As a soliloquy, the scene reenacts the previous failure of human communication with others and the inability to know oneself, particularly in the repeated question "How are you?" that humans seemed unable to pose or answer before. Here, the phrase is uttered, but the soliloquy prevents a response. Directed at the self, it becomes a meaningless figure of speech that communicates no real inquiry but only self-absorption.

In another description of an encounter between two humans, both the eroticization and failure of communication become more explicitly palpable:

> Ich weiß noch immer nicht, wie die Leute sich verständigen. Zwar nähern sie sich oft gegenseitig die Köpfe und entblößen die obere Zahnreihe, aber die Nasen scheinen mir zu kurz, um nach unserer Weise sich sofort zu orientieren. Dagegen entstürzen ihren Mündern ein ganzes Geknarr von Geräuschen, förmliche Mundsalven, denen fleißige Gesticulationen hinterdrein folgen. Aber zu einem Verständniß scheinen sie nicht zu gelangen, da das Gequatsch stundenlang dauert, heftiger wird, von Stampfen, Rücken, Stoßen und Zunge-Herausstrecken begleitet wird, bis Beide gehetzt mit dampfenden Mündern von einander scheiden. Armes Geschlecht, das du die Luft zerhackst und dein Gesicht verschneidest, um auszudrücken, was du willst. (TH, 56–57)

> I still don't know how people communicate. Even though they often approach each other's heads and expose the upper row of teeth, the noses seem too short to me to provide immediate orientation in our manner. Instead, an entire crackling of sounds is launched from their mouths, positively mouth-salvoes, followed by busy gesturing. Yet they don't seem to arrive at an understanding, since the chatter takes hours, becomes more intense, is accompanied by stomping, jiggling, pushing, and sticking out one's tongue, until both separate, hounded, with steaming mouths. Poor species, you hack apart the air and adulterate your face to express what you want.

Human speech is described as an embarrassing, ineffective endeavor that requires an enormous amount of energy only to produce an uncertain result.

Gestures are mingled with sounds, and the sheer physicality of this crackling, stomping, jiggling, pushing, steaming, and hacking enterprise seems daunting. The many rich onomatopoetic expressions trigger associations to all varieties of the animal kingdom as well as to the "chirping" and "exposing of teeth" of previous descriptions.[10] Exposing (*entblößen*—a term that will return repeatedly) one's teeth among humans designates a smile, while it usually signals aggression or fear among animals. This ambiguity adds to the impression of an altercation invoked by the term *mouth-salvoes*. Yet the many mechanistic sounds that describe this animated debate could just as well be read as an act of kissing and rhythmic sexual movement. Faces come together, mouths open, and teeth are exposed; an intense pounding, jiggling, pushing, and sticking out of tongues ensues. The accumulation of seemingly simple and straightforward words leaves the reader with uncertainty about what the dog observed. Nonetheless, the sheer orality and aurality of the passage betray aggression, not attraction. Whether it is read as a failure of human communication or of climax, the physical frustration conveyed in this paragraph is nonetheless a triumph of climactic narration, and hence of language, which simultaneously reverses notions of language failure and success in this story.

Similarly, the dachshund's claim about the failure of communication undermines itself because the language he deems ineffective is after all the one in which he displays exceeding eloquence. Even if language-based communication between humans fails, the dog nonetheless seems to have succeeded in communicating with us, his human readers, through language— a certain interpretative ambiguity notwithstanding. Ambiguous language and the strategy of defamiliarization are symptomatic of *die Groteske*, and Panizza's dachshund's style is an excessively concrete, rather ethnographic way of speaking, which suggests a dog's perspective by describing human concepts instead of using their names. The dachshund even occasionally describes things that he has named or defined abstractly before, thus seemingly bracketing what is known and indicating that his nonunderstanding might at times be disingenuous for the sake of a more thorough or different description and analysis of the object of his research. His choice of simple terms seems to indicate a refusal of abstract, possibly ambiguous human concepts, as if he were rejecting human language play in the context of the *Sprachkrise*. However, the dachshund's creative descriptions are themselves a continuous game with language. As perhaps the only anthropologist who does not belong to the human species and despite his seemingly clear-cut vocabulary, his account renders everyday items and actions defamiliarized and ambiguous. The additional creation of neologisms, such as "leg-shower" or "mouth-salvoes," which are based on the recombination of words and function as new technical terms, suggest a certain pliability and randomness of language that is as much a concern of the *Sprachkrise* as it is a central characteristic of *Grotesken*. Language is shown to "fail" at delivering clear, unambiguous results even in the description of the most mundane everyday circumstances. Yet because the framework of human references has been destabilized by the canine narrator, the defamiliarized descriptions open up new perspectives and multiple interpretations of human behavior, specifically their possession of language as a sign of superiority over other species.

Sexuality as Communication

As communication is eroticized by Panizza's canine narrator, sexuality is in turn depicted in the same terms as the communicative attempts. In one of the narrative's most central scenes, the dog witnesses a sexual encounter between humans, which is a traumatizing experience for him and highlights the disturbing effects sexuality appears to have on the dog:

> Die beiden nackten weißen abgezogenen Hasen schlüpften in das große weiße Haus hinein, in dem ich schon einmal meinen Herrn ertappte; und nun ging die Comödie erst recht an. Mein Herr beginnt heftig zu grimassieren mit Zuhilfenahme der Augenbrauen, und verschwendet eine unglaubliche Quantität hervorgezischter Luft; der Beinverstecker – oder wie soll ich ihn denn nennen, den Kerl; er steckte ja jetzt gerade die Beine wiederholt zum Gehäuse heraus, – diese Person da, benützte unter fleißigem Entblößen der oberen Zahnreihe, wie mir schien, die Handsprache, um etwas auszudrücken, was ich nicht verstand. Von Seite meines Herrn neue Grimasse. Dann plötzlich eine gilfende Mundsalve, spitzig und trillernd. Nun Zahn-Entblößung auf Zahn-Entblößung auf beiden Seiten. Zunge und Rachen werden sichtbar; Brust-Vorbeugungen und Kopf-Verrenkungen. Mein Herr verdreht plötzlich die Augen, bekommt Krämpfe und scheint das weiße Gehäuse in Stücke zerbrechen zu wollen. Sein *vis-à-vis* entrollt mit einemmal einen Haufen schwarzer, glänzender, lautloser Wellen, die aus dem Kopfe hervorsprudeln und wie Oel auf dem weißen Gehäuse schwimmen. [...] Ich hörte noch einen Schrei; dann wälzte die Nacht ihren schwarzen Mantel über die ganze Szene und ich kroch winselnd, erschöpft und zerknirscht unter das Bett. (TH, 76–77)

The two naked, white, skinned rabbits slipped into the big white house, in which I caught my master once already; and now the comedy got really started. My master begins to grimace intensely with the aid of his eyebrows, and he wastes an unbelievable quantity of hissing air; the leg-hider—or what should I call him, the fellow; he just now stuck his legs out of the house again,—this person there, while repeatedly exposing his upper row of teeth, seemed to use the hand language to express something that I did not understand. From my master's side more grimacing. Then suddenly a driveling mouth-salvo, pointy and warbling. Now teeth-exposure after teeth-exposure on both sides. Tongue and throat become visible; pushing out of chests and twisting of heads. My master's eyes suddenly roll back; he is convulsing and seems to want to break the white house into pieces. Suddenly, many black, shiny, soundless waves roll from his *vis-à-vis*; they spring from the head and swim like oil on the white house. [...] I heard one more scream; then the night rolled its black coat over the entire scene and I crawled under the bed, whimpering, exhausted, and hangdog.

Similar to previous accounts of human communication, the sexual act is described in excessive physicality, and it betrays an obsession with the oral, aural, and the climactic.[11] The gestures are understood as communication, most clearly in the neologism "hand language," and the vocabulary is almost identical to the previous descriptions of communicative attempts: neologistic "mouth-salvoes," the exposure (*Entblößung, entblößen*) of teeth and the body, grimacing, and gesturing. The orgasm is marked by sound and accompanied by physical contortions that, in all their obscurity, are perceived both as comical and disconcerting by the dog. Even more than the gestures of human communication, these twists and convulsions seem literally per-verted, and in the climactic ending of the scene, the human figure appears to lose control of its body altogether. The canine depiction of humans that are physically overwhelmed by pleasure both invokes and undermines the traditional distinction between instinctual animal reproduction and a controlled libidinal drive in humans.

The scene is shocking to the dog because it remains incomprehensible. The leading force of the encounter, sexual desire, remains inaccessible beneath the descriptions of its awkward physicality, and its eroticism is utterly uncomfortable for the dog. To the human reader, the physical detail suggests a fair amount of passion that prioritizes pleasure over reproduction. As the previous section has shown, the regulation of sexuality around 1900 was troubled by the ideas of "lust" and pleasure that conflicted with a sense of morality limited to married, heterosexual reproduction. The scene allows for wild speculation about these categories: the one-time occurrence of the act indicates that the dog's owner is a bachelor, like all the previous protagonists, and that his partner could be a sex worker—a common figure in Panizza's oeuvre and supported by the fact that the dog's master meets this person on the street.[12] Additionally, the guest is introduced as a "leg-hider"—that is, supposedly a woman (which the illustration supports), but in the same sentence described as "sticking his legs out" and referred to as *Kerl*, usually a term for men akin to "guy." This suggests that the act could be outside of the heteronormative realm and reinforces that the dog does not understand differences between sex or gender beyond clothing choices (which can be easily changed or disposed of, as this scene demonstrates). At the same time, the text says that "Beide sind vollständig gleich" (TH, 76; both are completely the same), representing "the human" rather than individuals. The dog's taxonomy of humankind has broken down as clothing differentiations disappeared, making the historical focus on sex and reproduction in classifications, such as Linnaeus' sexual system of plants, appear like a random, ill-fitting choice.[13] The supposed importance of sexual difference for studying humans and nature is thus simultaneously emphasized and undermined. Regardless of the sex or gender of the two people in this encounter, the "hand language" could be understood as manual stimulation, which moves this act into the pleasure-focused, nonreproductive realm no matter whether it is hetero- or homosexual.[14] The description remains distinctly unclear in many dimensions. Just as language is ambiguous, sexual desire does not follow the normative grammar of societal morality and therefore evokes an excess of meaning that obscures any single, clear-cut interpretation of the act. This leaves the dachshund at a loss of words and instead he lets out a whimpering sound, which is a suggestive communicative act that seems to respond to the orgasmic scream. Though he draws attention to his presence with the whimper, the dog also hides at this point, evoking the famous Derridean observation that animals have access to humans in the most intimate situations, like this encounter or the previous mirror scene, which would be drastically changed by the presence of another human.[15]

The sex scene had begun with a description of the naked owner and his companion as "skinned rabbits" (*abgezogene Hasen*): both an animal of prey and a symbol of copious sex and reproduction. If we are to take the disturbing term *skinned* to mean merely naked, the description of their intimate exposure (*Entblößung*) signals a combination of vulnerability and brazenness: the naked bodies are in their most unprotected state, yet they dare to put on display what is usually hidden by many carefully constructed layers of clothing and morality. The canine onlooker is unable to make sense of the nakedness on display, since exposing oneself is something animals cannot do. Clothing is a specifically human concept, associated with humankind's fall and a certain understanding of morality. Before Adam and Eve ate from the tree of knowledge that opened their eyes to self and other, their naked bodies did not have to be concealed. Their skin was their fur, feathers, and scales. As a kind of prelapsarian creature who lacks this understanding of self and other as sinful bodies, Panizza's dog seems to take clothing to be body parts. This is clear from his taxonomy of leg-showers and -hiders, and it further clarifies why the sexual scene that begins with the disrobing, or "skinning," of his master is so traumatic for him. To the dog, a hat is the same as a head (apparent in street scenes that involve greetings; see TH, 63–64), and undressing is consequently equal to the removal of limbs, or amputation. This frightening mobility of body parts, which comes with the loss of his taxonomic ability to differentiate between individuals once they take off their clothes, unsettles him deeply because it calls into question the (Aristotelian) form of another being—leading to an ontological and epistemological crisis. The implications of the dog's misconception become apparent most pointedly when he witnesses the theft of a wallet: "Der arme In-die-Hosentasche-Gelangte aber stand dort, bleich und zitternd. Offenbar war ihm eines der wertvollsten Organe abhanden gekommen, ohne das er unmöglich weiter leben kann, das Herz oder die Seele" (TH, 82–83; The poor person whose pocket had been picked stood there, pale and trembling. Apparently one of his most valuable organs had gone missing, without which he could not possibly live on, the heart or the soul). As comical as this satire of money or the dog's shock over the removal of clothing might seem at first glance, these vulnerable moments of *Entblößung* expose the norms and values regulating human behavior (such as sexual morality and capitalism) that the defamiliarizing canine perspective keeps satirizing. At the same time, these scenes ask about knowing the self and the other—making the dog wonder which parts are essential to a being and how we can know for certain.

Communication as Sexuality

These epistemological and ontological questions become increasingly more urgent as the text goes on, and they culminate in the dachshund's involuntary experience of canine sexual desire, which compromises the straightforward and efficient scent-based mode of dog communication and throws him into his own *Sprachkrise*. The intensity of the encounter brings the dog to the limits of language—he is lost for words in the face of an onslaught of sensory signals, similar to his encounter with human sexuality:

> ..... ich weiß nicht, wie ich mich ausdrücken soll, – – der kleine buschige Hund zitterte am ganzen Leib; halb Jauchzen, halb Schmerzen drückten seine Geberden, sein Blick aus; dumm, verzwickt, verlegen wurde seine Miene; sonderbar war, daß alle Begrüßungen, die ich bisher erlebte, einfach den Charakter gegenseitiger Informierung über den eigenen Zustand trugen; die diesmalige aber, diese Informierung für überflüssig haltend, sich in ganz anderen Empfindungen bewegte, und in mir eine neue stupende Idee weckte. Ja, um eine tolle aber kurze Ausdrucksweise zu gebrauchen: Mir kam vor, der Hund wolle ich sein, – oder mich sein; wie sagt man denn da? – Der buschige Hund wolle weniger über mich sich orientieren, wie meine Seele gestimmt sei, ob wir uns vertragen würden, und dergleichen, sondern er, der buschige Hund, wolle mich, der glatthaarige Hund, sein. Es klingt ganz verrückt. Ich geb es zu. Aber ich kann mich nicht anders ausdrücken. – Er beroch mich von hinten. Ich hielt dies früher immer für Spielerei. Aber ich muß sagen, es berührte mich eigentümlich. Mit Entsetzen merkte ich, wie in mir ein neues Hunde-Ich sich aufthat, welches meine Vergangenheit auszuwischen drohte. Ich machte die tollsten Sprünge und Körper-Verrenkungen. Ich kam mir wie ein Mensch vor. – (TH, 100–101)

> ..... I don't know how to express myself,——the small bushy dog's entire body was trembling; his gestures, his gaze expressed half jubilation, half pain; his face became dumb, dodgy, embarrassed; it was odd that all salutations I had experienced so far were simply characterized by mutual information about one's own well-being; this one however seemed to consider that information superfluous and moved within completely different sensations, and it awakened a new, stupid idea in me. To use a crazy but short expression: It seemed to me as if the dog wanted to be I,—or be me; how do you say this?—It seemed as if the bushy dog wanted less to orient himself about me, or the disposition of my soul, whether we would get along and such, but he, the bushy dog, wanted to be me, the straight-haired dog. It sounds absolutely crazy. I admit it. Yet I cannot express myself any other way.—He smelled me

from behind. In the past, I considered this to be shenanigans. Yet I have to say it touched me in a peculiar way. With horror I realized how a new Dog-I opened up inside of me, which threatened to wipe out the past. I did the craziest jumps and body twists. I felt [literally: appeared to myself] like a human.—

Overcome with what he considers a human desire that is very different from regular canine communication, the dog is horrified by the involuntary changes in his body and mind, as he jumps and twists in similarly per-verted physical contortions as the ones that humans performed during their sexual encounter. Ironically, the experience of "appearing like a human to himself" interferes both with his canine sense of self and with his most pronounced "human" ability: his linguistic eloquence. The dachshund is unsure how to describe with proper grammatical accuracy what is happening, specifically whether he is the subject (I) or object (me) of the other dog's desire to "be I,—or be me; how do you say this?" This is not just a grammatical problem on the sentence level but characteristic of the entire encounter: the canine narrator is losing control of his body, his feelings, his language, and the situation.

Human and canine forms of communication fail simultaneously in this scene. The sniffing of each other's hindquarters is turned from a mere opportunity to communicate facts (i.e., an immediate and satisfying olfactory answer to the question "How are you?" that lays bare one's soul) into an erotic encounter. Yet instead of exposing the soul as in canine communication, or exposing the body as in human sexuality, the other dog wants to "become him." "Becoming one" is a euphemism for intercourse, but the dachshund invokes the literal meaning of the other dog's intentions, in keeping with his concerns about differentiating self and other. He says that a "new Dog-I" opens up in him, which endangers his recently acquired self-awareness by "threatening to wipe out the past." The radical idea of "becoming another" scares the narrator because it threatens his self, and if it were to go along with a disrobing, or "skinning" as with humans, it would also undo the one visible difference between the two dogs, being bushy versus straight-haired, making them, too, "completely the same," or simply "*the* dog."[16]

The deconstruction of the canine I continues to play out in language, specifically the pronouns of the encounter. Pitted against the nominative *ich* or I is the accusative pronoun *mich* or me (twice *mich ausdrücken* [express myself]; twice *er wolle mich sein* [he wanted to be me]; and *weniger über mich sich orientieren* [less to orient himself about me]), which indicates the dog's status as direct object, both to himself and to others. On the other hand, there is the dative pronoun *mir*, which also translates to *me* in English (*weckte eine Idee in mir* [awakened an idea in me]; *ein neues Hunde-Ich that sich in mir auf* [a new Dog-I opened up inside of me]; *Mir kam vor* [It seemed to me]; *Ich kam mir vor* [I appeared to myself]), that seems indeed like a more indirect object form because it speaks of acts of becoming or "as if" scenarios. The direct object *mich* still contains the *ich*, whereas the more hypothetical and further removed indirect object *mir* deviates from this pattern of similarity and is on the verge of becoming something or someone else. The play with personal pronouns seems to reenact both the deconstruction of the self that occurs in this encounter between the two dogs and its potential result in the construction of one "new Dog-I."

Taken literally—the dachshund wants to express himself, appears to himself as a human, and it appears to him as if the other dog wants to become him or he—it becomes impossible to tell apart the multiple dogs that are facing each other. Yet at the same time, not a word is spoken in the entire scene: everything happens in one dog's mind. Read this way, the scene appears like a crisis of self that—if we take a cue from the plant section—could culminate in psychiatric institutionalization if the dog were indeed human. During the encounter, the dachshund fears that allowing his physical desire would undo the abilities of his mind—that is, end his possession of language and his ability to narrate, which he perceives as a complete loss of self. If language equals self-awareness or the I, this loss would be the end of his existence as a narrator and therefore the end of the story. This metacommentary on the creation and potential death of the first-person narrator highlights the role of language as the condition of narration in a similar manner to the first sentences of the text, and it points toward the end of the narrative, in which the dog learns about death and realizes that it entails the end of thought and narration.

Dogs and Not-Dogs

The dog's possession of language has led him into the same epistemological and linguistic crises as those of modernist human subjectivity at the time. The communicative encounter with another dog undid his sense of self and other, while disrupting his linguistic certainties, and when coming across a dead dog at the end of the text, he experiences another moment of becoming aware, this time not of the beginning but of the potential end of his life. Panizza's dachshund does not seem to know about death initially, which is why he understands human passing as "playing dead," a survival strategy of animals that he takes to be a comedic ritual among humans.[17] Yet when he sees the deceased dog toward the end of the text, he begins to grasp the horrifying nature of death because of the silence that surrounds him. To him, silence is not just the absence of speech; it is the loss of language and thought altogether—the end of narration and the death of the self, which explains his fear of losing his language skills during the encounter with the other dog:

> In der fürchterlichen Stille komme ich jetzt mehr zu mir selbst; und Gedanken der peinigendsten Art überfallen mich. [...] Jenes Denk-Wesen, jenes Tier, welches in unserem Kopfe steckt, und uns Alles befiehlt, zu riechen, zu fressen, zu laufen, auch gegen unsern Willen, hatte offenbar meinen armen Kameraden verlassen! [...] Wer ist jetzt der Hund? Das fortgelaufene Denk-Tier? Dann ist das, was da draußen liegt, der Nicht-Hund! Und was wird aus dem armen Kerl jetzt? – (TH, 113–39)

> In the horrible silence I increasingly came to myself; and thoughts of the most painful kind tortured me. [...] Said thought-creature, this animal, which is in our head, and tells us to do everything, to smell, to eat, to run, even against our will, it had apparently left my poor comrade! [...] Who is now the dog? The runaway thought-animal? But then, what is lying out there is the Not-Dog! And what will become of the poor fellow now?—

The dachshund has been convinced that he and other animals contain a *Denk-Tier* or thought-animal, which dictates dog behavior and can survive physical death (while it occasionally sounds like a Christian soul, dog souls have been defined as Aristotelian earlier). Leaving one's bodily shell behind seems entirely plausible because the dog has witnessed humans "take off body parts," so within this defamiliarized metaphor, abandoning one's physical self appears as an act of "undress" that exposes something else: the *Denk-Tier*, which raises questions about the true self. "Who is now the dog?" Is it the "thought-animal" and does that make the body a "Not-Dog"? The commanding *Denk-Tier* that makes dogs act "even against our will" also raises questions about unconscious drives, the control over one's body, and free will that have already come up in the canine erotic encounter, during which his self did not behave the way the dachshund wanted. Rather than a merging of two dogs as in that scene, however, the dog now seems split into two components, akin to body and mind (a distinction not needed in successful canine communication), which returns us to the Cartesian ideas present in the first sentences of the text.

Panizza's narrator is quite literally a "philosophical dog." He refers to the Cartesian *cogito* in the beginning, to the Aristotelian *anima* or canine soul in the encounter between the two dogs, and he defined the *Denk-Tier* with Fichte already before encountering the dead dog at the end of the text, as we will see in the next quote. Yet in all these instances, he struggles with applying traditional human philosophy to himself because it does not account for a dog in the subject position:

> Oft habe ich schon darüber nachgedacht, woher meine Hundegedanken kommen. Betrachte ich meine Pfoten, so sind es meine Pfoten; betrachte ich meinen Pelz, meinen Schwanz, so ist es mein Pelz und mein Schwanz; kurz, das ganze Hunde-Mich kann ich so zusammenfassen; und immer giebt es dann Pfoten, Pelz, Schwanz und dergl. – aber keine Gedanken. Woher kommen die Gedanken? Ich glaube, es ist ein Tier, welches mir unterm Kopfe steckt, und das diese rastlose, mühevolle Arbeit besorgt. Das, was zurückbleibt, wenn man vom Hunde alle äußeren Teile wegnimmt, ist, glaube ich, dieses Denktier, welches mich zwingt, seine Arbeit für die meine anzuerkennen. – Welche Entdeckung! / Mir kam es schon immer sonderbar vor, daß, wenn ich etwas tun wollte, es in mir bellte: Ich mag nicht. Und jedes Mal mußte ich folgen. Und umgekehrt, wenn ich zu träge war, vorübergehende Hunde zu beriechen, trieb mich oft dieses geheimnißvolle Denkwesen in meinem Innern auf, zur Geruchsarbeit zu gehen, die mir dann auch schmeckte. Welche elende Wirtschaft! Wenn der Hund nicht mehr thun darf, was der Hund will! Da sinkt ja der schöne, gefeierte Hund auf die elende Stufe einer pelzüberzogenen Marionette herab! Und der stille Commandeur im Innern, der läßt sich nie sehen. Dann besteht also der Hund aus A. + B., aus Hund + Nicht-Hund. Und dieser Nicht-Hund ist es, der die ganze Geschichte leitet. Er, der eigentlich für Alles verantwortlich ist, er heißt Nicht-Hund. Und gerade er sollte Hund heißen. Welch merkwürdiges Verhältniß! Welche Täuschung! Welche Infamie! So einen armen Hund herumlaufen, herumschnuppern zu lassen; ihn couragiert und stolz sein zu lassen, und ihm dann eines Tages zu zeigen, daß er gar nichts ist, und die Befehle eines andern sehr schlauen Commandeurs vollführt hat, und für die Zukunft vollführen wird. (TH, 84–85)

> Often, I've thought about where my canine thoughts come from. When I look at my paws, they are paws; when I look at my fur, my tail, they are my fur and my tail; in short, I can sum up the entire Dog-Me this way; and there are

always paws, fur, tail, and so forth—but no thoughts. Where do the thoughts come from? I think it is an animal, which is stuck in my head and takes care of this restless, cumbersome work. What remains when you take away all the outer parts of the dog is, I believe, this thought-animal, which forces me to acknowledge his work as mine.—What a discovery! / I had always found it peculiar that, when I wanted something, it barked inside of me: I don't like to. And every time I had to follow. And in reverse, when I was too lazy to take a smell at passing dogs, the mysterious thought-being inside of me urged me to go about my olfactory labor, which I then liked after all. What a miserable deal! If the dog cannot do anymore what the dog wants! Then the beautiful, celebrated dog sinks to the miserable level of a fur-covered marionette! And the silent commander on the inside always stays out of sight. Then the dog consists of A + B, of Dog and Not-Dog. And it is this Not-Dog who leads the whole story. He, who is actually responsible for everything, he is called Not-Dog. Yet it is him who should be called Dog. What a peculiar affair! What a delusion! What infamy! To let such a poor dog run around, sniff around; to let him be courageous and proud, and then show him one day that he is nothing and has been performing the orders of another very clever commander and will perform them in the future.

The dachshund appears to share the full weight of the human crisis of subjectivity at this point in his reflections. He questions the origin of his thoughts explicitly and implicitly also asks about his self-awareness, language, and ability to narrate. In response, he lays out familiar human concepts in dog terms: he begins by reenacting the Cartesian separation of body and mind as "paws, fur, and tail" versus "dog-thoughts." Then, he seems to allude to Fichte's concept of the *Ich* and *Nicht-Ich* (I and Not-I) by talking about the *Hund* and *Nicht-Hund* (Dog and Not-Dog), but he defines them against Fichte, and differently from his assessment in the aforementioned final encounter with the deceased dog, as the canine body (Dog) and consciousness or mind (Not-Dog).[18] This conflicts with both Fichte and the Cartesian mind-body separation, as the *cogito* locates the I in the mind—the place that the dog calls the "Not-I" or "Not-Dog" here. The narrator describes this "Not-Dog" as a puppet master that manipulates the "Dog"—that is, the body. Even *Geruchsarbeit*, which is the "olfactory labor" of canine communication, appears to be dictated by the *Nicht-Hund*. The dachshund identifies the "Not-Dog" with the *Denk-Tier*, or thought-animal, which makes the *Denk-Tier/Nicht-Hund*, in analogy to Fichte's "Not-I," everything that is not the I or self—that is, it is the other.

In this complex and confusing philosophical exercise, the dachshund has reasoned his self out of existence—he has literally lost his mind. Using reason to arrive at the opposite conclusion as the Cartesian *cogito* is as ironic and satirical as a speaking dog lamenting the obstacle that language poses to successful communication. His reattribution of philosophical terminology even seems to mock the destabilization of the relationship between signifier and signified in the *Sprachkrise*—terms can seemingly be applied to opposite concepts at random. Yet in another way, the dog has taken both Descartes and Aristotle by their word, since animals are mere bodies according to Descartes, and Aristotle defines the animal soul (*anima*) as lacking reason. That is why the narrator calls the dog's body, rather than the mind or *Denk-Tier*, the Dog or I. The traditionally anthropocentric perspective of institutions of human philosophy renders the animal a "Not-I," or an other to Man. In his philosophical exercise, the dog has therefore institutionalized himself by reasoning his mind out of existence. He speaks of himself as a *Hunde-Mich* (Dog-Me) in the accusative (a pronoun choice like the ones in the erotic canine encounter) since he finds that philosophy does not consider him a subject but an object. And subtle metacommentary gives away that the readers have been led astray alongside or by the narrator, since the text says that "it is this Not-Dog who leads the whole story." Panizza's "Not-Dog" underscores the unreliability of the narrative position of the *Groteske*, when the dachshund acts as a representative of the philosophically institutionalized tradition of anthropocentrism. At the same time, his doubt about the Dog and Not-Dog at the very end of the story, prompted by seeing a dead dog's body, points to both the limits of knowledge about the self and other and the dependence of narration on such an untrustworthy concept as language. Yet what might appear to be an acknowledgment of the dog as a creature without reason is not a mere acceptance of an anthropocentric view of animals; rather, presented by a speaking animal and discovered through philosophical *Denkarbeit* or thought labor, this traditional conception of animals, which serves to define humans against an other, is undermined and, at the end of the story, explicitly called into question ("Who is now the dog?").

As the unresolved crisis of subjectivity plays out in the dog's existential confusion about self and other, the narrator has consistently defined the *Denk-Tier* as an unconscious force that overrules both body and mind ("this animal, which is in our head, and tells us to do everything, to smell, to eat, to run, even against our will"). Around 1900, the discourse about the unconscious was rampant in philosophy and early psychology, which the psychiatrist Panizza followed closely.[19] If we recall—from the very first pages of this book—that Freud described the impact of the discovery of the unconscious on the human self-conception as a crisis of subjectivity, the third "narcissistic injury to humankind," we also see how closely it is related to the second, so-called Darwinian injury, which removed the constructed gap between humans and animals that had rendered Man the apex of creation. Just like the first, Copernican injury showed that the earth was not the center of the universe and thus ended Man's self-conception as lord and master of the world, the discovery of the unconscious demonstrates that neither the body (and its sexuality) nor the mind (and its language, one might add) are under full human control: "But both the explanations—that the life of the sexual impulses cannot be wholly confined; that mental processes are in themselves unconscious and can only reach the Ego and become subordinated to it through incomplete and untrustworthy perception—amount to saying that *the Ego is not master in its own house [das Ich nicht Herr sei in seinem eigenen Haus]*."[20] In Panizza's *Groteske*, the I is not master in its own body because the "Not-I," or "Not-Dog leads the whole story" in the form of the *Denk-Tier*, the unconscious. The developments that Freud describes as "injuries" strip humankind of their illusion of control of the world and themselves just like the canine perspective of the narrative does.

The text introduces a defamiliarizing dog's-eye view because it removes traditional assumptions about what it means to be human—and hence also animal. In the story, a dog ends up in the same modernist crisis of subjectivity as humans, and philosophy only makes it worse. On one level, this satire might suggest not to take ourselves as humans so seriously, yet on another, the narrative seems to say that such a crisis is unavoidable if you are a thinking, speaking, feeling creature. In doing so, the text follows the genre parameters of *die Groteske* through (1) its canine narrative perspective, which is fraught with a sense of built-in unreliability that makes the narrator both the representative of institutions (as "Not-Dog") and the nonhuman other (as "Dog"); (2) the way the narrator satirizes the conventions of human behavior, particularly their communication, that leads to his own crisis of communication and subjectivity; (3) the ambiguous and defamiliarizing language play about everyday interactions that literalizes the *Sprachkrise* especially in respect to communication; and (4) the way bodies and sexuality become entangled with the communicative attempts of relating to other and self. Written exactly thirty years later, in 1922, Kafka's *Groteske* takes up many of these ideas and strategies, as the next chapter shows exemplarily, yet in his dog's world, the crisis of self and other seems exacerbated, and the concerns about communication and language are met with resounding silence. One might even go so far as to say that the hermetic language of Kafka's text presents the failure of communication not only on the intradiegetic level but extends to the extradiegetic level, as its defamiliarizations often remain unresolvable.

EIGHT

Investigations/Researches of a Dog

Kafka's story also begins with a dog's account of his daily life without any explanation for his linguistic ability: "Wie sich mein Leben verändert hat und wie es sich doch nicht verändert hat im Grunde! Wenn ich jetzt zurückdenke . . ." (FH, 154; How my life has changed and yet has basically not changed! When I think back now . . .). Kafka's dog used to be "ein Hund unter Hunden" (FH, 154; a dog among dogs), but his titular investigations have rendered him solitary (see FH, 176–77) and the urgency of his questions is met with incomprehension and silence (see FH, 188–89), though there are encounters and conversations with other dogs in the text. While the dachshund's diary clearly includes humans, it is debatable whether humans exist in Kafka's text. Much of the scholarship engages with the canine narrator's failure to correctly interpret the effects of humankind's indirect or implicit presence.[1] This anthropocentric approach assumes that the canine narrator fails to perceive that humans are at the center of the world because his perception is impaired by his dog-ness. Yet the narrative is unambiguous about the fact that this dog's life does not revolve around a human master but is canine-centric instead, which suggests that the element of defamiliarization entailed in the premise of a narrating dog is not merely in place to be resolved into a human worldview.[2] Animal narration attempts to provide a nonhuman perspective, and once we are no longer impaired by our anthropocentrism, we might also spot humans in the texts—they are just not described in the way we think of ourselves. Most importantly, these creatures lack language: "Es gibt außer uns Hunden vielerlei Arten von Geschöpfen ringsumher, arme, geringe, stumme, nur auf gewisse Schreie eingeschränkte Wesen, viele unter uns Hunden studieren sie, haben ihnen Namen gegeben, suchen ihnen zu helfen, sie zu erziehen, zu veredeln u. dgl." (FH, 155–56; Aside from us dogs there are various kinds of creatures all around; poor, low, mute creatures, limited to certain cries; many among us dogs study them, have given them names, attempt to help them, to educate them, to refine them, etc.). In a canine-centric world, any nondog is just another animal—human or otherwise. Just like the dachshund in Panizza's *Groteske*, Kafka's dog finds humans in a low place, does not understand their communication, and instead sees a need to study and name them in the spirit of his Linnean and Adamic predecessors. Yet this endeavor does not take up much space in the text, as humans are simply not that important to the dog. The premise of a dog's-eye view once again overturns the traditional human–animal hierarchy and undermines human superiority, which is the satirical premise of canine narratives.

Communication and Sexuality

Similar to Panizza's *Groteske*, the dog in Kafka's text experiences a confusing yet formative encounter that involves sexual(ized) behavior, has traumatic effects on him, and momentarily affects his linguistic eloquence. In the text's perhaps most well-known scene, Kafka's dog meets the so-called *Musikhunde* or music(al) dogs, who are standing upright on two legs, like humans. What seems horrifying about the *Musikhunde* is that they do not behave like dogs and—more than that—do not adhere to the rules of communication:

> aber es waren doch Hunde, Hunde wie ich und du, man beobachtete sie gewohnheitsmäßig, wie Hunde, denen man auf dem Weg begegnet, man wollte sich ihnen nähern, Grüße tauschen [...]. Sie aber – unbegreiflich! unbegreiflich! - sie antworteten nicht, taten, als wäre ich nicht da. Hunde, die auf Hundeanruf gar nicht antworten, ein Vergehen gegen die guten Sitten, daß dem kleinsten wie dem größten Hunde unter keinen Umständen verziehen wird. Waren es etwa doch nicht Hunde? Aber wie sollten es denn nicht Hunde sein[?] (FH, 160–62)

> Yet they were dogs nevertheless, dogs like you and me; you observed them in the usual way, like dogs you meet on the street, you wanted to approach them and exchange greetings [...]. Yet they—incredible! incredible!—they did not answer, behaved as if I were not there. Dogs who make no reply to the call of other dogs are guilty of an offense against good manners for which the

smallest as well as the largest dog is not forgiven under any circumstances. Perhaps they were not dogs at all? But how should they not be dogs?

The young dog calls out to the other dogs, and their failure to respond leads him into an epistemological crisis: he not only asks if they are really dogs but also seems to wonder if he himself exists, because the others act like he is not there.[3] Communication serves to reaffirm the perception of oneself and the world, and here, its breakdown undermines both. The lack of affirmation of the self and the other through appellation in the *Musikhunde* scene raises questions about the possibility of creating an understanding or a connection between speakers at all. The text seems to suggest a pervasive inability to know someone else, which produces an all-encompassing crisis of epistemology, ontology, and language because it also entails the failure to know oneself and affirm one's existence with the help of a communicative or physical act performed by the other.

Panizza's dachshund had drawn attention to the way dogs can circumvent these problems by sniffing each other and instantly knowing the other's soul, but the *Musikhunde* encounter does not follow the laws of dog etiquette either. Kafka's canine narrator locates the reason for the breakdown in communication in their suggestive dance—a behavior that he considers a deviation from dog law and associates with sinful nakedness in the text:

> Diese Hunde hier vergingen sich gegen das Gesetz. Mochten es noch so große Zauberer sein, das Gesetz galt auch für sie, das verstand ich Kind schon ganz genau. Und ich merkte von da aus noch mehr. Sie hatten wirklich Grund zu schweigen, vorausgesetzt, daß sie aus Schuldgefühl schwiegen. Denn wie führten sie sich auf, vor lauter Musik hatte ich es bisher nicht bemerkt, sie hatten ja alle Scham von sich geworfen, die elenden taten das gleichzeitig Lächerlichste und Unanständigste, sie gingen aufrecht auf den Hinterbeinen. Pfui Teufel! Sie entblößten sich und trugen ihre Blöße protzig zur Schau [...] Ich konnte nicht weiter, ich wollte sie nicht mehr belehren, mochten sie weiter die Beine spreizen, Sünden begehen und andere zur Sünde des stillen Zuschauens verlocken, ich war ein so kleiner Hund, wer konnte so Schweres von mir verlangen? Ich machte mich noch kleiner als ich war, ich winselte. (FH, 162–64)

Those dogs were violating the law. Great magicians they might be, but the law applied to them too: that was something that I, a child, already understood very well. And from this point I now noticed even more. They really had good reason to remain silent, assuming that they remained silent from a sense of guilt. For how were they behaving; because of all the music I had not noticed it before, but they had flung away all shame, the wretched creatures were doing what is both most ridiculous and indecent; they were walking upright on their hind legs. Ugh, disgusting! They were exposing themselves and openly flaunting their nakedness, they prided themselves on it [...] I couldn't go any further, I did not want to instruct them anymore; even if they were to spread their legs further, commit sins, and tempt others to partake in the sin of silent on-looking; I was such a small dog, who could ask something so difficult of me? I made myself look even smaller than I was, I whimpered.

To the narrating canine, these other dogs act like "unrefined, limited, low, dumb creatures" by standing upright like humans, presenting their most vulnerable body parts in what can be a gesture of defeat in dogs.[4] This recalls the dachshund's horror at "appearing to himself like a human" in the eroticized encounter with the other dog. The scene also holds the potential of reversing the canine-centric species hierarchy if understood as trained behavior, signaling domestication and dependence on humans, since the posture invokes begging for a treat. Adding the "spreading of legs," which is associated with stereotypes about gender and sexuality, the dogs' behavior evokes submissiveness, recalling the phrase "hündisch ergeben" (submissive like a dog) that describes the condemned man Kafka's *In der Strafkolonie* (*In the Penal Colony*, 1919), who can be let loose but will return as soon as his executioners whistle.[5] Yet the "ridiculous and indecent" behavior of the dogs also appears shameless ("they had flung away all shame") to the young dog, and just like the dachshund's "skinned rabbits," they are described as simultaneously vulnerable and brazen ("they prided themselves on their nakedness [*Blöße*]"). The choice of words in the *Musikhunde* scene is familiar from Panizza's text, in which teeth and bodies are exposed with the same expression of *Entblößung*, and Ewers's plants were called "shameless" for making sexuality visible too. Panizza's text had suggested that undressing is a moment of *Entblößung* that is traumatic to dogs because they cannot do so themselves without removing body parts. Just like the dachshund had when he observed his owner's sex act, Kafka's dog whimpers and attempts to hide right after watching the *Musikhunde*. Unexpectedly observing a public display of exposed bodies associated with "shameless" sexuality unsettles onlookers across *Grotesken*, and the vulnerability of the exposed seems to be transferred to the viewers.

The young dog describes the *Musikhunde* as "silent from a sense of guilt," and his own "silent on-looking" makes him complicit in their "sin."[6] Vision, so central to human epistemology, contrasts here once again with the importance of scents for canine perception. In reference to Darwin, Freud takes the development of the upright posture to be a move from scent-centered interaction to visual stimuli (in the context of sexual attraction and distinguishing human from animal sexuality).[7] Watching the act silently makes the dog complicit both because he does not speak up against the sin and because the primacy of vision humanizes him just like the upright posture does the *Musikhunde*. The "sin of silent on-looking" conflates the realms of language (through its absence) and sexuality (the dog's witnessing gaze amplifies the transgression of the exposure). This recalls the policeman Jonathan from section 2, who is institutionalized as punishment for ending his self-censorship and speaking about—that is, reproducing—nonnormative sexuality, even though he does so to stop its occurrence. While the *Grotesken* in the plant section criticize and ridicule the fact that the censorship of literature and school curricula around 1900 condemned speaking about sexual aberrance more harshly than committing the act, the canine narrators in this section frequently conflate sexual activity and communication themselves. The act of witnessing, which is intricately connected to the sense of vision and the institution of the police, constitutes a transgression in all these texts. But *silent* witnessing becomes meaningless because the ability to report the incident is lost, which calls the occurrence of the *Musikhunde* encounter into question and suggests that it might all be in the narrator's mind—just like the encounter with the dog who wants to "become" the dachshund. This simultaneously evokes epistemological questions and the context of institutionalization and psychiatry from the previous section that is one of the characteristics of *Grotesken*. Not only does the complex encounter raise the question whether we can trust a canine narrator (a speaking animal that is supposed to be silent); we are moreover prompted to query the source of our own knowledge about the world and how to represent it in language, just like the narrating dogs do. Caught in the same crisis of subjectivity that the scene produces, the reader also becomes a complicit witness.

Silence and Hunger

In some ways akin to the dachshund's *Denk-Tier* or thought-animal, the reflections of Kafka's dog also produce the concept of a driving force that propels him forward and is trying to break the silence: the canine narrator is driven by what he calls his *Lufthunger* (literally: air hunger, or hunger for air, as the first word in a compound noun acts as the qualifier), which represents his metaphysical hunger for answers that urges him to conduct the story's titular investigations.[8] The term comes up once in the text, after the narrator wonders about the so-called *Lufthunde* (air-dogs, which are well-coiffed, small dogs moving through the air that he only ever hears stories about), and *Luft* and *Hunger* return frequently in his subsequent speculations about the origin of food, which he hopes will lead him to understand "das Wesen der Hunde" (FH, 210; dog nature).[9] *Lufthunger* is an old-fashioned term for dyspnea (i.e., shortness of breath) and is hence also associated with silence, as it suggests a potential inability to speak. The narrator identifies himself as among those "welche das Schweigen drückt, welche es förmlich aus Lufthunger durchbrechen wollen" (FH, 182; who are oppressed by the silence, who positively want to break through it because we hunger for air). In this sense, *Lufthunger* comes to signify not only his desire to speak with others but even more his longing to receive answers to his investigations. But the response to his research questions by other dogs continues to be "Schweigen, das allein ringsum mir noch antwortet. Wie lange wirst du es ertragen, daß die Hundeschaft, wie du dir durch deine Forschungen immer mehr zu Bewußtsein bringst, schweigt und immer schweigen wird. [. . .] Bollwerk des Schweigens, das wir sind" (FH, 174–75; silence that alone answers me all around. For how long will you bear it that the canine community [or: dogdom] is silent and will always be silent, as you are making yourself increasingly aware through your research. [. . .] bulwarks of silence that we are). Like the *Musikhunde*, other dogs do not respond to him, rendering "*the dog*" the supposedly mute animal of philosophical tradition—despite this one loquacious specimen.[10]

Just as silence is depicted as characteristic of dog-ness, so is the fact that no dog would ever go hungry willingly.[11] Yet in his quest to learn more about the origin of food, Kafka's canine undertakes physical hunger experiments (see FH, 195–96) that are reminiscent of Kafka's "Hungerkünstler" ("The Hunger Artist," 1922) but also evoke the behavioral dog experiments with food for which Ivan Pavlov received the Nobel Prize in 1904 (see FH, 193–94). Despite nearly starving to death and hallucinating the smell of food (see FH, 203), he does not stop his experiments. He seems compelled to fast by his investigative longing for answers, his *Lufthunger*, and it overrides the dog's physical hunger, or his instinct of self-preservation, because it is seductive: "Nun hätte ich ja wenigstens jetzt verspätet gehorchen und zu hungern aufhören können, aber mitten durch den Schmerz ging auch eine Verlockung, weiter zu hungern, und ich folgte ihr lüstern wie einem unbekannten Hund" (FH, 203; Now I could at least have obeyed, though tardily, and stopped fasting, but in the midst of my pain was a temptation to go on fasting, and I followed it as lecherously as if it were an unknown dog). This phrase evokes the encounter of Panizza's dachshund with an "unknown dog" who wanted to "become one" and awakened an eroticized, "lecherous" desire in him.[12] Once again, one dog appears as two, as if compelled by another (*Denk-Tier/Lufthunger*) to act against his body.

Indeed, the image of being or becoming one with hunger like a "burdensome lover" has come up before in Kafka's text:

> "Das ist der Hunger", sagte ich mir damals unzähligemal, so, als wollte ich mich glauben machen, Hunger und ich seien noch immer zweierlei und ich könnte ihn abschütteln wie einen lästigen Liebhaber, aber in Wirklichkeit waren wir höchst schmerzlich Eines und wenn ich mir erklärte: "Das ist der Hunger", so war es eigentlich der Hunger, der sprach und sich damit über mich lustig machte. (FH, 200)

> "That is the hunger," I told myself countless times back then, as if I wanted to convince myself that hunger and I were still two things and I could shake him off like a burdensome lover; but in reality we were very painfully one, and when I explained to myself: "That is the hunger," it was really the hunger speaking and making fun of me.

In this scene, the dog is speaking to himself—much like the man in the mirror or Panizza's dog in pronoun confusion. Once more, communication has turned into a soliloquy: the narrator tells himself (*sagte ich mir*), wants to make himself believe (*wollte ich mich glauben machen*), and explains to himself (*erklärte mir*). When he realizes that he and the hunger are, in fact, "very painfully" one, the delirium of hunger pangs seems to remind him that he is doing this to his own body, that his *Hunger* and *ich* are not *zweierlei*, or two things. Yet if deliberate fasting is not doglike, is *(Luft)Hunger* the Not-Dog? Has the *Denk-Tier* overridden his free will? The dog is putting his body through physical hunger experiments because his investigative longing for answers, his *Lufthunger*, compels him to, as if they were not one (*Eines*) and the same. Kafka's canine repeats in direct speech, "That is the hunger" (*Das ist der Hunger*) and then explains that "it was really the hunger speaking and making fun of me."[13] Who is speaking? The question seems insolvably lodged at the core of these texts narrated by dogs, yet it pokes fun not so much at dogs than at the human condition. If we take this moment to be the *Lufthunger* speaking for/in/as the dog (akin to a *Denk-Tier* or Not-Dog as in Panizza), then this drive to get responses to questions that cannot be answered has propelled the dog, his narrative, and us as his readers into a crisis of subjectivity. In the words of Panizza's dog, "It is this Not-Dog [*Nicht-Hund*] who leads the whole story," while Kafka's dog asks, "Perhaps they were not dogs [*nicht Hunde*] at all? But how should they not be dogs?" We end up with less certainty about ourselves and others than we had before—and perhaps with even less certainty about Kafka's text, whose seemingly simple language has undergone countless interpretations that accumulate meaning. As the two *Grotesken* have speaking dogs perform these problems of epistemology, ontology, and language philosophy, seemingly simple questions like "How are you?" and "Who is speaking?" are rendered utterly unanswerable.

NINE

Why Dogs?

Speaking animals seem to have trouble finding someone to talk to in a meaningful way. This soliloquist isolation is part of the modernist crisis of subjectivity, and it resonates not only with the *Grotesken* of the two authors but also with their private writings. Both Kafka and Panizza compared their state of mind repeatedly to that of an animal, and sometimes even specifically to a dog.[1] Panizza formulated the purpose of his literary production in his own diary in a way that resonates with his depiction of unsuccessful human and successful animal communication, which "lays bare the soul" in the dog's diary: "Ich will nur meine Seele offenbaren, dieses jammernde Tier, welches nach Hilfe schreit" (I only want to reveal my soul, this whining animal, which is crying for help).[2] Yet dogs mean something vastly different to Panizza and Kafka, respectively, and this is apparent in the differences between their *Grotesken*. Panizza lived with a dog named Puzzi, and one of his few extant photographs looks like a family portrait of the childless bachelor with his canine companion. His contemporaries were inspired to compare the ever-present dog at the side of the limping man to the appearance of Johann Wolfgang von Goethe's Mephisto in *Faust*, which corresponds with the presentation of the devil in Panizza's *Liebeskonzil* as a dog, whom many have identified with the author's voice.[3] When Puzzi died after eight years in February 1897, Panizza was devastated and remarked in a letter that the dog had become "ein menschliches Wesen" (a human being) to him. His diary adds that he loved his dog like "kaum ein anderes Wesen auf der Welt" (hardly another being in the world).[4] In the final words of the dachshund's diary, the canine narrator comes to realize his own mortality in a way that inspires such fellow feeling: "Ich wollte das Menschen-Geschlecht einteilen und ihre kuriosen Sonderbarkeiten untersuchen und sie verlachen und bin nur ein armer, kleiner Hund, der vielleicht bald krepiert" (TH, 116–17; I wanted to classify the human race and study their curious oddities and laugh about them and am only a poor, little dog, who might croak soon). Reminding us of our own impermanence, this dog is a kindred spirit, despite making fun of humans, who raises the question of what remains when our narrative ends.

The final words of Kafka's novel *Der Prozess* would answer this question with "shame." Famously, they have the protagonist describe his own violent death: "'Wie ein Hund!' sagte er, es war, als sollte die Scham ihn überleben" ("'Like a dog!' he said; it seemed as though the shame was to outlive him").[5] "Dying like a dog" is a shameful transgression for a human, or indeed Man. Yet when dogs act like humans, such as the upright *Musikhunde* who "had flung away all shame," they are considered shameless—not the opposite of shamefulness in a sense of liberation but rather an implication of the animal in human morality. Just as with the "shameless" plants in the previous section, the nonhuman other fails to adhere to human norms and thus calls them into question. While animality is famously a potent device in Kafka's oeuvre, his usage of dog imagery is usually distanced and often quite negative.[6] The most abject depiction of any animal in Kafka's writing is probably the dog in the aphorism "Ein Leben" ("A Life"):

> Eine stinkende Hündin, reichliche Kindergebärerin, stellenweise schon faulend, die aber in meiner Kindheit mir alles war, die in Treue unaufhörlich mir folgt, die ich zu schlagen mich nicht überwinden kann, vor der ich aber, selbst ihren Atem scheuend, schrittweise nach rückwärts weiche und die mich doch, wenn ich mich nicht anders entscheide, in den schon sichtbaren Mauerwinkel drängen wird, um dort auf mir und mit mir gänzlich zu verwesen, bis zum Ende – ehrt es mich? – das Eiter- und Wurm-Fleisch ihrer Zunge an meiner Hand.

> A stinking bitch, bearer of many children, already rotting in places, but which was everything to me in my childhood, which incessantly follows me faithfully, which I cannot bring myself to strike and before which, avoiding her breath, I move back step by step, and which, if I don't make a different decision, will force me into the already visible corner, so that there she may completely decay on me and with me, to the last—does it honour me?—the pus- and worm-filled flesh of her tongue on my hand.[7]

This old and sick dog behaves just like the formerly beloved pet she has been, but her loyalty and devotion now fill the speaker with dread and disgust. Feeling cornered by her pursuit of attention, yet unable to strike her because of his childhood feelings for her, the speaker withdraws from her touch, as her decaying body—worn out by copious reproduction—alerts him to his own physicality and mortality in a way that causes horror.

The loyalty and devotion of the dog in Kafka's aphorism highlights a relationship of dependence between species that is unlike any other. Dogs only exist because of humankind. Evolved from wolves, dogs were bred to fit humanity's needs, and they are trained to obey to such an extent that they override their own needs and urges for another species, even occasionally compromising their self-preservation instinct.[8] One might say that one of their defining species characteristics is their peculiar relationship to humans, who have found a multitude of ways to control them (as if taking on the role of the *Denk-Tier*). This raises the question of the unconscious and free will again, and Kafka's canine narrative ends with the dog lamenting the limits of his freedom: "Die Freiheit! Freilich die Freiheit, wie sie heute möglich ist, ein kümmerliches Gewächs. Aber immerhin Freiheit, immerhin ein Besitz" (FH, 211; Freedom! Certainly such freedom as is possible today, a stunted growth. Yet nevertheless freedom, nevertheless a possession). In reference to Pavlov's experiments with positive reinforcement in dogs (the famous bell that makes them salivate), behaviorists like B. F. Skinner have argued that human free will is an illusion too and all actions are stimulus–response reactions learned through repeated reinforcement. Critics accused him of "the taming of mankind through a system of dog obedience schools for all"[9]—thus faulting dogs for what humans have made them. This captures the ambivalence in Kafka's aphorism, where the speaker rejects what the beloved being has become in response to his behavior and fears the discovery of any similarities between the animal and the self.

As the most extended depiction of a dog in Kafka's writing, his researching canine is part of an entire zoo of animal protagonists, among them the eloquent ape Rotpeter in "Ein Bericht für eine Akademie" ("A Report for an Academy," 1917). So why not turn to apes for the crisis of subjectivity—a species that seems to be much more like our own and is not beholden to humans in obedience? It seems as if Rotpeter has already realized that humans—just like animals—are not as free as they like to think, for "mit Freiheit betrügt man sich unter Menschen allzuoft" ("human beings all too often deceive themselves about freedom"). Instead, the captured ape declares, "Nein, Freiheit wollte ich nicht. Nur einen Ausweg" ("No, it was not freedom I wanted. Just a way out").[10] His way out entails learning the human language:

> Ach, man lernt, wenn man muß; man lernt, wenn man einen Ausweg will; man lernt rücksichtslos. Man beaufsichtigt sich selbst mit der Peitsche; man zerfleischt sich beim geringsten Widerstand. Die Affennatur raste, sich überkugelnd, aus mir hinaus und weg, so daß mein erster Lehrer selbst davon fast äffisch wurde, bald den Unterricht aufgeben und in eine Heilanstalt gebracht werden mußte. (B, 564)

> Oh, you learn when you have to; you learn when you want a way out; you learn relentlessly. You supervise yourself, whip in hand; you tear yourself to pieces at the least sign of resistance. Ape nature, falling all over itself, raced madly out of me and away, so that I practically made a monkey of my first teacher, who was soon forced to give up training and had to be delivered to a sanatorium. (R, 83)

The need for a "way out" is so strong that Rotpeter becomes his own driver or master in the image of the cracking whip—outperforming his teacher with no need for a *Denk-Tier*. Meanwhile, his *Affennatur* or ape nature (akin to the term *Hundenatur*/dog nature in FH, 202) exits his body so rapidly that his teacher momentarily loses his mind and is institutionalized.[11] If an ape can imitate (or ape) humans so easily, as Rotpeter says and demonstrates in the text, then who is human and who is animal is no longer clear, so that the teacher becomes apelike (and indeed, several of the illustrations in Panizza's dog diary also show his owner with ape features). Perhaps he is "infected" by the *Affennatur* like the feverish, institutionalized Jonathan from the previous section was by plants. In any case, the place of the ape-ish is among the institutionalized "mad" in the asylum—a fate that the dog escapes precisely because he is not similar enough to the human.[12]

Kafka's and Panizza's narratives show that a canine perspective is uniquely suited for the kind of social critique *Grotesken* undertake, especially in the face of censorship. Unlike Kafka's ape, who is tasked with a report to an institution and has realized that he can never be free, "the dog" is not taken seriously enough to be institutionalized in the first place (hence the dismissal of the animal in philosophy), and Panizza's dog diary is in fact one of few texts that was ignored by his censors. Accordingly, the dog has been the image of the satirist since the notoriously "shameless" Cynic Diogenes, who was called "the Dog" (since cynic means "doglike," this nickname extends to all of them) and said, "The other dogs bite their enemies, but I my friends in order to save them."[13] Dogs maintain their loyalty and devotion even in criticism. Dog teeth are also bared (*entblößt*) in the trope of the "grinning dog," exemplifying both the laughter and the aggression of "biting satire."[14] As "honest dogs," satirists are said to be "lifting their legs and pissing against the world" with the help of the spoken or the written word.[15] Panizza's and Kafka's canine narrators do just that: they subvert the idea of human superiority and expose the failure of the various constructs on which humanity prides itself. Instead of championing the possession of language, the assumed control over sexuality, and the knowledge of death as superior and uniquely human characteristics, the texts use these concepts as springboards for the exploration of existential epistemological problems, which leads to the discovery of the way the unconscious controls body and mind, while limiting the freedom of will.[16] Additionally, human ways of interacting are shown not to succeed in transferring information or creating community; instead, human communication and sexuality are bound up with isolation and the failure to know oneself or the other. Human behavior thus appears as incomprehensible to the dogs as the act of sniffing another dog's hindquarters might be to humans. The texts suggest that humans need to reevaluate their relationship to themselves and the world around them to determine what it means to be human—a question whose increased urgency is at the center of the next section, and which extends eloquent Rotpeter's struggles with acceptance into a parable of "Jewish assimilation."

SECTION 4

THE HUMAN

Panizza, Friedlaender, and the Rise of Fascism

Since the mid-eighteenth century, debates about the civil, legal, and social status of Jews within Western European societies were subsumed under the label of the so-called Jewish Question, which later also included the idea of a Jewish state. In the mid-nineteenth century, the term was increasingly negatively appropriated by antisemites, and it would ultimately be taken up by the Nazis, who proposed their horrific "Final Solution" to the "Jewish Question" in 1941.[1] While the 1871 constitution of the German Empire had granted the Jewish population equal citizenship rights, Jews continued to be denied access to certain professions and experienced a range of social exclusions. Antisemitism remained commonplace, whether in the form of demanding that Jewish people and their cultures be expelled or instead expecting conversion and radical integration. Discourses about "Jewish assimilation" in both Wilhelmine and Weimar Germany focused on the relationship not only between German Christians and Jews but also between so-called assimilated Western German Jewry and newly arriving orthodox, Yiddish-speaking Jews from Eastern Europe.[2] These shifts complicated already complex notions of acculturation and belonging for the Jewish community in Germany around 1900. Accordingly, the image of a "Jewish other" was persistently present in aesthetic and literary representations of the time, among them also *Grotesken*, which comment on the political and cultural facets of contemporaneous discourses satirically.

In this section of the book, I examine such a pair of *Grotesken*—Oskar Panizza's "Der operirte Jud'" ("The Operated Jew," 1893) and Salomo Friedlaender's "Der operierte Goj: Ein Gegenstück zu Panizzas operiertem Jud" ("The Operated Goy": A counterpiece to Panizza's Operated Jew, 1922)—that were published almost thirty years apart, but in conversation with each other.[3] Panizza was raised within a family struggle between competing Christian denominations, censored for his irreverent criticism of the church and state, and called himself an atheist, while Friedlaender was a neo-Kantian philosopher and declared atheist born into the Jewish community. Both were critical of organized religion and national endeavors.[4] The two authors' divergent positionalities with respect to Jewish culture and the different sociopolitical settings of their texts within the Wilhelmine Empire and the Weimar Republic contribute to the understanding of the complex and shifting discourses about Jewish identity and belonging in the German context. Their two *Grotesken* address the belonging and exclusion of Jews in Germany during a crucial historical moment, and they ask who is considered a human being with equal rights and accepted as part of society. Reading the texts together shows that the exaggerated caricatures of stereotypes in the two narratives represent ways in which Jewish and German identities were imagined and constructed against and alongside each other at the time.

In Panizza's "Der operirte Jud'," a Jewish figure undergoes extreme physical operations, behavioral modifications, and speech training to pass as not Jewish. Yet the transformation ultimately fails, and at first glance, this story by a non-Jewish author suggests that any attempt at assimilation is doomed as an act of imitation, evoking the antisemitic stereotype of Jewish mimicry.[5] However, by going beyond the examination of the body of the protagonist that is popular in existing scholarship and including the language learning process in the analysis of the narrative, the upcoming chapter 10 demonstrates that the text also problematizes essentializing identity concepts and satirizes the paranoid imagination of German society. In Friedlaender's "Der operierte Goj," an early Nazi supporter falls in love with a Jewish woman and converts to Judaism in ways that are modeled on Panizza's protagonist. While the direction of the transformation in the text is the opposite, its narrative strategies are deliberately similar. The analysis of this text in chapter 11 shows that these parallels expand the satirical target of the text from

German society to the Jewish community, thus complicating what Friedlaender might mean by calling his narrative a "counterpiece" (*Gegenstück*) to Panizza's text in its subtitle. Addressing both inner-Jewish conflicts between Western and Eastern European Jewry and the Zionist project, Friedlaender's text suggests that German and Jewish nationalisms employ similar principles of exclusion based on the notion of an essentialized identity whose purity must be retained. As a set, the two *Grotesken* illustrate the complex problems that arose amid attempts to define German and Jewish identities and cultures in the early twentieth century.

Turning to the question of who is accepted as human from the point of view of Jewish characters showcases the urgency of the criticisms of *Grotesken*. Once again we find the typical characteristics of the genre: (1) seemingly trustworthy narrators, in this case representing medical institutions, who are exposed as unreliable and flawed when they attempt to enforce society's normative order; (2) an association of deviation and nonconformity with the marginalized human perspectives that leads to institutional, and here specifically biopolitical, interventions; (3) the genre's play with ambiguous, pliable language and even language learning; and (4) the focus on bodies and their sexual reproduction as a site of biopolitical control. Yet the exaggerations and stereotypes in these particular *Grotesken* produce more horrified than humorous responses today. As the beginning of this book outlines, the laughter about *Grotesken* tends to "get stuck in one's throat" out of shock, and especially the antisemitism in Panizza's text has a predominantly chilling effect. In this context, it is important to remember Gershom Scholem's words from the introduction: He commented that Friedlaender's *Grotesken* "almost knocked me off my chair with laughter at the time" but are "a literary form that became impossible after Hitler and is virtually inaccessible today."[6] As the first section of the book showed, the reception of *Grotesken* was fundamentally changed by the Holocaust, and this is certainly nowhere more apparent than in the case of these two examples, which require careful analysis to be made accessible in the context of their own time.

TEN

The Operated Jew

Oskar Panizza's narrative "Der operirte Jud'" satirizes discourses about "Jewish assimilation" at a time when equal citizenship rights for Jews had only been in place for a little more than twenty years. The Jewish protagonist of the text is an amalgamation of exaggerated stereotypes, and he appears like a collage of antisemitic insults. His name, Itzig Faitel Stern, is that of a nineteenth-century stock figure, and his appearance, from his hair to his feet, follows physiognomic typecasting.[1] Faitel's story is told by a nameless narrator, a fellow student of medicine in Heidelberg, who seems transfixed by Faitel's perceived physical and linguistic differences and reproduces them throughout the narrative, such as Faitel's desire "ßu werden aach a fains Menschenkind wie a Goj-menera, und aufßugeben alle Fisenemie von Jüdischkeit" (OJ, 144–45; "to become such a fine gentilman [literally: human child/being] just like a goymenera and to geeve up all fizonomie of Jewishness"; Z, 55). Several doctors assist Faitel with a gruesome Pygmalion-esque experiment to make this desired physiognomic passing possible: his bones are broken and straightened, his hair is dyed blond, and he practices a new set of gestures. Most significantly, he must learn to speak "proper" German because his diction supposedly gives away his descent. In the doctors' view, the ultimate success of the experiment can only be proven by procreation, and when the transformation seems complete, Faitel successfully woos a "blonde Germanin" (OJ, 155; "a blonde Germanic lass"; Z, 64). However, on his wedding day, he drinks too much, and his old language, behavior, and even appearance return, making the wedding party flee.

Panizza's *Groteske* is quite controversial and has often been discarded as an antisemitic diatribe.[2] Jack Zipes's 1991 translation of the text into English seems notably colored by this assumption, which forecloses other aspects of the narrative and likely shaped its US reception. The few scholars who engaged with "Der operirte Jud'," such as Sander Gilman, Eric Santner, and Jay Geller, have primarily focused on Faitel's body in the context of a variety of discourses in German Jewish studies.[3] In both English and German, there is little extended engagement with the text that takes Panizza's other writing into account, and the genre context of *die Groteske* is almost entirely absent.[4] Even though Friedlaender's narrative is mentioned in the existing scholarship, the question why he chose to write a "counterpiece" to Panizza's text in 1923 is not fully resolved beyond the increasing urgency of the topic of "Jewish assimilation" in his own time. While acknowledging the harmful antisemitism operating in and around these texts, this section of the book suggests that the targets of Panizza's *Groteske* are more varied and complex—something that Friedlaender's response recognizes and emphasizes within the same genre. At stake is the artificially constructed and exclusory nature of national identity concepts, exemplified by German society and its exclusion of Jews. Specifically, the languages and dialects of the narrative introduce a subtext that undermines both the German and Jewish stereotypes at play. While the degree of Faitel's difference is also measured in physical deviations, which become evident in the detailed descriptions of "dieses grauenhaften Stücks Menschenfleisch" (OJ, 141; "this dreadful piece of human flesh"; Z, 52), there is an even greater obsession with Faitel's hybrid language in the text. The French, Palatinate, and Yiddish elements of his speech, along with neologisms and mannerisms, are discussed at much more length than his physical traits. The narrator of the *Groteske* provides a detailed and derogatory description of the protagonist's hybrid mix of other languages and dialects, which this section contrasts with an analysis of the linguistic strategies of the text itself. *Hochdeutsch*, standard or literally "high" German, which is the superior language model that Faitel is supposed to acquire, emerges as fragmented and hybrid rather than "pure." The text questions the existence of such a language standard and the unified national identity with which it has become synonymous. Ultimately, *Hochdeutsch* and all that it stands for is exposed as an illusory construct, in line with the language play and criticism in other *Grotesken*. Panizza's narrative does not spare anyone from ridicule and complicates concepts such as identity, assimilation, cultural appropriation, passing, and multilingualism. Before turning to the topic of language to explicate these claims, the following pages first unfold how the narrator depicts Faitel's body (including sexuality) as an amalgamation of ultimate otherness. This raises the central question of the genre about what it means to be human explicitly, and, in a second step, it leads to the category of the soul (familiar from the previous section) in an attempt to find the "essence" of identity.

(De)Humanization

The descriptions of Faitel's body are caught between two seemingly competing strategies: on the one hand, the narrator dehumanizes him with derogatory details and even calls him a monster; on the other hand, Faitel's humanity is established frequently and explicitly in the text. Often, this happens in the same sentence—producing a disconcerting effect, such as when he was called a "gruesome piece of human flesh" earlier and professed his desire to become a "fine human being like a Goy." The description even questions his humanity outright, such as when scientists ask "ob es sicher sei, daß Itzig von menschlichen Eltern geboren" ("whether it was certain that Itzig's parentage was human"), which is immediately followed by "Dies konnte auf's unwiderleglichste nachgewiesen werden" (OJ, 143; "Of course, this could be proven without a doubt"; Z, 54). At other times, his appearance is likened to animals and plants: "Ein Gazellen-Auge von kirschen-ähnlich gedämpfter Leuchtkraft schwamm in den breiten Flächen einer sammtglatten, leicht gelb tingirten Stirn- und Wangen-Haut" (OJ, 136; "An antelope's eye with a subdued, cherry-like glow swam in wide apertures of the smooth velvet, lightly yellow skin of his temple and cheeks"; Z, 48).[5] This depiction includes different species (antelopes, cherries) but also stereotypes of racialized human bodies, such as "yellow skin." The narrator's paradoxical strategy suggests that the category of the human is fraught and has subgroupings, returning to the notion of Man as the only one considered fully human. Now that others are beginning to gain access to more human rights, Man (and the narrator as one of his representatives) must differentiate himself from these others to retain his privileges and power.

Establishing a facade of scientific inquiry and humanism that only amplifies its inherent racism and antisemitism, the narrator creates a division of "us versus an other" with descriptions like the following that are perhaps some of the most dehumanizing in the text:

> Es war gewiß viel, wie soll ich sagen, medizinische, oder besser anthropologische Neugierde dabei; ich empfand ihm gegenüber wie etwa bei einem N[...]. Mit Verwunderung beobachtete ich, wie dieses Monstrum sich die grauenhafteste Mühe gab, sich in unsere Verhältnisse, in unsere Art zu gehen, zu denken, in unsere Mimik, in die Aeußerungen unserer Gemüthsbewegungen, in unsere Sprechweise einzuleben. (OJ, 141)[6]

> There was certainly a great deal of what I would call medical or rather anthropological curiosity in this case. I was attracted to him in the same way I might be to a Negro [...]. Perhaps there was also some pity here, but not much. I observed with astonishment how this monster took terrible pains to adapt to our circumstances, our way of walking, thinking, our gesticulations, the expressions of our intellectual tradition, our manner of speech. (Z, 52)

In line with racial pseudoscience and the colonial endeavors of the time, Faitel is mapped and charted like foreign territory and other peoples. What the narrator seems to have found invokes a mythical creature from the edge of the world that can only be described by degree of difference and is devoid of any individuality: a monster.[7] The narrative shows that the definition of the self depends on the contrasting foil of such an "other," which is, however, quite variable—from cherries and antelopes to racialized humans and mythical beings, and later also women and dogs. Though clearly introducing a wide range of specifically antisemitic stereotypes too, as existing analyses of Faitel's body have shown, the text's discourse about the human evokes not just the context of "German versus Jewish" identity but also "Man versus the other" writ large. By painting an amalgamated image of the greatest degree of difference possible, a literal other, Faitel is introduced to the individual reader's imagination as "the most different" figure conceivable—a strategy that will recur in the discussion of language and betrays anxiety about the ability to define and clearly delineate the self. In fact, the narrator repeatedly emphasizes his difficulty with describing Faitel at all (a familiar problem with the limits of language), which seems to indicate that he is too different to be imagined but makes space for the imagination to run rampant with ideas of otherness.

What this contrastive description of the other leaves for the concept of the supposedly German "us," which is really only reserved for Man, is the caricature of a stereotype: Faitel "gefiel sich im heroisch-teutonischen Genre, wie in der blond-naiven, süßlächelnden Jünglings-Gangart" (OJ, 147; "imagined himself to be part of the heroic-Teutonic genre like some young stalwart, blond and naïve, who walked about smiling with great ignorance"; Z, 57; literally: liked himself in the heroic-Teutonic genre as well as in the blond-naive, sweetly smiling young man's bearing). Yet Faitel's transformation into this shallow blond "hero" comes not just at great financial but also physical cost, which he bears "mit größten Heroismus [. . .], um ein gleichwerthiger abendländischer Mensch zu werden" (OJ, 147; "great heroism so he could become the equivalent of an Occidental human being"; Z, 57; literally: an equivalent Occidental human being or a human being of equal value). Becoming heroic apparently requires inherent heroism, which raises questions about differentiating old from new and Man from other, while the theme of "the human" continues. When "Faitel war jetzt ein ganz neuer Mensch geworden" (OJ, 148; "Faitel was now an entirely new human being"; Z, 58), he names himself Siegfried Freudenstern (literally: victory-peace joy-star), thus moving from a Hebraic name infused with German dialect (Itzig) to one that consists of positively connoted German words yet remains true to his roots (his original last name Stern, a reference to the Star of David). Though he becomes unrecognizable to his old acquaintances after this transformation, he has retained not just the core of his heroism and last name but apparently also physical traces of his supposed "Oriental" Jewish self—evoking an antisemitic stereotype about the origin of Jews in Egypt:

> Freilich die Zahnbildung, die Lippenwülste, die Nasenlappung in Faitels Gesicht mußten stehen bleiben, wollte man nicht ein Scheußal zusammenoperiren; und wer ein Auge für derlei Dinge hatte, erkannte im Profil Freudenstern's das sinnliche, fleischige, vorgemaulte Sphinx-Gesicht aus Egypten. (OJ, 160)

> Of course, the formation of the teeth, the padded lips, the nasal pitch in Faitel's face had to remain absolutely fixed to prevent a monster from becoming visible [literally: if one wanted to avoid stitching together a monster]. And whoever had an eye for such things could recognize the sensual, fleshy, and jutting Sphinx-like face [missing: from Egypt] in Freudenstern's profile. (Z, 68)

Here, Faitel is no longer inherently monstrous; rather, changing him too much would result in monstrosity (*ein Scheußal*), which places a curious responsibility on his Frankenstein-esque surgeons and the choices made in the transformation process—a theme that will return in the context of language learning.[8] The passage suggests an understanding of "Jewish assimilation" as mimicry and evokes two seemingly contrasting antisemitic stereotypes:

a supposed Jewish unchangeability that points to problematic notions of an "essence" of identity and a deceptive ability to imitate others flawlessly. Accordingly, the narrator had cautioned the reader about Faitel's "pretense" earlier on by invoking contemporary antisemitic depictions of Jewish men as effeminate: "Nur das Weib darf lügen und sich in falsche Umhüllungen kleiden" (OJ, 158; "Only a woman may lie and cloak herself in false wrappings"; Z, 67). [9] These ideas betray his own insecurities (also about women) since they indicate that the fear of the other is really a fear of the other becoming unrecognizable as such. Once the other is no longer identifiable as different, the other has become like the self, so the narrator must insist on a residual difference.[10] The expression "having an eye for such things" in the passage indicates that racists and antisemites will always see what they believe to be true, no matter how much of a "new human" Faitel becomes. The repeated emphasis on Faitel's humanity is such a disconcerting strategy of dehumanization because it shows that the definition of Man rests exclusively on differentiation from all others and is hence inherently unattainable for them. Man might be blond, "Occidental," and a "Goy," but his main characteristic is having the institutionalized power to determine who belongs.

Just like the narrator, Faitel's doctors share in this power, and they are eager to complete the step that is needed to ensure the success of any scientific experiment: its reproducibility.

> Eines fehlte noch: Es galt diese kostbar-gewonnene Menschenrace fortzupflanzen. Mit dem feinsten abendländischen Reis sollte der neue Stamm oculirt werden. Eine blonde Germanin mußte die mit fabelhafter Mühe gewonnenen Resultate erhalten helfen. (OJ, 155)

> Only one thing was still missing, for it was also important to reproduce this human race, which it had cost so much to achieve. The new breed was to be grafted with the finest Occidental sprig. A blonde Germanic lass had to help preserve the results that had been garnered through fabulous efforts. (Z, 64)[11]

Notably, reproduction would render Faitel and his offspring still a seemingly separate kind of human—their own family tree. Nonetheless, the proximity to Man becomes threateningly close and the experiment must therefore fail—but it has to be Faitel's fault. Casting his transformation as surface-level mimicry, one drink too many turns Faitel back into to his old self on his wedding day—his linguistic and physical changes come undone. One aspect of his transformation was to stop his torso from moving back and forth—a reference to Jewish prayer—for which he put "ähnlich wie bei Hunden, ein Stachel-Halsband [...] auf den bloßen Körper" (OJ, 145; "a barbed wire belt similar to a collar [...] on his bare skin (as they do with dogs)"; Z, 56). This movement returns when he unravels and is resignified in a threateningly sexualized way that shows the reproduction fantasy in a different light: "schnalzend und gurgelnd und sich hin- und herwiegend, und mit dem Gesäß ekelhaft lüsterne, thierisch-hündische Bewegungen machend, sprang er im Saal herum: [...] Kellnererá, wo is mei copulirte, christliche Braut?" (OJ, 165; "clicking his tongue, gurgling, and tottering back and forth while making disgusting, lascivious and bestial canine movements with his rear end. [...] Waiterá, vere iss mine copulated Chreesten bride?"; Z, 73).[12] Adding animalistic sexualization and the potential "madness" of a rabid dog to the catalog of devices that have been used to dehumanize Faitel renders him a threat in ways that the description did not do before—one that calls up the need for the containment of institutionalization, though this *Groteske* does not spell it out.[13] Yet even now, Faitel is explicitly called human, while described in continuously gruesome ways: "ein blutrünstig angelaufenes, violettes Menschenantlitz mit speichelndem Mund, lappig hängenden Lippen und quellenden Augen" (OP, 164; "a bloodthirsty, swelling, crimson [missing: human] visage spewed saliva from flabby drooping lips, and gushing eyes glared at them"; Z, 72). Whether one simply sees the caricature of a drunk person or not depends on what one believes, as the narrator revealed earlier. The wedding party's verdict is clear: "Alles blickte mit starrem Entsetzen auf [...] de[n] Juden" (OJ, 166; "Everyone looked with dread at [...] the Jew"; Z, 73). Faitel himself repeatedly invokes his own humanity during his unraveling: "Bin ich ä Mensch aß gut und werthvoll als Ihr Alle!" (OP, 164; "I vant you shood know dat I'm a human bing jost as good for sumtink [literally: as good and valuable] as any ov you!"; Z, 72), but the narrator gets the final word, labeling him "ein verlogenes Stück Menschenfleisch, *Itzig Faitel Stern*" (OJ, 166; "a counterfeit [literally: lying piece] of human flesh, Itzig Faitel Stern"; Z, 74). Faitel's transformation was doomed from the beginning, as the other can never join the ranks of Man—just be marginalized and excluded over and over, despite being human.

Soul Searching

Beyond the antisemitic stereotype of the unchangeable Jew, the reemergence of Itzig Faitel Stern at the end of the narrative is tied to problematic ideas of an "essence" such as blood and, because of that, the soul. During his transformation, his experimenters had asked, "Hatte Faitel eine Seele?" (OJ, 149; "Did Faitel have a soul?"; Z, 59). The concept of a soul is familiar from the dog diary discussed in the previous section that Panizza wrote just one year before this text, and there are several resonances between the two *Grotesken* (not least the evocation of "leg-hiders" in the quote about women cloaking themselves in false wrappings).[14] Implicitly evoking the Cartesian "animal machine," the doctors consider "die primäre Seelen-Anlage bei Leuten wie Faiteles nicht als geistigen Besitz, sondern als mechanische Funktion" (OJ, 149–50; "the primary spiritual predisposition [literally: composition of the soul] of people like Faitel not as a *spiritual* possession but as a mechanical function"; Z, 59). But they deem Cartesian ideas about the location of the soul in the human pineal gland outdated and instead suggest that "der Sitz der Seele sei das Blut" (OJ, 150; "the abode of the soul could be located in the blood"; Z, 60). Even though the text says that Faitel has the soul necessary for expressing emotions and charity "wie jeder Andere" (OJ, 149; "like everyone else"; Z, 59), just as he has been human and heroic all along, he wants to attain the full extent "jener keuschen, undefinirbaren, germanischen Seele" (OJ, 149; "chaste, undefined [literally: undefinable] Germanic soul"; Z, 59) about which he has heard. To acquire this elusive "essence" of (the Ger)Man, Faitel's blood is exchanged for "German blood" donated by "mehrere kräftige Schwarzwälderinnen, die zur Messe gekommen waren" (OJ, 151; "seven [literally: several, and as the text makes clear later, eight] strong women from the Black Forest, who had come to mass"; Z, 60). In this context, the text briefly mentions that Faitel undergoes a formal religious conversion, and during the seemingly much more important blood exchange, Faitel nearly dies, signifying the death of his old self and his rebirth as a Christian, since he now has "christlich's Bluht" (OJ, 150; "Chreesten blud"; Z, 60). The text immediately casts doubt on the success of the procedure, calling his subsequent emotional recitals of sentimental poetry yet another attempt at attaining a soul and becoming "ein Gemüthsmensch durch und durch" (OJ, 152; "a man with a soul through and through"; Z, 62; literally: a sentimentalist, or a human of feeling). Together with the "female blood" he received, this soul-based sentimentality satirizes stereotypical concepts of Christian masculinity—that is, Man—along with blood-based ideas of an "essence," and it raises fundamental questions about what might make a soul or identity "Germanic."[15]

According to the story, Germans are overly sensitive and naive, shallow and stupid, uptight and greedy, along with many other negative qualities, yet the image of the blond German archetype is also destabilized by the diversity of the German population in the text itself. Eric Santner remarks, "What is at stake here, then, is not simply Panizza's ridicule of German vulgarity and stupidity, which is no doubt also present in the text, but rather his suggestion that, in a sense, 'the German' does not exist."[16] Identity categories are de- and reconstructed repeatedly across the text to show that defining belonging is an exercise of power. Satirizing what Faitel aspires to be is humorous and so are Faitel's often quite witty remarks in the text, yet many of the rampant antisemitic stereotypes across Panizza's *Groteske* do not seem comically exaggerated to today's readers because of the way the Nazis applied them to Jewish bodies in devastating ways. Jack Zipes writes in the postscript to his translation,

> Each step Faitel Stern takes to control and eliminate his Jewishness is laughable, not so much because his obvious stereotypical Jewish traits are ridiculous, but because the German qualities, which he wants to adapt, are preposterous. To become a blond, blue-eyed German stalwart means learning how to walk stiffly, utter pretentious phrases, dispense with critical thinking, and to pander to money, power, and the upper classes. In a way it is a credit to Faitel Stern's Jewish "essence"—his rebellious nature—that he cannot become German, that the experiment fails, and that human flesh proves stronger than a eugenic operation. (Z, 106)

This notion of an "essence," Jewish or otherwise, is problematic, and the narrative satirizes the idea of such an intrinsic quality in its discussion of the soul and blood in respect to the body—and it will do so for language too. The belief in an "essence" is tied to the racist and antisemitic convictions of the narrator and the other doctors. Their literally "fabulous efforts" (Z, 64) and the narrator's self-professed qualifications as an anthropologist and humanist are strategies of critique that comment on the physiognomic pseudoscience and rampant racism of the time (also by referencing historical physiognomists like Lavater explicitly). While the narrator introduced himself as Faitel's "friend" in the beginning, he is the one who suggests the transformation (see OJ, 135; and Z, 47), and his lengthy descriptions of Faitel's changes serve to establish difference more firmly. The narrator and the doctors as representatives of medical institutions therefore emerge as not trustworthy in this eugenic experiment because they tell Faitel that he might be able to belong if he only changes (and pays) enough, even though they know that an antisemitic differentiation between "us" and "them" makes any attempt to cross such a divide inherently impossible, no matter how one looks or speaks.[17] These critiques become more evident when turning from the physical reproduction of a nonexistent ideal to the aspect of linguistic reproduction in Panizza's *Groteske*.

Language Imitation

"Der operirte Jud'" reproduces an understanding of "Jewish assimilation" as imitation on multiple levels, most notably that of language. Even though the text consists of pages upon pages of descriptions of Faitel, the narrator repeatedly states that he himself is at a loss for words (like Jonathan when discovering the masturbating plants). From the beginning, he reflects on the difficulty of imitation in the context of language:

> Aber wer hilft mir die Sprache von Itzig Faitel Stern beschreiben? Welcher Philologe oder Dialektkenner würde sich unterstehen diese Mischung von Pfälzerisch, semitischem Geknängse, französischen Nasal-Lauten und einigen hochdeutsch mit offener Mundstellung vorgebrachten, glücklich abgelauschten Wortbildungen zu analysiren?! (OJ, 139)

> But who will help me describe Itzig Faitel Stern's speech? What philologist or expert in dialects would dare analyze this mixture of Palatinate Semitic babble, French nasal noises, and some high German vocal sounds that he had fortuitously overheard and articulated with an open position of the mouth? (Z, 50)

Faitel's hybrid language appears as different and amalgamated as his body, invoking the antisemitic caricature of the "mauschelnde Jude" (literally: "mumbling Jew," originally "speaking like Moses or Moische," meaning "speaking Yiddish" but also "to cheat," "to make secret agreements").[18] However, despite the narrator's professed difficulty to distill a "pure" language from Faitel's speech, he seems quite willing to experiment with unusual phonetics himself. In the narrator's experiment, it is not so much *Hochdeutsch*, or "high" German that is imitated as a variety of "lower" vocals, many of which are onomatopoetic reproductions. There are musical "Schnedderengdeng-Geräusche" (OJ, 138; "rhythmically uttered sounds like a trumpet"; Z, 50) and "Sing-Sang" (OJ, 146; "sing-song"; Z, 56), bodily sounds like "schneuzen," "näseln," "knängsen," "gröhlen," or "gurgeln," and animal noises like "miauen," "grunzen," "schnarren," "schnurren," and "meckern" (see OJ, 138–39 and 146; "nasal gurgling," "creaking," "bawling," "sneezing," and "meowing," "bleating," "rattling," "purring," "grunts"; see Z, 50–51 and 56) that convey "[seine Gedanken] immer exacter [...], als wenn er blos einige Worte hingeworfen" (OJ, 138; "even more [missing: exactly] [...] than mere words interjected here and there"; Z, 50). The first act of imitation in this story is thus not Faitel's but the narrator's seemingly oblivious attempt to reproduce and describe Faitel's phonetics, which defies his own standard of *Hochdeutsch* and makes him just as much a mimic and language learner as Faitel. From the start, language as an object of imitation therefore appears mutable, and other elements, like different languages or animal sounds, are considered part of it.[19]

Contrary to what the narrator says, Faitel is far from the only example of what is considered "compromised" or "aberrant" language in the text, as is evident from the sheer number of other languages, dialects, and phonetic spelling in it. Panizza officially adopted a unique phonetic spelling for his writing right before "Der operirte Jud'," and increasingly so until the end of his life.[20] His spelling resonates with his own Lower-Franconian dialect of German, and Panizza's maternal family heritage is French just like Faitel's. So, while the influence of French and Palatine elements indicates inferiority to the bourgeois German narrator of the story, the rampant yet cleverly constructed use of these elements counteracts his stance throughout the text. Moreover, *Hochdeutsch*'s definition as unified, standardized German is challenged by the suggestion that different dialects can fulfill the requirements of the abstract idea of *Hochdeutsch* proper:

> Wohl konnte Faiteles auch Hochdeutsch reden; aber dann war es eben nicht Faiteles, sondern eine Zierpuppe. Wenn Faitel für sich war, und sich nicht zu geniren brauchte, dann sprach er Pfälzisch und – noch etwas. (OJ, 137)
> Da es hoffnungslos war, ihn mit seinem Pfälzisch-Jüdischen auf ein nächstverwandtes reines Hochdeutsch zu bringen, so versuchte man, durch einen absoluten Gegensatz zu seinem bisherigen Sing-Sang, ihn auf rechte Bahn zu bringen; und besorgte einen hannoveranischen Hofmeister, dessen hell-näselnde, klirrende Sprechweise Itzig wie ein Schulknabe, Satz für Satz, nachzusprechen hatte, so daß er Hochdeutsch wie eine völlig fremde Sprache lernte. [...] Diese ganze Reihe von Maßnahmen war das Resultat einer sachgemäßen Besprechung mit dem berühmten *Tübinger* Linguisten damaliger Zeit [...]. Und nun wurde genau untersucht, welcher deutsche Dialect mit dem Pfälzisch-Jüdischen Faitel's die geringste Laut-Verwandtschaft besitze.

Man kam erst auf das Pommer'sche. Aber Faitel war dieß zu hart. Endlich einigte man sich über dem Hannoveran'schen. (OJ, 146–47)

Of course, Faitel could speak High German, yet it was not his language but that of a dressy doll. When Faitel was in private company and did not have to feel embarrassed, he spoke the dialects of the Palatinate—and something more than that. (Z, 49)

Since it was hopeless to raise the level of his Palatinate-Yiddish to that of the related pure high German, an attempt was made to bring his former sing-song on the right track through its direct opposite. A private tutor was engaged, and Itzig was to repeat his clear nasal-sounding manner of speech like a schoolboy, sentence by sentence, so that he learned High German like a totally new, foreign language. [...] This series of measures was the result of expert opinion gathered from the most famous linguist of that time in nearby Tübingen. [...] And now he was examined to determine which German dialect contained the least tonal affinity with Faitel's Palatinate-Yiddish. At first, the specialists considered Pomeranian. But this was too difficult [literally: too harsh] for Faitel. Finally, they agreed upon the Hanoverian dialect. (Z, 56)

Taught by a *Hofmeister*, a private tutor (literally: a court master), *Hochdeutsch* is representative of a society with institutionalized rules and conventions, yet it also seems surprisingly random because any German dialect qualifies as "proper" German if it is only different enough from Faitel's own and can, yet, be imitated by him with success. Even though the region around Hannover is often considered the "cradle of *Hochdeutsch*," the definition of *Hochdeutsch* seems to be rather found by negation, or degree of difference from Faitel's original manner of speech. As "undefinable" as the Germanic soul, *Hochdeutsch* is everything Faitel is not. Indeed, the text admits that Faitel both has a soul and can speak *Hochdeutsch* before each of these changes—demonstrating that the goal post for these standards of belonging is continually moved to keep them unreachable. Presented as a language that is acquired by way of repetition and imitation (i.e., institutionally sanctioned or even required mimicry), *Hochdeutsch* is meant to eradicate Faitel's French and Palatine speech elements as well as his *Jüdisch* or Yiddish (literally: his Jewish). Transliterated into Latin letters and therefore representing another layer of phonetic imitation, Faitel's use of Yiddish is often difficult to distinguish from dialectal variants of German in the text, which underscores the proximity between the two languages. While the spelling of *Hochdeutsch* and Yiddish appears mostly conflated in the narrative, there are nonetheless certain key words and some patterns of word order that can be identified as distinctly Yiddish and that are marked as "foreign" elements of Faitel's speech.

One of the words attributed to Faitel perfectly exemplifies his hybrid language, and its associations describe the very problems of assimilation presented here. Faitel uses the expression "Misemischine" (OJ, 142–43) or "Misemaschine" (OJ, 156), once to describe himself as a mess and once as a curse when his wedding goes awry. The first instance is entirely left out in Zipes's translation, and the second is translated as "Wot misery!" (Z, 73), demonstrating the untranslatability of the term. The word is nowhere else to be found in this particular spelling variation. It is reminiscent of the Hebraism *misso meschunno*, which literally describes a sudden unnatural death and is usually used as a curse word.[21] Panizza's specific spelling does, however, conjure up all kinds of associations. It evokes the German term *mischen*, *mies* and *Maschine* (to mix, mean/foul, and machine), and it is noteworthy in regard to the latter that Faitel is also identified as a Hoffmann-esque "Zierpuppe" (OJ, 137; "dressy doll"; Z, 49) with "Schnurr-Sprechwerkzeugen" (OJ, 156; "who purred when he spoke"; Z, 65; literally: purr-speech-tools), while his soul was supposedly a Cartesian "mechanical function or '*rotation work*'" (Z, 59).[22] *Misemaschine* also contains the French word *mise*, which denotes a whole range of meanings, the most notable in this context perhaps "appearance," "a stage setting," "insertion," and "being out of place," which evokes the idea of mimicry through performance and could also describe the process of being inserted into a machinery of braces and corsages as it happens during Faitel's physical transformation.[23] The term leads the reader to multiple etymologies and connotations. Thus, as language subverts standardization, it simultaneously mimics standard forms and makes creative connections in unexpected places that yield new meanings. Many of these meanings only become possible by fragmenting composite nouns—that is, hybrid terms, which are so typical for *Hochdeutsch*. Ultimately, it proves impossible to identify one conclusive meaning for *Misemaschine*, and it remains a composite that exudes general meaningfulness but does not communicate one specific or unambiguous idea—in line with the concerns of the *Sprachkrise* and typical for *Grotesken*. For the story's narrator and his bourgeois peers, such a fragmentation of semantic standards poses a threat to the perceived coherence of their linguistic identity. The narrative ridicules these fears by showing that there has never been *Hochdeutsch* in the first place but just a variety of interconnected German dialects that have produced a hybrid mix from the start. *Hochdeutsch* is itself a *Misemaschine*.

Schibboleth

The provocative nature of this claim about the illusory nature of *Hochdeutsch* becomes most obvious when the narrative combines questions of individual and national identity with language and religion. As we have seen, the soul is designated as a supposedly essential quality that defines identity:

> Aber Faitel hatte von jener keuschen, undefinirbaren, germanischen Seele gehört, die den Besitzer wie einen Duft umkleide, aus der das Gemüth seine reichen Schätze beziehe, und die das Schiboleth der germanischen Nationen bilde, jedem Besitzer beim Andern sofort erkennbar. Faitel wollte diese Seele haben. Und wenn er kein echtes Kölnisches Wasser haben konnte, wollte er das Nachgemachte. Er wollte wenigstens diese Seele in ihren Aeußerungen, in ihren Zutagetretungen sich aneignen. Man rieth ihm nach England zu gehen, wo der reinste Extrait dieser germanischen Seele zu finden sei. Sprachschwierigkeiten ließen diesen Plan bald wieder fallen. (OJ, 149)

> But Faitel had heard about the chaste, undefined [literally: undefinable] Germanic soul, which shrouded the possessor like an aroma. This soul was the source of the possessor's rich treasures and formed the *shibboleth* of the Germanic nations, a soul which was immediately recognized by all who possessed one. Faitel wanted to have this soul. And, if he could not have genuine eau de cologne, then he wanted the imitation. At the very least, he wanted to appropriate this soul in all its expressions and daily manifestations. So he was advised to go to England, where the purest effusion of this Germanic soul was to be found. Language difficulties soon caused this plan to be dropped. (Z, 59)

This reference to "language difficulties" as the obstacle to achieving "the imitation" (*das Nachgemachte*) seems to be a satire of the story itself. It emphasizes that the kind of national identity Faitel wants to adopt can only ever be an imitation, not because he is Jewish, as antisemitic stereotypes would have it, but because it is an "undefinable" construct. The advice to find the purest Germanic souls in England comically undermines the idea of Germanness. It alludes to the Hanoverian version of *Hochdeutsch* mentioned before and thus connects the idea of "pure" language with politics—that is, the closely related royals of the House of Hanover governing England and Germany at the time. What Faitel wants to "appropriate" is a constructed idea that can seemingly be attributed to different linguistic traditions; or, if English is in fact understood as a (more) Germanic language here, this claim of shared linguistic origins inherently undermines the concept of exclusive language purity in the first place. The word that makes this most obvious is schibboleth. Because it is etymologically a Hebraism, the phrase "das Schiboleth der *germanischen* Nationen" is an ironic commentary about the bourgeois fears of "Jewish assimilation." *Hochdeutsch* cannot do without foreign words to communicate specific expressions. The meaning of shibboleth, on the other hand, is the narrative in a nutshell: it is the part of speech that gives away one's social or regional origin. It is also a way to put someone to a test. Either it reveals him as a member of a community or it casts him out as a fraud.

Faitel's own shibboleth is analyzed by the narrator in great linguistic detail, which is worth quoting at length, in particular because the terms in question are neologisms that display the text's experimentation with language:

> Faitel Stern sagte z. B. wenn ich ihn über den ungeheuren Luxus in seiner Garderobe, seinen Toilettegegenständen, interpellirte, – "... was soll ech mer nicht kahfen ä neihes Gewand, ä scheene Hut – 'm e n e r á, faine Lackstiefelich, – 'm e n e r á, aß ech bin hernach ä fainer Mann! D e r a d á n g! D e r a d á n g! . . . ." [. . .] Der Leser wird hier mit Verwunderung zwei Wörter entdeckt haben, oder vielmehr ein Annexum, ein Anhängsel, und eine Interjection, die er in jedem Wörterbuch vergeblich suchen würde. "-m e n e r á", eine Art Schnurrwort, kurz-kurz-lang, mit dem Ton auf der letzten Silbe, (Anapäst) wurde Substantiven angehängt, und verlieh ihnen eine Art eigenthümlicher, pathetischer Bedeutung; schloß das Substantiv mit einem Consonanten, so wurde oft "-e m e n e r a" angehängt, und zwar mit solch rasselnder Geschwindigkeit, daß der Ton auf dem Substantiv blieb, und das Annex als vierkurzsilbiger Schnurrlaut (also: Doppelpyrrhichius) sich anschloß. (OJ, 139–40)

> Faitel Stern said something like this when I questioned him about the immense luxury of his wardrobe and toilet articles: "Why shoodn't I buy for me a new coat, a bootiful hat—menerá, fine wanished boots—menerá, me, too, I shood bicome a fine gentilman after this Deradáng! Deradáng!" [. . .] The reader will have discovered two surprising words here, or rather an annexation, an appendage, and an interjection which cannot be found in any dictionary. "Menerá," a kind of purring word, short-long, with the stress on the last syllable (anapest), was appended with substantives, which were

endowed with a consonant. Then "emenerá" was frequently added, but with such dazzling speed that the stress remained on the substantive, allowing the annex to attach itself as a purring sound with four short syllables [missing: thus: doubled pyrrhic]. (Z, 51)

The narrator analyzes linguistic elements with a range of phonetic, semantic, grammatical, and prosodic concepts that point to the emphasis *Grotesken* put on the role of language.[24] The two emphasizers *(e)menerà* and *Deradáng*, which have no apparent meaning of themselves but are added to Faitel's utterances to exude general meaningfulness like *Misemaschine* did, must be excised from his speech for him to pass as not Jewish. During his final drunk collapse, when asking for his bride, these linguistic "appendages" (*Anhängsel*) return and seem to mirror inversely something that is left unsaid in the text: his circumcised foreskin, the one appendage the transformation can or does not restore, would have given him away when exposing himself on his wedding night.[25]

The narrator's detailed analysis of Faitel's old speech serves to demonstrate his language learning success by way of contrast. As a final step, Faitel had received assistance from a profession that represents imitative art and underscores the performative aspect of identity and language use: *Hofschauspieler* (see OJ, 152), or court actors that recall the earlier tutor (*Hofmeister*). These imperial employees teach him how to act, presumably convincingly enough to pass in court—that is, in front of those who make the rules for all Germans. The reader suddenly *hears* a very different Faitel, and it is now that his old friends fail to recognize him. The stark contrast in language and gestures turns the text from a satire of one stereotype into that of another:

> Faitel brachte jetzt mit großem Geschick in seiner Diction Sätze vor, wie: "Ach, ich sag' Ihnen, wenn ich darüber nachdenke, wenn ich mir's überlege, es wird mir oft dunkel vor den Augen und mein Herz preßt sich zusammen ..."; – dabei einige brüske Bewegungen, beide Hände auf die linke Seite der Brust gepreßt, – (OJ, 152)

> Now Faitel could express statements with great adroitness in a discussion such as, "Oh, I must confess, when I reflect about this, when I consider this, everything seems gloomy to me, and my heart shudders." These words would be accompanied by some brusque movements, both hands pressed on the left side of the chest. (Z, 61)

It seems that Faitel is now "der dumbe, tappige Germanen-Jüngling" (OJ, 148; "the dumb, awkward German lad"; Z, 58) he wanted to become, though his sentimentality raises questions about (belonging to) the category of Man, just as Jonathan's effeminacy did in the plant chapter.

And indeed, shortly before, the narrator shared a secret observation of Faitel in front of a mirror (reminiscent of the dog story once again). This scene introduces yet another kind of language, which appears to represent the true Faitel for the first time, in particular because the quotation marks that usually frame his speech are suddenly absent:

> – Faiteles! Scheener Jüd', fainer Jüd', eleganter Jüd', – so sprach oft Faitel zu sich selbst, aber nur in der Gedankensprache, wenn er vor dem Spiegel stand, – biste jetzt geworden ä Christenmensch, frei von aller Jüdischkeit? Kannste jetzt hingehn, wo de willst, und dich hinsetzen zu de faine Leit, ohne daß Einer kann sagen: des is aach aner vun unnere Leit? – (OJ, 148–49)

> —Faiteles! Such a bootiful yid, such a fine yid! Such a elegant yid!—This was the way Faitel frequently spoke to himself when he stood in front of a mirror, but only in his thoughts,—So you tink now you're a Chreesten, wit no drop Jewishness? You tink you could go wearevver you want wot you shood take a seat wit de fine people wot everyone should tink [literally: without any one being able to say]: dat's one of us!—(Z, 59)

Zipes's erroneous translation of the final sentence suggests that Faitel is imitating the Germans ("de fine people" or "everyone"), who think that he is "one of us" (moreover ending with an exclamation rather than a question mark). This last phrase deviates most strongly from *Hochdeutsch* in the German original, thus supposedly indicating that the locals of Heidelberg around Faitel do not speak *Hochdeutsch* themselves (which they likely would not have), or at least that their *Gedankensprache*, or "thought language" is also not *Hochdeutsch*.[26] This reinforces the notion that *Hochdeutsch* is hardly the condition for belonging to German society that it is made out to be; rather, true shibboleth is the *right* regional dialect. However, the German original says "without any one being able to say: that's one of us" in a way that is more reminiscent of Faitel's previous way of expressing himself, which would indicate that Faitel is imitating other Jews in this line, who are no longer able to identify him as one of them. Ultimately, the passage remains ambiguous, showing just how indistinguishably similar certain German dialects and Yiddish can be (especially after multiple layers of imitation, as the narrator imitates Faitel's thoughts, and Panizza's spelling phonetically imitates spoken language).[27] Faitel's *Gedankensprache* or "thought language" is akin to his old language, and it literally and figuratively questions his transformation while simultaneously voicing the reasons for his imitation, as it addresses a sense of belonging that was historically unachievable for the European Jewry. As Faitel wonders whether he can pass successfully (admitting that he cannot yet right after the passage), he realizes that it goes along with losing his sense of belonging, since "his people" will no longer recognize him as one of them either. "Without anyone being able to say" that he is one of them, he belongs nowhere. As one of the connotations of *Misemaschine* suggested, Faitel remains "out of place," and he ultimately imitates both Germans and Jews.

Identity and Exclusion in Other *Grotesken*

Panizza exposes *Hochdeutsch* and German national identity as exclusory standards at a time when his own linguistic expression was censored heavily by the state, because of which he ultimately opted to give up his German citizenship and stopped speaking German altogether. A mere twenty years after Germany first became a nation, his *Groteske* insists that national identities are built on an illusion of purity and homogeneity. His writing also shows that those who expose this fiction will suffer the biopolitical consequences—whether it is the physical destruction and social rejection of Faitel, or, in the context of same-sex desire, the consequences for Jonathan's report about the plants, which prefigured Panizza's own end in the asylum. In other *Grotesken*, featuring an intersex individual, a Native American chieftain, and a Black dancer, Panizza negotiates similar ideas about identity and exclusion by showing how these figures are marginalized, dehumanized, and rejected by society.

"Eine N [...] geschichte" (A Negro story, 1893), for instance, tells the story of a Black dancer in Hamburg who realizes that his dance performances are valued by his white audience not because of his skill but because he is an exoticized attraction to them. In yet another mirror scene, he reproduces their view of him: "Ein schwarzes Scheusal! – Ein fletschender Gorilla! [...] schwarzes N [...] -Thier" (A black monster!—A teeth-baring gorilla! [...] black Negro-animal).[28] When he visits a doctor to seek an official certification that he is, in fact, as white as he considers himself, his consultation is interrupted by what he calls "schwarze[] Teufel" (EN, 27; black devils), who are the presumably white guards of an insane asylum to which he is returned—a familiar gesture from section 2. While this narrative about racial passing could be read as poking fun at the protagonist, the recurring unreliable narrator-physician and the invocation of the asylum in the context of the genre of *die Groteske* suggest otherwise. Accordingly, the story ends with the protagonist's "langen, schrecklichen, weißen Blick" (EN, 28; long, terrible, white look) that lingers reproachfully on narrator and reader alike. The narrative illustrates the brutality of racism and spells out the punitive measures for those who try to destabilize its underlying norms of racialization.

Similar literary strategies of rendering marginalized figures monstrous and animalistic also occur in Panizza's "Indianer-Gedanken" ([An] Indian['s] thoughts, 1893), where the colonized are exhibited in human zoos. Once again, a doctor is asked for help in this *Groteske*, this time by a Native American chief. He and his people have been suffocating their newborns and are resolved to kill themselves to escape their oppression. Seemingly inspired by both the revenge tales of Greek mythology and the Eucharist, the chief wants to feed the tribe's youth to "the white man," while the elders hang themselves. This scenario literalizes the genocide of Native Americans, and the chief despairs over finding a way to die that will ensure the tribe's happiness in the afterlife: We "sind doch noch zu sehr Menschen; wären wir Thiere! . . ." (are still too human; if only we were animals! . . .).[29]

Panizza's "Ein skandalöser Fall" ("A Scandal at the Convent," literally: A scandalous case, 1893), to give a final example, reimagines the discovery of the historical intersex individual Herculine Barbin (1838–1868), nicknamed Alexina, and the resulting scandal.[30] Alexina is a smart charity case at a convent school for noble daughters, whose intimate friendship with another pupil at first suggests a same-sex relationship. When the pair is found in bed, everyone immediately takes the poor, less normatively feminine and pleasing looking of the two girls to be a threat, and a mob with pitchforks and axes besieges the convent, saying that the devil resides there. To appease the crowd, the Abbé calls a doctor who is asked to look for the mark of the devil on Alexina's body, so that an exorcism can be performed. Instead, the examination brings to light Alexina's intersex physicality and, without being consulted, she is declared a man. Her existence is considered "a crime against nature," much like other expressions of sexuality and gender have been, and the story ends without further describing her fate in a society that is based so fundamentally on a binary of sexes that it has no space for her.[31]

While one might want to associate Panizza with the medical personnel in these texts due to his training as a psychiatrist, it is important to remember that *Grotesken* undermine the position of those representing institutions. Panizza left the profession quickly himself and ultimately became the patient. Though these *Grotesken* also reproduce the harmful discourses they satirize, just like the rampant antisemitism in "Der operirte Jud'," they demonstrate Panizza's deep-seated preoccupation with questions of identity and belonging. All four texts were published in the same 1893 collection, along with the story of the masturbating plants and potentially gay policemen as well as other texts about deviating from society's norms. By showing how identity is constructed and deconstructed with the help of language and on the basis of physical difference, Panizza's *Grotesken* provide the opportunity for a reconsideration of being and belonging altogether—a charge that Friedlaender, another former student of medicine, took up to advocate for an even more radical reassessment of identity concepts in his literary answer to "Der operirte Jud'."

ELEVEN

The Operated Goy

Friedlaender's story from 1922, "Der operierte Goj: Ein Gegenstück zu Panizzas operiertem Jud," is written in direct response to Panizza's text and turns its premise upside down. The story undoes the gruesome ending and instead presents German Jewish intermarriage as the path to an ideal society that no longer knows racialization. In Friedlaender's narrative, an Aryan nobleman converts to Judaism and lives out his life in Jerusalem with his Jewish bride and many children. Just like Faitel, he undergoes complicated operations to match a stereotypical physical image, and his transformation into a Jew is only complete and acceptable after he has learned Hebrew and Yiddish: "Er redete mit Armen, Beinen und der Zunge nach dem Herzen Jehovas" (OG, 604; "He talked with arms, legs, and tongue [added:, a man] after Jehovah's own heart"; Z, 84). The goal of his conversion is to attain his bride's hand in marriage with her parents' approval, so this case of successful linguistic reproduction ultimately also equals sexual reproduction and preserves his assimilation in future generations.

Friedlaender's *Groteske* reverses the outcomes of Panizza's to criticize Germany's increasingly paranoid view of Jews and assimilation. Written one year before the failed *Hitlerputsch*, the text reflects the worsening antisemitic climate of German society, but it also speaks to the contemporaneous Zionist project and comments on the relationship between so-called assimilated Western and orthodox Eastern European Jewry. To this end, Friedlaender's narrative introduces a semblance of the famous "two households, both alike in dignity" from the first line of the prologue in Shakespeare's *Romeo and*

Juliet, which are set up as opposites through their respective German and Jewish identities but are shown to have maintained the same values of "racial purity" for centuries:

> cf. Montecchi & Capuletti. Haus Gold-Isak war, was Rassereinheit anbelangt, das jüdische Gegenstück zum Geschlechte der Grafen Reschok: dito, seit der Zerstörung Jerusalems und der Zerstreuung des jüdischen Volkes durch alle Länder, hatte sich die Familie niemals mit fremdem Blute vermischt. (OG, 601)

> (cf. the Montagues and Capulets). As far as purity of race was concerned, the house of Gold-Isaac was the Jewish counterpart to the family of Count Rehsok: ditto, ever since the destruction of Jerusalem, and ever since the dispersion of the Jewish people in many different countries, the family had never become contaminated by alien blood. (Z, 79)

Just as Friedlaender's story is identified as a counterpiece or -narrative (*Gegenstück*) to Panizza's text in its subtitle, these two houses are called counterparts (*Gegenstücke*), yet their differences in heritage underscore the similarities in the manner they construct and preserve the "purity" of this heritage or bloodline. Both Friedlaender's and Panizza's texts criticize the concept of such purity by demonstrating with satirically exaggerated means how destructive it is. Even though Panizza's narrative depicts the failure or potential impossibility of assimilation and Friedlaender's story presents a successful transformation, both *Grotesken* show that these "pure" categories of the German and the Jew are socially constructed, based on racial pseudoscience, and meant to reinforce the self by excluding the other. Friedlaender's *Groteske* demonstrates that, thirty years after Panizza's text, the situation of the German Jewry had far from improved and organized antisemitism was on the rise. It points toward a terrifying future that even the exaggerations of *Grotesken* could not fully anticipate. Yet Friedlaender's narrative also extends the critique of exclusionary national identity to Jews and the contemporaneous Zionist debates. The following pages will first examine the depiction of the various German and Jewish bodies and then turn to the discourse about language in the text. Picking up on many ideas that are familiar from "Der operirte Jud'" but also introducing several complex additions, Friedlaender's *Groteske* negotiates how identity concepts derive their problematic "authenticity" from physical, cultural, and linguistics markers.

Reschok-Koscher

The two houses in Friedlaender's narrative are the noble German line von Reschok with their successful son Kreuzwendedich and the Jewish dynasty Gold-Isak with their beautiful daughter Rebecka. From their names to their physical features, both protagonists reinforce a slew of stereotypes about the kind of identity their families represent. The von Reschoks' military history dates to the Crusades, as the family has been furthering "die Bekämpfung der die zarten Arier so mörderlich bedrohenden Judenplage" (OG, 598; "struggle against the Jewish plague, which had threatened to wipe out the frail Aryans"; Z, 75). This satirized vision of "racial purity" is undermined from the beginning because Reschok reads *koscher* in reverse and thus already contains its other. The von Reschok family members are described as "Antisemitenhäuptlinge [. . ., die] speziell gegen die jüdisch-arischen Mestizen [eiferten]" (OG, 598; "eloquent leaders of the anti-Semitic movement [literally: antisemitic chiefs] [. . . who] especially inveighed against the Jewish-Ayrian [sic] mix-breeds"; Z, 75). The idea of "purity" that determines this family's identity is simultaneously constructed and deconstructed through not only this reference to the "racially hybrid Jewish-Aryan mestizo" but also the tribal metaphor of the "antisemitic chief," which paradoxically invokes the twelve tribes of the Israelites (as well as Native Americans and the colonial context of the time, as does "mestizo").

Despite this linguistic subversion, the von Reschoks' outward appearance matches the Aryan ideal to the letter, and like Faitel, just in reverse, it is contrasted by degree of difference from antisemitic stereotypes:

> Abstrahiert man sorgfältig von jedem jüdischen, jedem orientalischen Typus, so erhält man den der Grafen Reschok: sie trugen keine Pfropfenzieherlöckchen, sondern hatten sanft gewelltes, fast silberblondes Haar. Ihre weißen Stirnen steilten sich, statt schräg nach hinten zu sinken, wie Granitwände. Gegen sogenannte Adlernasen waren sie mißtrauisch; ihre Nasen waren unheimlich grade. Dünne Lippen, preußisches Kinn, stolzer Nacken, fabelhaft schlanke Haltung; Beine, die in ihrer Unschuld nicht X noch O kannten [. . .], auf aristokratischsten und zugleich pangermanischsten Füßen standen und mit ihnen einen Gang wie vom Olymp herab schritten. Vor allem aber hatten sie keine Schlitzaugen von schwarzbrauner Glut, sondern rein und eisig leuchtete offene, wahre Himmelbläue aus ihren herrischen Blicken, deren Gewalt durch das Monokel ins Unwahrscheinliche gesteigert wurde. (OG, 598)

If one carefully abstracted certain elements from each Jewish and each Oriental type [literally: every Jewish, every Oriental type], then one would be left with the type representative of the counts of Rehsok: they did not wear corkscrew locks, rather, their hair was soft and wavy, almost silvery blond. Their white foreheads dropped steeply like walls of granite instead of sinking and slanting toward the rear. They were suspicious of so-called eagle noses, for their noses were unbelievably straight. They all had thin lips, Prussian chins, proud necks, and fabulously slender builds, and their legs, which in their innocence did not know either X or O, stood simultaneously on aristocratic and pan-Germanic feet and took strides as though descending from Mount Olympus. Above all, they did not have narrow eyes with a dark brown glow but open, true [missing: sky-; or: heavenly] blue ones which glistened like pure ice, and the power of their imperious look was enhanced exceedingly by the monocle. (Z, 75–76)

The exaggerated description is oddly gripping, as if building toward a climax of violent intensity. The soft wavy hair is followed by increasingly hard lines: the stony foreheads, uncannily straight noses, proud necks, thin lips, and the straightest posture underline the image of military discipline, and as "the von Reschok type," or Man, they invoke an uncanny army of indistinguishable *Doppelgänger*, marching in step. Their "Prussian chins," "noble and pan-Germanic feet" simultaneously imbue them with ancient, national, and divine privilege that shines out of their "pure, icy-blue, authoritative eyes." The description of the bourgeois monocle, which supposedly multiplies their power (or violence, since *Gewalt* can mean both) by enlarging or doubling the eye, is also the ultimate tipping point into the ridiculous in the passage, emphasizing the absurd nature of these stereotypes, or indeed Aryan eyewear (though the monocle will come to be an appendage of Prussian identity to be removed like the foreskin during circumcision). Just like their name, this physical description of the perfect Prussian military specimen contains its opposing *Gegenstück*, or other. The contrastive figure that can be derived from the passage observes a different religion, is not white, has dark narrow eyes, and sports a crooked posture. Additional antisemitic stereotypes emerge by inverting the description of the von Reschoks, suggesting supposedly "weak chins" and "flat feet" that are reminiscent of Faitel's original body. Though the text leaves no doubt that this is meant to be the image of a Jew with "corkscrew locks," it also functions as an amalgamation of otherness that lumps together a range of different peoples.[1] Serving as a blueprint of difference from "every Jewish, every Oriental type" against which the

"Occidental," Christian, Aryan figure of Man is defined, it becomes the other writ large.

Kreuzwendedich

The particular von Reschok protagonist of the story has a telling first name that contains the entire story: Kreuzwendedich (cross-turn-around) von Reschok carries his impending conversion in his name, yet the *Kreuz* has multiple meanings.[2] As if the name were a *Stoßgebet* or devout ejaculation, it invokes Christian protection, but it also connotes the *Hakenkreuz* or swastika—symbols of the values passed on to Kreuzwendedich by his parents. They warn him to stay true to his Aryan, Christian self and simultaneously set up the expectations for what happens next by urging, "rasserein bleiben! Da gibt es jetzt monstros reiche Semitentöchter, die auf uns erpicht sind" (OG, 599; "Keep your blood pure! There are now enormously [literally: monstrously] rich Semitic daughters who are keen on our kind"; Z, 76). The antisemitic stereotype of the monstrously rich and money-grabbing Jew is deflated by the fact that the von Reschoks are themselves one of the richest families around. There also seems to be no need to worry about Kreuzwendedich's susceptibility to Jewish charms, since his world is kept—in what is now notorious Nazi terminology— "judenrein" (OG, 599; "completely cleansed [literally: purified] of Jewishness"; Z, 76).

His desire for "purity" goes so far that even his specially manufactured Bible contains no more Hebrew names, "so hieß der weise Salomo darin der weise Friederich" (OG, 599; "the wise Solomon was called the wise Friedrich"; Z, 76–77). This replacement of the author Friedlaender's namesake Salomo with the German king Friedrich der Weise (1463–1525) also invokes Gotthold Ephraim Lessing's enlightenment play *Nathan, der Weise* (1779), which advocates for religious tolerance through the figure of the Jew Nathan. His historical model was Moses Mendelssohn, who is often credited with bringing about Jewish emancipation in the eighteenth century. With this chain of associations (from Salomo to Friedrich to Nathan to Moses), Kreuzwendedich's renaming endeavor is implicitly rendered unsuccessful and it anticipates the name he will choose for himself after his conversion, Moische. In his religious devotion, he is suspicious of Christianity, to which the story refers as "'das jüdische Pfropfreis auf indischem Stamm'" (OG, 599; "'that Jewish offshoot [literally: graft] of an Indian tribe'"; Z, 77), a modified quote of Kant's "Pfropfreis auf einem anderen Stamm," a graft on another stem that is described as a parasitic appendage in §64 of *Kritik der Urteilskraft* (*Critique of Judgement*, 1790), which the neo-Kantian philosopher Friedlaender invokes here with another enlightenment association.[3] So instead of Christianity, Kreuzwendedich turns to Nordic mythology to cast his future family, which he wants to be exactly like Odin's, even in their names: "Frigga sollte die künftige Gattin heißen, die Kinder in spe Balder, Brage, Hermod, Thor und Tyr" (OG, 599; "His future wife was to be called Frigga; his children *in spe*, Balder, Braga, Hermod, Thor and Tyr"; Z, 77). Equipped with this hodgepodge of Christian and mythological Germanic heritage that is shown to be everything but "pure," Kreuzwendedich is introduced to the reader when he joins *Borussia Bonn*, the fraternity of the so-called *Bonner Preußen* (Prussians of Bonn), whose members consisted almost exclusively of Prussian nobility and particularly many relatives of the imperial family.[4]

In Bonn, Kreuzwendedich speaks "nur im Telegrammstil" (OG, 599; "only in the style of a telegram"; Z, 77) to give commands, and when he takes to the streets, he is sporting "das Hakenkreuz a[uf der] Rockklappe [...] und den weißen Stürmer auf dem blonden, durchgezogenen Scheitel, das Monokel im Auge" (OG, 599; "a swastika on the arm of his coat [literally: on his lapel] [...] with the customary white student cap on his blond parted hair, his monocle on his eye"; Z, 77).[5] These insignia emphasize both his militarism and antisemitism, and to all of Friedlaender's readers, they clearly outline the political position of a nobleman, fraternity member, and early Nazi supporter in the Weimar Republic, thus identifying the most obvious of the text's targets.[6] Kreuzwendedich is depicted as a "model antisemite," as he seeks to distance himself from any contact with Jews and Jewish culture with the help of a warning system that betrays pure paranoia. His servant, the bearlike "Riese Bör" (OG, 599; "giant Bor"; Z, 77; the name of Odin's father), carries two ravens with the same names as those of Odin. Together with Kreuzwendedich's dog, the ravens identify Jews from afar with a cacophony of sounds and even chirp an antisemitic song:

> vom galonierten Diener gefolgt, der, sobald sich etwas Hebräisches zeigte, aus silbernem Pfeifchen einen schrillen Triller herausgellte. Daß die englische Dogge des Grafen auf Judenwaden sorgfältig dressiert war, ist zu bemerken überflüssig. Konnte doch der Rabe Hugin den beliebten Borkumer Antisemitenchoral korrekt intonieren. (OG, 599–600)[7]

As soon as anything Hebrew showed itself, the servant made a shrill sound with a silver whistle. Of course, it would be superfluous to remark that the Count's Great Dane [literally: English bulldog, a much less imposing breed] was carefully trained to bite any Jew who came too close [literally: Jewish calves]. In addition, the raven Hugin could correctly chirp the well-known Borkum anti-Semitic hymn. (Z, 77)

This "protection mechanism" supposedly defeats any attempts at disguising "Jewishness," so "unbeirrbar zielsicher funktionierten hier die Instinkte" (OG, 600; "imperturbably sure were they [. . .] that their instincts functioned here perfectly"; Z, 78; literally: imperturbably unerring functioned the instincts). Spotting a Jew is seemingly such an instinctive action that even, or maybe especially, supposedly less intellectual creatures can accomplish it: "Wie ein Jude ausschaut, weiß jedes arische Kind, ja jedes Haustier wittert ihn euch heraus" (OG, 598; "Every Aryan child knows what a Jew looks like. Indeed, every domestic pet can scent out a Jew"; Z, 75). This grouping shifts the species barrier that usually separates humans from animals and instead reinforces a differentiation between Jews as the ultimate other and everyone else.

Kreuzwendedich's multispecies vanguard relies not only on visual cues but also on the supposedly unfailing "*foetor judaicus*" (OG, 600; "Foetor judaicus"; Z, 78), an antisemitic concept dating to the Middle Ages, according to which Jews have a distinctly different body odor, akin to excrement. This smell was said to cause contagious diseases and brings up the association of the aromatic with the sexual and animalistic from the previous two sections about plants and dogs.[8] The idea that "even a child or domestic pet" can "sniff out" one's identity invokes the principle of a Jewish and a German "essence" that both texts locate in the blood or soul (which is familiar from Panizza's encounter between the sniffing dogs, which lays bare their souls to each other). In fact, Panizza's "operirter Jud'" also contained a scented shibboleth: "the chaste, undefinable Germanic soul, which shrouded the possessor like an aroma" (in distinct contrast to the "unchaste smell" emanating from the plants). The soul and *foetor judaicus* come together in Gustav Jäger's chemical treatise on pheromones, *Die Entdeckung der Seele* (*The Discovery of the Soul*, 1880), in which he postulates the existence of a racial soul that has a distinctive odor, like *foetor judaicus*.[9] The mention of *foetor judaicus* in Friedlaender's "counterpiece" turns the aroma of the Germanic soul into a foul odor that underpins the criticism of a mythical, "pure" essence as the basis of identity in both *Grotesken*.

Rebecka

After introducing the caricature that is Kreuzwendedich, the reader meets another assemblage of stereotypes: the rich, beautiful, and Jewish Rebecka Gold-Isak, "eine schmachtende Odaliske mit Mandelschnitt-Augen, Ebenholzhaar, Elfenbeinhaut usw. usw." (OG, 600; "a languishing odalisque with eyes like almonds, ebony hair, ivory skin, etcetera, etcetera"; Z, 78). The description calls up the antisemitic notion and literary stock figure of the "beautiful Jewess," both with its reference to an odalisque, a harem concubine who was shown mostly as a near-naked, exoticized sexual object in nineteenth-century paintings, and because her name evokes *la belle juive* Rebecca in Sir Walter Scott's *Ivanhoe* (1819).[10] The "etcetera, etcetera" indicates that this description of "ebony hair and ivory skin" is a formula with which the reader is familiar, not just that of the "beautiful Jewess" but also that of the German fairy tale princess Snow White: "so weiß wie der Schnee, so roth wie das Blut, und so schwarz wie Ebenholz" (as white as snow, as red as blood, and as black as ebony).[11] The "etcetera" replaces the mention of blood, the supposed carrier of difference, but the three colors of the fairy tale also correspond to those of the flag of the German Empire (1871–1918), which had just undergone a controversial change to black-red-gold in the Weimar Republic, on which Friedlaender commented actively.[12] Combining both this "German" beauty and the exoticizing elements, Rebecka's description thus blurs the supposedly strictly divided, "pure" categories of "Jewish" and "German."

Rebecka is passionate, strong-willed, and holds her own. She is furious about Kreuzwendedich's antisemitic behavior and decides to confront him: "Diesen sauberen Vogel kaufe ich mir [. . .] und wenn ich ihn aus Rache heiraten müßte" (OG, 600; "I'm going to buy me this pompous turkey, [. . .] even if I have to marry him out of revenge"; Z, 78). The sentence is an amalgamation of polysemous idioms for which the translation cannot account: The combination of *komischer Vogel* (strange bird) and *sauberer Kerl* (good guy, literally: clean guy) into *sauberer Vogel* invokes hyperbolic "purity" that effectively designates a dirty character.[13] It is also an instance of mixing up idioms typical for multilingualism. "Ihr Papa besaß fast eine Milliarde" (OG, 600; "Her Papa was practically a billionaire"; Z, 78), yet the sentence is only outwardly about money: "to buy someone" implies a bribe, but the reflexive phrase *sich jemanden kaufen* means to give someone a piece of one's mind. This is Rebecka's intention, and the comical notion of potentially marrying Kreuzwendedich out of revenge is a "counterpiece" to his parents' fears of the "monstrously rich Semitic daughters," demonstrating the efficacy of her plan. While she says it in jest, it nonetheless foreshadows the course of events. To stage her intervention successfully, Rebecka must fool Kreuzwendedich's protection mechanisms. With a "tizian-bronzenen Perrücke" (OG, 600; "bronze wig like something painted by Titian"; Z, 78), she disguises herself as a Germanic Venus named "Baronesse Freia-Rotraut von Isagold" (OG, 600), another name loaded with associations, and thus undergoes the first transformation of the text.[14] Yet the detection system still finds her out, though with a moment's delay due to her great beauty, so that she succeeds in spitting into Kreuzwendedich's face. He is as awestruck by her allure as he is puzzled by the absence of *foetor judaicus*, and the incident becomes the talk of the town. Rebecka's act of revenge thus has an unexpected side effect: Kreuzwendedich falls for her.

Reproductive Rules

The two would-be lovers are struggling with the discovery of their affection. Kreuzwendedich is suffering from a "psychisches Trauma" (OG, 601; "psychological trauma"; Z, 79), and his "Oberbewußtsein" (OG, 601; "high consciousness"; Z, 79; a creative coinage that denotes the opposite of *Unterbewusstsein*, the subconscious) is keeping him from realizing that he has fallen for a Jewish woman. Her contradictory feelings, on the other hand, encompass a combination of repulsion and curious attraction that is similar to the feelings Faitel provoked in the narrator of his story and brings up assimilation explicitly: "fasziniert von seiner feindlichen Fremdartigkeit, empfand sie Haß, Eitelkeit, Wut mit Liebe zusammen und lechzte inbrünstigst nach Überwindung, d. h. aber nach gänzlicher Assimilation und Einverleibung des Gegners" (OG, 601; "Fascinated by his inimical strangeness, she felt hate, vanity, and fury mixed with love. She yearned ardently to overcome everything, that is, she yearned for complete assimilation and incorporation of the enemy"; Z, 79; *Einverleibung* also means ingestion). This uncanny image of consumption combines cannibalism and intercourse in a threatening melee, invoking the folktale of the *vagina dentata* and the connected psychoanalytical castration anxiety that foreshadows Kreuzwendedich's circumcision.[15]

The change of perspective in Friedlaender's *Groteske* would have us think that Kreuzwendedich, the Goy, should be the monstrous one, but in fact, the two potential lovers are "strange" to each other—which underlines that "the other" is a matter of perspective. Through the melding of the oppositions such as love and hate, death and life, devouring and giving birth, the notions of assimilation and annihilation become synonymous. While Faitel seemed to belong nowhere after his transformation unraveled, Kreuzwendedich is fully absorbed, indeed incorporated by the Jewish community at the end of the story. Initially only considering marriage out of revenge, Rebecka "wußte also mit der genauesten Bestimmtheit, sie werde nicht eher glücklich werden, als bis gräflich Reschok'sches Leben ihrem jüdischen Schoß entkeimte" (OG, 601; "knew with utmost certainty that she would not be happy until Count Rehsok's offspring sprouted from her Jewish womb"; Z, 80). Just as in the case of Faitel, reproduction becomes the explicit goal of the scheme she devises to turn Kreuzwendedich into a suitable suitor. While reproduction usually entails the mixing of genetic characteristics from mother and father, Rebecka seems to follow a plan of *Einverleibung*, or incorporation, which considers Kreuzwendedich the weaker party—that is, the one whose genes will be recessive—while the matrilinear tradition will render their offspring Jewish. Rebecka's sexual desire for Kreuzwendedich and her "Macht über ihn" (OG, 602; "power [. . .] over him"; Z, 79) are moreover depicted as stereotypically masculine characteristics, which emasculates/effeminates Kreuzwendedich (see OG, 602; and Z, 79–80) as "the weaker sex," since he is giving up his claim to the category of Man.

Operation Transformation

The parameters for Kreuzwendedich's conversion process are initially set by Rebecka's parents, who themselves serve to reinforce a wide array of Jewish stereotypes. When Rebecka tells them about her chosen groom, they are shocked, and the passage establishes the text's multiple concepts of Jewish identity, which is why it is worth quoting at length:

> Mutter Gold-Isak, Hagar geheißen, watschelte händeringend, mit beringten Händen, durch etwa drei Prachtsäle hin und her; sie rief dabei andauernd, und zwar in reinstem Hochdeutsch: "Wehe schrieen, du gerechter Gott, mein Kind ist mesch....!" / Papa Gold-Isak, dessen Vorname zufällig auch Isak war, trieb Realpolitik und stellte, indem er, im Klubsessel halb liegend, die Daumen um einander drehte, phlegmatische Fragen: "Heißt ä Sach'! Ausgerechnet die Reschok's! Mir gesagt! Nebbich sind'se noch reich obendrein; ich kann'se dir nich kaufen; ich kann dabei nix tun. Gut, mein Kind, obgleich sich mir der armen Mamme wegen – ächze nich' Hagarleben! – das Herz im Leibe rumkehrt, will ich dir nicht im Wege sein. Als er sich wird lassen

beschneiden, mit allem Zubehör, als Kaftan, Payes, Zizekanfaus. Rebecka, Grafen kannst'e haben, soviel de willst; ich kann mer kaufen fast den ganzen Gotha. Und selbst wenn'de könnt'st haben den Reschok – als er sich nich wird lassen beschneiden, wern wir dir geben unsern gut jüdischen Fluch: daß dein Schoß soll verdorren!" Rotraut erschrak. Isak Gold-Isak gehörte zum Unglück den Birnbaumianern an, die erst im Ostjuden den echten Juden schätzen; denen der westlich kultivierte Jude, z. B. der katholisierende Bubermartin, bereits den jüdischen Dekandent bedeutet. (OG, 602)

Mother Gold-Isaac, named Hagar, waddled about and wrung her hands studded with rings [missing: the chiasmus of hand-wringing her ringed hands is lost in translation]. Back and forth she went through [missing: circa] three grand parlors, continually crying out, to be sure, in the purest high German: "*Veh is mir* [literally: Woe is me! This should be in German instead of Yiddish, as the text expressly emphasizes.], dear God! My child is *meshu*...!" / Papa Gold-Isaac, whose first name was coincidentally Isaac, dealt in *Realpolitik*, and as he sat in his easy chair, half-lying and twiddling his thumbs, he posed phlegmatic questions: "What a situation! It had to be the Rehsoks! If you had asked me, they're all *nebbechs* and rich to boot. I can't buy them for you. There's nothing I can do here. Good, my child, even though my heart is breaking on account of your poor mother [literally: *mame*]—don't sob, Hagar dear—I won't stand in your way. If he has himself circumcised with everything that goes with it, caftan, *payess, tallith* tassels, Rebecca, you can have as many counts as you want. I can buy practically the whole [added: city] of Gotha. And, if I have to, I'll get you Rehsok—only he must let himself be circumcised. If not, we'll give you our good Jewish curse so that your womb will wither!" / Rotraut was horrified. Unfortunately, Isaac-Gold belonged to the sect of Birnbaumianers, who believe that the only real Jew is the East European Jew. The cultivated West European Jew [literally: Westernly cultivated Jew], for example the catholicizing Martin Buber, was already considered a decadent Jew. (Z, 80)

The mother's prioritization of *Hochdeutsch* associates her with the "Westernly cultivated,"—that is, the so-called assimilated German Jewry exemplified by Martin Buber here, whereas the father's Yiddish inflection signifies orthodox Eastern European Jewry, in line with political convictions that are exemplified by Nathan Birnbaum.[16] When a term of Yiddish origin, like *mesch(ugge)*, creeps into her "purest" *Hochdeutsch*, the mother stops and corrects, or censors, herself, while the father's diction displays Yiddish word order (e.g., the placement of the verb in the second position even in dependent clauses that the translation leaves out).[17] He throws in an array of Yiddish terms, such as calling von Reschok *Nebbich*, or simpleton. As a pair, the parents represent contemporary inner-Jewish conflicts about "authentic Jewishness," but while the two identities might disagree with each other, they are family. Shown as a stereotypical worrying Jewish *mame* and through her name Hagar a curious symbol of reproduction, the active, pacing mother is contrasted with the phlegmatic, sedentary father.[18] This imbalance mirrors the power dynamics in Rebecka and Kreuzwendedich's relationship and invokes matrilinearity once more, which makes women the carriers of Jewish identity, even though Kreuzwendedich will ultimately emulate the idea of Jewish identity that the father desires.

Rebecka's parents make clear that the formal conversion of the groom is required to ensure the Jewish identity of an intermarriage's offspring and to avoid a scandal in their community. The father lists orthodox requirements that change the male body and its outward appearance: circumcision, side locks (*Payes*), a Chassidic *Kaftan*, and *Zizekanfaus* (the fringed undergarment Zipes translates as "tallith tassels"; the term is crossed out in the manuscript and therefore does not appear in the print version in this place, possibly because Friedlaender suspected that his non-Jewish readers might not know its meaning). Because he cannot imagine that Kreuzwendedich would submit to any of these demands, particularly the first and most incisive, the father threatens to punish his daughter's unorthodox desire with a curse that would render her infertile.[19] This intermarriage proposal threatens the "purity" of the two equally strong Aryan and Jewish bloodlines: Isak's money cannot "buy" the von Reschoks because their noble title is still sufficiently funded, unlike many other dynasties that not only were troubled by debt but also faced the reproductive problem of ending bloodlines.[20] Therefore, Kreuzwendedich needs to convert "fully" to ensure that the matrilineal Jewish heritage prevails over his blood.

Yet before Kreuzwendedich can convert or change physically, he first needs to undergo a mental or psychological transformation and come to terms with the fact that he has, in fact, fallen in love with a Jewish woman in disguise. Rebecka is confident that she can turn him from a hateful antisemite into a convert because she knows, with military precision,

> daß sie den Kreuzwendedich ins Herz getroffen hatte. War nicht die radikale Judenverachtung das unheimlichste Mittel, um das Gegenteil heranzuzüchten: das jäheste Umschlagen ins andere Extrem? Der Antisemitismus ist womöglich noch jüdischer als das Judentum. Überhaupt, wer haßt und

verachtet, prädisponiert sich in aller Heimlichkeit langsam aber sicher zur
intimsten Blutverwandschaft, ja Identifikation mit den Objekten seines
Negierens. Brachte sie den jungen Grafen zur Selbstbesinnung, dann war
sie seiner sicher. Man mußte ihn zwingen, sich psychoanalysieren zu lassen.
(OG, 602)

> that she had captured Kreuzwendedich's heart. Wasn't it precisely the radical
> despising of Jews that could serve as the most unlikely means to produce the
> opposite? Couldn't it generate the quickest turnabout to the other extreme?
> Anti-Semitism is perhaps even more Jewish than Judaism. After all, whoever
> hates and despises predisposes himself in all secrecy, slowly but surely, for the
> most intimate ties of blood, indeed, for an identification with the object of his
> negation. If she could make the young count aware of all this, then she could
> be sure of him. Of course, the count would first have to feel how necessary it
> was [literally: One had to force him] to be psychoanalyzed. (Z, 81)

Just as hate had led her to love, she reasons that Kreuzwendedich's extreme
feelings could turn (*wenden*) too, as if two sides of the same coin. The symbolic charge of their German Jewish union is most palpable in the sentences
that allude to the problematic idea of Jewish self-hatred that became a popular concept during this time.[21] Radical hate entails a fixation that, according
to Rebecka's thought, can lead one to identify with its object. More than
identification, it becomes intimately related to the self in the way of family
(*Blutsverwandtschaft*, or ties of blood). If it becomes part of the self in this
way, then one needs only to become aware (*Selbstbesinnung*) of what has
happened. Her notion of *Selbstbesinnung* requires psychoanalysis because
Kreuzwendedich's strong predispositions make it impossible to rediscover
the other in the self without help. The hated other is eroticized here too, both
in the invoked "intimacy" and the phrase das *Objekt seines Negierens* ("the
object of his negation"), which invokes the psychoanalytic formulation das
Objekt seines Begehrens (the object of his desire) and conflates love and hate,
as Rebecka hopes.

And indeed, aided by her beauty and some monetary supplementation in
Bör's pockets, Rebecka succeeds, as Kreuzwendedich "Rekosch,"[22] whose
name is already one step closer to *koscher* at this point of the text, appears

> mit rätselhaften Seelenhemmungen im Ordinierzimmer des berühmten
> Freud [...]. Dieser echte Feigenblattvernichter beraubte die gräflich
> Reschok'sche Seele so anatomisch sicher ihres Schutzfells, daß der Graf mit
> einem furchtbaren Aufschrei in die Arme seines herbeieilenden Dieners sank.

> [...] Und nun war er auch mit Leib und Seele preisgegeben. Rotraut trat ihre vollkommene Herrschaft über ihn an[.] (OG, 602–3)
>
> in the office of the famous Dr. Freud, where the young man displayed some puzzling psychological inhibitions [literally: inhibitions of the soul]. In response, the authentic destroyer of subterfuges [literally: fig leaves] robbed Count Rehsok's psyche [literally: soul] of its protective cover in such a surehanded anatomical way that the count sank with a terrible cry into the arms of his servant [...]. Now he was prepared to surrender body and soul. Rotraut began to dominate him completely. (Z, 81)

It seems that Kreuzwendedich's process of *Selbstbesinnung* does not take long. With surgical precision, the most intimate is exposed by Sigmund Freud (the Jewish doctor par excellence, whose ideas are satirized all over the text), and all protection mechanisms are removed—his metaphorical *Schutzfell* ("protective cover," literally: protective fur; invoking *dickes Fell*, which is thick fur, i.e., thick skin) and Kreuzwendedich's *Scham* (shame but also euphemism for genitals, reinforced by the *Feigenblattvernichter* or destroyer of fig leaves Freud), which foreshadows his circumcision.[23]

While Kreuzwendedich is now set on marrying Rebecka, he still must convert, which requires changes to both his soul and his body. Pulling away from him (and rejecting sexual advances until he is circumcised), Rebecka now demands,

> Werde du erst Jude, schlechthin Jude, Jude bis zum Exzeß, mit Kaftan, Gebetriemen, langen Locken. Du liebst mich nicht restlos, wenn du nicht mit Haut und Haaren, bis ins Mark deiner arischen Knochen hinein Jude und aber Jude geworden sein wirst. (OG, 603)

> First become a Jew, completely Jewish, a Jew to the point of excess, with caftan, phylactery, and long locks of hair. You don't love me with all your heart [literally: with skin and hair] unless you become utterly Jewish deep in the marrow of your Aryan bones, a Jew and nothing but a Jew. (Z, 82)

To become Jewish "with skin and hair," from foreskin to side locks in the way Rebecka describes, requires a spiritual and intellectual first step—one that involves language learning. As a "counterpiece" to Panizza's texts, Friedlaender reverses the order of the transformation here and attends to language and "the soul" before the body. Kreuzwendedich learns Hebrew to study Jewish law, traditions, and prayers, after which he submits to his circumcision. Just like in Faitel's case, the complicated matter of religious conversion is negotiated matter-of-factly in no more than a few sentences (see OG, 603; and Z, 82). He takes on the new name Moses or Moische Mogandovidwendedich (*Mogandovid*, i.e., the Star of David, replaces the cross in his name) and reverses his last name from Reschok into Koscher, keeping his old roots in his name like Faitel did with Stern (star).

Yet his transformation does not suffice. When he returns to Rebecka, he is still sporting his monocle as a last visible remnant of his Aryan Prussianness, as if not all necessary appendages had been removed yet (recalling Faitel's linguistic remnants—the appendages *(e)menerà* and *Deradáng*—and the dachshund's confusion about clothing and accessories as body parts). She therefore demands a (re)turn to "more authentic" Eastern European Jewish roots that suggests an uneasy hybrid status for so-called assimilated Western Jewry, which includes Rebecka herself:

> Deine jüdische Seele hat ja den infernalisch arischen Rosche-Leib noch gar nicht recht ergriffen! Diese Gojimhaltung beleidigt das Andenken meiner Väter. Ist das Liebe? Kann ich so mit dir unter die Chuppe? Als Kalle eines solchen Choßn, wie du äußerlich noch scheinst? Bevor der ehemalige Reschok nicht wirklich so ausschaut wie die mosaischen Männer auf Steinhardt's, Artur Segal's oder Chagal's Gemälden, ist an unsere eheliche Verbindung nicht zu denken. (OG, 604)

> Your Jewish soul hasn't really taken complete hold of the infernally [missing: Aryan] Rehsok [literally: *Rosche*, or evil person] body yet! This goyim posture is an insult to the memory of my forefathers. Is that love? Do you think I could stand with you like that under the *chuppa*? Do you think I want to be wed to such a bridegroom looking the way you still look? Until the former Rehsok really looks like a Jewish man, like in the paintings of Steinhardt, Segal, or Chagall, you can forget all about marrying me! (Z, 82–83)

Rebecka wants her future husband to be an Eastern European Jew like her father desires. Her markedly increased use of Yiddish in this passage is all wedding vocabulary, using words like *Chuppe* (wedding canopy), *Kalle* (bride), and *Choßn* (groom), many of which Zipes's translation renders in English.[24] The use of Yiddish and emphasis on Kreuzwendedich's appearance are not only familiar from her father's language and demands but they also reveal that she, like him, considers Eastern European heritage to be the authentic, true Jewish shibboleth, both physically and linguistically. Because of her groom's transformation, she is herself changing, or rather showcasing her own mutability and multilingual heritage, which allows her to foreground her Yiddish-speaking, "more Jewish" self. The three contemporary Jewish painters mentioned all created quite expressionist figures that make anatomical modeling rather difficult, but Rebecka resolutely sends Kreuzwendedich to a prepaid, famous orthopedic surgeon with a word that seems to be taken out of the von Reschoks' dictionary and turns her back into Freia-Rotraut: "Marsch!" (OG, 604; "March!"; Z, 83).[25]

Kreuzwendedich obliges, and it is in the titular operations on the convert's body that the strongest similarities between the two texts can be found, as the surgeon turns Kreuzwendedich into the original Faitel. While Faitel's hair was turned blond and straight, and his nose, legs, and back straightened, the straight-lined stick figure of Kreuzwendedich is now curled, twisted, and rounded out with medical help. Eastern Europe is his next destination, "um bei dortigen Wunderrabis das Jiddisch und die dazu gehörige Gebärdensprache zu erlernen. Er redete mit Armen, Beinen und der Zunge nach dem Herzen Jehovas" (OG, 604; "to learn Yiddish from the wonder rabbis there as well as all the gestures that go along with it. He talked with arms, legs, and tongue [added:, a man] after Jehovah's own heart"; Z, 83–84). Learning Yiddish and what the text calls *Gebärdensprache* (meaning "sign language" but literally indicating a "gesture language" that is akin to the neologistic terms Panizza invented, like Faitel's *Gedankensprache* and the *Handsprache* in the dog diary) authenticates his intellectual, spiritual, and physical conversion.[26] He is now—in mind, soul, and body as well as German, Hebrew, and Yiddish—accepted as Jewish and can finally marry Rebecka, which will lead to the ultimate fulfillment of his transformation through reproduction. "Rebecka's Triumpf war unermeßlich" (OG, 605; "Rebecca's triumph was boundless"; Z, 84), and everybody talks about the social scandal. At this point, the text self-referentially comments on its own genre: "Die Groteske drang bis in die allerhöchsten Kreise" (OG, 605; "This grotesque affair [literally: *die Groteske*] reached the highest echelons"; Z, 84).

The humiliated von Reschoks plan to interfere with the wedding ceremony with the help of the fraternity and Bör, who is dressed up—or finally exposed—as one-eyed Odin: "als einäugiger Odin ver- oder vielmehr entkleidet" (OG, 605; "disguised or rather undisguised [literally: disrobed] as one-eyed Odin"; Z, 85). When Kreuzwendedich-Moische first sees him, he exclaims, "'Gott meiner Väter!' rief garnicht so unkorrekt Moische Koscher

[…]. 'Heißt ä Gott,' kreischte Gold-Isak, 'der nur ein Auge hat! Unter den blinden Gojim ist der König'" (OG, 605–6; "'God of my fathers!' Moishe Kosher exclaimed, not so incorrectly […] 'May God bless whoever has only one eye!' [literally: Whoever has only one eye is a god], screamed Gold-Isaac. 'He's king among the blind goyim'"; Z, 85). The adapted saying has Isak call those who worship one-eyed Odin—that is, the Aryan monocle-wearers of the growing Nazi movement—figuratively blind. Isak can successfully buy off Bör, and the ease with which the servant switches sides suggests that a lot of Nazi supporters are just following those who provide them with income. In the guise of Odin, god is now on the Jewish family's side (and indeed, the text suggests that he is the god of Isak's fathers too), as Bör kicks out his former masters and even the police lend institutional support and arrest them.

The wedding now goes off without a hitch and is described as an assemblage of signifiers of Jewish legitimation that includes the whole community.[27] Signaling looming sexual success and reproductive fulfillment, "Rebecka sah dabei selber zum Anbeißen aus" (OG, 605; "Rebecca herself was just about to take a bite"; Z, 84; literally: Rebecka looked scrumptious herself/good enough to eat), which makes her no longer the active part of the previously threatened act of *Einverleibung* (incorporation or ingestion). The success of his conversion seems to have reinstated Moische's masculinity, and he has "den Talles sonderbarerweise um die Lenden geschlungen" (OG, 606; "the tallith strangely wrapped around his loins"; Z, 85) instead of wearing his prayer shawl around the neck, indicating a residual unfamiliarity with Jewish custom and suggestively emphasizing his religiously reinforced masculinity with a display that is reminiscent of a bandage in the general area of his successful circumcision.

Not Quite "Reschok"

After these chaotic scenes, the story fast-forwards to the present-day consequences of the conversion case:

> Herr und Frau Moische Koscher bewohnen heute, als enragierte Zionisten, ein Landhaus bei Jerusalem. Ihre Nachkommen heißen zwar nicht Balder, Braga, Hermod, Thor und Tyr, aber dafür melodischer und ehrlicher: Schlaume, Schmul, Veigelche, Pressel und Jankef. – Die Grafen Reschok hingegen sind bisher vergebens um Änderung ihres Namens eingekommen und müssen es leiden, daß man in ihren Kreisen von etwas, das nicht ganz koscher ist, simpler sagt, es sei nicht ganz 'reschok'. (OG, 606)

> Now Mr. and Mrs. Moishe Kosher are living today as committed [literally: enraged] Zionists in a country villa near Jerusalem. To be sure their offspring are not called Balder, Braga, Hermond, T[h]or, and Tyr. Instead, they have more melodic and honest names: Shlaume, Shmul, Feigelche, Pressel, and Yankef.—The Rehsok clan has vainly sought to the present day to change its name and must consequently put up with the fact that, when something is not completely kosher, people in their circles say it is not completely 'rehsok.' (Z, 85)

In the case of the bourgeois-sounding Herr and Frau Koscher, the desired reproductive success has come true. They have five sons with "honest" Yiddish names, who are contrasted with Odin's mythological offspring, whose names Kreuzwendedich had once wanted to use for his Germanic sons. The family resides near Jerusalem as enraged (and specifically not just actively engaged) Zionists, which points to Friedlaender's criticism of the concept.[28] This corresponds to the narrative's critique of the idea of an inherent and exclusive "pure essence" of identity, which applies to both German and Jewish national projects. At the end of the text, the von Reschoks have lost not only their son (and therefore their lineage and supposedly their honor) but also their name—instead of changing it, they are stuck with its changed meaning, as language once again displays its mutability.

Friedlaender's story ends optimistically—on a utopian note, given Friedlaender's political farsightedness—by assessing the long-term effects of Kreuzwendedich's case on humankind. The text takes his successful transformation to be an example of humanity's ability to change—for the better:

> Seitdem ist der Antisemitismus merklich abgeflaut. Man ängstigt sich vor gewissen Orthopäden, denen keine noch so stolze Rassenreinheit widersteht. [...] Man baut nicht mehr dogmatisch auf Rassenunterschiede. Rassenblut hat aufgehört, ein besonderer Saft zu sein. Professor Friedlaender zieht es auf Flaschen und transfundiert es ungescheut genug. (OG, 606)

> Since then, anti-Semitism has noticeably slackened. Certain orthopedists are feared and resisted by people who are still proud of the purity of their race. [...] One no longer bases everything on racial differences. Racial blood has stopped being considered a special kind of vital juice. Meanwhile, Professor Friedlaender gathers it in bottles and continues to transfer it undauntedly from one vessel into another. (Z, 85–86)

In a world in which one's skin color can be changed like one's hair color, categories such as race lose their power. In Goethe's *Faust*, Mephistopheles famously says, "Blut ist ein ganz besondrer Saft" (blood is a very special juice), and invoking this reference makes race-based distinctions a satanic inheritance.[29] Kreuzwendedich's transformation results in a radical change of the way humankind conceives of identity: it is no longer understood as an unchangeable result of one's blood or physical properties; rather, it becomes mutable and mobile. At the forefront of this development is Professor Friedlaender, who is Kreuzwendedich's orthopedic surgeon and the author's namesake. He had initially been tasked with the "perverse Aufgabe [. . .], gewissermaßen umgekehrt, als Kakopäde zu verfahren" (OG, 604; "perverse task, in a certain way to do the reverse, that is, to act as a caco-orthopedist"; Z, 83) to facilitate Kreuzwendedich's transformation. While an orthopedist would "right" the body, the prefix *caco* introduces the reverse by indicating ugliness. This charge applies not only to the biopolitical operations conducted on Kreuzwendedich but also to the author Friedlaender, whose awareness of antisemitic stereotypes in addition to his familiarity with Jewish culture enabled him to take on the "perverse task" of creating the "best" antisemitic image.[30]

He did so to call attention to the increasing antisemitism of the unstable Weimar Republic but also pointed out that inner-Jewish conflicts as well as Zionism and other national projects were relying on similar notions of authenticity, "purity," and exclusion.[31] Rather than focusing on the supposed difference between nations, Friedlaender rejected the idea of a Jewish or other "essence" and wrote in 1936,

> Vernunft ist weder deutsch noch jüdisch, sondern sowohl die deutschen wie die jüdischen Leute täten gerade heut endlich wohl daran, wenn sie ihr Deutsch- oder Judentum der Vernunft anpaßten; wenn sie nicht immer von neuem auf Deutsch und Jüdisch herumritten, sondern sich von diesen bescheidenen Tieren endlich auf das hohe Roß der Menschheit schwängen. [. . .] '*Deutscher*' Staat, '*jüdischer*' Staat – Was ist das für ein subalterner Jargon! Das ist der *nationalistische* Jargon. [. . .] flugs wird *der* Jud fabriziert, wie es der Pöbel herzlich gerne macht. [. . .] Dieser jüdische Charakter ist ein empiristisches Pöbelprodukt. Ich bin nicht auf die Welt gekommen, um Juden zu verteidigen. Aber ich verteidige den erhabenen, schönen, guten, frommen, intelligenten MENSCHEN so sehr im Deutschen wie im N[. . .] wie im Juden.[32]

> Reason is neither German nor Jewish, yet both the German and the Jewish people would do well, especially these days, to adapt their German- or

Jewishness to reason; not to beat the dead horse that is German and Jewish, but to mount the noble steed of humanity instead of those wretched creatures. [...] *'German'* state, *'Jewish'* state—what kind of subaltern jargon is that?! It is the *nationalist* jargon. [...] immediately, it creates *the* Jew, as the mob loves to do. [...] This Jewish character is an empiristic product of the mob. I was not born to defend Jews. But I am defending the sublime, beautiful, good, pious, intelligent H U M A N   B E I N G as much in the German as in the Negro and the Jew.

In his *Grotesken*, Friedlaender "defended the human" with a strong dose of satirical laughter "by exaggerating the caricature [here of "the German" and "the Jew"] to the point of being grotesque, until it succeeds in driving [the philistine] out of the merely imagined paradise of his customs," as his definition of the genre put it.[33] The humanistic tone of his letter resonates with the hopeful ending of "Der operierte Goj," where science makes the world a place of equality. It is unclear whether we should believe this utopia, or whether it is rather another "caricature of genuine life," in which the philistine of the *Grotesken* definition "out of forgetfulness, naively feels good."[34] After all, orthopedist Dr. Friedlaender is a physician, whom we have learned not to trust in *Grotesken*, and his/the author's name is dangerously close to Dr. Frankenstein, who created monsters.[35]

Friedlaender published his *Groteske* in October 1922.[36] A year earlier, on September 28, 1921, Oskar Panizza had died, which has been largely ignored in the reception of Friedlaender's text.[37] From 1894 to 1895, Friedlaender spent almost a year in Munich, which was just one year after the publication of Panizza's "operirter Jud'" and at the height of his infamy and literary success among the Munich Moderns because of the ongoing *Liebeskonzil* trial.[38] As Friedlaender's title explicitly states, the story is a response to Panizza. It establishes the generic connection of Panizza's narratives to Friedlaender's *Grotesken* and shows a certain shared understanding with the older text.[39] Even though Friedlaender's and Panizza's stories end on vastly different notes, they nonetheless caricature the same paranoid fear of assimilation and expose the supposedly "pure essence" of both German and Jewish identities as an imaginary construct. Like the current of "counterpieces" that runs through the texts, these caricatures of society are mutually constitutive. Yet the reception of the two *Grotesken* has been changed by the devastating biopolitical deployment of the same antisemitic stereotypes by the Nazis. Scholem's altered assessment of Friedlaender's writing after the war, which went from "almost knocked me off my chair with laughter at the time" to "a literary form that became impossible after Hitler," demonstrates that the reception of *Grotesken* was fundamentally changed by the Holocaust.[40] The two *Grotesken* at hand make the reasons for this shift in reception quite clear, and at the same time, the case they make against limiting access to the category of the human for anyone aside from Man became even more imperative *because* of the experiences of the Shoah.

TWELVE

Why Humans?

In the *Groteske* "Der Beweis, daß die Deutschen dennoch Menschen sind" (The proof that the Germans are nonetheless human [beings], 1923) and the slightly changed version "Beweis, daß die Deutschen Menschen sind" (Proof that the Germans are human [beings], 1934), Friedlaender defines what it means to be human—proposing a satirical answer to the question so central to the genre of *die Groteske*:

> Eindeutig ist der echte Mensch dadurch definiert, daß er bereits im Mutterleib unverkennbar Antisemit ist; woraus erhellt, was man Deutschen, seien sie Menschen, Unmenschen oder nichts, gar nicht erst zu beweisen braucht, daß Juden, mögen sie sonst sein, was sie wollen, jedenfalls keine Menschen sind. Sie verdienen keinen Beweis, zumal ihre schamlose Behauptung, Menschen zu sein, sie vollends zu Nichtmenschen stempelt.[1]

> Clearly, the real human being is defined by the fact that he is unmistakably antisemitic already in the womb; which elucidates what one need not prove in the first place to the Germans—be they human, inhuman, or nothing—that the Jews—be they otherwise what they may—are in any case not human beings. They deserve no proof, the more so as their brazen claim that they are human declares them fully nonhuman.

Instead of setting out to prove that Jews are not human beings, at which the early Nazis tried their best at the time, Friedlaender reverses Nazi "logic" by saying that the true human is an antisemite, which makes all Germans humans and all Jews nonhumans (*Nichtmenschen*) or the ultimate other.

This tautology of oppositions nonetheless leaves room for *Unmenschen*, the inhumane, which Friedlaender defines not as the opposite of human beings but as their inherent nature, thus exposing humanistic ideals as fraught. The contrastive foil of humans are subhumans, *Untermenschen*—a Nazi term that is implicitly satirized in this *Groteske*. The repeated usage of "Q. e. d." gives the text a (pseudo-)scientific air, but all that has been demonstrated is that those who declare other people subhuman are inhumane themselves—which calls their humanity into question. The earlier rendering of the text was written in the same year as "Der operierte Goj" and demonstrates Friedlaender's clear political foresight. After going into exile in 1933, Friedlaender's 1934 version of the text bears witness to the nightmarish ways in which Nazi "logic" was becoming institutionalized.

Friedlaender mainly used comedic ways to explore the idea that people are judged by the way they look and are perceived, but his *Grotesken* nonetheless criticize the necessity to adhere to specific norms to fit in. "Die lüderliche Nase" (The cockish nose, 1919), for instance, implicitly takes up a German saying that suggests a correlation between nose and penis size because of which a young man is frequently seduced and subsequently dies a premature death.[2] While crude humor seemingly prevails in this narrative, its subtext references the antisemitic stereotype of the Jewish nose and the assumptions that come with thinking that one can recognize someone's "essence" by their physical features, or even smell it, as *foetor judaicus* suggested. Friedlaender's texts became more openly critical in exile, as Hitler's intentions became impossible to ignore. He directly addressed the persecution of Jews in *Grotesken* such as "Fast Nacht" (Almost night/Carnival, 1934) and "Totenlärm" (Dead noise, 1935) and presented his ideas for a new world order in "Die Letzten – die Ersten" (The last—the first, 1934) and "In spe" (To be, 1934).

One of Friedlaender's texts, "Tödliche Anprobe" (Deadly fitting, 1929), comments on the role of the genre of *Grotesken* in a world bound for the violent extermination of others. It tells the story of a dressmaker whose clothes do not merely make the man but render men gods ("Meine Kleider machen nicht nur Leute, sondern Götter").[3] Indeed, this "leg-shower," as Panizza's dachshund would say, confirms the canine assumption that clothes *are* people. Similar to the orthopedic doctors creating or undoing straight legs in "Der operirte Jud'" and "Der operierte Goj," this tailor considers himself tasked with an act of divine creation, compared to which the original body of his clients is a mere caricature:

> Meine Anprobe ist Schöpfung. Mit dem Ideal, das mir beim ersten Anblick eines Kunden sofort vorschwebt, verglichen ist der Leib Karikatur. Meine Fräcke, Sakkos, Westen erst entbuckeln; erst meine Hose bringt gerade Beine hervor. Fungier' ich orthopädisch, – [...] Sofort, wie gesagt, konzipiere ich die Norm[.] (TA, 337)
>
> My fittings are Creation. Compared to the ideal that I immediately envision when I first see a client, the body is a caricature. My dress coats, jackets, vests de-hunchback to begin with; only my pants create straight legs. If I function orthopedically,—[...] Immediately, like I said, I conceptualize the norm.

To have his norm-producing creations made, the tailor writes down descriptions of his clients' actual appearance for his workers, and these "satirisch-lakonisch[e...], literarisch wertvoll[e...] Zettel" (TA, 338; satirical-laconic, literary valuable slips of paper) are *Grotesken* that cause boundless laughter among his employees. When one of his notes is accidentally sent to his most narcissistic and supposedly malformed client, who looks like "ein Etwas [...], das ich zuerst für einen kompliziert verbogenen Laternenpfahl hielt" (TA, 338; a Something [...] that I initially thought to be a lamp post warped in complicated ways), the taunted man ends his life.

The text also ends on a lighter note than its plot warrants by saying "Wahrheit, gesprochen und gehört, tötet Eitelkeit" (TA, 340; truth, spoken and heard, kills vanity), which makes the story appear as if it only addressed fashion and beauty standards. Yet as his other writing shows, Friedlaender was fully aware that norms and their transgressions were much more serious problems. Omitting the object, the sentence "truth, spoken or heard, kills" could be the motto of his *Grotesken*, as he said in his definition of *die Groteske*: "Der Groteskenmacher ist davon durchdrungen, daß man diese Welt hier, die uns umgibt, gleichsam ausschwefeln muß, um sie von allem Ungeziefer zu reinigen; er wird zum Kammerjäger der Seelen" (The creator of *Grotesken* is permeated by the obligation that he has to fumigate this world that surrounds us, in order to clean it from all vermin; he becomes the exterminator of souls).[4] Friedlaender's *Grotesken* do not shy away from speaking the truth to prompt laughter about a horrifying reality in the hopes that its cathartic function will cleanse the soul. The *Grotesken* in this section expose mechanisms of exclusion from the category of the human and reveal their drastic biopolitical consequences. By asking what it means to be human, they do not aim to further limit or circumscribe this category but instead break open category constraints, question preconceived notions and norms, and expose the inhumane effects of social and political definitions of the self against the other. As Friedlaender described it, the definition of "us versus them" renders no one human: it designates "them" as subhuman, which makes "us" inhumane.

Conclusion

Die Groteske is a frequently censored short prose form that uses strategies such as exaggeration, defamiliarization, and ambiguity to provoke a reaction oscillating between horror and laughter, for the purpose of political criticism. As a genre, it contributes to the question what it means to be human around 1900. Responding to an interlocking set of crises—about the place of Man in the world, the subject's ability to know self and other, and the limits of language—*Grotesken* turn to nonhuman and marginalized human perspectives to highlight the underlying biopolitical norms that regulate the status of the human. From the vantage point of plants, animals, and people who are denied access to human rights and social belonging, the crisis of Man—a white, Western, Christian, straight, able-bodied, neurotypical, bourgeois or upper-class, cis-male archetype—becomes the subject of satire. No longer the center of the universe, the crown of creation, or even in full control of his own mind? Welcome to everyone else's world, where those who try to fit in are institutionalized for "madness" like Jonathan and the masturbating plants in section 2; chronicle their descent into an isolating epistemological and ontological crisis like the dogs in their diaries in section 3; and submit to changes that render them unrecognizable to anyone like the "operated Jew" in section 4. Those representing institutions and society, often physicians, priests, and policemen who serve as narrators of the texts, turn out to be unreliable and untrustworthy, as they reinforce the biopolitical regulation of bodies and minds. Language—the supposedly unreliable element—is in turn weaponized as a defamiliarizing, exaggerating, and ambiguous force that provides layers of new meaning in seemingly simple terms. While the defiance of rules is programmatic for *Grotesken*, these shared strategies are palpable across the texts in this canon, and this monograph provides the first book-length analysis of these narratives as a genre.[1]

Now forgotten, the genre proliferated in the fifty years between the 1890s and the beginning of the Second World War in Germanophone literature. Its success can be measured in its infamy, fueled by rampant censorship—from the courts of the Wilhelmine Empire to the book burnings of the Nazis. Oskar Panizza's pioneering, and as this book demonstrates, influential work at the end of the nineteenth century led to the longest censorship prison sentence under Kaiser Wilhelm II, and only a few decades later, literary histories declared him dead before his time, while he languished in one of the asylums that feature so prominently in his provocative texts. Hanns Heinz Ewers republished Panizza's writings and adapted the genre's potential for sensationalist shock value for other media, such as the cabaret and early film; yet in his best-selling success, he increasingly lost sight of the political targets that deserved support or criticism, and he was caught up in the propaganda machine of the Nazis. Salomo Friedlaender, on the other hand, who infused his many *Grotesken* with witty intellectual wordplay from the 1910s throughout the 1930s, demonstrated the genre's increasing relevance as a critical outlet for German Jewish authors and audiences in the very same time frame. Finally, the genre's critique of society's norms through the lens of animals and marginalized human beings took shape in the work of Franz Kafka, who is not usually considered a part of literary trends and traditions. Recontextualizing his oeuvre within the concerns of this network of authors, who all spelled out the idea of *die Groteske* in their own ways, illustrates both how his writing connects to a specific humorous view of a horrifying world and what kind of *Grotesken* would speak to a post-Holocaust society.

Gershom Scholem's 1975 diagnosis of *die Groteske* as "a literary form that became impossible after Hitler and is virtually inaccessible today," though it "almost knocked me off my chair with laughter at the time," has elucidated why most *Grotesken* and their humor have fallen out of favor.[2] Yet it also points to the ways in which the genre resonated with the Jewish experience in Weimar Germany and the Third Reich, as the contemporaneous assessments of Kurt Tucholsky, Walter Benjamin, and Salomo Friedlaender confirm. In line with its earlier iterations, the genre proved a provocative way for literary voices in the 1920s and 1930s to address the rise and spread of ideas of exclusion that would ultimately end in the fascist realization of many of the texts' biopolitical exaggerations. Especially Friedlaender's philosophy of laughter highlights the importance of these texts as a means of resistance on the eve of the Second World War, and as a self-declared "synthesis of Kant and Clown," he maintained the significance of laughter as a political statement even in the 1940s.[3] As the close readings in this book render the humor of a distinct historical moment legible again, they do so in the awareness that the genre's criticisms of the structures that enable fascism remain more pertinent than ever. This brings out the sustained urgency of a mode of address whose provocative existence between public success and state censorship demonstrates the political impact of literature.

Both the ways in which the genre "no longer works" and the ways in which it still does today raise questions about what kinds of texts or media of the present might have taken over their role or feel tasked with the obligation of the *Grotesken* writer "to fumigate the soul," as Friedlaender described it.[4] Which contemporary comedy negotiates the line between harmful offense and productive criticism successfully? Whose tales of society and institutions make us recognize ourselves in their grotesque exaggerations in a way that has "laughter get stuck in our throats"? These deliberations point to voices excluded from twentieth-century *Grotesken* that are exceedingly urgent for the twenty-first. The West is only beginning to grapple with the legacies of many biopolitical power structures of its making: from colonial endeavors that mapped, displaced, and exhibited the peoples, animals, and plants of the world in relation to a white self to the justification of racist, sexist, and ableist ideas by science and medicine, legal persecution of sexual orientation, and religious oppression of diverse gender identities. While some of these themes are negotiated in *Grotesken*, and each of the texts raises different questions about who gets to speak or write and why, it is quite noticeable that one large group is almost entirely absent from the genre: women. Neither among the writers of *Grotesken* nor in many of the texts themselves do women seem to have a place, and the lack of female experiences or subjectivity in the genre is glaring. Why did contemporaneous female-identifying authors not express or see themselves in these kinds of texts? Speculating about the reasons for this condition—aside from the structural barriers for women writers, let alone within censorship mechanisms—reinforces the centrality of Man to these discourses of crisis around 1900.[5] The writers who satirize this distinctly masculine loss of certainty and superiority missed their own share in the advantages of this group only narrowly—a sense of belonging that was denied to all four of the authors for different reasons at some point in their lives. All of this emphasizes the urgent need to expand the available voices, experiences, and subjectivities in the field of German and German Jewish literary and cultural studies and beyond—no matter the genre.[6]

Ideas of the human that tout exceptionalism and exclusion have persisted in various forms since the days of pseudoscientific physiognomy, colonial exploits, and world wars, and they continue to underpin a dominant paradigm that has historically been limited to Man at the cost of equitable rights for both humankind and more-than-human life in all its diverse dimensions. The legacy of these developments in the human self-conception is apparent not just in today's struggles over race, religion, gender, and sexuality around the globe but also in the ongoing environmental crisis caused by the exploitation of other life forms. The nonhuman figures in *Grotesken* address the unfolding catastrophe of the Anthropocene by highlighting that our current posthuman age continues to be engaged in an endeavor to define what it means to be in an anthropocentric way. While the Darwinian worldview arising in the nineteenth century generated the need to differentiate humans from animals all over again, the scientific, social, and environmental changes of our own age have brought different anxieties about human–animal relations to the forefront, be it our reliance on them as food or family—and the ethical conflicts that arise in the spaces between. The suffering of both humans and nonhumans irrevocably underpins the way we live in the West: no steak without the agony of animals—no coffee or chocolate without a global economy of exploitation that harms people and planet. While an increasingly industrialized environment around 1900 prompted the reformulation of Man's relationship to the natural world with a focus on a future of progress, the awareness of climate change and its devastating consequences dominates these discourses today. The realization of the violent underbelly of Western existence has seemingly inspired a longing to be closer to nature intellectually, emotionally, and physically that takes cues from centuries of non-Western and Indigenous knowledges and explores concepts like kinship and entanglement.[7] Excavating *die Groteske* grounds such ideas from animal, plant, and environmental studies in multispecies history—tracing how the human relationship to self and other has shifted over time and centering rather than marginalizing the nonhuman.

The book's rather taxonomical organization around the perspectives of plants, animals, and marginalized human beings might raise questions about reinforcing the hierarchical classification systems that many of these texts satirize, while at the same time noting the built-in problems that come with studying both humans and animals, let alone plants, side by side. Work at the intersection of race and animal studies cannot avoid the long history of people treating other humans like animals—from chattel slavery to cattle cars.[8] Scholars that engage with these discourses and practices of animalization must grapple with the ethical unease that surrounds placing the suffering of humans next to that of nonhumans. While comparison is not a productive approach when it comes to suffering or to valuing life, the strategy of *Grotesken* is to show shared underlying principles at work in the devaluation of anyone not perceived as "one of us," as the folks in Faitel's environment put it. Through the lens of an "us," the other is constructed as an amalgamation of difference that can consist of a variety of identities and life forms. The plant, animal, and human sections of this book focus on the specificity of each of these figurations to highlight what kind of criticisms they bring to the fore. Organizing the book around the voices of marginalized "others" is therefore ultimately not about similarity but solidarity.

NOTES

Introduction

1. Freud, *General Introduction*, 246–47.
2. See Küenzlen, *Der Neue Mensch*; Gelderloos, *Biological Modernism*; Glaser, "Kulturchronik 1900–2005"; and Bundeszentrale für politische Bildung, "Der neue Mensch." For the Dadaist New Man, see Benson, *Raoul Hausmann*.
3. In turning to plants, animals, and dehumanized people, *Grotesken* tie into the biopolitical force of rendering the nonhuman as central rather than marginal, which has been particularly well developed in respect to animality in Kafka's work (see exemplarily recent monographs such as Geller, *Bestiarium Judaicum*; Harel, *Kafka's Zoopoetics*; Pines, *The Infrahuman*; and Geier, *Kafka's Nonhuman Form*) and runs alongside a current about the creaturely (see Pick, *Creaturely Poetics*; and Santner, *On Creaturely Life*). This kind of research brings together (German) Jewish studies with animal studies, and in this book also the relatively recent field of plant studies.
4. Across her work in Black studies and post/decolonial theory, Sylvia Wynter's discussion of "the genre of Man" brings together the political with the ecological and points to the larger Western history of equating Man with the human and excluding everyone else. See exemplarily Wynter, "Unsettling the Coloniality"; Drexler-Dreis and Justaert, *Beyond the Doctrine of Man*; McKittrick, *Sylvia Wynter: On Being Human in Praxis* (in this volume, see especially Wynter and McKittrick, "Unparalleled Catastrophe for Our Species?"; Mignolo, "Sylvia Winter: What Does It Mean to Be Human"); and Parker, "Human as Double Bind."
5. von Hofmannsthal, "Letter," 121–22. See Nietzsche, "Ueber Wahrheit und Lüge."
6. Wolfgang Kayser diagnosed this problem in the Kafka reception already in his 1957 study on *The Grotesque*:

Thirty years have sufficed to blot out the memory of his contemporaries to such an extent that today he is often considered to have been unique and isolated in his own time. He has even been called a prophet without honor in his own country. When making such assertions, the older ones among us forget that a number of Kafka's most characteristic stories were published around 1920, and that Kafka himself was a well-known author who was supported by the publishers Kurt Wolff and Rowohlt. At that time his unusual voice still formed part of the chorus of contemporaries. (146)

7. Max Brod famously reports on Kafka's humorous understanding of his own texts: "When Kafka read aloud himself, this humor became perfectly clear. Thus, for example, we friends of his laughed quite immoderately when he first let us hear the first chapter of *The Trial*. And he himself laughed so much that there were moments when he couldn't read any further. Astonishing enough, when you think of the fearful earnestness" (*Franz Kafka*, 178). See also Parvulescu, "Kafka's Laughter."

8. Scholem, *Walter Benjamin: Geschichte einer Freundschaft*, 62; and Scholem, *Walter Benjamin: Story of a Friendship*, 58. The second volume of *Grotesken* in Friedlaender's collected works assembles a range of reviews, which demonstrate the immense laughter (and some indignation) that his texts produced in Germany before the Second World War, and some of the few postwar reviews confirm Scholem's verdict (see Friedlaender/Mynona, *Grotesken*, 2:479–518).

Section I: The Grotesque

1. Kayser highlights the first three years of the 1890s as the period that saw the production of all styles of modernist literature that would define the twentieth century, though he notably excluded the grotesque and locates it in the years between 1910 and 1925 (see *The Grotesque*, 130–31). Yet as this book shows, the grotesque was already present in the early 1890s, which is particularly apparent in Panizza's work.

2. See Vogl, Balke, and Siegert, *Kleine Formen*; and Locher, *Die kleinen Formen in der Moderne*. One of the exceptions to prove the rule of brevity for texts labeled *Grotesken* is Paul Madsack's 230-page crime novel *Die metaphysische Wachsfigur oder Auf Geisterfang mit Sir Arthur Conan Doyle: Eine magische Groteske* (1930).

3. A few examples will show the widespread modernist engagement with grotesque aesthetics while demonstrating the broad attribution of a vaguely defined concept: Grotesque poetry ranges from satirists like Wilhelm Busch to Dadaists such as Hugo Ball. Frank Wedekind stands exemplarily for the grotesque in the theater of the time, as Gustav Meyrink does for modernist novels. Alfred Kubin and George Grosz are just two creators of the grotesque in modernist art, and films such as *Das Cabinet des Dr. Caligari* (1920) and *Nosferatu* (1922) represent the many examples that develop the grotesque so typical of Weimar film (terms like *Filmgroteske* and *Groteskfilm* also circulate about Hollywood productions and in film criticism from Benjamin to Kracauer). See Baumgartner and Lawicki, *Satire – Ironie – Groteske*;

Dimić, "Das Groteske"; Haakenson, *Grotesque Visions*; Kort, *Comic Grotesque* and *Grotesk!*; and Zbytovský, "Formen des Grotesken in der frühexpressionistischen Lyrik."

4. Soergel, *Dichtung und Dichter der Zeit*, 859. Unless otherwise indicated, translations from German into English in this book are my own. Since language is centrally important to the genre and most of the *Grotesken* have never been translated before, primary texts for analysis, other writings by the four main authors, and central theoretical passages that will be referenced repeatedly will be given in both languages in full when first cited (like Scholem's in the introduction), while English-only passages include relevant original terms in brackets.

5. The references to Hoffmann and Panizza are particularly prevalent in *Grotesken* written before the First World War: Panizza dedicated his first collection of short prose to Poe and called it *Dämmrungsstücke* (Dusk pieces, 1890) in reference to Hoffmann's *Nachtstücke* (*Night Pieces*, 1817). He dedicated his second collection (*Visionen*, 1893) to Hoffmann. Ewers wrote several essays about Poe (e.g., *Edgar Allan Poe*, 1909) and republished Hoffmann's tales in the first volume of his book series *Galerie der Phantasten*—a series that later also included Panizza's stories. Walter Benjamin made the connection in 1930, when giving the opening talk of a series concerned with literary parallels about "E. T. A. Hoffmann und Oskar Panizza."

6. Lorenz, "Das Groteske," 2. The grotesque and the fantastic are frequently used synonymously (both during modernism and in studies of the time), and a differentiation is difficult to come by, which might have to do with definitory debates about the fantastic (see Brittnacher, "Auf der Rückseite von Ordnung und Vernunft"). In "Exkurs: Phantastik und Groteske," Thomas Wörtche undertakes an overview of previous attempts (see Pietzcker, Henniger, and Foster reprinted in Best, *Das Groteske*), and this is one of few studies to point to the neglected genre of *die Groteske*. Cornwell also provides a brief synopsis in *The Literary Fantastic* (4–11), focusing on the simultaneous usage of the fantastic and the grotesque in Kayser, Bakhtin, and other seminal works. See moreover Todorov, *The Fantastic*; and Durst, *Theorie der phantastischen Literatur*. My suggestion would be that the element of laughter sets the grotesque apart from the fantastic, moving it closer to political satire, while retaining its existential terror.

7. For a detailed differentiation of terms that have an affinity with the grotesque but do not share its propensity for horror, such as the carnivalesque, the absurd, and satire, see Fuß, *Das Groteske*, 134–36 and 142–43; Bakhtin, *Rabelais and His World*; Sorg, "Groteske"; Cornwell, *The Absurd in Literature*; Imm, *Absurd und Grotesk*; Heidsieck, *Das Groteske und das Absurde*; and Clark, *The Modern Satiric Grotesque*. Satire is frequently used in conjunction with the grotesque (and aptly describes how many *Grotesken* package their criticism), as Kayser (*The Grotesque*, 203) and Panizza's contemporary Schneegans attest (see *Geschichte der grotesken Satire*). Several

dissertations of the Weimar Republic also provide a contemporaneous understanding of the grotesque, such as Untermann, *Das Groteske*; and Vieth, *Beobachtungen zur Wortgroteske*.

8. The persistence of this program is probably best exemplified by the title of Friedlaender's last collection of *Grotesken*, called *Der lachende Hiob und andere Grotesken* (The laughing Job and other grotesques, 1936), which he published in Parisian exile from the Nazis. See Exner, *Fasching als Logik*, 323–24; and Velten, "Laughing at the Body."

9. Mynona, "Grotesk," 54a. This corresponds to a general tendency of grotesque art, since

> the grotesque necessarily refers to society: part of its structure is the horizon of expectations that is customary in the society the work targets. It attacks these expectations [...]. Insofar, the grotesque is critical of society, even if in some cases its criticism might only turn against the customary language of a society and the ideas that are related to it, for instance religious ones. Similarly, its criticism can target ideas, behaviors, and conditions that appear as already socially established, for instance belonging to a certain class, and finally, it can attack beliefs that have been recognized as ideological. (Pietzcker, "Das Groteske [1971]," reprinted in Best, *Das Groteske*, 85–102, here 93–94)

All ellipses in brackets are mine throughout, while those without brackets, including Panizza's frequent and many dots, follow the original.

10. The pejorative term *philistine* refers to those who feel comfortable with inherited ideas, do not pursue independent thought, and fail to appreciate innovative art, aesthetics, or philosophy. Emerging from the student milieu in the late eighteenth century, the image of the conservative bourgeois philistine was a popular target of satire and caricature among the romantics. Clemens Brentano's speech "Der Philister vor, in und nach der Geschichte" ("The Philistine before, in and after History," 1811), originally given at the antisemitic *Deutsche Tischgesellschaft* (German Table Society) and published anonymously as a "humorous treatise" in the same year, explicitly connected "the philistine" with "the Jew" as two ridiculed figures. In antisemitic satires written by the romantics, humor meets grotesque elements, which makes Friedlaender's choice of the term in his definition of *die Groteske* a reclamation of this form of literary expression from antisemites. See Nienhaus, *Geschichte der deutschen Tischgesellschaft*; and Oesterle, "Juden, Philister und romantische Intellektuelle."

11. In perhaps the most systematic overview approach to the genre, a short lexicon entry, Reto Sorg notes the absence of studies on *die Groteske* as a whole, while drawing on the few texts that approach aspects of the genre (mostly focusing on dramatic iterations), which are almost exclusively in German and date back predominantly to the 1960s and 1980s. His entry names all four authors at the center of this book as authors of *Grotesken*, confirms the same time line of genre formation with a beginning in the nineteenth century and demise after 1945, establishes

roots in romanticism and ties to the cabaret, and points to the frequent connection of the human with animals or plants. His description of the genre also aligns with mine when he writes, "Shorter text that combines heterogenous things in a vexing manner and creates effects that oscillate between humor and horror [*Komik und Grauen*]" ("Groteske," 748). Drawing on Sorg with a specific view to Panizza, Claudia Lieb also briefly confirms multiple claims of this section about the genre (including the connection to romanticism): "Panizza's own prose shows that the turn of the century formed its own tradition of *die Groteske*. *Grotesken* are mostly shorter texts that want to vex purposefully by producing chilling effects [*Schauereffekte*] between horror and comedy" ("Nachwort," 232–33). See also Lieb, "Der Fall Oskar Panizza," 355. Thomas O. Haakenson's recent study *Grotesque Visions* confirms the prevalence of the grotesque around 1900 with a focus on the visual (rather than the literary) grotesque. He begins with a chapter on Friedlaender, which sketches out important connections between the grotesque in the arts, film, literature, philosophy, and the sciences but does not account for the distinction between *das* and *die Groteske*, though Friedlaender used the latter consistently. We nonetheless portray two sides of the same coin of the grotesque writ large within the distinct historical context of German modernism when highlighting the important function of critical laughter and pinpointing a focus on bodies, sexuality, scientific knowledge, and institutions.

12. See "Das 'fonetische Schreibsistem,'" in Düsterberg, *"Die gedrukte Freiheit"*, 167–72.

13. The labeling issue applies to most of Panizza's and Kafka's works. Panizza's texts from the early 1890s are simply called *Erzählungen* (narratives), but two of his later, untitled manuscripts in the same style are labeled as *Grotesken*, though by whom and when is unclear. See the undated manuscripts L1484 "Groteske (ohne Titel)" and L1485 "Groteske (ohne Titel)" at the Literaturarchiv Monacensia, Munich. Later editions of Panizza's narratives take up the designation, such as, for instance, *Dämmerungsstücke: Groteske Erzählungen*, though this is one of the many republications that does not preserve Panizza's programmatic spelling deviations. Kafka's works are described as grotesque by others but are not labeled this way by himself. In the absence of this label, one commonality of writers of *Grotesken* are their publishers (such as Albert Langen, Georg Müller, Paul Steegemann, and Kurt Wolff)—a criterion that would potentially add figures like Alfred Döblin to the list of *Grotesken* authors.

14. Little-known authors such as Rudolf von Delius, Robert Forster-Larrinaga, Friedrich Freksa [Kurt Friedrich-Freksa], Fritz von Herzmanovsky-Orlando, Paul Mongré [Felix Hausdorff], Curt Schawaller, and Wilhelm von Scholz mostly wrote plays designated as *Grotesken*. There are a few better-known examples, such as Arthur Schnitzler's *Der grüne Kakadu: Groteske in einem Akt*, which presents one of the earliest uses of the genre label in 1899; Alfred Polgar and Egon Friedell's *Goethe [im*

Examen]: Groteske in zwei Bildern from 1908; and Joachim Ringelnatz's 1921 *Mannimmond: Eine einaktige Groteske* and *Bühnenstar und Mondhumor: Einaktige Groteske.* Hans Arp, Jakob van Hoddis, Alfred Lichtenstein, and Christian Morgenstern, for instance, wrote *Grotesken* in the form of poems (see Zbytovský, "Formen des Grotesken in der frühexpressionistischen Lyrik"), and there are also aphorism and lithography collections with that (sub)title. Some of Friedlaender's *Grotesken*, on the other hand, are instead given neologistic (sub)titles such as *Reklameske* (a combination of the words for advertisement, *Reklame*, and customer complaint or protest, *Reklamation*), *Alkoholeske*, and *Pithekanthropeske* (putting Kant in the *Pithecanthropus erectus*, today called *Homo erectus*), which shows that *die Groteske* as a text type was familiar enough to be defamiliarized at this time.

1. Characteristics of die Groteske

1. Since the texts often feature direct speech or homodiegetic narrators, these positions are not always exclusive to a narrative voice but can be shared with one or even more protagonists.

2. Kayser diagnoses this trait for Kafka in the context of grotesque aesthetics (see *The Grotesque*, 149), and representatives of institutions, such as judges, lawyers, administrators, doctors, ushers, messengers, doormen, clerks, and officers, are a staple of his writing.

3. The use of "madness" in this book is consistently set apart in quotation marks to flag an issue with language use: Rather than reinforcing neurotypicality and addressing modern conceptions of mental health, the term draws here both on its nineteenth-century history of romantic discourses about literary genius and on changing understandings of the mind in early psychology and the asylum around 1900. Fuß explains in *Das Groteske*, "Aside from psychoanalysis, Nietzsche's demise accelerated the re-evaluation of madness in modernism. This manifested itself among other things in the fact that art let itself be inspired by the creation of the so-called insane. This inversion of the conventional assessment is—just like the simultaneously awakening interest in the art of the so-called primitive—a form of recentralization of the marginalized and another argument for the complete equation of modernist art with the grotesque" (310). Drawing on his dual expertise as a psychiatrist and author, Panizza gave a talk about literary "genius and madness" at the Munich *Gesellschaft für modernes Leben* (Society for Modern Life) in 1891, which presented a thorough discussion of the close relation between the two (see "Genie und Wahnsinn," in Panizza, *Werke*, 3:5–48; and Jacobs, "Nachwort"). As this book shows, "madness" is explicitly tied to the notion of freedom of expression and dissent in Panizza's thought, and in my analysis, the term therefore comes up sparingly in its literal and figurative meanings as a concept that undermines "madness" as a derogatory category by applying it to those in power who traditionally determine who and what

counts as "mad" or "sane." This is a catch-22, however, since the usage nonetheless reinforces what it undermines, but as Foucault's work has also shown, there is no way around the asylum when assessing the interplay of power and language.

4. Kayser, *The Grotesque*, 61. This revaluation of "madness" and the asylum is a particularly prevalent feature of Panizza's writing, since he worked as a physician in a sanatorium and later became a patient. His notebooks show that he rejected the idea of pathology: "We speak of 'mental illness' [*'Geisteskrankheit'*] when we see that someone does not want to listen to reason [*Jemand gar keine raison annehmen will*] and relies firmly on his instinct—[. . .] but we cannot *objectively* assess any mental expression [*Geistesäußerung*] whatsoever, we can say of the mental states of our neighbors [*Geisteszuständen unserer Nebenmenschen*] only: that they are different from ours, and that they do not agree with the social and cultural life of our times." (Quoted in Bauer, *Oskar Panizza*, 51, where the italicized portions are underlined; this volume is an updated edition of Bauer's 1984 portrait of Panizza.) Panizza also described the state apparatus as "madhouse-y [*tollhäuslerisch*]" (quoted in Jaschke, "Neue Lebensflüsse," 109). For contemporary attempts to reclaim "madness," see Beresford, "'Mad,' Mad Studies."

5. Section 2 of this book discusses the role of mental institutions in greater detail, focusing on texts by Panizza and Ewers. For examples in Friedlaender's *Grotesken*, see Thiel, "Einleitung," 57–62. Some texts work with variations of the so-called insane asylum, which include, here exemplarily in Kafka's oeuvre, prison camps (*In der Strafkolonie*), cages ("Ein Bericht für eine Akademie"), confined rooms (*Die Verwandlung, Der Prozess, Das Schloss*, etc.), and burrows ("Der Bau"). Asylums also feature in the films of the time—for instance, in *Das Cabinet des Dr. Caligari*, which, as the surprise ending reveals, takes place in a patient's mind.

6. Fuß, who sees the grotesque as an anthropological constant of cultural transformation and creativity, describes its semiotics as follows: "As a generally meaningful sign without a specific meaning, the grotesque semion is the source of a plethora of potential meaning" (*Das Groteske*, 18). He discusses *die Groteske* only in passing and does not further differentiate the text type from the broader aesthetic phenomenon of the grotesque; nonetheless, he recognizes language play as one of its characteristics, especially in Friedlaender's iteration (see 339, 345, and 391). Pietzcker speaks specifically of the phenomenon of the *Sprachgroteske* (Language-*Groteske* in "Das Groteske," reprinted in Best, *Das Groteske*, 85–102, here 99), and one of the dissertations that appeared contemporaneously to the height of *Grotesken* production focused exclusively on *Beobachtungen zur Wortgroteske* (Observations on the Word-*Groteske* in Vieth).

7. The focus on bodies and bodily functions is a general staple of the grotesque writ large; see, for instance, Bakhtin's fifth chapter in *Rabelais and His World*, "The Grotesque Image of the Body and Its Sources." While sexual norms and aberrations

from this moral code are also generally prevalent themes in literature and society from the fin de siècle to the Weimar Republic, Huber sums up the specific preoccupation of *Grotesken* with sexuality in the term "Sexualgroteske" in *Mythos und Groteske*, 117. For a more in-depth discussion of the roles of sexology and psychology at the time, see section 2 of this book.

8. Bourgeois society around 1900 considered many of the topics of *Grotesken*, such as masturbation, fetishism, sex work, and same-sex encounters, amoral, but only the latter two were illegal. Yet in literature and public speech, the amoral *was* illegal, as its representation was censored, which led not only to the prohibition and destruction of literary works but also to court trials that resulted in monetary fines or the imprisonment of authors and publishers. For the details of censorship processes and laws, see section 2 of this book and Stark, *Banned in Berlin*.

9. Foucault, *History of Sexuality*, 1:18.
10. Foucault, *History of Sexuality*, 1:18.
11. Foucault, *History of Sexuality*, 1:105.

2. Grotesken *in a Nexus of Censorship*

1. The most important publishers of *Grotesken*, Georg Müller and Albert Langen (also the founder of the oft-censored journal *Simplicissimus*), suffered from frequent censorship just like their authors. A postcard Panizza sent from exile in Zurich in 1898 describes what had just become his own fate as well: "From Germany [*von Deutschland aus*], Albert Langen has been denied his citizenship identification card. As a result, he is 'writing-less' [*schriftenlos*, play on state-less] a. can be expelled from Zurich every day. He already received a citation [*Verwarnung*]!" Printed in Panizza, *Neues aus dem Hexenkessel*, 208.

2. Mehring, "Mynona: Bank der Spötter," 1. Author and artist Paul Scheerbart's official cause of death in 1915 was a stroke.

3. In the play, a demented God, imbecile Jesus, and callous Mary convince the devil to spread syphilis in the world to punish an orgy-prone pope. See Panizza, *Das Liebeskonzil*; Bauer, *Oskar Panizza*; Binder, "'Der zensierte Dämon'"; Boeser, *Der Fall Oskar Panizza*; Brown, *Oskar Panizza and The Love Council*; Mann, "Das Liebeskonzil"; Mitterbauer, "'Ihr Herrn'"; Pankau, "Oskar Panizza"; Schonlau, "Warum der Teufel Medizin studiert hat," and *Syphilis in der Literatur*; Tucholsky, "Panizza"; and Voß, "Die Darstellung der Syphilis." Panizza also commented explicitly on the devastating effects of literary censorship in his article "Kunst und Polizei."

4. Benjamin, "E. T. A. Hoffmann und Oskar Panizza," 644–45. The Panizza Society faltered when its Jewish chair, Emil Tuchmann, was forced into exile in Paris in 1933 (see Bauer, *Oskar Panizza*, 29).

5. For Friedlaender's commentary on censorship and retracted texts, see Thiel, "Einleitung," 68–69. For Ewers's experiences with censorship and typical ways in

which Weimar cabarets managed to avoid it by declaring their events private, see Kugel, *Der Unverantwortliche*, 70–71; and also Brömsel, "Stephen King des wilhelminischen Kaiserreichs."

6. See Kuxdorf, *Der Schriftsteller*, 6–7. The notion of degeneration or *Entartung* connects the social criticism of *Grotesken* with the discourse about "madness" in the influential work of Max Nordau, a Jewish contemporary of Panizza, who diagnosed fin-de-siècle art with the "mental illness" of degeneration in 1892 (just a year after Panizza's aforementioned talk about literary "genius and madness"); called for censorship of authors such as Oscar Wilde; and urged teachers, judges, and politicians to act as the psychiatrists of an increasingly urbanized society (see Nordau, *Entartung*). The Nazis appropriated his term for their own ends. See also Greenslade, *Degeneration*, for these effects beyond Germany.

7. See Voigt, "Bibliothek verbrannter Bücher." It nonetheless appears as if the Nazis initially attempted to capitalize on the success of *Grotesken* by giving some of their antisemitic films that designation, albeit distinctly marking it as a genre of the past—for instance, *Nur nicht weich werden, Susanne! Eine Groteske aus vergangener Zeit* (1935).

8. Panizza's paradoxical status is probably best exemplified by the fact that an entry in Ewers's *Führer durch die moderne Literatur*, honoring the three hundred most exceptional authors of modernism, claimed in the 1911 edition that the then institutionalized but very much alive author had died in 1909 (see 136). Ewers's epilogue to Panizza's oft-reprinted volume in the *Galerie der Phantasten* reiterates his assessment that Panizza was no longer well-known, though this text is generally full of criticism of Panizza. See Ewers, "Zum Epilog," 376.

9. While Panizza and Kafka both passed away in the early 1920s (and Bierbaum, Busch, Morgenstern, Scheerbart, Schmitz, and Wedekind in the decade before them), an entire generation of *Grotesken* writers perished during and after the Nazi dictatorship (many of them in exile, which severely limited their careers years before and after the Second World War, while others died by suicide or were murdered directly by the Nazis). The following somber list exemplifies this development and is perhaps the only place that groups these names together in order to outline the corpus and larger authorial network of the genre of *die Groteske*: Rieß († 1931), Forster-Larrinaga († 1932), Meyrink († 1932), Ernst († 1933), Kyber († 1933), Landsberger († 1933), Ringelnatz († 1934), Tucholsky († 1935), Kraus († 1936), Friedell († 1938), C. Einstein († 1940), Reiss († 1941), Mongré († 1942), Sternheim († 1942), Ewers († 1943), Adler († 1946), Friedlaender († 1946), Strobl († 1946), von Delius († 1946), Madsack († 1949), Ehrenstein († 1950), H. Mann († 1950), Herzmanovsky-Orlando († 1954), Freksa († 1955), Goetz († 1955), Th. Mann († 1955), and Polgar († 1955). Some of these authors were marginalized to such a degree that the year of their death is now unknown and information about them is nearly impossible to find, such as Curt Schawaller and Ferdinand Timpe.

10. Cited in full in the introduction and translated in Scholem, *Walter Benjamin: Story of a Friendship*, 58. Postwar *Grotesken*, such as Günther Neumann's *Ich war Hitlers Schnurrbart* (1950), which ties into the prewar tradition with references to Friedlaender and the cabaret, remain outliers. Kafka's writing, though burned by the Nazis, managed to carry some of the characteristics of *Grotesken* successfully into a postwar world, yet it lost its humorous effect in favor of the more existential aspects of the alienating experiences it addresses. Perhaps precisely because it felt appropriate after the Holocaust, the grotesque in the Kafkaesque vein was also successful on the German stage after the Second World War, in the works of, for instance, Bertolt Brecht, Friedrich Dürrenmatt, and Samuel Beckett. The label *Groteske* can still occasionally be found attached to short prose, feuilleton, cabaret, and theater in the second half of the twentieth century.

11. Haderlev, "Mynona," 39.

12. Richard Rieß is occasionally spelled Riess or misspelled Reiss in the few available sources about him. While these authors all explicitly called their short prose *Grotesken*, most of them produced only a few texts of this kind. Some, like Landsberger, also produced plays and musical pieces with that title. This list does not include the countless texts by authors that use the adjective *grotesk* in their subtitles at the time, though many of them would qualify for the genre, e.g., Arnold Hahn, *Die Bibse: Groteske Satiren* (1921) and Ferdinand Timpe, *Wendepunkte: Vier groteske Striche* (1921). More well-known authors of the time, such as Paul Adler, Carl Einstein, Paul Ernst, Herbert Eulenberg, Max Halbe, Alfred Kubin, Karl Kraus, the brothers Mann, Gustav Meyrink, Leo Perutz, Karl Hans Strobl, etc., did not use this generic label, though many of their texts would warrant it and have been called *Grotesken* by some, while others subsume the grotesque in their novellas/narratives, novels, and plays under a return to the fantastic. See Wünsch, *Fantastische Literatur*, 69–70.

13. See Fuß, *Das Groteske*, 30–32. This marginalization is mirrored in the aesthetic origins of the grotesque as plant-inspired ornaments (arabesques) that served to frame "actual" art, which seems to live on in the consideration of *Grotesken* in literature as a "low" and marginalized art form. See, for instance, Goethe's discussion of the arabesque in "Von Arabesken (1789)." See also Silhouette, "Von den Grottesken zum Grotesken."

14. On the notion of *Trivialliteratur* in respect to the best-selling author Ewers, see particularly the introduction to Murnane and Godel, *Zwischen Popularisierung und Ästhetisierung*. For more on the history of the cabaret, see Jelavich, *Berlin Cabaret*.

15. Deleuze and Guattari, *Kafka*. On the origin of this idea in Kafka's own work, see also Lowell, "Kafka on Minor Literature." Though not all four authors lived under conditions that were as multilingual and politically charged as Kafka's in respect to language, their texts make use of many other languages and dialects, and they take

part in the active de- and reconstruction of German itself. All three other authors were at least bilingual: Ewers lived in the US during the First World War, published in English, and traveled widely. Both Friedlaender and Panizza spent years in exile in Paris, and their texts also evidence their fluency in English. Later in life, Panizza only communicated in French and translated from Latin, and he was also fluent in his father's native Italian. "Panizza's ability to quote everything in its original language and immediately translate it perfectly and comment on it spontaneously caused astonishment and admiration everywhere." Ruch, "Wer ist Oskar Panizza?," ix.

3. A Literary Network of the Marginalized

1. See Kellermann, *Propaganda der Tat*.

2. See exemplarily Panizza's *Imperjalja* (including Kistner, "Der wackelnde Thron"; Meilicke, *Paranoia und technisches Bild*, and "Fotografie und 'Pseudizität'"; and Wurich, "Der halluzinierte Kaiser"); and Panizza, *Neues aus dem Hexenkessel*, 208. Panizza's notebooks profess anarchist sympathies (see Bauer, *Oskar Panizza*, 279), and his article "Mania anarchista progressiva" both embraces and pokes fun at the designation, as it gives satirical advice for "how princely personalities can most effectively protect themselves from anarchist attacks" (37; see also Jäger, "Flucht nach vorn"). The milieu of the cabaret, which was home to Ewers's and Friedlaender's *Grotesken*, engaged in similar criticism, be it of Kaiser Wilhelm II or, later, the Weimar Republic.

3. Max Stirner is the pseudonym of Johann Kaspar Schmidt. The name Stirner invokes the German idiom *jemandem die Stirn bieten*, that is, to stand up to or defy somebody, or, to preserve the metaphor of the forehead (*Stirn*), to make head against someone.

4. The pronounced similarities between the ideas of Stirner and Nietzsche were noted already during the latter's lifetime, though there has been much speculation about the reasons (see Brobjer's "Possible Solution to the Stirner-Nietzsche-Question"). While Nietzsche, the "Groteskkünstler" (grotesque artist, as Thomas Mann put it in "Betrachtungen eines Unpolitischen," 347), figures centrally for German literary modernism and his ideas resonate with many of the preoccupations of *Grotesken* (e.g., "madness"), the four authors took greatly varying positions vis-à-vis his work.

5. The book was printed with the date of the year prior, 1844, to confuse the Prussian censors, but it was immediately confiscated nonetheless. Panizza's short prison diary mentions that someone sent him the book (see "Ein Jahr Gefängnis," in *Das Liebeskonzil*, 172–73), and around the same time, he dedicated his only philosophical text to Stirner's memory (see "Der Illusionismus und Die Rettung der Persönlichkeit," in Panizza, *Werke*, 7:5–76; also Smiljanić, "Nachwort"; and Hertz, "Pathologie"). For a more detailed explication of Panizza's stance on Stirner, see Bauer, *Oskar Panizza*, 53; and Düsterberg, *"Die gedrukte Freiheit"*, 85–91.

6. Mackay, *Max Stirner*.

7. Much of his writing and about half of his *Grotesken* (e.g., the 1891 "Der Stationsberg" and the following from 1893: "Die Kirche von Zinsblech," "Das Wirtshaus zur Dreifaltigkeit," "Pastor Johannes," and "Die Wallfahrt nach Andechs") engage critically with religious themes, especially the Catholic Church. As a child, Panizza was at the center of the so-called *Bad Kissinger Konfessionsstreit* (Denomination Disagreement of Bad Kissingen). His Huguenot mother and Catholic father initially raised their children Catholic, but on his deathbed, Panizza's father granted his wife permission to give their children the Protestant upbringing he had originally promised and that had been subject of many fights and broken agreements over the years. A local priest took the issue to court, claiming that the father had not been in his right mind. During the drawn-out proceedings, Panizza's mother moved her children repeatedly to relatives in Protestant German states, appealed unsuccessfully to the Bavarian king, and refused to pay fines or comply with multiple verdicts. The accompanying press coverage only fueled the mother's religious zeal, which she expressed later in life in her own writing under the pseudonym Siona. Ultimately, Oskar attended a Pietist school, but he disappointed his mother's hopes that he might study theology. The Catholic Church and organized religion are consistently depicted negatively in Panizza's writing (in *Grotesken* and beyond), and while his position vis-à-vis religion can at times appear contradictory, Soceanu argues that, after his earlier identification with Protestantism, he became a "Radikalaufklärer" (radical enlightener) rather than someone who merely wanted to shock audiences with blasphemy (see "Oskar Panizza's Kampf um den Glauben," 142). See also Bauer, *Oskar Panizza*, 72–91; and Deschner, "Oskar Panizza."

8. See "Die Menschenfabrik" (1890), "Eine Mondgeschichte" (1890), and "Indianer-Gedanken" (1893).

9. Analogous to modernist artist communities in Berlin and Vienna around 1900, the *Münchner Moderne* is usually associated with Michael Georg Conrad (1846–1926), since he founded the influential though small and short-lived *Gesellschaft für modernes Leben* (Society for Modern Life, 1890–1893), which first brought together many Munich modernists, Panizza included, over their shared support of naturalism. The society's legacy lived on in several important Munich-based journals, such as *Moderne Blätter, Die Gesellschaft, Simplicissimus,* and *Jugend.* Panizza left Munich after his one-year censorship prison sentence, which, as his diary and subsequent writing show, seemed to have broken the once social man's spirit (see Panizza, *Abschied von München*; Bauer, *Oskar Panizza*, 249–50; and diary extracts printed in Panizza, *Das Liebeskonzil,* 169–86).

10. See Bauer, *Oskar Panizza*, 267–76; Düsterberg, *"Die gedrukte Freiheit"*, 87.

11. Panizza to Michael Georg Conrad on November 22, 1898, quoted in Panizza, *Neues aus dem Hexenkessel,* 208.

12. In his memories of Panizza, Ruch confirms the impact of this library, which is also apparent from the author's oeuvre: "His stupendous erudition and his unusual memory seemed astounding. He was a great reference book that one never asked in vain for information. He peppered his conversations with numerous examples from the literature of all countries and times" (ix). For the fate of Panizza's books, see Bauer, *Oskar Panizza*, 41–42; and Hildebrandt, "Oskar Panizza als Bibliophile."

13. Ruch, "Wer ist Oskar Panizza?," ix.

14. Benjamin, "E. T. A. Hoffmann und Oskar Panizza," 648; Tucholsky, "Oskar Panizza"; Fontane in a letter to Maximilian Harden on July 22, 1895, quoted in *Schriften zur Literatur*, 299.

15. Bierbaum, "Oskar Panizza," 982.

16. Only some of Panizza's texts have seen sporadic republication since the 1960s (see Bauer, *Oskar Panizza*, 35–48; and Stobbe, *Oskar Panizzas literarische Tätigkeit*), and an edition of his collected works by Peter Staengle and Günther Emig is appearing now, a century after his death, at merely one hundred copies per volume (see Panizza, *Werke*). A list of academic works about Oskar Panizza is consequently relatively short (for a bibliographic overview, see Bauer and Düsterberg, *Oskar Panizza*; Bauer, *Oskar Panizza*; Brown, *Oskar Panizza and* The Love Council; or, most recently, Jacobs, Klarić, and Thurn, "Auswahlbibliografie"). Those scholars who devoted their research to Panizza's writing rather than prioritizing his admittedly fascinating biography have predominantly focused on *Das Liebeskonzil*. Mostly compiled in the 1980s and early 1990s, as the play's focus on syphilis resonated with the HIV/AIDS epidemic (see also Jelavich, "Pan(dem)izza"), many of these research results have not been systematically revisited (with the exception of a 2021 lecture series on the one hundredth anniversary of Panizza's death; see https://sites.arizona.edu/panizza/), and comprehensive studies of many major aspects of Oskar Panizza's oeuvre have yet to be undertaken. Only a few individual texts from the corpus of Panizza's *Grotesken* in this book have been written about in more depth, and no more than two of his *Grotesken* have been translated into English (one via the French in a publication by Foucault and both featured in section 4 of this book).

17. A 1982 film version of the play, directed by Werner Schroeter, had to be withdrawn from theaters in Austria in 1985 for blasphemy once more—a verdict that was upheld by the European Court of Human Rights in 1994, a century after the first censorship trial. To date, this verdict has only been overturned in Switzerland, the original place of publication, in 1998. See Brown, "The Continuing Trials of Oskar Panizza"; Kuhlbrodt, "Tiroler Zensur"; and Berling, *Liebeskonzil*.

18. See Panizza, "Die Selbstbiographie," reprinted in Boeser, *Der Fall*, 8–14, here 14. He also notes that he had been rejected when he tried to commit himself earlier. The above "autobiography" was written in November 1904 in an abbreviated, diagnostic style and in the third person about the *Pazjent* (idiosyncratic spelling of

Patient) Panizza. It served as Panizza's explanation in the process of having himself committed, and it shows traces of both of his professional personas, the literary and the medical.

19. As a psychiatrist, Panizza knew just what to say to be admitted (see Bauer, *Oskar Panizza*, 303). One of the expert reports by Dr. Fritz Ungemach from December 6, 1904, quotes Panizza's words, which suggest a calculated decision: "Nobody wants to be declared mentally ill [*geistig krank*]. I considered myself mentally healthy but perceived the advantage that resulted from being declared mentally ill" (reprinted in Bauer, *Oskar Panizza*, 307). This resonates with a line in Panizza's 1897 *Dialoge im Geiste Huttens* (published after his devastating censorship prison sentence): "When someone utters a free thought out loud these days, he is limited to three choices: insane asylum, prison, or escape. If he admits madness openly, the district physician will turn a blind eye and—he disappears" (52).

20. The phrase "zur Diagnose der politischen Gehirnerkrankung" is part of the subtitle of Panizza, *Die kriminelle Psychose*, which reprints the text, whose original subtitle reads *Anleitung um die vom Gericht für notwendig erkanten Geisteskrankheiten psichjatrisch zu eruïren und wissenschaftlich festzustellen. Für Ärzte, Laien, Juristen, Vormünder, Verwaltungsbeamte, Minister etc.* (Instructions for the psychiatric determination and scientific discovery of those mental illnesses that the courts consider necessary. For doctors, laymen, jurists, guardians, administrative officials, ministers, etc.).

21. Panizza, "Psichopatia criminalis," in *Werke* 9:137–95, here 162. This diagnosis will be discussed in more detail in the context of institutionalization in the next section of this book. See also Bauer, *Oskar Panizza*, 52; Hertz, "Pathologie"; Steinlechner, *Fallgeschichten*; and Lang, "'Writing Back.'"

22. The debate about Oskar Panizza's alleged mental illness has been ongoing since his institutionalization. Since almost no writing from his sixteen years in the sanatorium exists, opinions about his state of mind are based on accounts of visiting friends and the institution's pastor, Friedrich Lippert, who became his confidant during his time in prison, though Bauer (*Oskar Panizza*, 45–48) gives reason to doubt the endurance of the friendship. See Lippert, *In Memoriam Oskar Panizza*; Friedrich-Wilhelm Kantzenbach, "Der Dichter Oskar Panizza"; Bauer, *Oskar Panizza*, 301–9; Lichti, *Der letzte Ausweg in die Freiheit*; Schneider, "Die Paranoia der Dichter"; and Müller, *Der Pazjent als Psichater*.

23. Panizza's family, particularly his devoutly religious mother Mathilde, had long hoped to contain her son's blasphemy and criticism of the Catholic Church. Together with lawyer Josef Popp, she motioned to have Panizza declared incompetent, and Popp, who had called Panizza insane in the press in the earlier context of Panizza's 1895 trial, became his legal guardian (see Bauer, *Oskar Panizza*, 43–45 and 307). Panizza had predicted this; a letter to Paul Ostermaier on September 20, 1900,

says, "The government has apparently no idea how my mother, and influenced by her, the entire family, has used the fact of the confiscation [of his estate] to wrestle me to the ground. My mother intends, because I attacked her protestant ideal, the German Kaiser, nothing less but to have me committed to an asylum!! . . ." (Panizza, *Neues aus dem Hexenkessel*, 236). The reasons for forcibly putting him under guardianship would be humorous, had they not been uttered in seriousness: According to Dr. Ungemach's report, Panizza had shown his insanity by "giving in to the direction of the so-called modernists in extreme ways" (quoted in Bauer, *Oskar Panizza*, 297) and by relinquishing his German citizenship. Moreover, his self-diagnosis with *Psichopatia criminalis* was taken seriously enough to be interpreted as a sign of insanity.

24. "Ein Poet, der umsunst gelebt hat" (manuscript from 1904, quoted in Bauer, *Oskar Panizza*, 309; see also Bauer, *Oskar Panizza*, 307; and Panizza, *Neues aus dem Hexenkessel*, 236). In Panizza scholarship, this act of defiance, which is also a form of self-censorship, has often been connected with a line spoken by the devil in *Das Liebeskonzil* that appears right after he asks for the uninhibited publication and circulation of his books: "If someone is thinking and is no longer allowed to communicate his thoughts to others, that's the ghastliest torture of all" (Brown, *Oskar Panizza and The Love Council*, 52).

25. See, for instance, the trial surrounding the poem cycle *Von der goldenen Kätie* (see Kugel, *Der Unverantwortliche*, 59) or his cabaret work (70). For the fainting incident, see 104. Ewers was even briefly suspected of being a serial killer (292).

26. Kugel's detailed biography gives evidence for Ewers's engagement with Stirner and Nietzsche as early as age sixteen in *Der Unverantwortliche*, 19. For Wilde, see 38.

27. He also produced a drama about a father's attraction to his son, called *Enterbt: Drama in vier Akten* (1903/1904), and a novella about same-sex love by the title "Armer Junge," first published in the journal *Der Eigene* in 1899. Ewers's sexual orientation has been subject of much speculation, but the evidence only points to frequent sexual escapades with women (see Kugel, *Der Unverantwortliche*, 82–85 and 255). Some of this speculation (which entangles it with that about his political convictions) is due to his proximity to the Nazi *Sturmabteilung* (SA), several leaders of which lived their same-sex attraction openly (see 82–84, 255, 296–97, 356, and 360).

28. *Lebensreform* is a turn-of-the-century movement that emphasized a return to nature through nudism (which Ewers's Capri pictures in the appendix of Kugel's *Der Unverantwortliche* demonstrate) and sexual liberation, alternative medicine and refusal of vaccinations, healthy eating (understood as raw, vegan/vegetarian, and organic diets), and—very much unlike Ewers, who is frequently depicted with his opium pipe (see Kugel)—abstention from drugs and alcohol. See also Carstensen and Schmid, *Literatur der Lebensreform*.

29. See Kugel, *Der Unverantwortliche*, 40–41, 90 ("Rausch und Kunst"), 107–8, 253, and 411.

30. For his time with the cabaret, see Kugel, *Der Unverantwortliche*, 63–65. Kugel also details Ewers's journeys across Europe, both American continents, Australia, China, India, and many other Southeast Asian nations. Ewers's travels were mainly funded by his journalistic work and the sponsorship of a passenger ship company, which he mentioned favorably in his feuilletons in return. On the racism in his travel reports, see 112–14.

31. See Kugel, *Der Unverantwortliche*, 184–86; and Loew, *Special Effects and German Silent Film*. *Der Student von Prag* was remade twice during his lifetime, in 1926 and 1935.

32. In "Zum Epilog," Ewers critically remarks on the difficulties of publishing Panizza (see 378)—both because of Panizza's idiosyncratic language use and because of the refusal of his family that would also stifle the attempts of Hermann Croissant, Gustav Landauer, Emil Tuchmann, Kurt Tucholsky, Walther von Hollander, Leo Weismantel, and Ewers himself to reproduce more of Panizza's writing or his collected works in the 1910s and 1920s. See Panizza, *Das Rothe Haus*, 16; Kugel, *Der Unverantwortliche*, 200; Bauer, *Oskar Panizza*, 35–41; Tuchmann, "Die Erben Panizzas vereiteln die Herausgabe des Nachlasses"; and Galle, "Oskar Panizza," 61. As section 2 of this book demonstrates, Ewers was influenced by Panizza in many ways, even though his criticism of Panizza seems to indicate otherwise.

33. See Kugel, *Der Unverantwortliche*, 216–18.

34. See Kugel, *Der Unverantwortliche*, 40–42 and 263–65.

35. See Kugel, *Der Unverantwortliche*, 302–4, 368, and 399–400. Many of Ewers's political changes appear opportunistic. See Kugel's documentation of this attitude in reference to Kaiser Wilhelm II (215), Walther Rathenau (162 and 399), and Hitler (368).

36. "Der Jude ein Pionier des Deutschtums" made the case for a German Jewish *Kulturnation* and provoked a strong reaction at the time (see Kugel, *Der Unverantwortliche*, 398–99). Ewers continued to write about contentious themes, such as gender-affirming surgery in *Fundvogel: Die Geschichte einer Wandlung* (1928). For his stance on Rathenau, see Kugel, 262–63. For attempts to expel Ewers from the Nazi Party, see 305, 321–22, and 331–32.

37. Horst Wessel was an SA man who was shot by a member of the Communist Party and subsequently stylized into a martyr of the Nazi movement. The strong embellishing influence of the Wessel family left Ewers severely frustrated with the project (see Kugel, *Der Unverantwortliche*, 324).

38. For the "putsch," which was a euphemistic name for the SS-run, simultaneous assassination of the chief of the SA, Ernst Röhm, and other people who had developed ideological and power-political differences with some of Hitler's directives, see Kugel, *Der Unverantwortliche*, 356. See 357–58 for the subsequent destruction of Ewers's livelihood.

39. He also managed to find a protected workplace for the Jewish woman with whom he had a relationship for the last four years of his life. See Kugel, *Der Unverantwortliche*, 362–63, 364–65, 367–68, and 377. Compared to his earlier writing, these later satires appear careful, which speaks to Ewers's awareness of his unsafe position. On Ewers's complicated stance toward Jews, Nazis, and his racism, see 398–99. Despite the many contradictions, there are multiple parallels between Ewers's life and another well-known *Grotesken* author of the time, Hans Reimann, who used "Hanns Heinz Vampir" as one of his pseudonyms.

40. Ewers's most successful novel, *Alraune* (1911, German word for mandrake, but translated as *Alraune* into English, as it is also the name of the protagonist, with two film versions in 1918 and one each in 1919, 1928, 1930, and 1952), was an immediate bestseller and is the only of Ewers's novels still well-known today. See Ashkenazi, *Weimar Film*; Janzen, *Media, Modernity and Dynamic Plants*; Kugel, *Der Unverantwortliche*, 165; Matzigkeit, *Literatur im Aufbruch*, 83; and Orich, "Artificial Aliens."

41. The contemporaries Ewers and Friedlaender knew many of the same people and one could read their work occasionally in the same publication, e.g., in the journal *Der Querschnitt* (1921–1936). A note in his autobiography indicates that Friedlaender even introduced a reading of Goethe's poetry by Ewers in Berlin (see Friedlaender/Mynona, *Ich*, 70). Since they (were) both identified with *Grotesken*, one might expect commonalities, yet on the contrary, each understood *Grotesken* and their function quite differently and used the genre to critique and satirize each other. Friedlaender particularly disliked the spiritualism Ewers reveled in (see Friedlaender/Mynona, *Grotesken*, 1:45), which comes out in some of his *Grotesken* with direct references to Ewers (see index of volume 2 of his *Grotesken* and Thiel, "Einleitung," 54–55). For instance, Ewers makes appearances as "the demonically squared Poe" (see "Im Bier-und Buchverlag G.m.b.H.: Für Leib und Seele," 1926) and "'Little Mandrake, the semi-world champion of eroticism.'— 'Called Poe-Poe [*Popo* is also a synonym for buttocks] here.'" ("Hab' Höhensonne im Herzen, sonst – ," 1928). With these references, Friedlaender criticizes the occult, violent, and erotic focus of Ewers's *Grotesken* that contrasts with his own emphasis on philosophical wordplay and laughter. Though as different as can be in many respects, the two authors were nonetheless influenced by several of the same writers and texts, and they shared a love for the cabaret and writing about the pursuit of women (see Kugel, *Der Unverantwortliche*, 82–84 and 255; and Friedlaender/Mynona, *Ich*).

42. I am spelling Friedlaender's name in accordance with his own rendering and the edition of his collected works (without the *Umlaut*), and I am using his given name instead of his pen name here and when discussing his literary texts to avoid confusion. For a discussion of his name and its versions, see Geerken, "Nachwort," 277. The publication of his collected works in a multivolume edition by the late

Hartmut Geerken and Detelf Thiel began in 2005 and is ongoing. The two volumes of *Grotesken* within his collected works contain 263 texts, though a few of these are drafts of the same work.

43. Review by Otto Best, quoted in Friedlaender/Mynona, *Grotesken*, 2:493–94, here 493. In the early 1910s, Friedlaender still had trouble finding publishers for his *Grotesken*, despite help from famous friends like Martin Buber (see Thiel, "Einleitung," 18–24), but with growing success, he produced more. His satirical style has been compared to anyone from Georg Christoph Lichtenberg to Heinrich Heine and Wilhelm Busch (see 17). After the Second World War, his contemporary Kurt Pinthus credited Friedlaender even with the creation of an entirely "new genre of literature [...] as a predecessor of Dadaism, surrealism, and especially today's literature of the absurd" in "Philosoph und Clown," n.p.

44. Friedlaender scholarship makes the "Kant and Clown" reference repeatedly without providing a source, but Kuxdorf (*Der Schriftsteller*, 3) locates it, for instance, in *Der Holzweg zurück oder Knackes Umgang mit Flöhen* (1931). For the performances of *Grotesken*, see Thiel, "Einleitung," 24–38, where Kafka is noted as an audience member (see 34). Friedlaender's foray into media like the radio is also an example of his keen interest in technology that renders some of his *Grotesken* veritable science fiction.

45. His *Grotesken* satirize Freud, e.g., *Nur für Herrschaften: Un-Freud-ige Grotesken* (Only for gentlemen: Un-Freud-ian/Un-joy-ful *Grotesken*, 1920) and *Das Eisenbahnglück oder der Anti-Freud* (The train luck or the anti-Freud, 1925), which is "dedicated to Professor S. Freud in Vienna with the most heartfelt 'I copulate, therefore I am!' [*Coeo, ergo sum!*]." For his criticism of organized religion, society, and other authors, see Thiel, "Einleitung," 47 and 52–57. Friedlaender also radically opposed militarism, racism, and any form of dictatorship (63–70).

46. See Kuxdorf, *Der Schriftsteller*, 2.

47. He founded both in 1919 with Anselm Ruest (pseudonym of Ernst Samuel, the brother of Friedlaender's brother-in-law). The journal is not to be confused with Ewers's activities for the gay journal *Der Eigene* that was also named after Stirner's book.

48. Friedlaender/Mynona, *Schöpferische Indifferenz*. See also Geerken, "Vorwort," 8–9; and Friedlaender, *Friedrich Nietzsche*.

49. See Kuxdorf, *Der Schriftsteller*, 70–71.

50. He even took his name literally as "peace-lands" and began to sign his letters from Paris as *Pax/Paixdespays* (see Kuxdorf, *Der Schriftsteller*, 87). His didactic impetus also shows in his schoolbook *Kant for Children*, published as *Kant für Kinder: Fragelehrbuch zum sittlichen Unterricht* in 1924.

51. Dodd, "The Case for a Political Reading," 131. Dodd provides a useful overview of approaches to Kafka as a political writer on the first pages.

Section II: The Vegetal

1. Panizza, "Das Verbrechen in Tavistock-Square," hereafter cited in the text as VTS. Ewers, "Die Petition" hereafter cited in the text as P. Also known as "Die Bittschrift."
2. For more details about *Das Liebeskonzil*, see the previous section.
3. Rather than the uniform concern to hide sex, rather than a general prudishness of language, what distinguishes these last three centuries is the variety, the wide dispersion of devices that were invented for speaking about it, for having it be spoken about, for inducing it to speak of itself, for listening, recording, transcribing, and redistributing what is said about it: around sex, a whole network of varying, specific, and coercive transpositions into discourse. Rather than a massive censorship, beginning with the verbal proprieties imposed by the Age of Reason, what was involved was a regulated and polymorphous incitement to discourse. (Foucault, *History of Sexuality*, 1:34)

4. The Crime in Tavistock-Square

1. See Panizza, "Die Selbstbiographie," in Boeser, *Der Fall*, 8–14, here 9; Bauer, *Oskar Panizza*, 172; and Jacobs, "'Verbrechen wider die Natur.'"
2. In Germany, a variety of formulations emerged from the Latin *vitium contra naturam*, ranging from "Laster wider die Natur" to "widernatürliche Unzucht" in the heading of the famous §175 of the German Criminal Code, which made "sodomy," meaning here both sex between men and with animals, a crime between 1871 and 1994 (see Beachy, *Gay Berlin*; Craft, *Another Kind of Love*; Sutton, *Sex between Body and Mind*; and Linge, *Queer Livability*). The term *crime against nature* is still used in social controversies today, such as the debate about marriage equality, in which many argue with ideas of naturalness. See, for instance, Haskell's "Nature's Case for Same-Sex Marriage," which quotes US chief justice Roy S. Moore calling a same-sex relationship "a crime against nature" in a custody trial. Biologist Haskell counters with a description of the diverse and varied concepts of sex and sexuality in nature, arguing that these are far from human binaries and morality. His turn to plant reproduction is one of many connections between this contemporary approach and the *Grotesken*, as will become apparent in this section. In addition to the plants and the subtext of same-sex desire, Panizza's story also contains a British police chief who becomes chief justice, like Roy Moore, because he persecutes sexual behaviors. Panizza's censorship trials took place in the same decade as Oscar Wilde's highly publicized 1895 London trials for "gross indecency with men" (on occasion of which the recent law graduate Ewers publicly spoke up for decriminalization)—showing that these topics characterized the period and that the case of the plants is always also about the sexual freedom of humans.

3. Kraus, "Oscar Panizza," 143.

4. See, for instance, intersex identity in "Ein skandalöser Fall," sex work and the police in "Ein criminelles Geschlecht," and fetishism in "Der Corsetten-Fritz" (all 1893); see also Lasse, "Sexualität."

5. See Bland and Doan, *Sexology Uncensored*; and Beachy, *Gay Berlin*. Early sexology publications were struggling with censorship too.

6. See Sutton, *Sex between Body and Mind*; and Linge, *Queer Livability*.

7. See Foucault, *History of Sexuality*, 1:51–74 and 105. See also Marcus, *The Other Victorians*.

8. For a history of the transgressive cultural function of masturbation, see Laqueur, *Solitary Sex*.

9. For a history of censorship, see Kanzog, "Literarische Zensur"; and Schneider, "Literarische Zensur."

10. In Catholic states like Bavaria, where Oskar Panizza stood trial, crimes committed in print had to be tried in public before a jury (*Schwurgericht*), which was often more inclined to act on charges of blasphemy but less so in cases of lèse-majesté or crimes against morality. Increasingly frustrated with low conviction rates, some prosecutors encouraged courts to declare defendants incompetent to stand trial to create the possibility of a permanent ban of the work without risking an acquittal. For the details of censorship processes and laws, see Stark, *Banned in Berlin*, 2–9 and 157.

11. See Kanzog, "Literarische Zensur"; Schneider, "Literarische Zensur"; and Stark, *Banned in Berlin*.

12. Mincing Lane is geographically and socially as far removed from the police station in "*Marylebone-Street*" (VTS, 109) as it is from Tavistock Square in London, where the plants pursue their pleasure near colleges, museums, and writers' residences (ranging from Charles Dickens to Virginia Woolf in the nineteenth and early twentieth centuries).

13. For the impact of biology on German thought of the time, see Craig and Linge, *Biological Discourses*; Gelderloos, *Biological Modernism*; and Nyhart, *Modern Nature*.

14. For a discussion of Panizza's multilingualism, well-stocked library, and ability to cite in the original from memory, see section 1.

15. See Foucault, *History of Sexuality*, 1:106.

16. While Ewers was married and quite vocal about sexual freedom, as the previous section discusses, there is no indication that Panizza was ever in love or in a relationship, though his expulsion from Zurich associates him with a female sex worker (see Brown, *Oskar Panizza and The Love Council*, 112). He states that he was infected with syphilis as a student, but this is debated by scholars as a potential stylization of artistic genius (resonating with the topic of *Das Liebeskonzil*) rather than

a real diagnosis or cause of his limp (see Panizza, "Die Selbstbiographie," reprinted in Boeser, *Der Fall*, 8–14, here 2; and Düsterberg, "Panizza, Oskar"). Kafka, who is central to the next section of the book, famously remained a bachelor as well, and his diary shows that he struggled with the idea of marriage and the negative impact he anticipated it to have on his writing, which resulted in multiple broken engagements. Many of his texts present bachelors (*Junggesellen*), such as "Das Unglück des Junggesellen" (1913) and "Blumfeld, ein älterer Junggeselle" (1915), whose name translates to "flower field" and who explicitly opts against animals or plants as companions. See also Corngold, "Kafka & Sex."

17. Most *Grotesken* authors in this book wrote other texts that point to the contemporary preoccupation with the plant–human relationship and include women: Hanns Heinz Ewers's *Alraune* (1911), though a novel, explores the myth of the mandrake-turned-woman (see also Janzen, *Media, Modernity, and Dynamic Plants*), and in his *Groteske* "Aus dem Tagebuch eines Orangenbaumes" (From the diary of an orange tree, 1907), a young fraternity brother in a mental institution is tasked to put in writing how a woman turned him into an orange tree, which invokes famous mythical predecessors of the idea of vegetal metamorphosis, such as Apollo and Daphne (see also Leskau, "Botanical Perversions"). In Friedlaender's "Die betrunkenen Blumen und der geflügelte Ottokar" (The drunk flowers and the winged Ottokar, 1911), "drunk flowers" turn into young women, and "Die vegetabilische Vaterschaft" (The vegetable paternity, 1919) tells the story of a rose bush fathering a daughter with a young woman (both in *Grotesken*, vol. 2). In *Le monstre, le singe et le fœtus*, Stead briefly comments on the exceptional status of Ewers's and Panizza's texts in respect to gender to support her claim for a specifically female representation of monstrous flowers at the time (see 259–60).

18. See Taiz and Taiz, *Flora Unveiled*; and Sandford, *Vegetal Sex* for a history of the discovery of sexual reproduction in plants and its cultural effects.

19. See Jacobs, "Plant Parenthood," "Phytopoetics," and "'These Lusting, Incestuous, Perverse Creatures'" for the concept of vegetal eroticism.

20. See Fara, *Sex, Botany and Empire*; and Schiebinger, *Nature's Body*, chap. 1.

21. In addition to the sources mentioned in the three previous notes, see Browne, "Botany for Gentlemen"; Connelly, "Flowery Porn"; George, *Botany, Sexuality, and Women's Writing*; and Shteir, *Cultivating Women, Cultivating Science*.

22. For a fuller version of this argument, see Jacobs, "'These Lusting, Incestuous, Perverse Creatures.'" See also Mortimer-Sandilands and Erickson, *Queer Ecologies*; Heinemann, "Fucking Pansies"; Bondestam, "When the Plant Kingdom Became Queer"; and Linge, *Queer Livability*.

23. See Peterson, "Brain Fever."

24. The policemen tried to keep Jonathan from going to the chief by saying (in English with German translation in the original text): *"Don't! Don't! Don't! Tell us*

stories! Don't slander!.... Etwa: Um Gotteswillen, Freund, halt ein! Schwätz' keinen Unsinn! Hör' auf!...." (VTS, 114; .... Something along the lines of: For God's sake, friend, hold off! Don't talk nonsense! Stop!....). In more recent translations, the famous first sentence of Kafka's novel *Der Prozess* has been rendered as "Someone must have slandered Joseph K...." (*Trial*, 3). This word choice has led to an assumption that the protagonist might have slandered himself (see Agamben, "K"). Self-slander is a distinct possibility in this scenario as well. Jonathan might be reporting his own transgressions in the guise of a "story," as his colleagues say, about plants. Slander was also illegal under censorship law (see Stark, *Banned in Berlin*, 2), so his report constitutes a crime (just like "Das Verbrechen in Tavistock-Square" itself), not only because he describes aberrant sexual acts.

25. In the introduction to *Solitary Sex* (2003), Laqueur describes various ways of increasing the stigmatization of masturbation in the past—for example, by branding it as a pathological weakness or disease, which can be understood as either hereditary, in keeping with Darwinian ideas, or infectious, similar to the way Jonathan's speech is affected by what he has seen.

26. Regarding the relationship of Panizza's *Grotesken* to film, see Lieb, "Nachwort"; and Schmidt, "Ende der Vorstellung."

27. Panizza ridicules the police's flawed powers of deduction and limited investigative prowess also in "Ein criminelles Geschlecht" (1893, in Panizza, *Werke*, 4:29–47), in which a police commissioner (a pious bachelor who is in many ways like the police chief in this text) is tasked with arresting a group of perpetrators but does not know how to identify them. The government instructions are not explicit enough, and he tries to explain his directives to the narrator, a student of medicine similar to the narrator of "Das Verbrechen." Yet like Jonathan, he is unable to find the "right" words and fills page upon page with an extremely suggestive, halting description of the criminals and their crime (making references, for instance, to venereal disease). He even wonders whether the perpetrators are actually human (see 42). The conversation leads to the commissioner's mental breakdown, but when the narrator meets him several weeks later, the commissioner looks much better and proudly shows off a newspaper clipping that details the arrest of French sex workers, both men and women—the target of his search.

28. In *Grotesque Visions*, Haakenson shows that a turn-of-the-century emergence of scientific attempts to help audiences "learn to see" was met by avant-garde art's "grotesque vision" "to challenge not only the dissemination of science's supposed visual evidence but also the conflation of such an optical orientation with 'truth'" (19–20). The narrative's repeated emphasis on eyes and Jonathan's struggle with the "blinding lantern" (see also the following note) evokes the concept of "plant blindness" (Wandersee and Schussler, "Preventing Plant Blindness" and "Toward a Theory of Plant Blindness"), which is central to plant studies and describes cognitive,

evolutionary, and cultural reasons for the human lack of plant awareness (for critiques and alternatives to the ableist term, see McDonough MacKenzie et al., "We Do Not Want"; Parsley, "Plant Awareness Disparity"; see also Montgomery, *Lessons from Plants*; and Aloi, *Why Look at Plants*).

5. The Petition

1. The motif of damaged health caused by writing at night reoccurs in the story and recalls a Panizza manuscript from 1904 (L1227 "Für 'Petroleumdichter'" at the Literaturarchiv Monacensia Munich, published recently as Panizza, "Für 'Petroleumdichter'"; and contextualized in Jacobs, "Oskar Panizzas Manuskript") that plays with the terms *petroleum lights* (*Petroleumlichter*) and *petroleum poets* (*Petroleumdichter*), who are said to "reek of the lamp" to indicate that their late-night work is spoiling their writing. The importance of smell (the "unchaste" one of plants, and later that of dogs and people) increasingly challenges the human primacy of vision in subsequent chapters of this book, and the *Petroleumlichter/dichter* turn the aforementioned "blinding lantern" from Jonathan's unreliability as a witness into the unreliability of literary language.

2. See Trommer, *Natur im Kopf*, 194. See also the "Lippstädter Fall" (Lippstadt Case, 1879) concerning flower ecologist Hermann Müller who was caught up in a media frenzy over teaching Darwin and Haeckel. This case later inspired the satirical play *Der Probekandidat* (1900) by Max Dreyer. See also Daum, *Wissenschaftspopularisierung im 19. Jahrhundert*; and Sommerey, "'Illegal Science.'"

3. The priest's criticism seems to be modeled on the dramatizing language of the historical school censorship debates—for example, conservative *Reichstag* representative Wilhelm Joachim von Hammerstein addressing minister of education Adalbert Falk: "If it is allowed that Haeckel-Darwinism becomes part of the curriculum in our schools, if it is allowed to inoculate the adolescent pupils of our public educational institutions with materialism, then the education authorities are not doing their duty. And in that case, they are responsible if a generation is raised in our homeland whose creed will be atheism and nihilism and whose political opinion will be communism" (quoted in Blumberg, "Der 'Fall' Müller," 40).

4. See also Jacobs, "Pollen."

5. This extends to ever-higher ranks as the police chief was, in fact, recommended to the narrator by the state secretary of the ministry of justice in the very beginning of Panizza's story—a gesture that explicitly aims to establish these figures of authority as trustworthy, so that the reader's disappointment in them might be all the more profound.

6. Koschorke, "Schmutz," 3.

7. Panizza, "Das rothe Haus," 17. See also Schmiedebach, "Hirne."

8. Panizza, "Psichopatia criminalis," in *Werke* 9:137–95, here 149–50.

6. Why Plants?

1. Haeckel, *History of Creation*, 2:264.

2. "Oskar Panizza—'our own notorious writer of—obscene plays and satires—in banishment here in Paris. He is an alienist, a madman who studies the mad.' 'An anarchist [...] who believes all is permitted. [...] a fellow *poète maudit*, who is surprised by no human habit, and has studied them all—'" (Byatt, *Children's Book*, 270).

3. The gate itself is inspired by radiolara. See Proctor, "Architecture from the Cell-Soul." The idea of a "World's Fair" goes hand in hand with other colonial exploits of the time, such as plant hunters, who brought "exotic" specimens to European botanical gardens. In addition, an unprecedented burst of horticulture and the growing popularity of *Schrebergärten* (allotment gardens) and *Wandervereine* (rambling clubs) in the context of the *Lebensreform* (Life Reform) movement promoted ongoing interaction with nature and botanical knowledge.

4. For the opposite understanding of plants, one only needs to look to the contemporary field of plant studies, which shows that plants are active, intelligent, and, as many of the previously referenced sources in this chapter and my own work demonstrate, sexual. See exemplarily Gagliano, Ryan, and Vieira, *Language of Plants*; Hall, *Plants as Persons*; Mancuso and Viola, *Brilliant Green*; Marder, *Plant-Thinking*; and Pollan, "Intelligent Plant." For a literary take on plants in that vein, see exemplarily Jacobs, Kranz, and Nitzke, *Plant Poetics*; Kranz, Schwan, and Wittrock, *Floriographie*; Laist, *Plants and Literature*; McHugh, "Plants and Literature"; and Nitzke and Braunbeck, "Arboreal Imaginaries." For more information about plant studies as a field, see the bibliography of the Literary and Cultural Plant Studies Network at https://sites.arizona.edu/plants/bibliography/.

5. In contrast to the Latin roots of the vegetal vocabulary (*vegetabilis* = animating, *vegetare* = to enliven, *vegere* = to excite), it seems that this word family was influenced by medical and early psychological terminology concerning the nervous system (e.g., to vegetate) in the second half of the nineteenth century, possibly also in response to the debates surrounding vitalism (see Mitchell, *Experimental Life*). The first attested use of *vegetable* as "dull, uneventful, like a vegetable" can be found in 1854, and the clinical usage of *vegetative* as brain-dead or mentally inert is first documented in 1893—one year after Panizza wrote "Das Verbrechen in Tavistock-Square." In 1921, the expression was applied to individuals as "persons who lead a monotonous life" (*Online Etymology Dictionary*, s.v. "vegetable" and "vegetative").

6. For a cultural history of roses, see Jacobs, "Rose," and for the associations of flowers and other components of plants more broadly, see Jacobs, "Plant Parts."

7. For a history of concerns about vegetal eroticism since its beginnings in the eighteenth century, and for the discourses forming around tropes like flowers across the sciences and the arts, see Jacobs, "'These Lusting, Incestuous, Perverse Creatures.'"

8. This power is an example of what I call "phytopoetics," that is the impact of plants on the human imagination, which results in the making (*poiesis*) of texts, ranging from the literary examples in this section to the legislation that surrounded them. For a more detailed discussion of this term, see Jacobs, "Phytopoetics," and "'These Lusting, Incestuous, Perverse Creatures'"; as well as the introduction to Jacobs, Kranz, and Nitzke, *Plant Poetics*.

9. While the phytopoetic impact of plants on the human imagination draws on plant behavior and capabilities just as much as on the ways humans imagine plants to be and act, plants can of course also have a strong impact on mental processes in the form of medications and drugs, relating to the psychiatric context of the asylum.

Section III: The Animal

1. Tucholsky, "Der Prozeß," 383.

2. See also my previous engagement with these texts from various angles in Jacobs, "'Waren es etwa doch nicht Hunde?,'" "The Grammar of Zoopoetics," "Separation Anxiety," and "Nachwort."

3. Panizza, "Aus dem Tagebuch eines Hundes," hereafter cited in the text as TH. The text includes drawings by Reinhold Hoberg (1859–1932), whose works also appear in the journals associated with the Munich Moderns. These illustrations are comparable to Wilhelm Busch's style, and while worthy of analysis in their own right (especially when merging human and animal features), there is only room to mention them here when they provide additional context. Kafka, "Forschungen eines Hundes," hereafter cited in the text as FH. I translated the excerpts myself, rather literally, to account for original pronouns and punctuation, specific terms that are central to my argument, and particular stylistic means that make this text a *Groteske*. In doing so, I am indebted to the following two translations: Willa and Edwin Muir's "Investigations of a Dog" and Stanley Corngold's "Researches of a Dog."

4. Systematic censorship of the kind introduced in section 2 only applies to Panizza's text, but during his lifetime, Kafka reflected repeatedly on outward constraints on his literary production in Prague, and when he decided to read the manuscript of *In der Strafkolonie* publicly in Munich on November 10, 1916, for instance, he knowingly risked German censorship interference. The (political) shock value of the text and the evening of the reading is discussed in varying accounts, such as Pulver, "Spaziergang mit Franz Kafka"; Brod, *Über Franz Kafka*; and Born, *Franz Kafka*.

5. Hamilton, "Die Erziehung des Teufels," 84.

6. I am referring to the two canine narrators with typically "human" pronouns in English (i.e., he, him, his, and who rather than it and that) because it reflects the usage in the original texts (i.e., a dog's grammatical gender in German) and supports the acceptance of the cognitive and linguistic abilities of the canine narrators.

7. Nineteenth- and early twentieth-century experiments that attempted to teach dogs to communicate took a variety of shapes, such as *Wunderhund* (wonder dog) curiosities like the philosophizing terrier Rolf, who was one of the most prominent subjects of the flourishing *Neue Tierpsychologie* (New Animal Psychology), which was significantly impacted by Pavlov's turn-of-the-century behaviorist studies on dogs, or *Tiersprechschule Asra* (Animal Speech School Asra), which has been claimed to be a Nazi effort to breed an army of speaking super dogs. These dogs communicated through knock signals, but it has been shown that they reacted more to their trainer's gestures than speech commands. This nonetheless demonstrates an extraordinary degree of attunement to human behavior. See the "Clever Hans Fallacy" in Hearne, *Adam's Task*, 4–5; Bondeson, *Amazing Dogs*; von den Berg, "*Neue Tierpsychologie*"; and Moekel, *Mein Hund Rolf*. See also Ritvo, *Animal Estate*.

8. Walzel, "Neue Dichtung vom Tiere," 53. See also Lickart, "Hunde in der Literatur der Weimarer Republik." Literary examples of first-person canine narratives published in the years between Panizza's and Kafka's include Marie More Marsh's *Vic: The Autobiography of a Fox Terrier* (1892), Marshall Saunders's *Beautiful Joe: An Autobiography* (1893), Anatole France's "Riquet" (1901, as a chapter of *Monsieur Bergeret à Paris*) and "Meditations of Riquet" (1904), Mark Twain's "A Dog's Tale" (1903), Reginald Pelham Bolton's *The Autobiography of an Irish Terrier* (1904), Olive Evelyth Hurd Bragdon's *Pup: The Autobiography of a Greyhound* (1905), O. Henry's [William Sydney Porter] "Memoirs of a Yellow Dog" (1906), Esther M. Baxendale's *Yours with All My Heart: Her Own Story, as Told by the Beautiful Italian Gazelle-Hound Fairy* (1904) and *Fairy: The Autobiography of a Real Dog* (1907), Jacinto Benavente y Martínez's *New Dialogues of the Dogs* (1908), Miguel de Unamuno's *Mist* (1907/14) and "Berganza and Zapirón" (1909), Carrie Gates Niles Whitcomb's *The Autobiography of Jeremy L.: The Actor Dog* (1910), Barbara Blair's *The Journal of a Neglected Bulldog* (1911), Octave Mirbeau, *Dingo*, etc. This list could arguably be extended by a range of twentieth-century texts appearing shortly after Kafka's, for instance, Albert Payson Terhune's *Lad: A Dog* (1919), Mikhail Bulgakov's *The Heart of a Dog* (1925, censored until 1987), Sewell Collins's *The Rubáiyát of a Scotch Terrier* (1926), Virginia Woolf's *Flush* (1933), Italo Svevo's "Argo and His Master" (1934), etc., but the majority of these texts move away from the first-person narrative position so central to the cluster around 1900. Contemporaneous to the narratives around 1900 are also nonfiction texts such as Thomas Mann's *Herr und Hund* (1918).

9. Ziolkowski, "Talking Dogs," 118. See also Brown, *Homeless Dogs and Melancholy Apes*, 113–44; Kuzniar, *Melancholia's Dog*; Kohlhauer, "Wenn Hunde erzählen"; Neumann, "Der Blick des Anderen"; Prawer, "'Ein poetischer Hund'"; and Giardina, *Le parole del cane*.

10. See discussions about narrating animals in Jacobs, *Animal Narratology*; and Middelhoff et al., *Texts, Animals, Environments*.

11. See Pascal, *Kafka's Narrators*, 189; Harel, "Investigations of a Dog," 52, and *Kafka's Zoopoetics*, 109.

7. From the Diary of a Dog

1. The formats of Panizza's dog diary and Kafka's rather monologic canine investigations allow for the possibility of having no addressee other than the self. While the dogs can converse with other animals within the texts, each narrator addresses dogs directly and specifically only once, yet neither of these instances clearly designates them as the recipients of the narratives: see "ihr Hunde" (FH, 205; you dogs) and "Nun glaubt vielleicht Eins von Euch, Hündchen" (TH, 100; Now one of you, little dogs, might believe).

2. See Descartes, *Discourse on the Method*.

3. The title "Forschungen eines Hundes" was added by Brod for the posthumous 1931 publication and rendered as "investigations" in the Muir translation, until Corngold translated it as "Researches of a Dog." While *investigations* could pertain to a dog's activity of tracing scents, *research* has specifically human connotations, which highlights a deliberate juxtaposition of human and animal behavior inherent in the title and the text.

4. Derrida criticizes the notion of "the animal" as a homogenized construct in *The Animal That Therefore I Am* and instead suggests the term *animot*, which is a combination of *animaux*—animals—and *mot*—word—that makes visible the role of language in the construction of human self and animal other.

5. See Vroon, Amerongen, and de Vries, *Smell*.

6. The canine ability to instantly know, through scent, who one is, is a popular trope, for instance in Homer's *Odyssey*, where the dog Argos is the only one to recognize his disguised master Odysseus after his twenty-year absence. Knowing who one is, on a fundamental level, is also invoked in Levinas's account of Bobby, the dog that recognizes concentration camp prisoners as men despite their dehumanization (see "Name of a Dog").

7. See Aristotle, *De Anima*, II.1 and II.2.

8. While human reproduction can be decoupled from the traditional set of parents today, this was not possible at the time, but the self-pollination of plants in section 2 provides a possible inspiration for such a process. The notion of repetition embedded in this idea of the reproduction of the human species through an individual evokes the disproven biological theory of recapitulation, put succinctly by Haeckel in *Generelle Morphologie* (1866) as "ontogeny recapitulates phylogeny," which states that animals resemble their remote ancestors in their developmental stages from embryo to adult, thus representing millennia of evolution in one lifespan.

9. In reference to the Cartesian "animal machine," Agamben talks about "the anthropological machine" in *The Open*, which he describes as an "optical machine

constructed in a series of mirrors in which man, looking at himself, sees his own image always already deformed in the features of an ape" that facilitates his recognition of himself "in a non-man in order to be human" (26–27). The mirror is a prominent theme in psychoanalysis, especially in Lacan's work, but it also shows up in animal experiments that aim to prove subjectivity through self-recognition in a mirror (some animal species, like great apes, dolphins, and magpies, have passed this test, while dogs and cats fail). In respect to animals and language, Lacan "defines the animal by its lack of language thus impeding its experience of the mirror stage, the subject of signifier, etc." (Beaulieu, "Status of Animality," 72–73).

10. Descriptions of human communication as ineffective, while gestures and sounds prevail, are also a staple of colonial and racist encounters with unfamiliar languages. Darwin, for instance, writes about his arrival in Tierra del Fuego on the *Beagle* in 1832, "The language of these people, according to our notions, scarcely deserves to be called articulate." He goes on to describe their ability to imitate gestures, facial expressions, and sounds by saying, "They are excellent mimics [...] All savages appear to possess, to an uncommon degree, this power of mimicry" (*Narrative*, 229). Imitation, mimicry, and language learning will return at the end of this section in the discussion of Rotpeter and are central to the *Grotesken* about "Jewish assimilation" in the next section.

11. There is one other instance of a possible sexual nature later in the text. The description suggests violence, and it could be read as a scene of rape, murder, or a physical fight (see TH, 104–5).

12. On bachelors, sex workers, and Panizza's own complicated sexuality, see section 2 of this book and Brown, *Oskar Panizza and The Love Council*, 112.

13. See Jacobs and Seymour, "Asexual Ecologies."

14. The destabilization of gender roles and normative sexuality becomes much clearer when adding the context of Panizza's other *Grotesken*. Several texts that are published in 1893, a year after the dog's diary, focus explicitly on this topic: "Ein skandalöser Fall" critically recounts the public reaction to an intersex person and what is perceived as a same-sex relationship; "Der Corsetten-Fritz" tells the story of a young man with a fetish for corsets, which he takes to be an attractive species; and "Ein criminelles Geschlecht," which entails sex work and same-sex attraction, is prefaced by a sentence about Kaspar Hauser that applies equally to the dachshund: "Er wußte Nichts von den Geschlechts-Unterschieden der Menschen, und unterschied die Leute nur nach den Kleidern" (Panizza, *Werke*, 4:29–47, here 29; He knew nothing of the sex differences of human beings and distinguished people only according to their clothing).

15. See Derrida, *Animal*.

16. The *Groteske* "Ich möchte bellen" (I want to bark, 1920) by Friedlaender puts a particular spin on "becoming an other" in the context of humans, animals, sexuality,

and language: A young man wants to learn how to imitate animal sounds, particularly the barking of dogs. He only succeeds when he has intercourse for the first time. His orgasms give him access to all animal languages, which leaves his successful linguistic and sexual reproduction entirely in the realm of the nonhuman:

> Wer [. . .] will es ihm verübeln, daß er sich des Aktes möglichst oft als Mittels bediente, um beileibe nicht der Wollust, wohl aber der Wollust des Bellens, Wieherns, Summens, Iahens usw. zu frönen? Welchen Tierlaut er wählte, kam auf das Weib an, das ihm just unterlag; [. . .] heute [ist er] der wohlbestallte Vater von etlichen Mißgeburten, die zwar nicht sprechen, desto wundervoller aber heulen grunzen, quieken, quaken, vorzüglich aber bellen können[.] (Friedlaender/Mynona, "Ich möchte bellen," in *Grotesken*, 1:469–73, here 473)

> Who [. . .] would resent him for using the act as often as possible as a means of indulgence in, not lust, but the desire to bark, neigh, buzz, hee-haw, etc.? Which animal sound he chose was dependent on the woman succumbing to him at that moment; [. . .] today [he is] the well-appointed father of several monstrosities, which might not be able to speak, but so much the better grunt, squeal, quack, and bark most exquisitely.

Friedlaender also named one of his *Grotesken* collections *Für Hunde und andere Menschen* (For dogs and other humans, 1914), after one of his texts.

17. Man sollte nicht glauben, wie weit es diese Comödianten treiben! Komm ich da neulich mit meinem Herrn in ein fremdes Haus, wo ich schon früher war, und wo ein Kerl wohnte, der mir immer Bisquit gegeben. Schon als die Thüre geöffnet wurde, stunden zwei dort, denen Rotz und Thränen über's Gesicht liefen; und dabei ein Schneuzen und Augen-Verdrehen, daß es nimmer schön war. Dachte mir schon, daß wieder eine große Comödie los. Komm ich hinein, liegt der Kerl (der Bisquit-Mensch) nicht stocksteif in einem schwarz-lackirten Kasten, und verstellt sich, hält den Atem an, und rührt sich nicht. – Eine solche Comödie! Nun glaubt vielleicht Eins von Euch, Hündchen, der Lump wäre nach einiger Zeit aufgesprungen, hätte seinen Mit-Bein-Zeigern die Hand gegeben, und unter entsprechenden Knixen und Zahn-Entblößungen gesagt: Alles war nur Scherz, und, sie sollten zufrieden sein? Nein, der Kerl läßt den Kasten über sich zumachen, zuschrauben, die Stiege heruntertragen, und auf einen phantastischen Wagen mit zwei lahmen Pferden eine Stunde vor die Stadt hinaus spazieren fahren! – Welch ein Spaß! – (TH, 100)

You wouldn't believe how far these comedians go! The other day I go with my master to a different house, to which I have been before and in which lives a fellow who always gave me biscuits. Already when the door was opened, there were two standing there who had snot and tears running over their faces; and with it a sniffling and eye-rolling that was not nice no more. Thought already that this must be yet another comedy. I enter, and the fellow (the biscuit-man) is lying not rigid in a box that is painted black, and pretends, holds his breath and doesn't move.—Such a comedy! Now maybe one of you, little dogs, believes maybe the rascal might have jumped up after a little while, shaken hands with his fellow-leg-showers, and said with the appropriate bowing and exposing of teeth: Everything was just a joke, and they should be content? No, the fellow lets the box be closed over him, screwed shut, carried down the stairs, and driven around on a fantastical wagon with two lame horses to a place an hour outside of the city!—What a joke!—

18. See Fichte, *Grundlage der gesammten Wissenschaftslehre*.

19. Ffytche traces the development of the concept of the unconscious in German intellectual history from the 1800s to Freud in *Foundation of the Unconscious*.

20. Freud, "One of the Difficulties of Psycho-Analysis," 23, and "Eine Schwierigkeit der Psychoanalyse," 7.

8. Investigations/Researches of a Dog

1. For an overview, see Berg, "Forschungen eines Hundes."

2. For a similar interpretation, see Harel, "Investigations of a Dog," 52, which anticipates her larger project of rejecting the allegorical character of Kafka's animals in *Kafka's Zoopoetics* (see chap. 4, and for narrative unreliability in the text, 109–13). See also Wiehl, "Die Poetologie der Biologie"; and Jobst, "Pawlow, Uexküll, Kafka," who both approach the perspectives in the text with the help of Jakob von Uexküll's concept of "Umwelt."

3. The notion of *Anrufung* or interpellation (see the *Hundeanruf*, the call of/by/to dogs, in the *Musikhunde* scene) is a central concept in Lacanian and Althusserian theory that goes back to Fichte's concept of *Aufforderung* (summons). Althusser describes how interpellation by an other constructs the subject through language in "Ideology and Ideological State Apparatuses."

4. Exposing their stomach and reproductive organs can be a sign of defeat or trust in dogs (see Horowitz, *Inside of a Dog*, 110). While standing upright is usually considered an evolutionary advantage of humans, it also constitutes a unique vulnerability that entails the loss of speed and other qualities. See Darwin's formulation of this evolutionary change of posture in *Descent of Man*, vol. 1, chap. 2. See also Gehlen's concept of the human as *Mängelwesen* (flawed being) that is based on a physical and morphological inferiority to animals in *Der Mensch*.

5. Kafka, *In der Strafkolonie*, 6.

6. In Panizza's dog diary, only humans can sin. The narrator says about the dead dog: "Hat vielleicht mein Kamerad auch gesündigt wie die Menschen? Aber das kann er ja nicht" (TH, 115; Did my friend maybe sin like the humans? But he can't do that).

7. See Freud, *Das Unbehagen in der Kultur*, sec. 4. The ties of smelling to sexuality are particularly prevalent in the work of Freud's mentor, ear-nose-throat doctor Wilhelm Fließ. The upright posture of the *Musikhunde* also calls up Freud's account

of the *Wolfsmann*, a patient who dreamed of an encounter with several threatening wolves who looked more "like dogs," which Freud interpreted as a representation of the patient's suppressed trauma of having witnessed a primal scene—that is, his parents having "doggy style" sex. While the source of the canine narrator's trauma is clearly erotic, his inability to communicate in this scene of silent witnessing is extremely suggestive and renders the text itself a form of talking cure. Freud, "From the History of an Infantile Neurosis."

8. Zimmer also interprets *Lufthunger* as his research drive (see *Leerkörper*, 171).

9. See Nägele, "I Don't Want to Know That I Know." The term *Lufthunde* and the unmoored investigations of the dog resonate with the Yiddish *luftmentsh*, whose origin can be traced back to Max Nordau (at the Fifth Zionist Congress in Basel in 1901) and is sometimes translated as "airhead" in English today. According to Aschheim in *Brothers and Strangers*,

> Today it has come to mean a kind of spiritual, rootless, intellectual figure, but this is not the meaning that Nordau originally gave to it. The luftmensch was a specifically East European Jewish phenomenon. *Luftmenschen* were an entire class of grown, tolerably healthy men who were unemployed and wandered around in the hope of obtaining a piece of bread by the end of the day. Nordau was careful to distinguish the luftmensch from other marginal and itinerant social types such as the English loafer and the Neopolitan *lazzerone*. Unlike them, the luftmensch was honest and able to work but simply lacked the opportunity. The Jews of the ghetto had become a *Luftvolk*—they had no capital for the present and no reserves for the morrow. (87)

10. In *Hunger Artist*, Ellmann has made a connection between self-starvation and increasing loquacity in respect to Kafka's dog.

11. The search for the origin of food is one of the central concerns of the canine researches throughout Kafka's story, but from the beginning, the narrator describes himself as "zu wenig um Nahrung besorgt" (FH, 170; too little concerned with sustenance) in comparison to other dogs, though scents tempt him repeatedly. According to the text, he is breaking physical and metaphysical laws with his hunger experiment: going against the powerful urge to eat goes against the law of his *Hundenatur* or canine nature (see FH, 202) not only because it suppresses his instinct of self-preservation but also because there is a canine prohibition against starvation that is laid out like Talmudic commentary (see FH, 201–3). While all the dogs in Kafka's text are skinny or gaunt (*mager*), Panizza's dog is told to abandon philosophy for the sake of food by a fat dog who is reminiscent of the police-chief-turned-fat-judge in the plant section (see TH, 78–79 and 90). At the end of Panizza's text, the dog attempts to feed the deceased dog a piece of juicy meat to bring him back to life, but when this fails, his own hunger subsides as he realizes his mortality. Just like hunger, silence is associated with death in Kafka's narrative (see FH, 174–75 and 204–5), as it was for Panizza's dachshund.

12. The connection of physical hunger and sexual hunger (i.e., the urge for self-preservation and the libidinal drive toward self-reproduction) is a familiar analogy in the Freudian oeuvre. "Hunger and love are popularly distinguished as the representatives of the instincts which ensure self-preservation and propagation respectively. In acknowledging this obvious division, we distinguish in Psycho-Analysis also between instincts of self-preservation or Ego-tendencies on the one hand, and sexual impulses on the other. We call the mental aspect of the sexual instinct *Libido* (sexual hunger), this being analogous to hunger, desire for power, etc. in the sphere of the Ego-tendencies" (Freud, "One of the Difficulties," 17).

13. This is not the only time that hunger is "speaking," if you will, as the dog describes hearing noises from his belly (see FH, 203). However, noise (*Lärm*) and music (*Musik*) often, though not always, coexist with silence in the text, pointing to its dual meaning as a generalized absence of sound (more likely *Ruhe, Stille* in German) or someone's lack of response (*Schweigen*).

9. Why Dogs?

1. See, for instance, Brown, *Oskar Panizza and The Love Council*, 89; Bauer, *Oskar Panizza*, 71; Binder, *Kafka-Kommentar*, 263; Schneider, "Kafkas Tiere und das Unmögliche"; and Fingerhut, *Die Funktion der Tierfiguren*.

2. Quoted, for instance, in Düsterberg, *"Die gedrukte Freiheit"*, 30; and Bauer, *Oskar Panizza*, 71. Bauer additionally details the figure of "the animal" in Panizza's oeuvre (100–105).

3. See, exemplarily, Brown, *Oskar Panizza and The Love Council*, 51 and 89.

4. Both reprinted in Bauer, *Oskar Panizza*, 265.

5. Kafka, *Proceß*, 241, and *Trial*, 231. During Panizza's *Liebeskonzil* censorship trial, the jury is said to have deliberated on the author's sentence by saying, "Wenn der Hund in Niederbayern verhandelt würde – der käm' nicht lebendig vom Platz!" (quoted in Ewers, "Zum Epilog," 379; If that dog had gone to trial in Lower Bavaria—he wouldn't have gotten away alive!).

6. See, exemplarily, Geller, *Bestiarium Judaicum*; Harel, *Kafka's Zoopoetics*; Pines, *The Infrahuman*; and Geier, *Kafka's Nonhuman Form*. To see all appearances of dogs in Kafka's writing, refer to Yarri, "Index to Kafka's Use of Creatures," 280. Kafka's letters also demonstrate the versatility of the image, as they contain *arme Hunde* (poor dogs); *Höllenhunde* (hell hounds); *Jagdhunde* (hunting dogs); *Lumpenhunde* (rascals); *innere Hunde* (inner dogs/demons); and the image of being eaten piecemeal by a dog as if a roast (see Franz Kafka, *Briefe*). Despite high numbers of dog ownership in German-speaking countries across history, many German-language dog metaphors are coined pejoratively, such as *auf den Hund kommen/vor die Hunde gehen* (to go to the dogs), *Hundeleben* (a dog's life), *hündisch* (cowardly, excessively obedient), *Hundsfott* (scoundrel), etc. In Jewish culture, the keeping of dogs as pets was considered a

goyishe naches (gentile pleasure) for the longest time, and dogs carried largely negative associations because of their use in the persecution of Jews and, figuratively, as antisemitic insults (Ackerman-Lieberman and Zalashik, *A Jew's Best Friend?*, 5).

7. Kafka, *Nachgelassene Schriften*, 36–37 and 114–15 (it appears twice in Kafka's manuscripts) and translated in Robertson, "Kafka as Anti-Christian," 112. In *Sünden-Fälle*, Möbus notes that the second appearance of the aphorism in Kafka's notebooks is in the context of human sexuality, and he reads the dog's dying and decay as an allegory of human sexuality or intercourse (see 147–48). The change of the dog from beloved pet to disgusting creature also evokes Cixous's "Stigmata, or Job the Dog" (1998), a text in which Jewish identity, persecution, and "madness" come together in the figure of a dog (see also Gerhardt, "Narrating Entanglement").

8. See Clutton-Brock, "Origin of the Dog," 7–20.

9. Bjork, *B. F. Skinner*, 201.

10. Kafka, "Bericht," 561, and "Report," 79 and 80, hereafter cited in the text as B and R, respectively.

11. These terms also resonate with the respective narrators' professed distance from *Affentum* or apedom (see, e.g., B, 559; and R, 76) and *Hundeschaft* or dogdom (see, e.g., FH, 154; this term was coined in Corngold's translation).

12. One of the consequences of the ape's language learning or becoming human is that he covers his nakedness with clothes, as if he recognized the exposure of his genitals as inappropriate. Since he now has clothes, Rotpeter can expose himself, and he arguably even denies that he has genitals any longer: "Ich, ich darf meine Hosen ausziehen, vor wem es mir beliebt; man wird dort nichts finden als einen wohlgepflegten Pelz und die Narbe" (B, 560). "I, I have the right to lower my pants in front of anyone I like; there is nothing to see there other than a well-groomed pelt and the scar" (R, 78).

13. Aristotle, *Rhetoric*, III.10, 1411a25. Stobaeus, *Florilegium*, III, 13.44, translated in Fiske, *Lucilius and Horace*, 279. Diogenes literalized the gesture of exposure by walking around naked and is even said to have masturbated in public like the plants in the previous section (on Diogenes, shamelessness, and the Cynics as dogs, see Turp, "Shameless Dogs"). Panizza compares himself to Diogenes in the previously mentioned manuscript fragment "Für 'Petroleumdichter'" (see Jacobs, "Oskar Panizzas Manuskript").

14. The nuances of meaning surrounding literary dogs are explicated by Empson's "English Dog" and "Timon's Dog" in *Structure of Complex Words*. He demonstrates that in Elizabethan times, "the grin of dogs seems then to have been part of their reputation for satire," whereas "the idea of the dog as a cynic [. . .] seems to be in part a learned innovation" (164). "The notion that the dog blows the gaff on human nature somehow attached itself to the ambition of the thinker to do the same" (169). "Before the Restoration the dog of metaphor, by and large, is snarling, a sycophant, an

underdog, loose in sex and attracted by filth, cruel if it dare" (163). In the eighteenth century, the metaphor shifts from that of an outsider to a form of praise for a respectable character, yet it maintained "the independence of the outcast [. . .]; he does not hide the truth about himself and thereby shows the truth about us all" (168). This contrasts starkly with the idea of "the kept dog" whose flattery is a lie (see 165 and 176–77).

15. *Return from Parnassus* (1601), quoted in Empson, "English Dog," 165.

16. Dogs and the unconscious go together, according to Empson in *Structure of Complex Words*, who argues that humans have been choosing dogs to represent the unconscious because they are conceived of as pastoral creatures: The Dog

> stood for the Unconscious; for the source of the impulses that keep us sane, and may mysteriously fail as in drought. Its process of thought is a mystery, but the results are homey and intelligible; it makes what we do not know about the roots of our own minds seem cheerful and not alarming. [. . .] the trouble about Evolution was that one could not feel the same way about monkeys. [. . .] There is a curious agreement, at any rate, that if we are animals this [the dog] is the kind of animal we would like to be. (169–70; see also Brown, *Homeless Dogs and Melancholy Apes*; and Kuzniar, *Melancholia's Dog*)

This notion of the dog also invokes the possibility of "madness" that lingers in all of these texts.

Section IV: The Human

1. For this complex topic, see exemplarily Bein, *The Jewish Question*; and for a different take, Geller, *The Other Jewish Question*.

2. See Aschheim, *Brothers and Strangers*.

3. Panizza, "Der operirte Jud'," hereafter cited in the text as OJ. Friedlaender/Mynona, "Der operierte Goj," hereafter cited in the text as OG. Initially called *Seitenstück* (sidepiece or side play), Friedlaender changed the subtitle to *Gegenstück*. Older print versions still show the original subtitle, but I am citing Friedlaender's *Collected Works*, which follow the updated manuscript, indicating all changes in the commentary (see Friedlaender/Mynona, *Grotesken*, 1:687–89). Both texts are translated in Jack Zipes, *The Operated Jew*, hereafter cited in the text as Z. Where his translation deviates from the original in meaningful ways, I am adding my own, marked with the terms *literally*, *added*, or *missing*, depending on the case. A first deviation is the absence of Friedlaender's subtitle in the translation.

4. The first section of this book provides more information about Panizza's complicated religious upbringing. In his court defense for the *Liebeskonzil* trial, he states, "Ich erkläre, daß ich Atheist bin" (quoted in Bauer, *Oskar Panizza*, 18; I declare that I am atheist). Friedlaender discusses religion in his autobiography and says, "Ich verfiel auf Atheismus" (Friedlaender/Mynona, *Ich*, 12; I came to be an atheist).

5. See Geller, "Of Mice and Mensa"; Krčal, *Nachahmen und Täuschen*; and Wallach, *Passing Illusions*.
6. Scholem, *Walter Benjamin: Story of a Friendship*, 58.

10. The Operated Jew

1. The name Itzig V/Feitel Stern is first used as an antisemitic pseudonym in the eighteenth century (see Althaus, *Mauscheln*, 145). Stern alludes to the Star of David and was a popular choice among Ashkenazi Jews who adopted German names during Jewish emancipation (if they were given a choice). The name *Itzig* is an abbreviated Yiddish form of the first or last name Isaac, which turned into a metonym for a Jewish person and associated stereotypical characteristics (see Althaus, *Mauscheln*). The name is given to literary figures like Veitel Itzig in Gustav Freytag's 1855 novel *Soll und Haben* and, in reference to this tradition, to the Nazi Max Schulz, who takes on the identity of the murdered Jewish barber Itzig Finkelstein in Edgar Hilsenrath's grotesque novel *Der Nazi und der Friseur* (1971).

2. In a posthumous appropriation, the narrative was printed in the *Münchner Beobachter* in 1927, a local supplement of the Nazi paper *Völkischer Beobachter*. Bauer details multiple falsifications that led to the stylization of Panizza as a nationalist and antisemite in *Oskar Panizza*, 27–33. While there are clear indications against nationalism, other texts from 1893 suggest that Panizza was actively engaging with the typical antisemitic stereotypes of this time, though this engagement has been interpreted in various ways in Panizza scholarship (the texts are the essay "Prolegomena zum Preisausschreiben: Verbesserung unserer Rasse", the *Groteske* "Der Goldregen", and the pamphlet "Mach' Mores, Jud'!" [Behave, Jew!], which first appeared posthumously in another Nazi publication in 1943; see Eggers, *Oskar Panizza*). For more details about the contemporaneous reception of "Der operirte Jud'," including Jewish voices (such as Berg, "Visionen"), see Jacobs and Thurn, "'Ein antisemitisches Kunstwerk'?"; Stähler, "Author's *Derrière*," and *Zionism, the German Empire, and Africa*.

3. See Geller, *On Freud's Jewish Body* and *The Other Jewish Question*; Gilman, *The Case of Sigmund Freud*, *Jewish Self-Hatred*, and *Freud, Race, and Gender*; and Santner, *My Own Private Germany*. For a notable exception to the US context and body focus, see Althaus, *Mauscheln*. While my own bibliography cannot assemble all of Panizza scholarship, it does attempt to list all analyses of "Der operirte Jud'," an endeavor that can only ever fall short.

4. Aside from my own work, exceptions can be found in Krčal, *Nachahmen und Täuschen*; Stähler, "Author's *Derrière*," and *Zionism, the German Empire, and Africa*; Thurn, *"Falsche Juden"*; and Reichwald, *Das Phantasma*.

5. Peter D. G. Brown has pointed out that Christ's eyes in Panizza's *Liebeskonzil* are described with the same animal metaphor in *Oskar Panizza and The Love Council*, 19.

6. I am not spelling out the German n-word here and later in accordance with current scholarship practices. See Kelly, "Das N-Wort." This passage also reveals the narrator's supposed main motivation for his interactions with Faitel, which is learning more about the Talmud, while admitting that rumors accuse him of being more interested in Faitel's money.

7. Fuß describes the relationship of the monstrous to the grotesque as follows: "The monstrous dilutes the classical dichotomous structure in favor of the grotesque structure of the A-as-well-as-B, which is a neither-nor. The giant is neither big, nor small; he is gigantic. The monstrous is neither beautiful, nor ugly; neither good, nor bad; it is monstrous. Something does not disappear in its opposition (because it is rather preserved it its negation), but it disappears in its rampant exaggeration" (*Das Groteske*, 312). In *Monster Theory*, Cohen speaks similarly about monsters as cultural warning signs: "By revealing that difference is arbitrary and potentially free-floating, mutable rather than essential, the monster threatens to destroy not just individual members of a society, but the very cultural apparatus through which individuality is constituted and allowed" (12). See also Stähler, *Zionism, the German Empire, and Africa*.

8. For the manifold connections between Frankenstein and Freudenstern, see Jacobs, "Jewish Frankenstein," and for my other engagement with this text, Jacobs, "Assimilating Aliens," "'... und die ganze pfälzisch-jüdische Sündfluth,'" and "Function of Monsters."

9. See Gilman, *Freud, Race, and Gender* for the stereotype of Jewish effeminacy. Recalling the dachshund's difficulty with differentiating men and women when they are not wearing clothing and his desire to lay bare the soul in successful canine communication in the previous section, this reference to clothing (and perhaps makeup, with its historical association with sex workers) makes it a means of deception that hides someone's true nature (one's "essence," or perhaps soul). The phrase also designates women as the ultimate other.

10. While the topic of racial passing is more prevalent in US literature of the time, see Wallach, *Passing Illusions*, for Jewish passing in Weimar Germany. Just like Faitel is described as retaining physical aspects of his old self, he occasionally expresses himself as before during the language learning process; or rather, he imitates various versions of "Jewish speech" with which he grew up, thus commenting quite literally on "Jewish mimicry" and simultaneously diversifying the idea of "the Jew" in the text. During these episodes, he mimics his very first learning experience, hearing about creation and procreation from his Rabbi in *shul*, and this anticipates his sexualized unraveling at the story's end: "mit veränderter, mäckernder Rabbinerstimme [...] 'Wie lang copuliert der hailige Gott die Männer und die Waiber?'" (OJ, 152–53; "with an altered, carping Rabbi's voice [...] 'How long doth the holy Lord copulate the men and women?'"; Z, 62), to which he responds in the voices of various schoolboys.

11. They find the "arme, aber schöne, flachshärige Beamtenstochter *Othilia Schnack*" (OJ, 155; "poor, but beautiful flaxen-haired daughter of a civil servant, Othilia Schnack"; Z, 64), who is chosen as the unwilling Germanic princess of this grotesque fairy tale for her bourgeois mediocrity. Geller has suggested that her namesake is Ottilie in Goethe's *Wahlverwandtschaften* (1809), whose "image is imprinted upon the child without the mediation of biology or sexuality. And such is no doubt the chimerical hope of Faitel" ("The Unmanning," 241). She also invokes the patron saint Ottilia of Cologne, a martyr who was killed by "barbarians" for defending her Christian beliefs and virginity. Even though her "starke[r] Mädcheninstinkt" (OJ, 156; "strong woman's intuition"; Z, 65) makes her wary of her suitor, both the money and extraordinary popularity that go along with Faitel's courtship win her parents over.

12. The phrasing of Faitel's request for his bride calls up a scene in E. T. A. Hoffmann's "Die Abenteuer der Sylvester-Nacht" (1815, first printed in the same volume as his canine narrator Berganza), especially when also considering Panizza's usage of "Der Tausend! Der Tausend!" (OJ, 159; "the devil!"; Z, 67; literally: A thousand!). "Der Tausend" is a homophonous euphemism for "der Teufel." See also OJ, 140; and Z, 52, where it is mistranslated, and the next note. Hoffmann's text says, "At this very moment there tottered into the room a spindle-shanked cretin, eyes a-pop like a frog's, who said, in a mixture of croak and cackle, 'Where the Devil [*Wo der tausend*] is my wife?'" ("A New Year's Eve Adventure," 108). This evokes the motif of the "animal bridegroom" (ATU tale type 425a) in fairy tales such as "The Frog Prince." Unlike an animal bridegroom, however, Faitel is not given a chance of redemption through love, aligning him more with the monster in Shelley's *Frankenstein*, who cannot find his bride, since she has been killed to prevent reproduction (see Jacobs, "Jewish Frankenstein").

13. The image of the hydrophobic dog is usually associated with "madness" (the German term for rabies, *Tollwut*, connotes "madness" with both the notion of *toll sein* and *wüten*), which invokes the persistent theme of the asylum as well as the dogs discussed in the previous section (see Empson, *Structure of Complex Words*, 165).

14. The similarity between the two texts is probably most apparent in the following passage that sounds like it could be from the dog diary but instead comes from Faitel's story and immediately follows the "false wrappings," which are notably for the soul:

> Hast Du vielleicht, lieber Leser, schon Thiere mit einander sprechen sehen? [. . .] Nicht wahr, wie sie gurren, schnattern, kläffen, winzeln, wedeln und Körperkrümmungen machen! Glaubst Du, daß sie sich verstehen? Gewiß! Gewiß! Jeder weiß im Nu, was das Andere will. Aber zwei Menschen? Wenn sie schnüffelnd die Köpfe gegeneinanderstrecken, und sich ankieken; und dann ihre Gesichts-Taschenspielereien beginnen blinzeln; äugeln, schwere und leichte Falten aufziehen, die Backen blähen,

> knuspern, leer kauen, "Papperlapapp", und "Der Tausend! Der Tausend!" winzeln? Was thun sie? Verstehen sie sich wohl? Unmöglich! Sie wollen ja nicht. Sie können und dürfen ja nicht. Die *Lüge* hindert sie ja daran. (OJ, 158–59)

> Perhaps, my dear reader, you have seen animals talking among themselves. [...; missing: Indeed, how they are cooing, quacking, yapping, whimpering, wagging, and bending their bodies!] Do you think [literally: believe] they understand each other? Certainly! Certainly! Each knows what the other wants in a flash. But two people? When they stretch their heads toward one another, sniff and peep at each other and then begin their facial magic tricks, blinking, ogling, [missing: drawing up difficult and easy wrinkles, ballooning their cheeks, munching,] [added: rubbing,] chewing thin air, and whimpering "fiddlesticks" and "the devil!"—what are they doing? Do they actually understand each other? Impossible! They don't want to. They can't and are not allowed to. The lie prevents them from doing this. (Z, 67)

The figure of the Jew as/and dog (or animality writ large) also appears in Ackerman-Lieberman and Zalashnik, *A Jew's Best Friend?*; Benjamin, *Of Jews and Animals*; Geller, *Bestiarium Judaicum*; Cixous, "Stigmata, or Job the Dog"; and Pines, *The Infrahuman*.

15. While the blood transfusion coagulates a claim of gender crossing, it also carries associations of male menstruation, along with blood-related antisemitic horror stories of ritual murder and human sacrifice (see Gilman, *Creating Beauty to Cure the Soul*).

16. Santner, *My Own Private Germany*, 127.

17. See also Axel Stähler's discussion of eugenics in relation to Panizza and this text in *Zionism, the German Empire, and Africa*.

18. See Althaus, *Mauscheln*.

19. The same applies to nonverbal expressivity. The narrator says about Faitel:

> Wenn er aber eifrig wurde, und gute Opportunitäts-Gründe in's Feld zu führen hatte, dann bäumte er auf, hob den Kopf empor, zog die fleischige, wie ein Stück Leder sich bewegende Oberlippe zurück, so daß die obere Zahnreihe entblößt wurde, spreizte mit zurückgebeugtem Oberkörper beide Hände fächerförmig nach oben, knaukte mit dem Kopf gegen die Brust zu einigemal auf und ab, und ließ rythmisch abgestoßene Schnedderengdeng-Geräusche hören. Bis zu diesem Moment hatte mein Freund noch gar Nichts gesagt. (OJ, 138)

> But when he became zealous and had a good opportunity to wage an argument, then he reared up, raised a hand, pulled back his fleshy volatile upper lip like a piece of leather so that the upper row of teeth became exposed, spread open both his hands like fans pointing upward with his upper body leaning backward, bobbed his head up and down against his breast a few times, and rhythmically uttered sounds like a trumpet. Up to this moment my friend may not have said a thing. (Z, 50)

The narrative, however, has said plenty.

20. See "the fonetic writing sistem [*fonetische Schreibsistem*]" in Düsterberg, *"Die gedrukte Freiheit"*, 167–72.

21. See Althaus, *Mauscheln*, 152.

22. English terms like *rotation work* in the original German seemingly introduce international expertise in the text. This dehumanizing mechanistic view of Faitel invokes speaking machines such as in Hoffmann's "Der Sandmann" (1816) and "Die Automate" (1814) and foreshadows creations such as the *Maschinenmensch* Maria in Fritz Lang's *Metropolis* (1927) and the machinery that creates the monster in James Whale's film adaptation of *Frankenstein* (1931).

23. See *mise en machine; mise-en-scène; ne pas être de mise*, since French is one of Faitel's and Panizza's languages.

24. Other texts by Panizza contain similar deliberations—for instance, about the phonetics of a marionette representing Christ in "Das Wachsfigurenkabinett" (1890, see Panizza, *Werke*, 2:7–40, here 12–13).

25. The epigraph to Panizza's text (omitted in Zipes's translation) cites Bürger's "Lenore" (1774), revealing her bridegroom to be dead: "Zum Schädel, ohne Schopf und Zopf, / Zum nackten Schädel ward sein Kopf" (OJ, 135; A skull, without skin and hair, a naked skull became his head.). As Geller has suggested in *The Other Jewish Question* (see 75), this introduces the idea of circumcision implicitly, which comes up explicitly as the need for transforming "skin and hair" (foreskin and sidelocks) in Friedlaender's narrative, whose anticipation of circumcision plays with the absence of restoring Faitel's missing foreskin in Panizza's, thus highlighting the absence of an absence (see also Geller, "Unmanning," and *On Freud's Jewish Body*).

26. In *Hochdeutsch*, "des is aach aner vun unnere Leit" would read "das ist auch einer von unseren Leuten."

27. This reading differs somewhat from what I argued in Jacobs, "'. . . und die ganze pfälzisch-jüdische Sündfluth,'" demonstrating my own struggle with the persistent ambiguity of this passage.

28. Panizza, "Eine N [. . .] geschichte," in *Werke*, 4:18–28, here 25, hereafter cited in the text as EN. See also Wipplinger, "Racial Ruse"; Stähler, *Zionism, the German Empire, and Africa*; and Wallach, *Passing Illusions*.

29. Panizza, "Indianer-Gedanken," in *Werke*, 4:76–85, here 83.

30. Panizza, "Ein skandalöser Fall," in *Werke*, 4:86–134. Translated from German to French by Sophie Wilkins and from this French version into English by Richard McDougall as Panizza, "A Scandal at the Convent" in Foucault, *Herculine Barbin*, 155–99. Aside from Zipes's translation of "The Operated Jew," this is the only other *Groteske* by Panizza that has been translated into English. See also Gronau, "Der Psychiater als Literat"; Ketterl, "Von Hegemonie und Unentscheidbarkeit," and "Skandalöses Erzählen"; and Jacobs and Lasse, "Making Intersex Identity ILLegible."

31. "For a long time hermaphrodites were criminals, or crime's offspring, since their anatomical disposition, their very being, confounded the law that distinguished the sexes and prescribed their union" (Foucault, *History of Sexuality*, 1:38).

11. The Operated Goy

1. The description of the eyes, *Schlitzauge*, is an anti-Asian stereotype that will return in Rebecka's "almond shaped eyes" (*Mandelschnittaugen*) later, while also carrying the connotation of the *Schlitzohr*, or swindler. It calls up Faitel's "yellow skin," who was moreover called an "asiatisches Bild" (OJ, 166; "Asiatic image"; Z, 74) at the end of his story, and all these racialized markers contribute both to the common identification of Jews as "Oriental" and the amalgamation of otherness in the descriptions.

2. Kreuzwendedich is a rare, archaic name that was mostly popular as a middle name with Prussian Pietist nobility and sometimes given to children whose older sibling had passed away. In this sense, it is an invocation: "cross that we have to bear, make a turn for the better!" As a name, it is literally a cross to bear because it is the constant reminder of the child one replaced (see Heintze, *Die deutschen Familien-Namen*, 51).

3. Grafting involves adding a "foreign" branch to a tree and results in a hybrid, or perhaps monstrous plant. *Stamm* means both trunk and tribe, bringing together the previously mentioned Jewish with Germanic tribes, while India additionally invokes the shared origin of Indo-Germanic languages that Panizza's narrative pointed to when saying that "the purest effusion of the Germanic soul was to be found" in England. Recall also that Faitel's bride Othilia was "the finest Occidental sprig [*Reis*]" with which Faitel's "Stamm" is to be "grafted" to ensure his transformation's success through reproduction. Here, the association with Ottilie in Goethe's *Wahlverwandtschaften* brings up connections to plant reproduction and grafting in the novel (see Zumbusch, "Metamorphoses of Ottilie"; and Jacobs, "Eden's Heirs").

4. For this reason, the fraternity was often the target of satire—for instance, in the modernist magazine *Simplicissimus*—and it is the same fraternity that is made fun of in Ewers's "Aus dem Tagebuch eines Orangenbaumes" (see plant section). It should be noted, however, that the fraternity chose to resolve itself in 1934/1935 rather than excluding its comparatively high number of Jewish members.

5. "Der Stürmer" is the typical fraternity hat. The color (here white) indicates not only the fraternity but also the idea of purity, and the name now associates the Nazi publication *Der Stürmer*, which was, however, founded a year after the story's publication.

6. In the instability of the early years of the Weimar Republic, putsch attempts, separatist movements, street fights, and political murders committed by various

ideological factions abounded. Kreuzwendedich personifies a typical member of a *Freikorps* (war veterans who banded together into right-wing paramilitary groups) or the early Nazi SA, who were involved in these fights (see Sauer, "Freikorps und Antisemitismus").

7. At the end of the nineteenth century, many health resorts, particularly the island Borkum, advertised that they would host no Jews. The Borkum song, which was played daily by the health resort band and sung by the guests, says in its third stanza (in my rather literal translation): "On this green Island rules a truly German spirit. Therefore, everyone who is related to us by blood flocks here joyously. There is only Germanness on Borkum's beaches, only the German banner flies. We keep Germania's noble crest pure forever! But who approaches you on flat feet, with crooked noses, and curly hair shall not enjoy your beach; out with him, out with him!" (see Bajohr, *"Unser Hotel ist judenfrei"*).

8. As Geller says in *The Other Jewish Question*, "the repulsive, feminized, and often sexualized 'odor' that pervaded the popular and scientific imagination of postemancipation Europeans: the innate stench of the Jew, the *foetor Judaicus*" (273). See also Geller, "(G)nos(e)ology," "Aromatics of Jewish Difference," and "Unmanning."

9. See Jäger, *Die Entdeckung*, 106–9.

10. "There is in the words 'a beautiful Jewess' a very special sexual signification [...] This phrase carries an aura of rape and massacre" (Sartre, *Anti-Semite and Jew*, 48). For the odalisque, see DelPlato, *Multiple Wives, Multiple Pleasures*. The "almond shape" of the eyes reinforces the racial connotations and, while reminiscent of the anti-Asian stereotype about eyes earlier in the text, adds another element of erotic exoticization.

11. Grimm and Grimm, *Kinder- und Hausmärchen*, 1:238.

12. While nationalists favored the black-white-red combination (and the Nazis brought it back), the Weimar Republic went with the black-red-gold combination of the German Confederation before the Wilhelmine Empire, which led to the so-called flag fight that embroiled everyone, from parliament to street factions, in varying degrees of physical altercations. One of Friedlaender's collections of wartime *Grotesken* is called *Black-White-Red*, and he says in its preface that "Germany wears Goethe's colors" (Mynona, *Schwarz-Weiss-Rot*, 5). In reference to Goethe's *Zur Farbenlehre* (*Theory of Colors*, 1810), he comments on the ongoing First World War that led everyone to perceive the world in black and white and produced red bloodshed. See also Haakenson's discussion of the symbolic importance of the *Farbenlehre* for Friedlaender's worldview in *Grotesque Visions*, 36–43.

13. The formulation easily implies its opposite in phrases such as *er ist nicht ganz sauber* (something is not quite right about him/he might have a hidden agenda or be a criminal), *das geht nicht mit sauberen Dingen zu* (it is not legal/it is not done on the up and up), or *Bleib sauber!* (Keep your nose clean!).

14. Friedlaender's wordplay and layers of associations are at times overwhelming, as the character names in this *Groteske* show exemplarily: Freia and Rotraut are the Nordic equivalents to the dangerously attractive Venus, the goddess of beauty, sexuality, and fertility but also death. The seductive Venus imagery reappears in the observation that "Kreuzwendedich war [...] traumhaft von ihr bezaubert worden" (OG, 601; "Kreuzwendedich, enchanted by her, was in a trance"; Z, 79), evoking Tannhäuser's legend of the Venus Mountain (*Venusberg*), which is also the name of an area in Bonn, where the story takes place. The legend and its many romantic adaptations say that Venus lures mortal men into the mountain to lead a life of pleasure from which they cannot return. Freia is also the goddess of gold, so the name Freia Rotraut von Isagold contains a distinct color scheme with two references to gold (symbolizing wealth, the blond hair color of the Aryan ideal, and the missing color of Weimar Germany's flag according to an earlier note) and one mention of red (as blood) in *Rot*raut. Gold is also part of Rebecka's Jewish family name Gold-Isak, which she has simply reversed into Isagold to make the Jewish reference to "Israel" disappear (which nonetheless shows up in the first names of her father Isak and Itzig Faitel Stern). The Isar is a German river, and in combination with "gold," it evokes the title of Richard Wagner's *Rheingold* (*Rhine Gold*, 1869), and with it the Germanic *Nibelung* myth (as did Faitel's new name Siegfried). Rebecka's first name connects her ancestry to the biblical Rebecca/Rebekah, who was barren at first but then bore her husband Isaac twin sons (and this is not the only time when father and husband take on an uncanny oedipal tinge in the subtext of the story). The twin son Jacob is the father of the twelve tribes of Israel. Rotraut, on the other hand, is an old Germanic name that means *Ruhm* (hruod = glory) and *wehrhaft* (trud = well-fortified/strong) (see Gerr, *Das große Vornamenbuch*), but as typical Friedlaender wordplay, it also invites comparisons to the German dish *Rotkraut* (pickled red cabbage), which is one of the many cabbage-based dishes that give Germans the nickname *krauts*.

15. According to Cohen's sixth thesis in the introduction to *Monster Culture*, "fear of the monster is really a kind of desire" (16). Cannibalism "is the place where desire and dread, love and aggression meet [... and it] involves both the establishing of absolute difference, the opposites of eater and eaten, and the dissolution of that difference, through the act of incorporation which identifies them, and makes the two one" (Kilgour, "Function of Cannibalism," 240). After ripping apart her beloved Achilles together with her dogs, Heinrich von Kleist's Penthesilea similarly suggests that *Küsse* (kisses) and *Bisse* (bites) rhyme (*Penthesilea*, scene 24). The myth of the toothed vagina that would castrate any "intruder" was used as a cautionary tale to prevent rape (see Voegelin, "Vagina Dentata").

16. Nathan Birnbaum (1864–1937) coined the terms *Zionismus* and *Ostjudentum* (Eastern European Jewry). He was the first secretary general of the Zionist Organization and initially a representative of Theodor Herzl's political Zionism, but he later

became a strong proponent of cultural Zionism (i.e., life in Palestine even without a formal state) and moreover supported Yiddish, Chassidism, and *Ostjudentum* in a variety of ways (see Olson, *Nathan Birnbaum*; and Aschheim, *Brothers and Strangers*).

17. *Meschugge* had become part of standard German already at this point, which demonstrates once more that processes of cultural and linguistic blending are inherent to identity concepts and language development (see Althaus, *Zocker, Zoff und Zores*).

18. The choice of Hagar for a name is curious, as she was an Egyptian slave and her son with Abraham did not become the progenitor of the Israelites. In other words, neither she nor her offspring is Jewish.

19. The print version omits the actual curse, "daß dein Schoß soll verdorren" (that your womb shall wither), based on later manuscript edits. The plant imagery of reproduction (*Fortpflanzung*, containing the word *plant*) and fertility (*Fruchtbarkeit*, literally: fruitfulness) comes full circle in this line, when the potential offspring that was supposed to sprout (*entkeimen*, see OG, 601) from Rebecka's womb is threatened to wither, or dry up like a plant.

20. The father's professed ability to "buy" Gotha would require near limitless wealth, since the city had the reputation as a rich industrial hub at the time (see Stasjulevics, *Gotha*), while the *Gothaischer Hofkalender* (*Almanach de Gotha*, 1785–1944), which his phrase more likely refers to, given the grammatical gender in the original, annually assembled information about European royalty and higher nobility as a kind of "Who Is Who" of the upper classes. Yet Gotha also invokes the Sachsen-Gotha-Altenburg dynasty, whose two last representatives died without male heirs, so that Gotha was incorporated (*einverleibt*) into the Sachsen-Coburg area in 1826 (see Beck, *Geschichte des gothaischen Landes*).

21. The concept that a Jewish person would have antisemitic notions originated from inner-Jewish conflicts about the "proper" Jewish lifestyle in the nineteenth century, which finds itself repeated in the conflicts between so-called assimilated German Jewry and orthodox Eastern European Jews in the text. Weininger's *Geschlecht und Character* (1903) is often referenced as an example of the phenomenon. In his 1921 book *Juden und Deutsche*, Kuh suggested the usage of the term *Jewish self-hatred* rather than *Jewish antisemitism*, which fully came into use with Th. Lessing's 1930 *Der jüdische Selbsthaß*. It was also discussed in conjunction with anti-Zionism—for instance, in Herzl's polemic of the "anti-Semite of Jewish origin" in *Der Judenstaat* (1896). See Gilman, *Jewish Self-Hatred*; and Reitter, *Origins of Jewish Self-Hatred*.

22. There are two instances of the changed name (paragraphs 3 and 9 of Friedlaender's text) that are corrected in the print version but remain in the manuscript. It is unclear whether this transformation of the name was at any point intended or rather "just" a Freudian slip.

23. On Friedlaender's general tendency to satirize Freud as well as on Bierbaum's notion that Panizza was lacking the required "fig leaf," see section 1. Also note the

discussion of *Entblößung* (in regard to both physical nakedness and the soul) in section 3.

24. Asking, "Kann ich so mit dir unter die Chuppe?" is reminiscent of the expression *unter die Decke* (under the blanket), which implies intercourse.

25. For a discussion of the other painters mentioned in the two texts, see Jacobs, "Jewish Frankenstein."

26. In the beginning of act 3, scene 1 of *Das Liebeskonzil*, Panizza describes the devil (the figure with whom he was often associated) as "reminiscent in his gestures of a refined Jew" (Brown, *Oskar Panizza and The Love Council*, 46). Gesturing as an antisemitic and racist stereotype reinforces the association of mimicry with Jews (see Geller, "Of Mice and Mensa"; Krčal, *Nachahmen und Täuschen*; and Wallach, *Passing Illusions*).

27. An der Hochzeitstafel im Palais Gold-Isak war nicht nur die engere Kille [community], sondern der Vorstand der jüdischen Gemeinde versammelt. Die Hausorgel erdröhnte von Mendelssohn'schen und Bruch'schen Harmonien. Gegen ein Dutzend Rabbinen hielten, nachdem sie das junge Paar in der Synagoge eingesegnet hatten, fast zugleich ihre Festreden. (OG, 605)

At the wedding table in Gold-Isaac's mansion, the close relatives were seated alongside [literally: not only the immediate community but also] the president of the Jewish congregation. The house organ played music by Mendelssohn and Bruch. After a dozen or so rabbis had blessed the young couple in the synagogue[,] they all held celebration speeches almost at the same time. (Z, 84)

By contrast, Faitel's wedding location is signified as Christian to excess: "Im Gasthaus zum 'weißen Lamm' in der Martergasse" (OJ, 159; "In the Inn of the White Lamb, which was on the Martergasse [literally: Martyr's Alley]"; Z, 68). The "vorwiegend germanischer Charakter des Hochzeitsschmauses" (OJ, 161; "predominantly German character of the wedding banquet"; Z, 69) was ensured by plenty of stereotypical *Sauerkraut* and decidedly not kosher pork.

28. In his notes, Friedlaender pokes fun at Zionism—for instance, with the term *Zionanie*, a combination of *Zionismus* (Zionism) and *Onanie* (onanism). See Geerken, "Nachwort," 302.

29. In *Goethes Werke*, 3:57.

30. In this respect, there is a notable difference to Panizza's text, as Friedlaender makes use of authentic markers of Jewish identity, which is a form of shibboleth. They mostly relate to outward or physical appearance, so the assumption that all his readers would recognize at least most of them points to cultural coexistence within German society. It is also a sign that this text is addressing the Jewish community in a specific way, both to warn against rising antisemitism and as a commentary on inner-Jewish conflicts between assimilated Western and Eastern European Jewry and the question of Zionism.

31. In *Joseph Roths Auseinandersetzung mit dem Antisemitismus*, Ochse remarks, Kreuzwendedich's "assimilation process would additionally have increased the awareness of non-Jewish readers for the imposition that the assimilation demand for Jews constitutes. At the same time, Mynona [Friedlaender's pen name] ridicules the ideology of purity, maintained by antisemites and orthodox Jews alike, with his description of von Reschok's development" (97).

32. Letter to Fritz Lemke on February 29, 1936, in Friedlaender/Mynona, *Briefwechsel*, 5:300–302. This statement comes from a letter in which Friedlaender expresses his unhappiness about another letter (not to Friedlaender) that Kurt Tucholsky had written shortly before his suicide in exile in 1935. The Nazis publicized an abridged version that emphasized Tucholsky's criticism of Zionism and the absence of a Jewish uprising against Hitler (see Gilman, *Jewish Self-Hatred*). Friedlaender and Tucholsky disliked each other following a public dispute about Erich Maria Remarque's novel *Im Westen nichts Neues* when it appeared in 1929 (see Kuxdorf, "Mynona versus Remarque, Tucholsky, Mann and Others"). In contrast, Tucholsky was one of Panizza's greatest proponents. Just four months before Friedlaender's "Der operierte Goj," Tucholsky published the first in a popular series of caricatural narratives about an assimilated Jewish figure of his own, named Herr Wendriner (invoking the turning or conversion that is also inherent in Kreuzwendedich's name). Zipes has suggested that Friedlaender's "Der operierte Goj" might also be a reaction to Tucholsky's Wendriner figure because Friedlaender calls him the "Wendriner-Tucholsky" in his 1936 letter (see Z, 122–23). Yet this is unlikely because at the time when Friedlaender published "Der operierte Goj" in October 1922, only Tucholsky's first text of this series, "Herr Wendriner telefoniert" (published as "Zehn Minuten" on July 6, 1922), could have been known to him, and this short piece about Rathenau's death unfolds only minimally what the Wendriner character would ultimately come to stand for.

33. For the definition in the original, see section 1 or Mynona, "Grotesk," 54a.

34. Mynona, "Grotesk," 54a. For the relationship of the grotesque in modernism with science, including Friedlaender, see Haakenson, *Grotesque Visions*.

35. See also Jacobs, "Jewish Frankenstein."

36. See Friedlaender/Mynona, *Grotesken*, 1:687.

37. The notable exception is Thiel's introduction to Friedlaender's *Grotesken*, in which he demonstrates this oversight convincingly and suggests that the text was, in fact, written shortly after Panizza's death ("Einleitung," 76).

38. See Friedlaender/Mynona, *Ich*, 38–39.

39. The two texts have been received very differently, and "Der operirte Jud'," taken out of the context of Panizza's other *Grotesken*, was probably the main reason for Panizza's postwar reputation as an antisemite (see one of the first notes in chapter 10), which would likely have puzzled the many Jewish proponents of his work, such as Benjamin, Tucholsky, and Tuchmann, the chair of the short-lived Panizza Society

(see section 1). However, the answer to such a complex, much-discussed question like this cannot be simply reversed either, and it will likely remain unsolvable to a degree. Yet a nuanced assessment of Panizza's text needs to consider the previously ignored prewar reception and the context of other *Grotesken* (see Jacobs and Thurn, "'Ein antisemitisches Kunstwerk'?"; Stähler, "Author's *Derrière*," and *Zionism, the German Empire, and Africa*).

40. Scholem, Walter Benjamin: Story of a Friendship, 58.

12. Why Humans?

1. Friedlaender/Mynona, "Beweis, daß die Deutschen Menschen sind," in *Grotesken*, 2:452–53.

2. *An der Nase eines Mannes erkennt man seinen Johannes* (one can tell about a man's Johnson from his nose).

3. Friedlaender/Mynona, "Tödliche Anprobe," in *Grotesken*, 2:337–40, here 337, hereafter cited in the text as TA.

4. Mynona, "Grotesk," 54a.

Conclusion

1. Of course, the texts chosen for analysis in this book necessarily represent a specific subset of *Grotesken* that focuses on certain themes. One dimension of the genre that deserves more attention is its criticism of the church and organized religion, which is particularly apparent in Panizza's writing. Similarly, a closer examination of the genre's aesthetic proximity not only to Weimar cabaret and romantic literature but also to early science fiction and expressionist film would certainly prove fruitful, given Ewers's work as a film director and scriptwriter, Friedlaender's interest in futuristic science, Panizza's literary engagement with the moon, and Kafka's distinct style. Such an examination might also expand the canon of the genre and include other writers of the time, such as Alfred Döblin (see also Haakenson, *Grotesque Visions*; and Leskau, "Botanical Perversions").

2. Scholem, *Walter Benjamin: Story of a Friendship*, 58. This aspect of the genre's reception history raises the question why earlier genocides (e.g., of the Herero and Nama) have not compelled Germans to reckon with the violence they inflicted on others to such an extent or until now. To return to the introduction of this book, decolonial thinking calls everyone into the responsibility of engaging with the harmful consequences that result from equating Man with the human. See exemplarily Wynter, "Unsettling the Coloniality"; Drexler-Dreis and Justaert, *Beyond the Doctrine of Man*; and Mignolo, "Sylvia Wynter: What Does It Mean to Be Human?"

3. See Kuxdorf, *Der Schriftsteller*, 3; Exner, *Fasching als Logik*, 323–24; and Velten, "Laughing at the Body."

4. See Mynona, 54a.

5. For an exploration of the German Jewish context in conjunction with feminism and animal rights, see Lorenz, "Man and Animal." For gender in the context of the grotesque writ large (*das Groteske*), see Russo, *The Female Grotesque*.

6. See the ongoing work of the Diversity, Decolonization, and the German Curriculum collective at https://diversityingermancurriculum.weebly.com/.

7. See exemplarily the reception of Kimmerer's *Braiding Sweetgrass*.

8. See, exemplarily, Bennet, *Being Property Once Myself*; Boisseron, *Afro-Dog*; Chen, *Animacies*; Jackson, *Becoming Human*; McHugh, *Love in a Time of Slaughters*; Thurston-Torres, *Animals and Race*; as well as Ackerman-Lieberman and Zalashnik, *A Jew's Best Friend?*; Benjamin, *Of Jews and Animals*; Cooper, "Writing Humanimals"; Geller, *Bestiarium Judaicum*; Gross, *Question of the Animal*; and Pines, *The Infrahuman*. For ways of thinking about slavery and the Holocaust together, see Groves, "Low Tide, Black Shoals."

BIBLIOGRAPHY

Ackerman-Lieberman, Phillip, and Rakefet Zalashik. *A Jew's Best Friend? The Image of the Dog throughout Jewish History*. Eastbourne: Sussex Academic, 2013.
Adams, Carol J. *The Sexual Politics of Meat: A Feminist-Vegetarian Critical Theory*. New York: Continuum, 1990.
Agamben, Giorgio. "K." In *The Work of Giorgio Agamben: Law, Literature, Life*, edited by Nicholas Heron, Justin Clemens, and Alex Murray, 13–27. Edinburgh: Edinburgh University Press, 2008.
———. *The Open: Man and Animal*. Stanford, CA: Stanford University Press, 2004.
Allred, Mason. "Foreign Bodies: Border Control, Jewish Identity and *Der Student von Prag* (1913)." *Jewish Studies Quarterly* 21, no. 3 (2014): 277–95.
Aloi, Giovanni. *Why Look at Plants: The Botanical Emergence in Contemporary Art*. Boston: Brill, 2018.
Althaus, Hans Peter. *Mauscheln: Ein Wort als Waffe*. Berlin: De Gruyter, 2002.
———. *Zocker, Zoff und Zores: Jiddische Wörter im Deutschen*. Munich: Beck, 2002.
Althusser, Louis. "Ideology and Ideological State Apparatuses." In *Lenin and Philosophy*, translated by Ben Brewster, 127–86. New York: Monthly Review, 1971.
Anderton, Joseph. "Dogdom: Nonhuman Others and the Othered Self in Kafka, Beckett, and Auster." *Twentieth Century Literature* 62, no. 3 (2016): 271–88.
Aristotle. *De Anima*. Translated by J. A. Smith. Oxford: Clarendon, 1931.
———. *Rhetoric*. Translated by W. Rhys Roberts. New York: Modern Library, 1954.
Aschheim, Steven E. *Brothers and Strangers: The Eastern European Jew in German and German-Jewish Consciousness, 1800–1923*. Madison: University of Wisconsin Press, 1982.

Ashkenazi, Ofer. *Weimar Film and Modern Jewish Identity*. New York: Palgrave Macmillan, 2012.

Bajohr, Frank. *"Unser Hotel ist judenfrei:" Bäder-Antisemitismus im 19. und 20. Jahrhundert*. Frankfurt am Main: Fischer, 2003.

Bakhtin, Mikhail. *Rabelais and His World*. Bloomington: Indiana University Press, 1984.

Barasch, Frances K. *The Grotesque: A Study in Meanings*. The Hague: Mouton, 1971.

Baßler, Moritz. *Deutsche Erzählprosa 1850–1950: Eine Geschichte literarischer Verfahren*. Berlin: Erich Schmidt, 2015.

Bauer, Michael. *Oskar Panizza: Exil im Wahn: Eine Biografie*. Munich: Allitera, 2019.

Bauer, Michael, and Rolf Düsterberg, eds. *Oskar Panizza: Eine Bibliographie*. Frankfurt am Main: Peter Lang, 1988.

Baumgartner, Michael, and Rainer Lawicki, eds. *Satire – Ironie – Groteske: Daumier, Ensor, Feininger, Klee, Kubin*. Bielefeld: Kerber, 2013.

Beachy, Robert. *Gay Berlin: Birthplace of a Modern Identity*. New York: Vintage, 2014.

Beaulieu, Alain. "The Status of Animality in Deleuze's Thought." *Journal for Critical Animal Studies* 9, no. 1–2 (2011): 69–88.

Beck, August. *Geschichte des gothaischen Landes*, vol. 1. Gotha: E. F. Thienemann, 1868.

Bein, Alex. *The Jewish Question: Biography of a World Problem*. Translated by Harry Zohn. Vancouver: Fairleigh Dickinson University Press, 1990.

Benjamin, Andrew. *Of Jews and Animals*. Edinburgh: Edinburgh University Press, 2010.

Benjamin, Walter. "E. T. A. Hoffmann und Oskar Panizza." In *Gesammelte Schriften*, vol. 2, edited by Rolf Tiedemann and Hermann Schweppenhäuser, 641–48. Frankfurt am Main: Suhrkamp, 1991.

Bennet, Joshua. *Being Property Once Myself: Blackness and the End of Man*. Cambridge, MA: Harvard University Press, 2020.

Benson, Timothy O. *Raoul Hausmann and Berlin Dada*. Ann Arbor: University of Michigan Press, 1987.

Beresford, Peter. "'Mad,' Mad Studies and Advancing Inclusive Resistance." *Disability & Society* 35, no. 8 (2020): 1337–42.

Berg, Leo. "Visionen: Erzählungen und Skizzen von Oskar Panizza." *Der Zuschauer: Monatsschrift für Kunst, Litteratur und Kritik* 1, no. 7 (1894): 323–25.

Berg, Nicolas. "Forschungen eines Hundes." In *Kafka-Handbuch: Leben, Werk, Wirkung*, edited by Manfred Engel and Bernd Auerochs, 330–36. Stuttgart: Metzler, 2010.

Berger, John. "Why Look at Animals?" In *About Looking*, 1–28. New York: Pantheon, 1980.

Berkowitz, Beth. "Jews and Animals." *Oxford Bibliographies Online: Jewish Studies.* Oxford University Press, 2023, https://www.oxfordbibliographies.com/view/document/obo-9780199840731/obo-9780199840731-0229.xml.

Berling, Peter. *Liebeskonzil: Filmbuch.* Munich: Schirmer-Mosel, 1982.

Best, Otto F., ed. *Das Groteske in der Dichtung.* Darmstadt: Wissenschaftliche Buchgesellschaft, 1980.

Bierbaum, Otto Julius. "Oskar Panizza." *Die Gesellschaft* 3 (August 1893): 977–89.

Binder, Frauke. "'Der zensierte Dämon': Oskar Panizzas Liebeskonzil und die Mechanismen der Zensur." MA thesis, Universität Hannover, 1996.

Binder, Hartmut. *Kafka-Kommentar zu sämtlichen Erzählungen.* Munich: Winkler, 1975.

Bischoff, Doerte. *Poetischer Fetischismus: Der Kult der Dinge im 19. Jahrhundert.* Paderborn: Wilhelm Fink, 2013.

Bjork, Daniel W. *B. F. Skinner: A Life.* Washington, DC: American Psychological Association, 1997.

Bland, Lucy, and Laura Doan, eds. *Sexology Uncensored: The Documents of Sexual Science.* Chicago: University of Chicago Press, 1998.

Blumberg, Bernhard. "Der 'Fall' Müller: Lippstadt (1877) und die Lehrplanänderung von 1882." *Biologie in der Schule* 26, no. 1 (1977): 38–43.

Bodemann, Y. Michal. *Jews, Germans, Memory: Reconstructions of Jewish Life in Germany.* Ann Arbor: University of Michigan Press, 1996.

Boeser, Knut. *Der Fall Oskar Panizza: Ein deutscher Dichter im Gefängnis.* Berlin: Edition Hentrich, 1989.

Boisseron, Bénédicte. *Afro-Dog: Blackness and the Animal Question.* New York: Columbia University Press, 2018.

Bondeson, Jan. *Amazing Dogs: A Cabinet of Canine Curiosities.* Ithaca, NY: Cornell University Press, 2011.

Bondestam, Maja. "When the Plant Kingdom Became Queer: On Hermaphrodites and Linnean Language of Nonnormative Sex." In *Illdisciplined Gender: Engaging Questions of Nature/Culture and Transgressive Encounters,* edited by Jacob Bull and Margaretha Fahlgren, 115–36. Cham: Springer, 2016.

Borgards, Roland, ed. *Tiere: Ein kulturwissenschaftliches Handbuch.* Stuttgart: Metzler, 2015.

———. "Tiere in der Literatur: Eine methodische Standortbestimmung." In *Das Tier an sich: Disziplinenübergreifende Perspektiven für neue Wege im wissenschaftsbasierten Tierschutz,* edited by Herwig Grimm and Carola Otterstedt, 87–118. Göttingen: Vandenhoeck & Ruprecht, 2012.

Borgards, Roland, and Nicolas Pethes, eds. *Tier – Experiment – Literatur: 1880–2010.* Würzburg: Königshausen & Neumann, 2013.

Born, Jürgen, ed. *Kafka, Franz: Kritik und Rezeption zu seinen Lebzeiten: 1912–1924.* Frankfurt am Main: Fischer, 1979.

Brittnacher, Hans Richard. "Auf der Rückseite von Ordnung und Vernunft: Überlegungen zur Phantastik." *literaturkritik.de*, March 8, 2018. https://literaturkritik.de/public/rezension.php?rez_id=24270.

Brobjer, Thomas H. "A Possible Solution to the Stirner-Nietzsche-Question." *Journal of Nietzsche Studies* 25 (Spring 2003): 109–14.

Brod, Max. *Franz Kafka: A Biography.* New York: Schocken, 1960.

———. *Über Franz Kafka.* Frankfurt am Main: Fischer, 1974.

Brömsel, Sven. "Stephen King des wilhelminischen Kaiserreichs." *Deutschlandfunk Kultur*, October 17, 2020. https://www.deutschlandfunkkultur.de/autor-hanns-heinz-ewers-stephen-king-des-wilhelminischen-100.html.

Brown, Laura. *Homeless Dogs and Melancholy Apes: Humans and Other Animals in the Modern Literary Imagination.* Ithaca, NY: Cornell University Press, 2010.

Brown, Peter D. G. "The Continuing Trials of Oskar Panizza: A Century of Artistic Censorship in Germany, Austria, and Beyond." *German Studies Review* 24, no. 3 (October 2001): 533–56.

———. *Oskar Panizza and* The Love Council: *A History of the Scandalous Play on Stage and in Court, with the Complete Text in English and a Biography of the Author.* Jefferson, NC: McFarland, 2010.

———. *Oskar Panizza: His Life and Works.* New York: Peter Lang, 1983.

Browne, Janet. "Botany for Gentlemen: Erasmus Darwin and *The Loves of the Plants*." *Isis* 80, no. 4 (1989): 593–621.

Bruce, Iris. "'Aggadah Raises Its Paw against Halakha': Kafka's Zionist Critique in 'Forschungen eines Hundes.'" *Journal of the Kafka Society of America* 16, no. 1 (1992): 4–18.

Bühler, Benjamin, and Stefan Rieger. *Das Übertier: Ein Bestiarium des Wissens.* Frankfurt am Main: Suhrkamp, 2006.

Bundeszentrale für politische Bildung, ed. "Der neue Mensch." Special issue, *Aus Politik und Zeitgeschehen* 66, nos. 37–38 (2016).

Byatt, A. S. *Children's Book.* New York: Random House, 2009.

Carstensen, Thorsten, and Marcel Schmid, eds. *Die Literatur der Lebensreform.* Bielefeld: transcript, 2016.

Chen, Mel. *Animacies: Biopolitics, Racial Mattering, and Queer Affect.* Durham, NC: Duke University Press, 2012.

Clark, John R. *The Modern Satiric Grotesque and Its Traditions.* Lexington: University Press of Kentucky, 1991.

Clutton-Brock, Juliet. "Origin of the Dog: Domestication and Early History." In *The Domestic Dog: Its Evolution, Behaviour and Interactions with People*, edited by James Serpell, 7–20. Cambridge: Cambridge University Press, 2002.

Cohen, Jeffrey Jerome, ed. *Monster Theory: Reading Culture*. Minneapolis: University of Minnesota Press, 1996.
Connelly, Tristanne. "Flowery Porn: Form and Desire in Erasmus Darwin's *The Loves of the Plants*." *Literature Compass* 13, no. 10 (2016): 604–16.
Cooper, Andrea Dara. "Writing Humanimals: Critical Animal Studies and Jewish Studies." *Religion Compass* 13, no. 2 (2019): 1–11.
Corngold, Stanley. *Franz Kafka: The Necessity of Form*. Ithaca, NY: Cornell University Press, 1988.
———. "Kafka & Sex." *Daedalus* 136, no. 2 (2007): 79–87.
———. *Lambent Traces: Franz Kafka*. Princeton, NJ: Princeton University Press, 2004.
Corngold, Stanley, and Benno Wagner. *Franz Kafka: The Ghosts in the Machine*. Evanston, IL: Northwestern University Press, 2011.
Cornwell, Neil. *The Absurd in Literature*. Manchester: Manchester University Press, 2006.
———. *The Literary Fantastic*. Hertfordshire: Harvester Wheatsheaf, 1990.
Craft, Christopher. *Another Kind of Love: Male Homosexual Desire in English Discourse, 1850–1920*. Berkeley: University of California Press, 1994.
Craig, Robert, and Ina Linge, eds. *Biological Discourses: The Language of Science and Literature around 1900*. Oxford: Peter Lang, 2017.
Darwin, Charles. *The Descent of Man, and Selection in Relation to Sex*, vol. 1. London: John Murray, 1871.
———. *Narrative of the Surveying Voyages of His Majesty's Ships Adventure and Beagle*, vol. 3. London: Henry Colburn, 1839.
Daum, Andreas. *Wissenschaftspopularisierung im 19. Jahrhundert: Bürgerliche Kultur, naturwissenschaftliche Bildung und die deutsche Öffentlichkeit*. Munich: Oldenbourg Wissenschaftsverlag, 2002.
Dekel, Edan, and David Gantt Gurley. "Kafka's Golem." *Jewish Quarterly Review* 107, no. 4 (2017): 531–56.
DeKoven, Marianne. "Kafka's Animal Stories: Modernist Form and Interspecies Narrative." In *Creatural Fiction: Human-Animal Relationships in Twentieth- and Twenty-First-Century Literature*, edited by David Herman, 19–40. New York: Palgrave Macmillan, 2016.
Deleuze, Gilles, and Félix Guattari. *Kafka: Toward a Minor Literature*. Minneapolis: University of Minnesota Press, 1986.
DelPlato, Joan. *Multiple Wives, Multiple Pleasures: Representing the Harem, 1800–1875*. Madison, NJ: Fairleigh Dickinson University Press, 2002.
Densky, Doreen. *Literarische Fürsprache bei Franz Kafka: Rhetorik und Poetik*. Berlin: De Gruyter, 2020.
Derrida, Jacques. *The Animal That Therefore I Am*. New York: Fordham University Press, 2008.

Descartes, René. *A Discourse on the Method of Correctly Conducting One's Reason and Seeking Truth in the Sciences*. Translated by Ian Maclean. Oxford: Oxford University Press, 2008.

Deschner, Karlheinz. "Oskar Panizza." In *Das Christentum im Urteil seiner Gegner*, vol. 2, edited by Karlheinz Deschner, 7–27. Wiesbaden: Limes, 1971.

Dimić, Colette. "Das Groteske in der Erzählung des Expressionismus: Scheerbart, Mynona, Sternheim, Ehrenstein und Heym." PhD diss., Universität Freiburg, 1960.

Dodd, Bill. "The Case for a Political Reading." In *The Cambridge Companion to Kafka*, edited by Julian Preece, 131–49. Cambridge: Cambridge University Press, 2002.

Donahue, William Collins. *The End of Modernism: Elias Canetti's Auto-da-Fé*. Chapel Hill: University of North Carolina Press, 2001.

Drexler-Dreis, Joseph, and Kristien Justaert, eds. *Beyond the Doctrine of Man: Decolonial Visions of the Human*. New York: Fordham University Press, 2019.

Driscoll, Kári, and Eva Hoffmann, eds. *What Is Zoopoetics? Texts, Bodies, Entanglement*. New York: Palgrave Macmillan, 2018.

Durst, Uwe. *Theorie der phantastischen Literatur*. Berlin: Lit, 2007.

Düsterberg, Rolf. "'Die Auferstehung des Schweins in München': Eber und Sau in den Schriften Oskar Panizzas." In *Die Zoologie der Träume: Studien zum Tiermotiv in der Literatur der Moderne*, edited by Dorothee Römhild, 124–33. Opladen: Westdeutscher Verlag, 1999.

———. *"Die gedrukte Freiheit": Oskar Panizza und die Zürcher Diskußjonen*. Frankfurt am Main: Peter Lang, 1988.

———. "Moral und Sexualität in den Schriften Oskar Panizzas." *Zeitschrift für Sexualforschung* 1, no. 4 (1988): 365–78.

———. "Panizza, Oskar." *Datenbank Schrift und Bild 1900–1960*. http://www.polunbi.de/pers/panizza-01.html.

Edmunds, Lowell. "Kafka on Minor Literature." *German Studies Review* 33, no. 2 (2010): 351–74.

Edwards, Justin, and Rune Graulund. *Grotesque*. Milton Park: Taylor & Francis, 2013.

Eggers, Kurt. *Oskar Panizza: Aus Werk und Leben*. Berlin: Nordland, 1943.

Ellmann, Maud. *The Hunger Artist: Starving, Writing, and Imprisonment*. Cambridge, MA: Harvard University Press, 1993.

Empson, William. *The Structure of Complex Words*. Cambridge, MA: Harvard University Press, 1989.

Eschweiler, Christian. *Kafkas Dichtung als Kosmos: Der Schlüssel zu seinem Verständnis*. Bonn: Bouvier, 1993.

Ewers, Hanns Heinz. "Aus dem Tagebuch eines Orangenbaumes." In *Das Grauen*, 135–70. Munich: Georg Müller, 1912.

———. "Die Petition." *Jugend* 2, no. 35 (1904): 708–11.

———. *Führer durch die moderne Literatur: Dreihundert Würdigungen der hervorragendsten Schriftsteller unserer Zeit*. Berlin: Globus, 1911.

———. "Zum Epilog: ein paar Worte des Herausgebers." In Oskar Panizza, *Visionen der Dämmerung*, edited by Hanns Heinz Ewers, 375–80. Munich: Georg Müller, 1917.

Exner, Lisbeth. *Fasching als Logik: Über Salomo Friedlaender/Mynona*. Munich: belleville, 1996.

Fara, Patricia. *Sex, Botany and Empire: The Story of Carl Linnaeus and Joseph Banks*. Cambridge: Icon, 2003.

Feldt, Jakob Egholm. *Transnationalism and the Jews: Culture, History and Prophecy*. New York: Rowman & Littlefield, 2016.

Ffytche, Matt. *The Foundation of the Unconscious: Schelling, Freud and the Birth of the Modern Psyche*. Cambridge: Cambridge University Press, 2011.

Fichte, Johann Gottlieb. *Grundlage der gesammten Wissenschaftslehre*. Leipzig: Christian Ernst Gabler, 1794.

Fickert, Kurt. *End of Mission: Kafka's Search for Truth in His Last Stories*. Columbia: Camden House, 1993.

———. "Kafka's Search for Truth in 'Forschungen eines Hundes.'" *Monatshefte* 85, no. 2 (1993): 189–97.

Fingerhut, Karl-Heinz. *Die Funktion der Tierfiguren im Werke Franz Kafkas*. Bonn: Bouvier, 1969.

Fischer, Alexander M. "Renaissancismus als Terrorismus? Oskar Panizza und 'Das Liebeskonzil.'" In *Der Renaissancismus-Diskurs um 1900*, edited by Thomas Althaus and Markus Fauser, 199–224. Bielefeld: Aisthesis, 2017.

Fischer, Jens Malte. "Deutschsprachige Phantastik zwischen Décadence und Faschismus." In *Phaïcon: Almanach der phantastischen Literatur*, edited by Rein A. Zondergeld, 93–130. Frankfurt am Main: Suhrkamp, 1978.

Fiske, George Converse. *Lucilius and Horace: A Study in the Classical Theory of Imitation*. Madison: University of Wisconsin Press, 1920.

Flaig, Paul. "Weimar Slapstick: American Eccentrics, German Grotesques." PhD diss., Cornell University, 2013.

Fontane, Theodor. *Schriften zur Literatur*. Edited by Hans-Heinrich Reuter. Berlin: Aufbau, 1960.

Förderer, Manuel. "'Nun kommen aber die Fehler hintennachgehinkt': Zur Poetologie des Defekten bei Oskar Panizza." In *Kann das weg? Literarisierungen des Defekten und Defizitären*, edited by Dennis Borghardt and Florian Lehmann, 91–114. Hannover: Werhahn, 2022.

Foucault, Michel. *The History of Sexuality*, vol. 1, *The Will to Knowledge*. London: Penguin, 1998.

Freud, Sigmund. *Das Unbehagen in der Kultur*. Vienna: Internationaler Psychoanalytischer Verlag, 1930.

———. "Eine Schwierigkeit der Psychoanalyse." *Imago: Zeitschrift für Anwendung der Psychoanalyse auf die Geisteswissenschaften* 5 (1917): 1–7.

———. "From the History of an Infantile Neurosis ['The Wolf Man']." In *The Freud Reader*, edited by Peter Gay, 400–426. New York: W. W. Norton, 1989.
———. *A General Introduction to Psychoanalysis*. New York: Boni and Liveright, 1920.
———. "One of the Difficulties of Psycho-Analysis." *International Journal of Psycho-Analysis* 1, no. 1 (1920): 17–23.
Friedlaender, Salomo. *Friedrich Nietzsche: Eine intellektuelle Biographie*. Leipzig: Oskar Brandstetter, 1910.
Friedlaender/Mynona, Salomo. *Briefwechsel*, vol. 5, edited by Hartmut Geerken, Detlef Thiel, and Sigrid Hauff, 300–305. Herrsching: Waitawhile, 2019.
———. *Das Eisenbahnglück oder der Anti-Freud*. Berlin: Elena Gottschalk, 1925.
———. "Der operierte Goj: Ein Gegenstück zu Panizzas operiertem Jud." In *Grotesken*, vol. 1, edited by Hartmut Geerken and Detlef Thiel, 598–606. Herrsching: Waitawhile, 2008.
———. "Grotesk." In *Der Querschnitt durch 1921*, edited by Alfred Flechtheim, 54–55. Düsseldorf: Propyläen, 1922.
———. *Grotesken*, vol. 1. Edited by Hartmut Geerken and Detlef Thiel. Herrsching: Waitawhile, 2008.
———. *Grotesken*, vol. 2. Edited by Hartmut Geerken and Detlef Thiel. Herrsching: Waitawhile, 2008.
———. *Ich (1871–1936): Autobiographische Skizze*. Edited by Hartmut Geerken. Bielefeld: Aisthesis, 2003.
———. *Schöpferische Indifferenz*. Edited by Hartmut Geerken and Detlef Thiel. Herrsching: Waitawhile, 2009.
———. *Schwarz-Weiss-Rot*. Leipzig: Kurt Wolff, 1916.
Fromm, Waldemar. "Nachwort." In Oskar Panizza, *Werke*, vol. 4 (*Visionen*), edited by Peter Staengle and Günther Emig, 221–35. Niederstetten: Günther Emigs Literatur-Betrieb, 2020.
Fuß, Peter. *Das Groteske: Ein Medium des kulturellen Wandels*. Cologne: Böhlau, 2001.
Gagliano, Monica, John C. Ryan, and Patrícia Vieira, eds. *The Language of Plants: Science, Philosophy, Literature*. Minneapolis: University of Minnesota Press, 2017.
Galle, Heinz J. "Oskar Panizza: Ein Porträt." *Fantasia* 91/92 (1994): 55–100.
Geerken, Hartmut. "Nachwort." In Mynona, *Prosa*, vol. 2, 277–318. Munich: edition text+kritik, 1980.
———. "Vorwort." In Salomo Friedlaender, *Briefe aus dem Exil, 1933–1946*, edited by Hartmut Geerken, 7–14. Main: v. Hase & Koehler, 1982.
Gehlen, Arnold. *Der Mensch: Seine Natur und seine Stellung in der Welt*. Berlin: Junker & Dünnhaupt, 1940.
Geier, Ted. *Kafka's Nonhuman Form: Troubling the Boundaries of the Kafkaesque*. New York: Palgrave Macmillan, 2016.

Gelderloos, Carl. *Biological Modernism: The New Human in Weimar Culture*. Evanston, IL: Northwestern University Press, 2019.
Geller, Jay. "The Aromatics of Jewish Difference: Or, Benjamin's Allegory of Aura." In *Jews and Other Differences: The New Jewish Cultural Studies*, edited by Daniel Boyarin and Jonathan Boyarin, 203–56. Minneapolis: University of Minnesota Press, 1996.
———. *Bestiarium Judaicum: Unnatural Histories of the Jews*. New York: Fordham University Press, 2018.
———. "(G)nos(e)ology: The Cultural Construction of the Other." In *The People of the Body: Jews and Judaism from an Embodied Perspective*, edited by Howard Eilberg-Schwartz, 243–82. Albany: State University of New York Press, 1992.
———. "Of Mice and Mensa: Anti-Semitism and the Jewish Genius." *Centennial Review* 38, no. 2 (Spring 1994): 361–85.
———. *On Freud's Jewish Body: Mitigating Circumcision*. New York: Fordham University Press, 2007.
———. *The Other Jewish Question: Identifying the Jew and Making Sense of Modernity*. New York: Fordham University Press, 2011.
———. "The Unmanning of the Wandering Jew." *American Imago* 49, no. 2 (1992): 227–62.
George, Sam. *Botany, Sexuality, and Women's Writing, 1760–1830: From Modest Shoot to Forward Plant*. Manchester: Manchester University Press, 2007.
Gerhardt, Christina. "Narrating Entanglement: Cixous' 'Stigmata, or Job the Dog.'" *Humanities* 6, no. 4 (2017): 1–11.
Gerr, Elke. *Das große Vornamenbuch*. Hannover: Humboldt, 2008.
Giardina, Andrea. *Le parole del cane: L'immagine del cane nella letteratura italiana del Novecento*. Florence: Le Lettere, 2009.
Gilman, Sander L. "Anti-Semitism and the Body in Psychoanalysis." *Social Research* 57, no. 4 (1990): 993–1017.
———. *The Case of Sigmund Freud: Medicine and Identity at the Fin de Siècle*. Baltimore, MD: Johns Hopkins University Press, 1993.
———. *Creating Beauty to Cure the Soul: Race and Psychology in the Shaping of Aesthetic Surgery*. Durham, NC: Duke University Press, 1998.
———. *Franz Kafka: The Jewish Patient*. New York: Routledge, 1995.
———. *Freud, Race, and Gender*. Princeton, NJ: Princeton University Press, 1993.
———. *Jewish Self-Hatred: Anti-Semitism and the Hidden Language of the Jews*. Baltimore, MD: Johns Hopkins University Press, 1986.
Glaser, Hermann. "Kulturchronik 1900–2005: So viel Neuer Mensch war nie wie nach 1900." *Du: Die Zeitschrift der Kultur* 767 (2006–2007): 66–73.
Greenslade, William M. *Degeneration, Culture, and the Novel: 1880–1940*. Cambridge: Cambridge University Press, 1994.

Grimm, Jacob, and Wilhelm Grimm. *Kinder- und Hausmärchen*, vol. 1. Berlin: Realschulbuchhandlung, 1812.

Gronau, Magdalena. "Der Psychiater als Literat – der Literat als 'Psichopat' – der 'Psichopat' als Psychiater: Zu den Fallgeschichten des Falls Oskar Panizza: Mit einem Seitenblick auf Foucaults 'Hermaphrodismus.'" In *Fallgeschichte(n) als Narrativ zwischen Literatur und Wissen*, edited by Thomas Wegmann and Martina King, 195–223. Innsbruck: Innsbruck University Press, 2016.

Groves, Jason. "Low Tide, Black Shoals: Toward Offshore Formations in Celan Studies." *The Germanic Review: Literature, Culture, Theory* 98, no. 4 (2023): 447–61.

Haakenson, Thomas O. *Grotesque Visions: The Science of Berlin Dada*. New York: Bloomsbury, 2021.

———. "'The Merely Illusory Paradise of Habits': Salomo Friedländer, Walter Benjamin, and the Grotesque." *New German Critique* 36, no. 1 (106) (Winter 2009): 119–47.

Haderlev, Jürgen. "Mynona: Rosa, die Frau des Flickschusters." *Konkret: Unabhängige Zeitschrift für Kultur und Politik* 12 (December 1965): 39.

Haeckel, Ernst. *Generelle Morphologie*. Berlin: Georg Reimer, 1866.

———. *The History of Creation*, vol. 2. Translated by E. Ray Lankester. New York: D. Appleton, 1880.

Hall, Matthew. *Plants as Persons: A Philosophical Botany*. Albany: State University of New York Press, 2011.

Hall, Sara F. "Prussian Police Reform and the Modernization of the Academy Classroom: The Advent of the German Police Training Film, 1919–20." In *Policing Interwar Europe*, edited by Gerald Blaney Jr., 69–89. London: Palgrave Macmillan.

Hamilton, John. "Die Erziehung des Teufels: Über Hoffmanns Berganza-Novelle." *Hölderlin-Jahrbuch* 36 (2009): 75–84.

Hampe, Aron. "Der operierte Goj (Kurzgeschichte von Salomo Friedlaender, 1922)." In *Handbuch des Antisemitismus: Judenfeindschaft in Geschichte und Gegenwart*, vol. 7, *Literatur, Film, Theater und Kunst*, edited by Wolfgang Benz, 373–75. Berlin: De Gruyter, 2015.

———. "Der operierte Jud' (Kurzgeschichte von Oskar Panizza, 1893)." In *Handbuch des Antisemitismus: Judenfeindschaft in Geschichte und Gegenwart*, vol. 7, *Literatur, Film, Theater und Kunst*, edited by Wolfgang Benz, 375–77. Berlin: De Gruyter, 2015.

Haraway, Donna. *The Companion Species Manifesto: Dogs, People, and Significant Otherness*. Chicago: Prickly Paradigm, 2005.

Harel, Naama. "Investigations of a Dog, by a Dog: Between Anthropocentrism and Canine-Centrism." In *Speaking for Animals: Animal Autobiographical Writing*, edited by Margo DeMello, 49–59. Routledge: New York, 2013.

———. *Kafka's Zoopoetics: Beyond the Human-Animal Barrier*. Ann Arbor: University of Michigan Press, 2020.

Harpham, Geoffrey G. *On the Grotesque: Strategies of Contradiction in Art and Literature*. Princeton, NJ: Princeton University Press, 1982.

Haskell, David George. "Nature's Case for Same-Sex Marriage." *New York Times*, March 30, 2013. http://www.nytimes.com/2013/03/30/opinion/natures-case-for-same-sex-marriage.html?ref=opinion&_r=1&.

Hearne, Vicky. *Adam's Task: Calling Animals by Name*. New York: Skyhorse, 2007.

Heidsieck, Arnold. *Das Groteske und das Absurde im modernen Drama*. Stuttgart: W. Kohlhammer, 1969.

Heinemann, Caspar. "Fucking Pansies: Queer Poetics, Plant Reproduction, Plant Poetics, Queer Reproduction." BA thesis, Goldsmiths, University of London, 2016. https://www.academia.edu/32408905/FUCKING_PANSIES_Queer_Poetics_Plant_Reproduction_Plant_Poetics_Queer_Reproduction.

Heintze, Albert. *Die deutschen Familien-Namen: geschichtlich, geographisch, sprachlich*. Halle an der Saale: Verlag der Buchhandlung des Waisenhauses, 1882.

Heller, Erich. "Investigations of a Dog and Other Matters." In *The World of Franz Kafka*, edited by Joseph P. Stern, 103–11. New York: George Weidenfeld and Nicolson, 1980.

Heller, Paul. *Franz Kafka: Wissenschaft und Wissenschaftskritik*. Tübingen: Stauffenburg, 1989.

Hertz, Gal. "Pathologie des modernen Selbst: Oskar Panizzas *Das Liebeskonzil* und *Psichopatia criminalis*." *Text+Kritik* 7, no. 243 (2024): 10–17.

———. "The Pathologization of Everyday Life: Panizza's Syphilitic Literature." In *Religion und Wahnsinn um 1900: Zwischen Pathologisierung und Selbstermächtigung*, edited by Lutz Greisinger, Sebastian Schüler, and Alexander van der Haven, 139–66. Würzburg: Ergon, 2017.

Hildebrandt, Günther. "Oskar Panizza als Bibliophile." *Die Bücherstube: Blätter für Freunde des Buches und der zeichnenden Künste* 1, nos. 3–4 (1920): 92–98.

Hoffmann, E. T. A. "A New Year's Eve Adventure." In *The Best Tales of Hoffmann*, edited by Everett Franklin Bleiler, 104–29. New York: Dover, 1967.

Horowitz, Alexandra. *Inside of a Dog*. New York: Scribner, 2009.

Huber, Ottmar. *Mythos und Groteske: Die Problematik des Mythischen und ihre Darstellung in der Dichtung des Expressionismus*. Meisenheim am Glan: Anton Hain, 1979.

Hulfeld, Stefan, Rudi Risatti, and Andrea Sommer-Mathis, eds. *Grotesk! Ungeheuerliche Künste und ihre Wiederkehr*. Vienna: Hollitzer Wissenschaftsverlag, 2022.

Imm, Karsten. *Absurd und Grotesk: zum Erzählwerk von Wilhelm Busch und Kurt Schwitters*. Bielefeld: Aisthesis, 1994.

Isenberg, Noah William. *Between Redemption and Doom: The Strains of German-Jewish Modernism*. Lincoln: University of Nebraska Press, 1999.

Jackson, Frank. *Faithful Friends: Dogs in Life and Literature*. New York: Carroll & Graf, 1997.

Jackson, Zakiyyah Iman. *Becoming Human: Matter and Meaning in an Antiblack World*. New York: New York University Press, 2020.

Jacobs, Joela, ed. "Animal Narratology." Special issue, *Humanities* (Fall 2016–Spring 2018). https://www.mdpi.com/journal/humanities/special_issues/animal_narratology.

———. "Assimilating Aliens: Imagining National Identity in Oskar Panizza's Operated Jew and Salomo Friedlaender's *Operated Goy*." In *Alien Imaginations: Science Fiction and Tales of Transnationalism*, edited by Ulrike Küchler, Silja Mähl, and Graeme Stout, 57–71. New York: Bloomsbury Academic, 2015.

———. "Eden's Heirs: Biopolitics and Vegetal Affinities in the Gardens of Literature." In *Why Look at Plants? The Botanical Emergence in Contemporary Art*, edited by Giovanni Aloi, 120–23. Boston: Brill, 2019.

———. "The Function of Monsters: Loci of Border Crossing and the In-Between." In *Monstrosity in Art, Psychoanalysis and Philosophy*, edited by Gerhard Unterthurner and Erik M. Vogt, 71–88. Vienna: Turia + Kant, 2012.

———. "The Grammar of Zoopoetics: Human and Canine Language Play." In *What Is Zoopoetics? Texts, Bodies, Entanglement*, edited by Kàri Driscoll and Eva Hoffmann, 63–80. New York: Palgrave Macmillan, 2018.

———. "A Jewish Frankenstein: Making Monsters in Modernist German Grotesques." In *Monsters, Demons, and Wonders in European-Jewish History*, edited by Iris Idelson-Shein and Christian Wiese, 102–17. New York: Bloomsbury Academic, 2019.

———. "Nachwort." In Oskar Panizza, *Werke*, vol. 3 (*Genie und Wahnsinn; Aus dem Tagebuch eines Hundes; Die unbefleckte Empfängnis der Päpste*), edited Peter Staengle and Günther Emig, 267–79. Niederstetten: Günther Emigs Literatur-Betrieb, 2020.

———. "Oskar Panizzas Manuskript 'Für "Petroleumdichter."'" *Text+Kritik* 7, no. 243 (2024): 5–9.

———. "Phytopoetics: Upending the Passive Paradigm with Vegetal Violence and Eroticism." *Catalyst: Feminism, Theory, Technoscience* 5, no. 2 (2019): 1–18.

———. "Plant Parenthood, or the Fear of Vegetal Eroticism." In *Imperceptibly and Slowly Opening*, edited by Caroline Picard, 166–72. Chicago: Green Lantern, 2016.

———. "Plant Parts: Vegetal Tropes and Their Phytopoetic Resonances across Botany and Culture." *Plant Perspectives* 1, no. 2 (2024): 277–92.

———. "Pollen." In *Microbium: The Neglected Lives of Micro-Matter*, edited by Joela Jacobs and Agnes Malinowska, 101–14. Santa Barbara, CA: punctum, 2023.

———. "Rose." In *The Mind of Plants: Narratives of Vegetal Intelligence*, edited by John C. Ryan, Patrícia Vieira, and Monica Gagliano, 307–16. Santa Fe, NM: Synergetic, 2021.

———. "Separation Anxiety: Canine Narrators and Modernist Isolation in Woolf, Twain, and Panizza." In *Literatur für Leser:innen* 39, no. 2 (2018 as 2016): 153–68.

———. "'These Lusting, Incestuous, Perverse Creatures': A Phytopoetic History of Plants and Sexuality." *Environmental Humanities* 14, no. 3 (2022).

———. "'. . . und die ganze pfälzisch-jüdische Sündfluth kam dann heraus': Monstrosity and Multilingualism in Oskar Panizza's *Der operirte Jud'*." In *Zeitschrift für interkulturelle Germanistik* 3, no. 2 (2012): 61–73.

———. "'Verbrechen wider die Natur': Oskar Panizza's First Encounter with Censorship." In *Protest and Reform in the German Literature and Visual Culture, 1871–1918*, edited by Godela Weiss-Sussex and Charlotte Woodford, 125–38. Munich: Iudicum, 2015.

———. "'Waren es etwa doch nicht Hunde? Aber wie sollten es denn nicht Hunde sein?' Kommunikation, Epistemologie und Willensfreiheit in Kafkas Forschungen eines Hundes." In *Kafkas Tiere: Forschungen der deutschen Kafka-Gesellschaft*, vol. 4, edited by Harald Neumeyer and Wilko Steffens, 293–306. Würzburg: Königshausen & Neumann, 2015.

Jacobs, Joela, Tamara Klarić, and Nike Thurn. "Auswahlbibliografie." *Text+Kritik* 7, no. 243 (2024): 84–91.

Jacobs, Joela, Isabel Kranz, and Solvejg Nitzke, eds. *Plant Poetics: Literary Forms and Functions of the Vegetal*. Boston: Brill, 2025.

Jacobs, Joela, and Bastian Lasse. "Making Intersex Identity ILLegible: Oskar Panizza's 'Ein skandalöser Fall.'" In *Handbook to the Health Humanities in German Studies*, edited by Stephanie Hilger, 289–302. London: Bloomsbury, 2024.

Jacobs, Joela, and Nicole Seymour. "Asexual Ecologies." In *Asexualities: Feminist and Queer Perspectives, Revised and Expanded Ten-Year Anniversary Edition*, edited by KJ Cerankowski and Megan Milks, 23–36. New York: Routledge, 2024.

Jacobs, Joela, and Nike Thurn. "'Ein antisemitisches Kunstwerk'? Oskar Panizzas 'Der operirte Jud'.'" *Text+Kritik* 7, no. 243 (2024): 54–61.

———, eds. "Oskar Panizza." Special issue, *Text+Kritik* 7, no. 243 (2024).

Jäger, Christian. "Flucht nach vorn: Die anarchische Junggesellenmaschine Oskar Panizzas." In *Kulturrebellen: Studien zur anarchistischen Moderne*, edited by Christine Magerski and David Roberts, 83–98. Wiesbaden: Springer, 2019.

Jäger, Gustav. *Die Entdeckung der Seele*. Leipzig: Ernst Guenter, 1880.

Jahraus, Oliver, and Bettina von Jagow. "Kafkas Tier- und Künstlergeschichten." In *Kafka-Handbuch: Leben – Werk – Wirkung*, edited by Oliver Jahraus and Bettina von Jagow, 530–52. Göttingen: Vandenhoeck & Ruprecht, 2008.

Jakob, Hans-Joachim. "Tiere im Text: Hundedarstellungen in der deutschsprachigen Literatur des frühen 20. Jahrhunderts im Spannungsfeld von 'Human-Animal Studies' und Erzählforschung." *Textpraxis: Digitales Journal für Philologie* 8, no. 1 (2014).

Janzen, Janet. *Media, Modernity and Dynamic Plants in Early 20th Century German Culture*. Boston: Brill, 2016.

Jaschke, Gerhard. "Neue Lebensflüsse und Nahrung für unsere Nerven: Von der Notwendigkeit gezielter Skandale: Über Oskar Panizza." *Freibord: Zeitschrift für Literatur und Kunst* 9, no. 40 (1984): 107–9.

Jelavich, Peter. "Am Anfang war Panizza." *Herzattacke* 100 (2018): 94–99.

———. *Berlin Cabaret*. Cambridge, MA: Harvard University Press, 1996.

———. *Munich and Theatrical Modernism: Politics, Playwriting, and Performance, 1890–1914*. Cambridge, MA: Harvard University Press, 1985.

———. "Pan(dem)izza: Panizza lesen in der Pandemie." In *Freunde der Monacensia e.V. – Jahrbuch*, edited by Gabriele von Bassermann-Jordan, Waldemar Fromm, and Kristina Kargl, 169–80. Munich: Allitera, 2021.

Jobst, Kristina. "Pawlow, Uexküll, Kafka: Forschungen *mit* Hunden." In *Kafkas Tiere: Forschungen der deutschen Kafka-Gesellschaft*, vol. 4, edited by Harald Neumeyer and Wilko Steffens, 307–33. Würzburg: Königshausen & Neumann, 2015.

Kafka, Franz. *Briefe 1902–1924*. New York: Schocken, 1958.

———. *Der Proceß*. Frankfurt am Main: Fischer, 2000.

———. "Ein Bericht für eine Akademie." *Der Jude: Eine Monatsschrift* 2, no. 8 (November 1917): 559–65.

———. "Forschungen eines Hundes." In *Beim Bau der Chinesischen Mauer*, edited by Max Brod and Hans Joachim Schoeps, 154–211. Berlin: Gustav Kiepenheuer, 1931.

———. *In der Strafkolonie*. Leipzig: Kurt Wolff, 1919.

———. "Investigations of a Dog." In *The Complete Stories*, edited by Nahum N. Glatzer, 310–46. Translated by Willa and Edwin Muir. New York: Schocken, 1988.

———. *Nachgelassene Schriften und Fragmente II*. Edited by Jost Schillemeit. Frankfurt am Main: Fischer, 1992.

———. "A Report for an Academy." In *Kafka's Selected Stories*, edited and translated by Stanley Corngold, 76–83. New York: Norton, 2007.

———. "Researches of a Dog." In *Kafka's Selected Stories*, edited and translated by Stanley Corngold, 132–60. New York: Norton, 2007.

———. *The Trial*. Translated by Breon Mitchell. New York: Schocken, 1998.

Kant, Immanuel. *Kritik der Urteilskraft* [1790]. Edited by Heiner F. Klemme. Annotated by Piero Giordanetti. Hamburg: Meiner, 2009.

Kantzenbach, Friedrich-Wilhelm. "Der Dichter Oskar Panizza und der Pfarrer Friedrich Lippert." *Zeitschrift für Religions- und Geistesgeschichte* 26 (1974): 125–42.

Kanzog, Klaus. "Literarische Zensur." In *Reallexikon der deutschen Literaturgeschichte*, vol. 4, edited by Klaus Kanzog and Achim Masser, 998–1049. Berlin: De Gruyter, 1984.
Kayser, Wolfgang. *Das Groteske in Malerei und Dichtung.* Oldenburg: Gerhard Stalling, 1957.
———. *The Grotesque in Art and Literature.* New York: Columbia University Press, 1981.
Kellermann, Philippe, ed. *Propaganda der Tat: Standpunkte und Debatten (1877–1929).* Münster: Unrast, 2016.
Kelley, Theresa M. *Clandestine Marriage: Botany and Romantic Culture.* Baltimore, MD: Johns Hopkins University Press, 2012.
Kelly, Natasha A. "Das N-Wort." In *Rassismus auf gut Deutsch: Ein kritisches Nachschlagewerk zu rassistischen Sprachhandlungen*, edited by Adibeli Nduka-Agwu and Antje Lann Hornscheidt, 157–66. Frankfurt am Main: Brandes & Apsel, 2010.
Ketterl, Anja. "Skandalöses Erzählen: Panizza—Bernhard—Walser." PhD diss., University of Maryland, 2017.
———. "Von Hegemonie und Unentscheidbarkeit: Oskar Panizzas 'Ein scandalöser Fall.'" *Aussiger Beiträge* 10 (2016): 99–114.
Kilgour, Maggie. "The Function of Cannibalism at the Present Time." In *Cannibalism and the Colonial World*, edited by Francis Barker, Peter Hulme, and Margaret Iversen, 238–59. Cambridge: Cambridge University Press, 1998.
Kimmerer, Robin Wall. *Braiding Sweetgrass: Indigenous Wisdom, Scientific Knowledge, and the Teachings of Plants.* Minneapolis, MN: Milkweed Editions, 2013.
Kistner, Ulrike. "Der wackelnde Thron: Gott, Kaiser und Vaterland bei Oskar Panizza." *Acta Germanica* 17 (1984): 99–114.
Kittler, Wolf, and Gerhard Neumann, eds. *Franz Kafka: Schriftverkehr.* Freiburg im Breisgau: Rombach, 1990.
Kleinhans, Belinda. "Addressing the Modern Crisis of Language and Meaning through Kafka's and Aichinger's Literary Animals." In *Glaubenssysteme: Belief Systems in Austrian Literature, Thought and Culture*, edited by Michael Boehringer, A. G. Cattell, and Belinda Kleinhans, 129–51. Vienna: Praesens, 2017.
Koelb, Clayton. *Kafka: A Guide for the Perplexed.* New York: Continuum, 2010.
———. *Kafka's Rhetoric: The Passion of Reading.* Ithaca, NY: Cornell University Press, 1989.
Kohlenbach, Margarete. "Religious Dogs in Nietzsche and Kafka." *Oxford German Studies* 39, no. 3 (2010): 213–27.
Kohlhauer, Michael. "Wenn Hunde erzählen: Miguel de Cervantes' *Coloquio de los perros* und die Tierliteratur." *Iberoromania* 56 (2002): 51–81.

Könemann, Sophia. "Von 'Menschen-Bälgen', 'kostbaren Rassen' und 'Canarienvögeln': Fetischismus in Oskar Panizzas Erzählung 'Der Corsetten-Fritz.'" In *Das Geschlecht der Anderen: Figuren der Alterität: Kriminologie, Psychiatrie, Ethnologie und Zoologie*, edited by Sophia Könemann and Anne Stähr, 171–86. Bielefeld: transcript, 2011.

Kort, Pamela, ed. *Comic Grotesque: Wit and Mockery in German Art, 1870–1940*. Munich: Prestel, 2004.

———, ed. *Grotesk! 130 Jahre Kunst der Frechheit*. Munich: Prestel, 2003.

Koschorke, Albrecht. "Schmutz." In Oskar Panizza, *Das Schwein in poetischer, mitologischer und sittengeschichtlicher Beziehung*, edited by Rolf Düsterberg, 7–17. Munich: Belleville, 1994.

Kranz, Isabel, Alexander Schwan, and Eike Wittrock, eds. *Floriographie: Die Sprachen der Blumen*. Paderborn: Wilhelm Fink, 2016.

Kraus, Karl. "Oscar Panizza: Der teutsche Michel und der römische Papst." *Die Zeit*, December 1, 1894, 143.

Krčal, Katharina. *Nachahmen und Täuschen: Die 'jüdische Mimikry' und der antisemitische Diskurs im 19. und 20. Jahrhundert*. Hildesheim: Olms, 2022.

Kristeva, Julia. *Power of Horror: An Essay on Abjections*. New York: Columbia University Press, 1980.

Kucher, Primus-Heinz. "'Scheiterhaufen' oder 'Denkmal,' 'Provokateur' oder 'häretischer Heiligenbildmaler'? Radikale Realitätssicht in Texten von Oskar Panizza." In *Germanistik: Traditionspflege und neue Herausforderungen*, edited by Erzsébet Forgács, 117–27. Szeged: Grimm Kiadó, 2003.

Küenzlen, Gottfried. *Der Neue Mensch: Zur säkularen Religionsgeschichte der Moderne*. Munich: Wilhelm Fink, 1993.

Kugel, Wilfried. *Der Unverantwortliche: Das Leben des Hanns Heinz Ewers*. Düsseldorf: Grupello, 1992.

Kuhlbrodt, Dietrich. "Tiroler Zensur." *Konkret* 2 (2006).

Kuxdorf, Manfred. *Der Schriftsteller Salomo Friedlaender/Mynona: Kommentator einer Epoche*. Frankfurt am Main: Peter Lang, 1990.

———. "Mynona versus Remarque, Tucholsky, Mann and Others: Not So Quiet on the Literary Front." In *The First World War in German Narrative Prose*, edited by Heinz Wetzel and Charles N. Genno, 71–92. Toronto: University of Toronto Press, 1980.

Kuzniar, Alice. *Melancholia's Dog*. Chicago: University of Chicago Press, 2006.

Laist, Randy, ed. *Plants and Literature: Essays in Critical Plant Studies*. Boston: Brill, 2013.

Lang, Birgit. "'Writing Back': Literary Satire and Oskar Panizza's *Psichopatia criminalis* (1898)." In *A History of the Case Study: Sexology, Psychoanalysis, Literature*, edited by Birgit Lang, Joy Damousi, and Alison Lewis, 90–118. Manchester: Manchester University Press, 2017.

Laqueur, Thomas W. *Solitary Sex: A Cultural History of Masturbation*. New York: Zone, 2003.
Lasse, Bastian. "Sexualität im Werk Oskar Panizzas." In *Text+Kritik* 7, no. 243 (2024): 46–53.
Lawson, Richard H. *Franz Kafka*. New York: Ungar, 1987.
Lazardzig, Jan. "Performing *Ruhe*: Police, Prevention, and the Archive." In *Theatre/Performance Historiography*, edited by Rosemarie K. Bank and Michal Kobialka, 123–51. New York: Palgrave Macmillan, 2015.
Leadbeater, Lewis W. "Platonic Elements in Kafka's 'Investigations of a Dog.'" *Philosophy and Literature* 11, no. 1 (1987): 104–16.
———. "The Sophistic Nature of Kafka's 'Forschungen eines Hundes.'" *German Life and Letters* 46, no. 2 (1993): 145–55.
Leskau, Lina. "Botanical Perversions: On the Depathologization of Perversions in Texts by Alfred Döblin and Hanns Heinz Ewers." In *Biological Discourses: The Language of Science and Literature around 1900*, edited by Robert Craig and Ina Linge, 211–34. Oxford: Peter Lang, 2017.
———. *Sadismus und Masochismus: Zur Subversion der Sexualwissenschaft im Frühwerk Alfred Döblins*. Cologne: Böhlau, 2020.
Levinas, Emmanuel. "The Name of a Dog, or Natural Rights." In *Difficult Freedom: Essays on Judaism*, translated by Seán Hand, 151–53. Baltimore, MD: Johns Hopkins University Press, 1990.
Levine, Michael G. "'A Place So Insanely Enchanting': Kafka and the Poetics of Suspension." *Modern Language Notes* 123, no. 5 (2008): 1039–67.
Lichti, Marion. *Der letzte Ausweg in die Freiheit: Oskar Panizza: Ein Fall für sich*. Norderstedt: GRIN, 2007.
Lickart, Maren. "Hunde in der Literatur der Weimarer Republik: Erich Maria Remarques 'Station am Horizont' und Ruth Landshoff-Yorcks 'Die Vielen und der Eine.'" *literaturkritik.de*, February 8, 2018. https://literaturkritik.de/public/rezension.php?rez_id=24125.
Liddell, Henry George, and Robert Scott. *A Greek-English Lexicon*. Oxford: Clarendon, 1940.
Lieb, Claudia. "Der Fall Oskar Panizza: Skandalisierung des Skandals um das *Liebeskonzil* durch Recht und Bild." In *Skandalautoren: Zu repräsentativen Mustern literarischer Provokation und Aufsehen erregender Autorinszenierung*, vol. 1, edited by Andrea Bartl and Martin Kraus, 349–72. Würzburg: Königshausen & Neumann, 2014.
———. "'Ein Geschlecht läuft neben uns her, seltsam gebildet, die Blicke dunkel und verzehrend': Oskar Panizzas Hoffmann-Rezeption und die Münchner Neuromantik." *E. T. A. Hoffmann-Jahrbuch* 19 (2011): 90–112.
———. "Freedom of Satire? Oskar Panizza's Play *Das Liebeskonzil* in a Series of Trials in Germany and Austria." In *Exceptio Artis and Theories of*

Literature in Court, edited by Ralf Grüttemeier, 107–22. London: Bloomsbury, 2016.

———. "Nachwort." In Oskar Panizza, *Werke*, vol. 2 (*Dämmrungsstücke*), edited by Peter Staengle and Günther Emig, 223–38. Niederstetten: Günther Emigs Literatur-Betrieb, 2019.

———. "Window Dressing: Fetishistic Transactions in Fictional Prose by Oskar Panizza and Thomas Mann." In *Communication of Love: Mediatized Intimacy from Love Letters to SMS*, edited by Eva Lia Wyss, 307–20. Bielefeld: transcript, 2014.

———. "Window-shopping: Fetishistic Transactions in Fictional Prose of the 'Münchner Moderne.'" *Philologie im Netz* 52 (2010): 35–49.

Linge, Ina. *Queer Livability: German Sexual Sciences and Life Writing*. Ann Arbor: University of Michigan Press, 2023.

Lippert, Friedrich. *In Memoriam Oskar Panizza*. Munich: Horst Stobbe, 1926.

Locher, Elmar, ed. *Die kleinen Formen in der Moderne*. Bozen: Edition Sturzflüge, 2001.

Loew, Katharina. *Special Effects and German Silent Film: Techno-Romantic Cinema*. Amsterdam: Amsterdam University Press, 2021.

Lorenz, Dagmar C. G. "Man and Animal: The Discourse of Exclusion and Discrimination in a Literary Context." *Women in German Yearbook* 14 (1998): 201–24.

Lorenz, Felix. "Das Groteske." In *Das Buch der Grotesken: Eine Sammlung phantastischer und satirischer Erzählungen aus der Weltliteratur*, 1–6. Munich: Georg Müller, 1914.

Lothe, Jakob, Beatrice Sandberg, and Ronald Speirs, eds. *Franz Kafka: Narration, Rhetoric, and Reading*. Columbus: Ohio State University Press, 2011.

Mackay, John Henry. *Max Stirner: Sein Leben und sein Werk*. Berlin: Schuster & Loeffler, 1898.

Mancuso, Stefano, and Alessandra Viola. *Brilliant Green: The Surprising History and Science of Plant Intelligence*. Washington, DC: Island, 2015.

Mann, Thomas. "Betrachtungen eines Unpolitischen (1918)." In *Gesammelte Werke in 13 Bänden*, vol. 12, edited by Hans Bürgin and Peter de Mendelssohn, 9–589. Frankfurt am Main: Fischer, 1990.

———. "Das Liebeskonzil." *Das Zwanzigste Jahrhundert* 5 (1895): 522.

Marcus, Steven. *The Other Victorians: A Study of Sexuality and Pornography in Mid-Nineteenth Century England*. New Brunswick: Transaction, 2009.

Marder, Michael. *Plant Thinking: A Philosophy of Vegetal Life*. New York: Columbia University Press, 2013.

Matzigkeit, Michael. *Literatur im Aufbruch: Schriftsteller und Theater in Düsseldorf zwischen 1900 und 1933*. Düsseldorf: Verlag der Goethe-Buchhandlung, 1990.

McDonough MacKenzie, Caitlin, Sara Kuebbing, Rebecca S. Barak, Molly Bletz, Joan Dudney, Bonnie M. McGill, Mallika A. Nocco, Talia Young, and Rebecca K. Tonietto. "We Do Not Want to 'Cure Plant Blindness,' We Want to Grow Plant Love." *Plants, People, Planet* 1, no. 3 (2019): S.139–41.

McElroy, Bernard, and Cara Delay. *Fiction of the Modern Grotesque*. London: Palgrave Macmillan, 1989.

McHugh, Susan. *Love in a Time of Slaughters: Human-Animal Stories against Genocide and Extinction*. Philadelphia: Penn State University Press, 2019.

———. "Plants and Literature." In *Oxford Research Encyclopedia of Literature*. August 31, 2021. https://doi.org/10.1093/acrefore/9780190201098.013.1267.

McKittrick, Katherine, ed. *Sylvia Wynter: On Being Human as Praxis*. Durham, NC: Duke University Press, 2014.

Mehring, Walter. "Mynona: Bank der Spötter." *Literarische Rundschau: Beilage zum Berliner Tageblatt* 382, no. 2 (August 15, 1920): 1.

Meilicke, Elena. "Fotografie und 'Pseudizität': Paranoia als Medienwissen in Oskar Panizas 'Imperjalja.'" *Text+Kritik* 7, no. 243 (2024): 26–36.

———. *Paranoia und technisches Bild: Fallstudien zu einer Medienpathologie*. Berlin: De Gruyter, 2021.

Merkl, Helmut. "Von der Mission des Mitleids im Puppenland: Eine Studie zur Erzählkunst Oskar Panizzas." *Michigan Germanic Studies* 22, no. 1 (1996): 22–40.

Middelhoff, Frederike, Sebastian Schönbeck, Roland Borgards, and Catrin Gersdorf, eds. *Texts, Animals, Environments: Zoopoetics and Ecopoetics*. Freiburg im Breisgau: Rombach, 2019.

Mignolo, Walter. "Sylvia Wynter: What Does It Mean to Be Human?" In *Sylvia Wynter: On Being Human as Praxis*, edited by Katherine McKittrick, 106–23. Durham, NC: Duke University Press, 2014.

Mitchell, Robert. *Experimental Life: Vitalism in Romantic Science and Literature*. Baltimore, MD: Johns Hopkins University Press, 2013.

Mitterbauer, Helga. "'Ihr Herrn, mir scheint, der Streit geht schon zu weit': Performative Konstruktion von Blasphemie am Beispiel von Oskar Panizzas 'Liebeskonzil.'" In *Literatur als Skandal: Fälle – Funktionen – Folgen*, edited by Stefan Neuhaus and Johann Holzner, 247–56. Göttingen: Vandenhoeck & Ruprecht, 2007.

Mladek, Klaus, ed. *Police Forces: A Cultural History of an Institution*. New York: Palgrave, 2007.

Möbus, Frank. *Sünden-Fälle: Die Geschlechtlichkeit in Erzählungen Franz Kafkas*. Göttingen: Wallstein, 1994.

Moekel, Paula. *Mein Hund Rolf: Ein rechnender und buchstabierender Airedale-Terrier*. Stuttgart: R. Lutz, 1920.

Montgomery, Beronda L. *Lessons from Plants*. Cambridge, MA: Harvard University Press, 2021.

Mortimer-Sandilands, Catriona, and Bruce Erickson, eds. *Queer Ecologies: Sex, Nature, Politics, Desire*. Bloomington: Indiana University Press, 2010.

Müller, Burkhard. "Trost im Fell des Nachbarn: Zu Kafkas Tierparabeln." In *Lufthunde: Portraits der deutschen literarischen Moderne*, 137–68. Springe: zu Klampen, 2008.

Müller, Jürgen. *Der Pazjent als Psichater: Oskar Panizzas Weg vom Irrenarzt zum Insassen*. Bonn: Edition Das Narrenschiff im Psychiatrie-Verlag, 1999.

Müller-Schwefe, Moritz. "'Im Banne dieses wunderlichen Menschen.'" *Metamorphosen* 3, no. 33 (2013): 36–38.

———. "Urszenen des Tabus um 1900: Ästhetik des Tabus bei Panizza, Wedekind und Schnitzler." *Germanistische Mitteilungen* 41, no. 1 (2015): 59–73.

Murnane, Barry, and Rainer Godel, eds. *Zwischen Popularisierung und Ästhetisierung: Hanns Heinz Ewers und die Moderne*. Bielefeld: Aisthesis, 2014.

Nägele, Rainer. "I Don't Want to Know That I Know: The Inversion of Socratic Ignorance in the Knowledge of the Dogs." In *Philosophy and Kafka*, edited by Brendan Moran and Carlo Salzani, 19–31. Lanham, MD: Lexington, 2013.

Neau, Patrice. "Antisemitismus und Antikatholizismus bei Oskar Panizza." *Acta Germanica* 24 (1996): 21–33.

Neumann, Gerhard. "Der Blick des Anderen: Zum Motiv des Hundes und des Affen in der Literatur." *Jahrbuch der deutschen Schillergesellschaft* 40 (1996): 87–122.

———. *Kafka-Lektüren*. Berlin: De Gruyter, 2013.

Nicolai, Ralf R. "Wahrheit als Gift: Zu Kafkas 'Forschungen eines Hundes.'" *Modern Austrian Literature* 11, no. 3/4 (1978): 179–97.

Nienhaus, Stefan. *Geschichte der deutschen Tischgesellschaft*. Tübingen: Niemeyer, 2003.

Nietzsche, Friedrich. "Ueber Wahrheit und Lüge im aussermoralischen Sinne." In *Sämtliche Werke*, vol. 1, edited by Giorgio Colli and Mazzino Montinari, 873–90. Berlin: De Gruyter, 1980.

Nitschke, Peter, ed. *Die deutsche Polizei und ihre Geschichte: Beiträge zu einem distanzierten Verhältnis*. Hilden: Deutsche Polizeiliteratur, 1996.

Nitzke, Solvejg, and Helga G. Braunbeck, eds. "Arboreal Imaginaries." Special issue, *Green Letters* 25, no. 4 (2021).

Nordau, Max. *Entartung*. Berlin: Duncker, 1892.

Norris, Margot. *Beast of the Modern Imagination: Darwin, Nietzsche, Kafka, Ernst, and Lawrence*. Baltimore, MD: Johns Hopkins University Press, 1985.

Nyhart, Lynn K. *Modern Nature: The Rise of the Biological Perspective in Germany*. Chicago: University of Chicago Press, 2009.

Ochse, Katharina. *Joseph Roths Auseinandersetzung mit dem Antisemitismus.* Würzburg: Königshausen und Neumann, 1999.

Oeser, Erhard. *Hund und Mensch: Die Geschichte einer Beziehung.* Zurich: Primus, 2004.

Oesterle, Günter. "Juden, Philister und romantische Intellektuelle: Überlegungen zum Antisemitismus in der Romantik." *Athenäum: Jahrbuch der Friedrich Schlegel-Gesellschaft* 2 (1992): 55–89.

Olson, Jess. *Nathan Birnbaum and Jewish Modernity: Architect of Zionism, Yiddishism, and Orthodoxy.* Stanford, CA: Stanford University Press, 2013.

Orich, Annika. "Artificial Aliens: Reproductive Imaginations in German Culture." PhD diss., University of California, Berkeley, 2017.

Ortlieb, Claudia. "Kafkas Tiere." *Zeitschrift für deutsche Philologie* 126 (2007): 339–66.

Ossar, Michael. "Kafka and the Reader: The World as Text in 'Forschungen eines Hundes.'" *Colloquia Germanica* 20, no. 4 (1987): 325–37.

Panizza, Oskar. *Abschied von München: Ein Handschlag.* Zurich: Schabelitz, 1897.

———. "Aus dem Tagebuch eines Hundes." In *Werke*, vol. 3, edited by Peter Staengle and Günther Emig, 49–129. Niederstetten: Günther Emigs Literatur-Betrieb, 2020.

———. *Dämmerungsstücke: Groteske Erzählungen.* Bremen: Europäischer Literaturverlag, 2013.

———. *Das Liebeskonzil und andere Schriften.* Edited by Hans Prescher. Neuwied: Luchterhand, 1964.

———. "Das rothe Haus." In *Düstre Lieder.* Leipzig: Albert Unflad, 1886.

———. *Das Rothe Haus: Ein Lesebuch zu Religion, Sexus und Wahn.* Edited by Michael Bauer. Munich: Allitera, 2003.

———. "Das Verbrechen in Tavistock-Square." *Modernes Leben: Ein Sammelbuch der Münchner Modernen* 1 (1891): 109–118.

———. "Der operirte Jud'." In *Werke*, vol. 4, edited by Peter Staengle and Günther Emig, 135–66. Niederstetten: Günther Emigs Literatur-Betrieb, 2020.

———. *Dialoge im Geiste Huttens.* Edited by Bernd Mattheus. Munich: Matthes & Seitz, 1979.

———. "Für 'Petroleumdichter.'" *Text+Kritik* 7, no. 243 (2024): 3–4.

———. "Kunst und Polizei." *Die neue Rundschau* 5 (1894).

———. "Mania anarchista progressiva." *Zürcher Diskußionen* 3, nos. 28–32 (1900): 37–39.

———. *Neues aus dem Hexenkessel der Wahnsinns-Fanatiker.* Edited by Michael Bauer. Neuwied: Luchterhand, 1986.

———. *Psychopathia Criminalis: Die kriminelle Psychose, genannt Psichopatia criminalis: Hilfsbuch für Ärzte, Laien, Juristen, Vormünder, Verwaltungsbeamte, Minister, etc. zur Diagnose der politischen Gehirnerkrankung.* Munich: Matthes & Seitz, 1978.

———. "A Scandalous Case." Translated by Sophie Wilkins. In *Herculine Barbin: Being the Recently Discovered Memoirs of a Nineteenth-Century Hermaphrodite*, edited by Michel Foucault, translated by Richard McDougall, 155–99. New York: Pantheon, 1980.

———. *Werke*. Edited by Peter Staengle and Günther Emig. Niederstetten: Günther Emigs Literatur-Betrieb, 1919–.

Pankau, Johannes G. "Oskar Panizza: Tabubruch und Aufklärung." In *Sexualität und Modernität: Studien zum deutschen Drama des Fin de Siècle*, edited by Johannes G. Pankau, 308–39. Würzburg: Königshausen & Neumann, 2005.

Parker, Emily Anne. "The Human as Double Bind: Sylvia Wynter and the Genre of 'Man.'" *Journal of Speculative Philosophy* 32, no. 3 (2018): 439–49.

Parsley, Kathryn M. "Plant Awareness Disparity: A Case for Renaming Plant Blindness." *Plants, People, Planet* 2, no. 6 (2020): 598–601.

Parvulescu, Anca. "Kafka's Laughter: On Joy and the Kafkaesque." *PMLA* 130, no. 5 (2015): 1420–32.

Pascal, Roy. *Kafka's Narrators: A Study of His Stories and Sketches*. Cambridge: Cambridge University Press, 1982.

Peterson, Audrey C. "Brain Fever in Nineteenth-Century Literature: Fact and Fiction." *Victorian Studies* 19, no. 4 (1976): 445–64.

Pick, Anat. *Creaturely Poetics: Animality and Vulnerability in Literature and Film*. New York: Columbia University Press, 2011.

Pines, Noam. *The Infrahuman: Animality in Modern Jewish Literature*. Albany: State University of New York Press, 2018.

Pinthus, Kurt. "Philosoph und Clown." *Die Zeit*, November 18, 1966. https://www.zeit.de/1966/47/philosoph-und-clown.

Pocai, Susanne. "System-Wahn: Oskar Panizza und Oswald Spengler als Meister der inneren Katastrophe." In *Literarische Katastrophendiskurse im 20. und 21. Jahrhundert*, edited by Ewa Wojno-Owczarska, 77–96. Berlin: Peter Lang, 2019.

Pollan, Michael. *The Botany of Desire: A Plant's-Eye View of the World*. New York: Random House, 2001.

———. "The Intelligent Plant." *New Yorker*, December 15, 2013. https://www.newyorker.com/magazine/2013/12/23/the-intelligent-plant.

Porter, Theodore M. *Genetics in the Madhouse: The Unknown History of Human Heredity*. Princeton, NJ: Princeton University Press, 2018.

Powell, Matthew T. "Bestial Representations of Otherness: Kafka's Animal Stories." *Journal of Modern Literature* 32, no. 1 (2008): 129–42.

Prawer, Siegbert. "'Ein poetischer Hund': E. T. A. Hoffmann's *Nachrichten von den neuesten Schicksalen des Hundes Berganza* and Its Antecedents in European Literature." In *Aspekte der Goethezeit*, edited by Stanley Corngold, Michael Curschmann, and Theodore Ziolkowski, 273–93. Göttingen: Vandenhoeck & Ruprecht, 1977.

Proctor, Robert. "Architecture from the Cell-Soul: René Binet and Ernst Haeckel." *Journal of Architecture* 11, no. 4 (2006): 407–24.
Pulver, Max. "Spaziergang mit Franz Kafka." In *"Als Kafka mir entgegenkam..." Erinnerungen an Franz Kafka*, edited by Hans-Gerd Koch, 130–35. Berlin: Wagenbach, 1995.
Reichwald, Anika. *Das Phantasma der Assimilation: Interpretationen des "Jüdischen" in der deutschen Phantastik 1890–1930*. Göttingen: Vienna University Press, 2017.
Reitter, Paul. *On the Origins of Jewish Self-Hatred*. Princeton, NJ: Princeton University Press, 2012.
Rettinger, Michael L. *Kafkas Berichterstatter: Anthropologische Reflexionen, zwischen Irritation und Reaktion, Wirklichkeit und Perspektive*. Frankfurt am Main: Peter Lang, 2003.
Ritvo, Harriet. *The Animal Estate: The English and Other Creatures in Victorian England*. Cambridge, MA: Harvard University Press, 1989.
Robertson, Ritchie. "Kafka as Anti-Christian: 'Das Urteil,' 'Die Verwandlung,' and the Aphorisms." In *A Companion to the Works of Franz Kafka*, edited by James Rolleston, 101–22. Rochester: Camden House, 2006.
———. *Kafka: Judaism, Politics, and Literature*. Oxford: Oxford University Press, 1985.
Rösler, Walter. "Ein bißchen Gefängnis und ein bißchen Irrenhaus: Der Fall Oskar Panizza." *Sinn und Form* 32, no. 4 (1980): 840–55.
Ruch, Hannes. "Wer ist Oskar Panizza?" In Oskar Panizza, *Visionen der Dämmerung*, edited by Hanns Heinz Ewers, vii–xv. Munich: Georg Müller, 1917.
Russo, Mary. *The Female Grotesque: Risk, Excess, Modernity*. New York: Routledge, 1995.
Sandford, Stella. *Vegetal Sex: Philosophy of Plants*. New York: Bloomsbury, 2022.
Santner, Eric. *My Own Private Germany: Daniel Paul Schreber's Secret History of Modernity*. Princeton, NJ: Princeton University Press, 1996.
———. *On Creaturely Life: Rilke, Benjamin, Sebald*. Chicago: University of Chicago Press, 2006.
Sartre, Jean-Paul. *Anti-Semite and Jew*. Translated by George J. Becker. New York: Schocken, 1948.
Sauer, Bernhard. "Freikorps und Antisemitismus in der Frühzeit der Weimarer Republik." *Zeitschrift für Geschichtswissenschaft* 56, no. 1 (2008): 5–29.
Schaumann, Caroline, and Heather I. Sullivan, eds. *German Ecocriticism in the Anthropocene*. New York: Palgrave Macmillan, 2017.
Schiebinger, Londa. *Nature's Body: Gender in the Making of Modern Science*. Boston: Beacon, 1993.
Schmidt, Dietmar. "Assimilations-Experimente: Oskar Panizza liest Karl Marx." In *Experimentalanordnungen der Bildung: Exteriorität – Theatralität – Literarizität*,

edited by Bettine Menke and Thomas Glaser, 225–49. Paderborn: Wilhelm Fink, 2014.

———. "Ende der Vorstellung: Oskar Panizzas 'Das Wachsfigurenkabinet' und die Erfindung des Kinos." *Text+Kritik* 7, no. 243 (2024): 37–45.

Schmiedebach, Heinz-Peter. "Hirne, die in's Kraut schießen: Das Irrenhaus als Ort der Freiheit und Bohème? Oskar Panizza und Franziska zu Reventlow." In *Oskar-Panizza-Reihe*. Edited by Joela Jacobs and Nike Thurn. *Literaturportal Bayern* (blog), August 13, 2021. https://www.literaturportal-bayern.de/journal?task=lpbblog.default&id=2406.

Schneegans, Heinrich. *Geschichte der grotesken Satire*. Strasburg: Karl J. Trübener, 1894.

Schneider, Ivan. "Narrative Complexity in the Talking-Dog Stories of Cervantes, Hoffmann, Gogol, Bulgakov, and Kafka." MA thesis, Harvard University, Extension School, 2012.

Schneider, Manfred. "Das Notariat der Hunde: Eine literaturwissenschaftliche Kynologie." *Zeitschrift für deutsche Philologie* 126 (2007): 4–27.

———. "Die Paranoia der Dichter (1): Oskar Panizza." In *Das Attentat: Kritik der paranoischen Vernunft*, 209–17. Munich: Matthes & Seitz, 2010.

———. "Kafkas Tiere und das Unmögliche." In *Menschengestalten: Zur Kodierung des Kreatürlichen im modernen Roman*, edited by Rudolf Behrens and Roland Galle, 83–102. Würzburg: Königshausen & Neumann, 1995.

Schneider, Uwe. "Literarische Zensur und Öffentlichkeit im Wilhelminischen Zeitalter." In *Naturalismus, Fin de Siècle, Expressionismus 1890–1918*, edited by York-Gothart Mix, 394–409. Munich: Hanser, 2000.

Scholem, Gershom. *Walter Benjamin: Die Geschichte einer Freundschaft*. Frankfurt am Main: Suhrkamp, 1975.

———. *Walter Benjamin: The Story of a Friendship*. New York: New York Review of Books, 2012.

Schonlau, Anja. *Syphilis in der Literatur: Über Ästhetik, Moral, Genie und Medizin (1880–2000)*. Würzburg: Königshausen & Neumann, 2005.

———. "Warum der Teufel Medizin studiert hat: Antidogmatisches Lachen in Oskar Panizzas Dramensatire *Das Liebeskonzil*." In *LachArten: Zur ästhetischen Repräsentation des Lachens vom späten 17. Jahrhundert bis zur Gegenwart*, edited by Arnd Beise, Ariane Martin, and Udo Roth, 165–85. Bielefeld: Aisthesis, 2003.

Schroeter, Werner, dir. *Liebeskonzil*. Berlin: Saskia Film GmbH, 1982.

Schuhbeck, Birgit. *Paradise Lost: Das Denkmodell des Tabu/Bruchs in Drama, Theater und Gesellschaft um 1900*. Würzburg: Königshausen & Neumann, 2018.

———. "Urszenen des Tabus um 1900: Ästhetik des Tabus bei Panizza, Wedekind und Schnitzler." *Germanistische Mitteilungen* 41, no. 1 (2015): 59–73.

Shteir, Ann B. *Cultivating Women, Cultivating Science: Flora's Daughters and Botany in England, 1760–1860*. Baltimore, MD: Johns Hopkins University Press, 1996.

Siemann, Wolfram. *"Deutschlands Ruhe, Sicherheit und Ordnung." Die Anfänge der politischen Polizei 1806–1866*. Tübingen: Max Niemeyer, 1985.

Silhouette, Marielle. "Von den Grottesken zum Grotesken oder Das Spiel mit den Konventionen." In *Konvention und Konventionsbruch: Wechselwirkungen deutscher und französischer Dramatik 17.–20. Jahrhundert*, edited by Horst Turk and Jean-Marie Valentin, 202–19. Bern: Peter Lang, 1992.

Smiljanić, Damir. "Nachwort." In Oskar Panizza, *Werke*, vol. 7 (*Der Illusionismus und Die Rettung der Persönlichkeit; Ein guter Kerl; Abschied von München; Dialoge im Geiste Hutten's*), edited by Peter Staengle and Günther Emig, 221–52. Niederstetten: Günther Emigs Literatur-Betrieb, 2021.

Soceanu, Marion. "Oskar Panizza's Kampf um den Glauben." *Colloquia Germanica* 14 (1981): 142–57.

Soergel, Albert. *Dichtung und Dichter der Zeit: Im Banne des Expressionismus*. Leipzig: A. Voigtländer, 1925.

Sommerey, Constance. "'Illegal Science': The Case of Ernst Haeckel (1834–1919) and German Biology Education." *Shells and Pebbles* (blog), August 4, 2014. http://www.shellsandpebbles.com/2014/08/04/illegal-science-the-case-of-ernst-haeckel-1834-1919-and-german-biology-education/.

Sorg, Reto. "Groteske." In *Reallexikon der deutschen Literaturwissenschaft*, vol. 1, edited by Klaus Weimar, 748–51. Berlin: De Gruyter, 2007.

Spörl, Uwe. "Die Entmündigung eines Autors: Oskar Panizza als unzurechnungsfähiges 'Genie.'" In *Unzurechnungsfähigkeiten: Diskursivierungen unfreier Bewußtseinszustände seit dem 18. Jahrhundert*, edited by Michael Niehaus, 237–63. Frankfurt am Main: Peter Lang, 1998.

Stach, Reiner. *Die Kafka-Biographie in drei Bänden*. Frankfurt am Main: Fischer, 2017.

Stadler, Ulrich. "Kafkas Experimente." In *"Es ist ein Laboratorium, ein Laboratorium für Worte": Experiment und Literatur III: 1890–2010*, edited by Michael Bies and Michael Gamper, 139–61. Göttingen: Wallstein, 2011.

Stähler, Axel. "The Author's *Derrière* and the Ludic Impulse: Oskar Panizza's 'The Operated Jew' (1893) and Amy Levy's 'Cohen of Trinity' (1889)." In *Internal Outsiders – Imagined Orientals? Antisemitism, Colonialism and Modern Constructions of Jewish Identity*, edited by Ulrike Brunotte, Jürgen Mohn, and Christina Späti, 111–28. Würzburg: Ergon, 2017.

———. *Zionism, the German Empire, and Africa: Jewish Metamorphoses and the Colors of Difference*. Berlin: De Gruyter, 2019.

Stark, Gary D. *Banned in Berlin: Literary Censorship in Imperial Germany, 1871–1918*. New York: Berghahn, 2009.

Stasjulevics, Heiko. *Gotha, die Fliegerstadt*. Bad Langensalza: Rockstuhl, 2001.

Stead, Evanghélia. *Le monstre, le singe et le fœtus: tératogonie et décadence dans l'Europe fin-de-siècle*. Geneva: Librairie Droz, 2004.

Stegmann, Kathrin. *Halluzinatorisches Sehen: Augenblicke des Wahns bei Oskar Panizza und Georg Heym*. Würzburg: Königshausen & Neumann, 2019.

Stehle, Maria. *Plants, Places, and Power: Toward Social and Ecological Justice in German Literature and Film*. Rochester: Camden House, 2023.

Steinlechner, Gisela. *Fallgeschichten: Krafft-Ebing, Panizza, Freud, Tausk*. Wien: WUV-Universitätsverlag, 1995.

Stephan, Sigmund Jakob-Michael. "Ansätze zu einer (posthumanistischen) Tier-Umwelt-Poetik: Kafkas Tiergeschichten und Yoko Tawadas Etüden im Schnee." PhD diss., University of Waterloo, 2019.

Stirner, Max. *Der Einzige und sein Eigentum*. Stuttgart: Reclam, 1991.

Stobbe, Horst. *Oskar Panizzas literarische Tätigkeit: Ein bibliographischer Versuch*. Munich: Horst Stobbe, 1925.

Sutton, Katie. *Sex between Body and Mind: Psychoanalysis and Sexology in the German-Speaking World, 1890s–1930s*. Ann Arbor: University of Michigan Press, 2019.

Taiz, Lincoln, and Lee Taiz. *Flora Unveiled: The Discovery and Denial of Sex in Plants*. Oxford: Oxford University Press, 2017.

Taylor, Seth. *Left-Wing Nietzscheans: The Politics of German Expressionism 1910–1920*. Berlin: De Gruyter, 1990.

Thermann, Jochen. *Kafkas Tiere: Fährten, Bahnen und Wege der Sprache*. Marburg: Tectum, 2010.

Thiel, Detlef. "Einleitung: Ich verlange ein Reiterstandbild: Mynonas gesammelte Grotesken." In Salomo Friedlaender/Mynona, *Grotesken*, vol. 1, edited by Hartmut Geerken and Detlev Thiel, 13–81. Herrsching: Waitawhile, 2008.

Thompson, Philip. *The Grotesque in German Poetry, 1880–1933*. Melbourne: Hawthorne, 1975.

Thurn, Nike. *"Falsche Juden": Performative Identitäten in der deutschsprachigen Literataur von Lessing bis Walser*. Göttingen: Wallstein, 2015.

Thurston-Torres, Jonathan W., ed. *Animals and Race: The Animal Turn*. Ann Arbor: Michigan State University Press, 2023.

Todorov, Tzvetan. *The Fantastic: A Structural Approach to a Literary Genre*. Cleveland, OH: Case Western Reserve University Press, 1973.

Totzke, Ariane. "Der 'transnationale Körper' als Kampfplatz: Oskar Panizzas antisemitisches Panoptikum in 'Der operirte Jud'." *literaturkritik.de*, June 4, 2013. https://literaturkritik.de/public/rezension.php?rez_id=17983.

———. "Schwindsüchtige Erlöser, psychotische Pfaffen und 'Der Fall Barbin': Oskar Panizzas ästhetischer Vandalismus im Deutschen Kaiserreich." In

Religion und Literatur im 20. und 21. Jahrhundert: Motive, Sprechweisen, Medien, edited by Tim Lörke and Robert Walter-Jochum, 277–95. Göttingen: V&R unipress, 2015.

Trommer, Gerhard. *Natur im Kopf: Die Geschichte ökologisch bedeutsamer Naturvorstellungen in deutschen Bildungskonzepten*. Weinheim: Deutscher Studienverlag, 1993.

Tuchmann, Emil. "Die Erben Panizzas vereiteln die Herausgabe des Nachlasses." *Die literarische Welt* 5, no. 31 (1929): 8.

Tucholsky, Kurt [Hauser, Kaspar, pseud.]. "Zehn Minuten [Herr Wendriner telefoniert]." *Die Weltbühne* 18/2, no. 27 (July 6, 1922): 19.

——— [Panter, Peter, pseud.]. "Der Prozeß." *Die Weltbühne* 22/1, no. 10 (March 9, 1926): 383.

——— [Wrobel, Ignaz, pseud.]. "Die genialen Syphilitiker." *Die Weltbühne* 23/1, no. 6 (August 2, 1927): 212.

——— [Wrobel, Ignaz, pseud.]. "Oskar Panizza." *Freiheit* 3, no. 272 (July 11, 1920): 2.

——— [Wrobel, Ignaz, pseud.]. "Panizza." *Die Weltbühne* 15/2, no. 38 (September 11, 1919): 321–25.

Turp, Michael-John. "Shameless Dogs: Cynics and Nonhuman Animal Ethics." *Society & Animals* 32 (2024): 1–15.

Uhall, Michael. "Creaturely Conditions: Acknowledgment and Animality in Kafka, Cavell, and Uexküll." *Configurations* 24, no. 1 (2016): 1–24.

Untermann, Mally. *Das Groteske bei Wedekind, Thomas Mann, Heinrich Mann, Morgenstern und Wilhelm Busch*. Saalfeld: Günthers Druckerei, 1929.

Velten, Hans Rudolf. "Laughing at the Body: Approaches to a Performative Theory of Laughter." *Journal of Literary Theory* 3, no. 2 (December 2009): 353–73.

Vieth, Ludger. *Beobachtungen zur Wortgroteske*. Euskirchen: Euskirchener Volksblatt, 1931.

Voegelin, Erminie W. "Vagina Dentata." In *Funk & Wagnalls Standard Dictionary of Folklore, Mythology and Legend*, edited by Maria Leach, 1152. New York: Funk & Wagnalls, 1972.

Vogl, Joseph, Friedrich Balke, and Bernhard Siegert. *Kleine Formen*. Berlin: Vorwerk 8, 2021.

Voigt, Frank, ed. "Bibliothek verbrannter Bücher." *Moses Mendelssohn Zentrum für europäisch-jüdische Studien*. www.verbrannte-buecher.de.

von den Berg, Britt. *Die "Neue Tierpsychologie" und ihre wissenschaftlichen Vertreter (von 1900 bis 1945)*. Berlin: Tenea, 2008.

von Goethe, Johann Wolfgang. "Faust." In *Goethes Werke: Hamburger Ausgabe in 14 Bänden*, vol. 3, edited by Erich Trunz, 9–364. Hamburg: Wegner, 1948.

———. "Von Arabesken (1789)." In *Gedenkausgabe der Werke, Briefe und Gespräche*, vol. 13, edited by Christian Beutler, 62–66. Zurich: Artemis, 1954.

von Hofmannsthal, Hugo. "A Letter." In *The Lord Chandos Letter and Other Writings*, translated by Joel Rotenberg, 117–28. New York: New York Review of Books, 2005.

von Kleist, Heinrich. *Penthesilea: Ein Trauerspiel: Tübingen: 1808*. Edited by Joseph Kiermeier-Debre. Munich: Deutscher Taschenbuch-Verlag, 1998.

Voß, Hendrik Christian. "Die Darstellung der Syphilis in literarischen Werken um 1900: Auswirkung wissenschaftlicher Konzepte und sozialer Ideen." PhD diss., Universität Lübeck, 2004.

Vroon, Piet A., Anton van Amerongen, and Hans de Vries. *Smell: The Secret Seducer*. Translated by Paul Vincent. New York: Farrar, Straus & Giroux, 1997.

Wakefield, Andre. *The Disordered Police State: German Cameralism as Science and Practice*. Chicago: Chicago University Press, 2009.

Wallach, Kerry. *Passing Illusions: Jewish Visibility in Weimar Germany*. Ann Arbor: University of Michigan Press, 2017.

Walzel, Oskar. "Neue Dichtung vom Tiere." *Zeitschrift für Bücherfreunde* 10 (1918): 53–58.

Wandersee, James H., and Elisabeth E. Schussler. "Preventing Plant Blindness." *American Biology Teacher* 61, no. 2 (1999): 82–86.

———. "Toward a Theory of Plant Blindness." *Plant Science Bulletin* 47, no. 1 (2001): 2–9.

Wels, Ulrike. "Der individualistische Dämon: Oskar Panizzas dramatische Selbstinszenierung bis zur Katastrophe." In *Skandalautoren: Zu repräsentativen Mustern literarischer Provokation und Aufsehen erregender Autorinszenierung*, vol. 1, edited by Andrea Bartl and Martin Kraus, 323–48. Würzburg: Königshausen & Neumann, 2014.

Werner, Renate. "Geschnürte Welt: Zu einer Fallgeschichte von Oskar Panizza." In *Romantik und Ästhetizismus*, edited by Bettina Gruber and Gerhard Plumpe, 213–32. Würzburg: Königshausen & Neumann, 1999.

Wiehl, Klaus. "Die Poetologie der Biologie: Franz Kafkas 'Forschungen eines Hundes' und Jacob von Uexkülls Umweltforschung." In *Kafkas narrative Verfahren: Forschungen der deutschen Kafka-Gesellschaft*, vol. 3, edited by Harald Neumeyer and Wilko Steffens, 205–25. Würzburg: Königshausen & Neumann, 2015.

Williams, Eric. "Of Cinema, Food, and Desire: Franz Kafka's 'Investigations of a Dog.'" *College Literature* 34, no. 4 (2007): 92–124.

Winkelman, John. "Kafka's 'Forschungen eines Hundes.'" *Monatshefte* 59, no. 3 (1967): 204–16.

Winter, Marcel. *Das Individuum und die Gesellschaft: Herrschaftsmechanismen, Machtstrukturen und Diskurspraktiken im Werk Oskar Panizzas (1853–1921)*. Würzburg: Königshausen & Neumann, 2023.

Wipplinger, Jonathan. "The Racial Ruse: On Blackness and Blackface Comedy in 'fin-de-siècle' Germany." *German Quarterly* 84, no. 4 (Fall 2011): 457–76.
Wörtche, Thomas. "Exkurs: Phantastik und Groteske." In *Phantastik und Unschlüssigkeit: Zum strukturellen Kriterium eines Genres: Untersuchungen an Texten von Hanns Heinz Ewers und Gustav Meyrink*, 245–60. Meitingen: Corian-Verlag, 1987.
Wünsch, Marianne. *Die Fantastische Literatur der frühen Moderne (1890–1930): Definition, denkgeschichtlicher Kontext, Strukturen*. Munich: Wilhelm Fink, 1991.
Wurich, Marc. "Der halluzinierte Kaiser: Oskar Panizzas 'Imperjalja' (1901–04): Zwischen Ideologie und Poetologie." In *Herrschaftserzählungen: Wilhelm II. in der Kulturgeschichte (1888–1933)*, edited by Nicolas Detering, Johannes Franzen, and Christopher Meid, 143–65. Würzburg: Ergon, 2016.
Wynter, Sylvia. "Unsettling the Coloniality of Being/Power/Truth/Freedom: Towards the Human, after Man, Its Overrepresentation—An Argument." *New Centennial Review* 3, no. 3 (2003): 257–337.
Yarri, Donna. "Index to Kafka's Use of Creatures in His Writings." In *Kafka's Creatures: Animals, Hybrids, and Other Fantastical Beings*, edited by Marc Lucht and Donna Yarri, 269–83. Lanham, MD: Lexington, 2010.
Zbytovský, Štěpán. "Formen des Grotesken in der frühexpressionistischen Lyrik." *Germanistica Pragensia* 22 (2012): 143–79.
Ziener, Birgit. *Avantgarde avant la lettre: Strategien literarischer Popularisierung im Werk von Otto Julius Bierbau*. Vienna: Böhlau, 2022.
Zimmer, Christina. *Leerkörper: Untersuchung zu Franz Kafkas Entwurf einer medialen Lebensform*. Würzburg: Königshausen & Neumann, 2006.
Zimmermann, Hans Dieter. "Gegenwelten: Hugo Ball und Oskar Panizza: Rom und Anti-Rom." *Hugo Ball Almanach* 9 (2018): 70–87.
Ziolkowski, Theodore. "Talking Dogs: The Caninization of Literature." In *Varieties of Literary Thematics*, edited by Theodore Ziolkowski, 86–122. Princeton, NJ: Princeton University Press, 1983.
Zipes, Jack. "The Operated German as Operated Jew." *New German Critique* 21 (1980): 47–61.
———. *The Operated Jew: Two Tales of Anti-Semitism*. New York: Routledge, 1991.
Zumbusch, Cornelia. "The Metamorphoses of Ottilie: Goethe's Wahlverwandtschaften and the Botany of the Eighteenth Century." *European Romantic Review* 28, no. 1 (2017): 7–20.

INDEX

"Die Abenteuer der Sylvester-Nacht" (Hoffmann), 213n12
ableism, 4, 91, 174
Abschied von München (Panizza), 25
aesthetics, 6, 9–10; of the grotesque, 16, 19, 182n2, 183n6, 186n13; of modernism, 178n3; vegetal, 34, 78. See also *das Groteske* (aesthetic style in art and literature); *die Groteske* (literary microgenre)
Agamben, Giorgio, 203n9
Alraune (Ewers), 193n40, 196n17
Althusser, Louis, 206n3
ambiguity, 1, 35–36, 65, 95, 172, 215n27. See also language; narration
anarchism, 23–24, 26, 31, 187n2
animals: and humans, 89, 153, 174, 175; and language, 203n4, 204n16, 213n14; perspective of, 82–84, 173; in philosophy, 88, 92, 106–7, 120, 203n9; taxonomy of, 48, 89–90, 98. See also apes; dogs; narration; nonhuman figures

animal studies, 82, 176, 177n3
Anthropocene, 175
anthropocentrism, 82, 84, 91, 106, 109; satirizing of, 94. See also Man, paradigm of
antisemitism, 5, 25, 30, 123–25, 211n1; and dogs, 208n6, 209n7; in film, 185n9; in Germany, 147–48, 165, 217n7, 220n30; of Jewish people, 219n21; in Panizza's work, 128, 129–30, 146, 211n2; satirizing of, 152, 168, 180n10; stereotypes of, 131–32, 135, 136, 150, 151, 154, 214n15, 217n8, 220n26. See also Jewish people
apes, 93, 119–20, 203n9, 210n16. See also animals; nonhuman figures
Aristotle, 92, 99, 103–4, 106
Art Forms of Nature (Haeckel), 78. See also Haeckel, Ernst
art nouveau *(Jugendstil)*, 34, 50, 78. See also *Jugend*
arts and crafts, 78

asylum, the, 18, 47, 182n3, 183n5, 201n9; and dogs, 120, 213n13; in *Grotesken*, 15, 34, 36, 38, 73–75, 144–45; and Panizza, 27–28, 173, 183n4, 190n19, 190n23; and sexuality, 45, 49, 58. *See also* institutionalization; "madness"
atheism, 24, 124, 199n3, 210n4
"Aus dem Tagebuch eines Hundes" (Panizza), 82–85, 162, 172, 201n4, 204n11, 205n17; and communication, 91–102, 121, 203n1; dog behavior in, 112, 206n4, 207n11; human taxonomy in, 89–91, 212n9; illustrations in, 120, 201n3; narration of, 87–89, 102–8, 116, 117–18. *See also* dogs
"Aus dem Tagebuch eines Orangenbaumes" (Ewers), 72, 197n17, 216n4
authority figures, 13–14, 15, 44–45; institutionalization of, 34, 79; language use by, 17–18; unreliability of, 16, 59, 62–63, 125, 135–36, 145, 199n5. *See also* Man, paradigm of; medicine; physicians; police; priests; religious institutions; state, the
autoeroticism, 38, 93. *See also* masturbation
"Die Automate" (Hoffmann), 215n22

bachelorhood, 49–50, 67, 98, 196n16, 198n27; and sexuality, 43, 45
Barbin, Herculine, 145
Bavaria, 23–24, 68–69, 196n10
"Beer Hall Putsch," 24, 216n6
Benjamin, Walter, 6, 20–21, 26, 173, 179n5, 221n39
"Ein Bericht für eine Akademie" (Kafka), 119–20, 183n5, 209n12
"Die betrunkenen Blumen und der geflügelte Ottokar" (Friedlaender), 197n17

"[Der] Beweis, daß die Deutschen [dennoch] Menschen sind" (Friedlaender), 168
Bierbaum, Otto Julius, 21, 27, 219n23
biopolitics, 1, 4–7, 22, 75, 125, 172; of the body, 165; consequences of, 170, 174; and sexuality, 17–18, 39. *See also* asylum, the; institutionalization; state, the
Birnbaum, Nathan, 157, 218n16
Black studies, 177n4
Black-White-Red (Friedlaender), 217n12. *See also* German flag colors
blasphemy, 17, 19, 27, 188n7, 189n17; prosecution of, 20, 39, 196n10. *See also* censorship
body, the, 42, 183n7; and communication, 83, 92, 100–101; control of, 121, 125; and identity, 99, 112, 135, 158; and otherness, 120, 129–30, 135, 158; separation from mind of, 103–7; and sex, 58, 97; transformation of, 160–62, 165
botany, 50, 68–69, 71, 73, 200n3. *See also* Linnaeus, Carl; plants; science
Brod, Max, 31, 178n7, 203n3
Buber, Martin, 30, 157, 194n43
Byatt, A. S., 78, 200n2

cabaret, 5, 10, 11, 12, 21, 22; censoring of, 184n5; *Grotesken* and, 28, 60, 173, 180n11, 222n1; performance in, 30, 173; and satire, 187n2
Das Cabinet des Dr. Caligari, 178n3, 183n5
cannibalism, 155, 218n15
capitalism, 25, 99
Cartesian *cogito*, 87–88, 104–6, 194n45; and the "animal machine," 134, 139, 203n9, 215n22

Catholic Church, 25, 67, 69, 70, 72, 188n7. *See also* Christianity; priests; religious institutions
censorship, 1, 4–5, 7; avoidance of, 84, 120; of education, 68–69, 199n3; futility of, 79; of *Grotesken*, 19–22, 27, 32, 173; of knowledge, 73, 74–75; and language use, 16, 28, 34–36, 53–55, 63–64, 113; laws of, 39–41, 42–43, 51, 70, 184n8, 196n10; paradox of, 59, 67; of politics, 24–25; of science, 69; of sexuality, 17–18, 37–39; of slander, 197n24; and voice, 82. *See also* blasphemy; "crime against nature"; lèse-majesté
Cervantes, Miguel de, 84
Christianity, 49, 56, 65, 151–52; conversion to, 134; imagery from, 42, 66. *See also* Catholic Church; Protestantism; religious institutions
church. *See* religious institutions
circumcision, 155, 215n25; and identity, 142, 150, 157–58, 160–61, 163
class, 42, 48–49, 65
climate change, 175
colonialism, 2, 25, 174–75, 177n4, 200n3; and language, 204n10; and race, 130, 149
comedy, 5–6, 9, 10–11, 21, 173–74, 180n11; in Friedlaender's work, 29, 169; and Kafka, 178n7, 186n10. *See also* horror; laughter
communication, 16, 82–85, 107–8; animal, 91–92, 104, 117; failure of, 88, 94–95, 106, 111; human, 90, 121, 204n10; one-way, 115; sexuality as, 96–97, 100–101, 113. *See also* language; *Sprachkrise*
Conrad, Michael Georg, 188n9. *See also Münchner Moderne* (Munich Moderns)
Copernican revolution, 2, 77, 79, 107

"Der Corsetten-Fritz" (Panizza), 196n4, 204n14
"crime against nature," 37–38, 46, 53, 54, 70; in Germany, 195n2 (chap. 4); of plants, 78; and sexuality, 145. *See also* censorship
"Ein criminelles Geschlecht," (Panizza), 196n4, 198n27, 204n14
Cynics, 120–21, 209nn13–14

Dadaism, 16, 178n3, 194n43
Dämmrungsstücke (Panizza), 179n5, 181n13
Darwin, Charles, 2, 3, 46–48, 65, 90; on communication, 204n10; impact of, 34, 77, 107, 113, 175; teaching of, 69, 199nn2–3. *See also* science
Darwin, Erasmus, 50
death, 83, 85, 92, 207n11, 218n14; knowledge of, 102, 103, 121, 205n17
decolonization, 177n4, 222n2, 223n6
"degenerate art," 20–21, 185n6
Deleuze, Gilles, 22, 186n15
Derrida, Jacques, 203n4
Diogenes, 120–21, 209n13
disease, 25, 27, 47, 92, 153, 198n27
Döblin, Alfred, 181n13, 222n1
dogs, 82–84, 119, 172; behavior of, 110–12, 202n7, 206n4; communication between, 91–92; in human cultures, 208n6–209n7, 209n14, 210n16; meaning of, 117; as narrators, 87–89, 113, 201n6, 202n8; perspective of, 120; in philosophy, 114; and recognition, 203n6. *See also* animals; "Aus dem Tagebuch eines Hundes" (Panizza); "Forschungen eines Hundes" (Kafka); *Für Hunde und andere Menschen* (Friedlaender); "Ich möchte bellen" (Friedlaender); nonhuman figures
Dreyer, Max, 199n2

education, 36, 62, 68–69, 70–74, 199n3
Ego and Its Own, The (Stirner), 25
Der Eigene, 28, 191n27, 194n47
Der Einzige, 30, 194n47
Der Einzige und sein Eigentum (Stirner), 25
Eisenbahnglück oder der Anti-Freud (Friedlaender), 194n45
Elisabeth of Austria (Sisi), 25–26
Engels, Friedrich, 24–25
England, 37, 41, 48, 140–41, 216n3
Die Entdeckung der Seele (Jäger), 153
environmental crisis, 175
epistemology, 4, 83, 84, 89; crisis of, 102, 111, 116, 121, 172; foundations of, 92; and the senses, 113
eugenics, 2, 47, 48
evolution, theory of, 46–47, 69, 77, 203n8, 206n4, 210n16. *See also* Darwin, Charles; Haeckel, Ernst; science
Ewers, Hanns Heinz, 5, 6, 28–29, 112, 173, 191n25; censorship of, 20–21; and film, 222n1; and Friedlaender, 193n41; influences on, 24, 179n5, 185n8, 192n32; language use by, 16, 186n15; politics of, 192n35–193n39, 195n2 (chap. 4); sexuality of, 191n27, 196n16; travels of, 192n30; works of, 193n40, 197n17. *See also* "Aus dem Tagebuch eines Orangenbaumes" (Ewers); "Die Petition" (Ewers)
exceptionalism, 2, 48, 175. *See also* Man, paradigm of
exposure, physical (*Entblößung*), 94–97, 99, 112–13, 205n17, 209n12

fairy tales, 154, 213n11, 213n12
fantastic, literary, 10, 179n6, 186n12
Zur Farbenlehre (Goethe), 217n12
fascism, 24, 123, 174

Faust (Goethe), 117, 164
femininity, 50, 145. *See also* women
fetishism, 18, 184n8, 204n14
Feuerbach, Ludwig, 24
Fichte, Johann Gottlieb, 104–5, 206n3
film, 10, 16, 22, 28–29, 173; antisemitic, 185n7; censoring of, 189n17; grotesque genre of, 178n3, 180n11, 183n5, 193n40, 215n22, 222n1
"Final Solution," 123. *See also* Holocaust; "Jewish Question"
"*foetor judaicus,*" 153, 169, 217n8
Fontane, Theodor, 27
"Forschungen eines Hundes" (Kafka), 82, 83, 109–10, 201n3, 203n3; canine narrator of, 110–16, 119, 121, 203n1, 206n7, 207n10; food and hunger in, 207n11, 208n13
Foucault, Michel, 17–18, 35, 182n3, 189n16. *See also* biopolitics
Frankenstein, 131, 166, 212n8, 213n12, 215n22. *See also* monstrous, the
fraternity, 152, 162, 197n17, 216n4
free will, 103, 115, 119, 121
Freikorps, 216n6
Freud, Sigmund, 1–3, 24, 38, 79, 113, 208n12; satirizing of, 160, 194n45, 219n23; and the unconscious, 107, 206n7
Friedlaender, Salomo, 5, 6, 11, 29–30, 124, 173, 193n41–194n45; and animals, 204n16; censoring of, 20–21; definition of *die Groteske* of, 170–71; and Ewers, 193n41; influences on, 24, 152, 221n32; and the "Jewish Question," 128, 220n30; language use by, 16, 183n6, 186n15, 218n14; and laughter, 125, 174, 178n8; and nationalism, 221n31; politics of, 164–65, 168–69, 217n12, 219n23, 220n28; publications

of, 180n8, 194n47, 194n50, 210n3, 217n12; religious beliefs of, 210n4; and science, 222n1. *See also* "Der operierte Goj: Ein Gegenstück zu Panizzas operiertem Jud" (Friedlaender)
Fundvogel: Die Geschichte einer Wandlung (Ewers), 192n36
Für Hunde und andere Menschen (Friedlaender), 204n16
"Für 'Petroleumdichter'" (Panizza), 199n1, 209n13

Galerie der Phantasten, 28, 179n5, 185n8
Gehlen, Arnold, 206n4
gender, 4, 25, 43, 91; binariness of, 72, 98, 145, 214n15; destabilization of, 204n14; and oppression, 174–75; and plants, 50, 56, 197n17; stereotypes of, 112. *See also* Man, paradigm of; masculinity; women
genocide, 145, 222n2
German Empire. *See* Wilhelmine Empire (*Kaiserreich*)
German flag colors, 154, 217n12, 218n14
German Jewish studies, 128, 175, 177n3, 223n5
Germany, 7, 23, 26, 140, 217n12; censorship in, 20, 28; education in, 69; Jewish community in, 124, 147; modernism in, 27, 28; national identity of, 144; reception of *Grotesken* in, 178n8. *See also* Third Reich; Weimar Republic; Wilhelmine Empire (*Kaiserreich*)
Gesellschaft für modernes Leben, 182n3, 188n9. *See also Münchner Moderne* (Munich Moderns)
gestures, 51, 112, 209n13, 220n26; censoring of, 63; communication through, 90, 92, 95, 97, 100, 202n7; and identity, 127, 142, 162; and the limits of language, 53, 57, 59, 204n7. *See also* imitation; mimicry; performance
Goethe, Johann Wolfgang von, 117, 164, 213n11, 216n3, 217n12
das Groteske (aesthetic style in art and literature), 9–10, 178n1, 178n3, 180n9, 180n11, 183n6
die Groteske (literary microgenre), 1, 6–7, 9–12, 13, 172–75; and censorship, 19, 32, 82; characteristics of, 33, 36, 59, 65, 125; decline of, 21; and defamiliarization, 84, 95–96, 107, 109; definition of, 170–71, 179nn6–7, 180n11; and language, 139, 142, 183n6; marginalization of, 22, 186n13; narrative critiques of, 4; reception of, 166–67, 222n1; and sexuality, 112, 183n7; themes of, 2–3, 75–76, 144–46, 168, 222n1
Grotesken (literary texts), 1, 5, 12, 178n2; authors of, 21, 178n2, 181n14, 185n9, 186n10, 186n12, 193n39; censoring of, 19, 22; examples of, 181n14; political context of, 23, 186n10; popularity of, 10; publishers of, 184n1
grotesque, the. *See das Groteske* (aesthetic style in art and literature); *die Groteske* (literary microgenre); *Grotesken* (literary texts)
Guattari, Félix, 22, 186n15
Gulliver's Travels (Swift), 84

Haeckel, Ernst, 69, 77–78, 90, 199nn2–3, 203n8
Hebrew, 141, 147, 151, 160, 162
Herzl, Theodor, 218n16, 219n21
heterosexuality, 51, 98
Hoberg, Reinhold, 201n3
Hochdeutsch, 128, 136–41, 143, 144, 157

Hoffmann, E. T. A., 10, 20, 84, 179n5, 213n12, 215n22
von Hofmannsthal, Hugo, 3
Holocaust, 5, 11, 21, 167, 186n10
homosexuality, 98. *See also* same-sex relationships; sexuality
horror, 9, 10–11, 29, 179n7, 214n15; experience of, 101, 112, 119; and laughter, 1, 13, 125, 170, 180n11. *See also* comedy
Horst Wessel (Ewers), 29, 192n37
human figures: behavior of, 84, 96, 99, 119–20; evolutionary inferiority of, 206n4; humanity of, 168–69, 170–71; satirizing of, 107; taxonomy of, 48, 89–91, 109–10. *See also* anthropocentrism; Man, paradigm of; marginalized human figures; narration
humanism, 129, 135, 166, 168–69
human rights, 2, 3, 129, 172
humor. *See* comedy
"Der Hungerkünstler" (Kafka), 114, 207n10. *See also* "Forschungen eines Hundes" (Kafka)

"Ich möchte bellen" (Friedlaender), 204n16
identity, 124–25, 128–29, 130, 132; blending of, 219n17; "essence" of, 134–35, 153, 164–65, 166; Jewish, 156–58, 220n30; and language, 139, 142–43, 146; national, 140, 144, 148; stereotypes of, 149–50
imitation, 124, 136–38, 140, 143–44, 204n10. *See also* mimicry
In der Strafkolonie (Kafka), 112, 201n4
"Indianer-Gedanken" (Panizza), 145
individualism, 24, 30, 31
"In spe" (Friedlaender), 169
institutionalization, 6, 14–15, 18, 27, 180n11; of authority figures, 34, 36, 73–74, 79, 172; as a characteristic of *Grotesken*, 59, 113, 125, 146; in Kafka's work, 31; from loss of mind, 102, 106, 120; of the marginalized, 133, 144, 145; and power, 132; and social control, 49, 51, 58, 75. *See also* asylum, the
intersex, 144, 145, 174, 204n14, 216n31
In the Penal Colony (Kafka), 112, 204n1
"Investigations/Researches of a Dog" (Kafka). *See* "Forschungen eines Hundes" (Kafka)
Ivanhoe (Scott), 154

Jewish people: "assimilation" of, 127, 131–33, 136, 139, 140–41, 143–44, 147–48, 221n31; assimilation to, 156, 160–63; and dogs, 208n6, 209n7; in Germany, 123–25, 157–58, 165–66, 211n1; marginalization of, 21, 153; ridicule of, 180n10; and self-hatred, 219n21; stereotypes of, 130, 135, 151, 212n9, 216n1, 217n10. *See also Ostjudentum*
"Jewish Question," 3, 123
journals and magazines, 70, 184n1, 188n9, 192n30, 193n41, 194n47, 201n3. *See also Der Eigene; Der Einzige; Jugend; Simplicissimus*
Judaism, 1, 3, 124, 147, 159
"Der Jude ein Pionier des Deutschtums" (Ewers), 29, 192n36
Jugend, 67, 70, 78, 188n9. *See also* art nouveau (*Jugendstil*)

Kafka, Franz, 5, 6, 14–15, 31–32; animals in the work of, 87, 89, 117–21, 177n3, 208n6, 209n7; censoring of, 20–22, 201n4; humor of, 5, 178n7, 186n10; language use by, 16, 108, 116, 222n1; literary themes of, 60, 81–85, 173,

182n2, 183n5; reception of, 23, 177n6, 181n13; sexuality of, 196n16. *See also* "Forschungen eines Hundes" (Kafka)
Kant, Immanuel, 30, 124, 152, 174, 181n14, 194n44
kleine Formen, 10, 186n15
Krafft-Ebing, Richard von, 27, 38, 74
Kraus, Karl, 37, 186n12
Kulturkampf, 69, 70, 77
Kunstformen der Natur (Haeckel), 78
"Kunst und Polizei" (Panizza), 184n3

Lacan, Jacques, 203n9, 206n3
Der lachende Hiob und andere Grotesken (Friedlaender), 180n8
Lang, Fritz, 215n22
Langen, Albert, 181n13, 184n1
language, 3–4, 6, 22; ambiguity of, 15–16, 19, 63–65, 164; and animals, 203n9, 204n16, 209n12; and censorship, 35–36, 54–55, 72, 74; and colonialism, 204n10; failure of, 92–93, 94–96, 100–102, 111, 116; force of, 172–73; and identity, 140–44, 146; imitation and mimicry of, 136–40, 204n10, 212n10, 214n19; learning of, 124, 127, 147, 160–62, 212n10; limits of, 52–54, 82–84, 88; loss of, 103; multilingual use of, 46, 128–29, 154, 186n15, 219n17; and otherness, 130–31; and power, 107, 182n3; regulation of, 7, 17–18, 58–59; and sexuality, 59, 113; and subjectivity, 206n3; unreliability of, 106, 199n1. *See also* communication; Hebrew; *Hochdeutsch*; performance; *Sprachkrise*; Yiddish
Laughing Job and Other Grotesques, The (Friedlaender), 180n8
laughter, 11, 22, 30, 179n6, 180n11; in Friedlaender's work, 166, 170, 178n8; inappropriateness of, 61, 125; in Kafka's work, 178n7; politics of, 174. *See also* comedy
"Ein Leben" (Kafka), 118–19
Lebensreform, 28, 191n28, 200n3
lèse-majesté, 17, 19, 26, 39, 196n10. *See also* censorship
Lessing, Gotthold Ephraim, 151
"Die Letzten – die Ersten" (Friedlaender), 169
Levinas, Emmanuel, 203n6
Lex Heinze, 40, 60, 70. *See also* censorship
Das Liebeskonzil (Panizza), 20, 27, 34, 184n3, 189n16; censorship of, 40, 189n17; devil in, 117, 220n26; trial of, 166, 208n5
"Life, A" (Kafka), 118–19
Linnaeus, Carl, 48, 50, 72, 78, 89–90, 98. *See also* botany
London, 37, 41, 42, 196n12
Love Council, The (Panizza). See *Das Liebeskonzil* (Panizza)
"Loves of Plants, The" (Darwin), 50
"Die lüderliche Nase" (Friedlaender), 169

"madness," 14–15, 18, 73–75, 172, 182n3–183n4; in art, 185n6; and dogs, 120, 133, 210n16, 213n13. *See also* asylum, the; institutionalization
magazines. *See* journals and magazines
Man, paradigm of, 2–4, 13, 150–51, 172, 175, 177n4; belonging to, 143; challenge to, 34, 46, 48, 77, 107; decentering of, 222n2; exclusion from, 5, 106, 129–33, 169, 171; inversion of, 89–91, 93, 110, 118, 156; and nature, 78–79; satirizing of, 94, 134, 174. *See also* New Human

Mängelwesen, 206n4
Marcus, Ernst, 30
marginalized human figures, 1, 2–3, 125, 172, 207n9; dehumanization of, 132–33, 144–46, 170–71; exclusion of, 174; perspectives of, 4, 13, 14–15, 18, 173; taxonomies of, 48. *See also* human figures; Jewish people; "madness"; otherness
Marx, Karl, 24
masculinity, 48, 72, 134, 156, 163, 174
masturbation, 18, 37–39, 49, 51–54, 67; anxieties about, 50, 59; legality of, 184n8; stigmatization of, 198n25. *See also* autoeroticism
media, 10, 22, 194n44. *See also* cabaret; film; journals and magazines; radio
medicine, 127, 146, 174. *See also* authority figures; physicians
Metropolis (Lang), 215n22
militarism, 25, 30, 152, 194n45
mimicry, 124, 131–32, 138–39, 204n10, 212n10, 220n26. *See also* imitation
modernism, 9, 10, 16, 27; authors of, 185n8; crisis of, 117; language crisis (*Sprachkrise*) of, 18, 82; in literature, 178n1, 178n3, 187n4; "madness" in, 182n3, 190n23. *See also* journals and magazines; *Münchner Moderne* (Munich Moderns)
modernist art, 3, 178n3, 182n3
monstrous, the, 129–31, 144, 155, 212n7, 213n12; fear of, 218n15; reproduction of, 216n3
morality: Christian, 56; crimes against, 37, 39, 54, 57, 69–70, 196n10; critique of, 34; enforcement of, 61; individual, 24, 31; sexual, 98–99; threats to, 78–79. *See also* censorship; "crime against nature"

Müller, Georg, 28, 181n13, 184n1
Müller, Hermann, 199n2
Münchner Moderne (Munich Moderns), 25, 27, 166, 188n9, 201n3
Mynona. *See* Friedlaender, Salomo

Nachtstücke (Hoffmann), 179n5
narration, 6, 13–14, 182n1; authority of, 15, 59, 62–63; canine, 82, 84, 107, 109, 115–16, 201n6, 202n8; end of, 103; and language, 87–88, 95, 102; theatrical, 60; untrustworthiness of, 83, 106, 113, 125, 135–36, 145, 172, 212n6
Nathan, der Weise (Lessing), 151
nationalism, 25, 30, 125, 128, 166, 211n2. *See also* identity
Native Americans, 144, 145, 149
natural sciences, 69, 77, 83, 89. *See also* botany
Nazi Party, 21, 29, 192n36. *See also Sturmabteilung* (SA)
Nazis, 3, 5, 202n7; antisemitism of, 135, 168–69; and censorship, 20–21, 173; and the grotesque, 185n7; and the "Jewish Question," 123, 166–67; satirizing of, 29, 30, 152, 163
Der Nazi und der Friseur (Hilsenrath), 211n1
Neue Tierpsychologie (New Animal Psychology), 202n7
New Church, 45. *See also* Swedenborg, Emmanuel
New Human (*neuer Mensch*), 2, 24
"Eine N[...]geschichte" (Panizza), 144
Nietzsche, Friedrich, 2, 3, 24, 187n4
Night Pieces, The (Hoffmann), 179n5
nihilism, 24, 199n3
nonhuman figures, 3, 10, 172, 175–76, 177n3; and language, 204n16; and "madness," 14–15, 133; as narrators,

87–88, 107, 118; parallels with humans of, 46–47, 53, 78; perspectives of, 4, 13–14, 18, 83, 109; plants as, 38–39, 56–57; sexuality of, 34; taxonomy of, 48. *See also* animals; apes; "Aus dem Tagebuch eines Hundes" (Panizza); dogs; "Forschungen eines Hundes" (Kafka); "Die Petition" (Ewers); plants; "Das Verbrechen in Tavistock-Square" (Panizza)

Nordau, Max, 185n6, 207n9

November Revolution (Bavaria), 23

Nuremberg Laws, 29

Nur für Herrschaften: Un-Freud-ige Grotesken (Friedlaender), 194n45

On the Origin of Species (Darwin), 46–47

ontology, 4, 83, 111, 116, 172

"Der operierte Goj: Ein Gegenstück zu Panizzas operiertem Jud" (Friedlaender), 124, 147–48, 172, 210n3, 219n20, 219n22; context of, 221n32; protagonists of, 149–56; reception of, 166–67; transformation in, 156–63, 164–65; wedding scene in, 220n27

"Der operirte Jud'" (Panizza), 124, 127–33, 172, 211nn1–3; concept of the soul in, 134, 153, 215n22; and language, 136–44, 212n10, 213n14, 215nn23–24; narrator of, 212n6; reception of, 221n39; satire in, 135, 146; transformation in, 214n15, 215n25; wedding scene in, 213nn11–12, 220n27

Original Sin, 46, 73. *See also* Christianity

Ostjudentum, 157, 207, 218n16, 219n21, 220n30. *See also* Jewish people; Yiddish

otherness, 130, 133, 176, 212n9; construction of, 150, 156, 159, 216n1; fear of, 132. *See also* marginalized human figures

pacifism, 20, 30

Panizza, Oskar, 5, 6, 9, 25–28, 178n1, 181n13, 200n2, 209n13; academic study of, 189n16, 211nn2–3; antisemitism of, 125, 221n39; arrest and trial of, 34, 37, 173, 208n5; censoring of, 20–21, 24, 184n3; and dogs, 117–18; on identity, 144–46, 148, 166; influences on, 78, 179n5, 187n5, 189n12; institutionalization of, 74, 189n18–190n19; language use by, 16, 137, 139, 144, 162, 186n15, 215nn23–24; and "madness," 182n3–183n4; mental health of, 190nn22–23; as playwright, 60; politics of, 187n2; as a psychiatrist, 38, 107; publication of, 192n32; and religion, 124, 188n7, 210n4, 222n1; and self-censorship, 28, 191n24; and sexuality, 49, 196n16, 204n14; status of, 81, 185n8. *See also* "Aus dem Tagebuch eines Hundes" (Panizza); *Das Liebeskonzil* (Panizza); "Der operirte Jud'" (Panizza); "Das Verbrechen in Tavistock-Square" (Panizza)

Panizza Society, 20, 184n4, 221n39

Pavlov, Ivan, 83, 114, 119, 202n7

performance, 11, 13, 29, 37; of identity, 139, 142, 144, 162; and narrative, 59–60, 63; in place of language, 51–54, 55, 57–59. *See also* gestures; *Sprachkrise*

"Die Petition" (Ewers), 34, 36, 66–69, 195n1, 199n1; and authority, 199n5; and censorship, 73–74, 199n3; language use in, 69–73; and "madness," 75–76

philistine, the, 11–12, 13, 180n10

physicians, 14–15, 63, 145, 166, 172. See also authority figures; medicine
"phytopoetics," 201nn8–9
"plant blindness," 198n28
plants, 34, 36, 77–79; censoring of, 73; collecting of, 200n3; exclusion of, 174; grafting of, 216n3; and humans, 201n8–9; masturbation by, 51–54, 55–56; perspective of, 84; reproduction of, 195n2 (chap. 4), 203n8, 219n19; sexuality of, 38–39, 50–51, 71–72, 200n4; smell of, 153; taxonomy of, 48, 57, 98. See also "Die betrunkenen Blumen und der geflügelte Ottokar" (Friedlaender); nonhuman figures; "Die Petition" (Ewers); "Das Verbrechen in Tavistock-Square" (Panizza)
plant studies, 50, 177n3, 198n28, 200n4
Poe, Edgar Allan, 10, 179n5
poetry, 10, 12, 16, 178n3, 181n14
police: authority of, 43–45, 56; and censorship, 17, 34–35, 39–41, 74; satire of, 37, 42, 60–62, 198n27; unreliability of, 63, 172; and witnessing, 113. See also authority figures
posthumanism, 175
poverty, 47, 65
priests, 3, 14–15, 34, 36, 66–69, 172. See also authority figures; religious institutions
Der Probekandidat (Dreyer), 199n2
Protestantism, 188n7
Der Prozess (Kafka), 81, 118, 178n7, 183n5, 197n24
Prussia, 69, 150
pseudoscience, 4, 48, 90, 175; of race, 130, 135, 148. See also eugenics
Psichopatia criminalis (Panizza), 27, 74, 190n21, 190n23
psychiatry, 4, 18, 38, 113, 146, 190n19
psychoanalysis, 1, 3, 17, 89, 159, 203n9

psychology, 17, 107, 182n3, 202n7
Psychopathia sexualis (Krafft-Ebing), 27, 38, 74
publishers, 21, 40, 184n1, 184n8

queer identities, 50–51. See also gender; intersex; same-sex relationships

race, 91, 129–30, 148, 149, 164–65; and the soul, 153; stereotypes of, 216n1, 217n10, 220n26
racial passing, 145, 212n10
racism, 28, 129–30, 132, 135, 174–75, 194n45; and identity, 135, 144–45; and language, 204n10
radio, 10, 11, 30, 194n44
Reimann, Hans, 21, 193n39
religion, 25, 45; anxiety about, 46–47; and conversion, 161; critique of, 65, 222n1; decline of, 77; and identity, 140; and oppression, 174–75; and Panizza, 188n7; satire of, 89–90. See also atheism; Christianity; Judaism
religious institutions: authority of, 25, 33–34, 77; and censorship, 74–75; critique of, 4, 43, 65; separation from state of, 70. See also Catholic Church
"Report for an Academy, A" (Kafka). See "Ein Bericht für eine Akademie" (Kafka)
Röhm-Putsch, 29, 192n38, 216n6
romanticism, 9, 180nn10–11, 222n1
"Das rothe Haus" (Panizza), 74
Russian Revolution, 23

same-sex relationships, 3, 18, 28, 38, 195n2 (chap. 4); anxieties about, 50; legality of, 184n8; marginalization of, 21, 49; oppression of, 174; in Panizza's work, 144, 145, 204n14

"Der Sandmann" (Hofmann), 215n22
satire, 1, 5, 11, 172, 179nn6–7, 180n10;
of censorship, 54; censorship of, 20;
and dogs, 120–21, 209n14; of human
behavior, 84; of identity, 135, 142–43,
168; of institutions, 83; of knowledge,
106; language of, 22, 41; of race, 149;
and reproduction, 146; and sexual
taboos, 17. *See also* comedy; laughter
"Scandal at the Convent, A" (Panizza).
See "Ein skandalöser Fall" (Panizza)
Scheerbart, Paul, 20, 21, 184n2, 185n9
Scholem, Gershom, 5, 21, 125, 166, 173
Schöpferische Indifferenz (Friedlaender), 30
science, 1, 2, 4, 174, 180n11; and aesthetics, 78; anxiety about, 34, 46–47; censorship of, 36, 73; and race, 130, 132, 135, 148; and religion, 65; satire of, 89–90, 169; teaching of, 68–69; and truth, 198n28; utopia of, 166. *See also* botany; Darwin, Charles; evolution, theory of; natural sciences; pseudoscience
science fiction, 222n1
Scott, Walter, 154
sexism, 174
sexuality, 6, 16–18, 28, 180n11, 183n7;
as communication, 96–97, 100–101;
control of, 37–39, 59, 75, 77, 107;
dehumanization of, 133, 145; human,
121, 204n14, 208n6–209n7, 208n12;
oppression of, 174–75; outlets for, 49,
67; of plants, 34, 36, 50–51, 71–72, 78,
195n2 (chap. 4); religious beliefs about,
45; and smell, 92, 153, 206n7; speaking about, 35–36, 59, 63, 73, 195n3;
stereotypes of, 112; and vision, 113. *See also* exposure, physical (*Entblößung*);
gender; same-sex relationships

sex work, 40, 98, 196n4, 196n16, 204n14, 212n9; regulation of, 18, 184n8
Shoah. *See* Holocaust
Simplicissimus, 184n9, 188n9, 216n4
"Ein skandalöser Fall" (Panizza), 145, 196n4, 204n14, 215n30
slander, 197n24
smell/scent, 91–92, 100, 113, 199n1; of flowers, 71, 78; and recognition, 140, 153, 169, 203n6, 217n8. *See also* "*foetor judaicus*"
Social Darwinism, 46, 48
sociopolitical criticism, 1, 13, 14, 18, 22; censorship of, 19; of grotesque art, 180n9; of Weimar Germany, 30. *See also* satire
soul, the: of animals, 84, 91–92, 100–101, 103–4, 106; exterminator of, 170, 174; of humans, 99, 117; and identity, 129, 133–35, 138–39, 140, 212n9, 213n14, 216n3; smell of, 111, 153; transformation of, 160–62
Species Plantarum (Linnaeus), 48
Sprachkrise, 3, 16, 18, 33, 36, 53–54; and communication, 82–83, 100, 107, 139; and meaning, 59, 65, 88–89, 93, 95–96, 106. *See also* language
state, the: authority of, 33–34, 77; and censorship, 74–75; critique of, 4, 36, 43, 65; "madness" of, 73, 183n4; separation from church of, 70. *See also* biopolitics; police; Weimar Republic; Wilhelmine Empire (*Kaiserreich*)
Stirner, Max, 24–25, 28, 30, 74–75, 187nn3–5
Stirner-Bund, 30, 194n47
Der Student von Prag (Ewers), 28, 192n31
Sturmabteilung (SA), 191n27, 192nn37–38, 216n6. *See also* "Beer Hall Putsch"; Nazi Party; Nazis; *Röhm-Putsch*

surrealism, 194n43
swastika, 151–52
Swedenborg, Emmanuel, 45, 47, 56, 62
Swift, Jonathan, 84
Systema Naturae (Linnaeus), 48

theater, 10, 12, 178n3, 181n14; censorship of, 40; narrative strategy of, 60; postwar, 186n10. *See also* cabaret
Third Reich, 24, 173
Tiersprechschule Asra, 202n7
"Tödliche Anprobe" (Friedlaender), 169–70
"Totenlärm" (Friedlaender), 169
Trial, The (Kafka). *See Der Prozess* (Kafka)
Tuchmann, Emil, 21, 184n4, 221n39
Tucholsky, Kurt, 21, 26, 81, 173, 221n32, 221n39
Twain, Mark, 84, 202n8

Überbrettl, 28. *See also* cabaret
Übermensch. *See* Man, paradigm of
unconscious, the, 79, 103, 106–7, 121, 210n16. *See also* Freud, Sigmund; psychoanalysis
Untermensch. *See* Man, paradigm of: exclusion from

"Die vegetabilische Vaterschaft" (Friedlaender), 197n17
"vegetable," 78, 200n5
"Das Verbrechen in Tavistock-Square" (Panizza), 34–35, 75–76, 172; and censorship, 37–39, 40–41, 51–59; influence of, 66; narration of, 59–65, 198n27; police in, 42–43, 48–50, 197n24
violence, 24, 28, 150, 222n2; of police, 43; sexual, 204n11

vision, 92, 112–13, 198n28, 199n1
Visionen (Panizza), 179n5
visual arts, 9, 10, 180n11. *See also* art nouveau *(Jugendstil)*

"Das Wachsfigurenkabinett" (Panizza), 215n24
Die Wahlverwandtschaften (Goethe), 213n11, 216n3
Weimar Republic, 10–11, 24, 154, 173, 216n6; antisemitism in, 165; censorship in, 20; flag of, 217n12, 218n14; *Grotesken* in, 29–30; Jewish population of, 123–24, 212n10; Nazis in, 152; satirizing of, 187n2. *See also* Germany; state, the
Wilde, Oscar, 185n6, 195n2 (chap. 4)
Wilhelm I (Kaiser), 23
Wilhelm II (Kaiser), 20, 23, 24, 26, 41; satirizing of, 187n2, 191n23
Wilhelmine Empire *(Kaiserreich)*, 24, 25, 154, 217n12; censorship in, 19, 20, 40–41, 173; Jewish population of, 123–24, 128; policing of, 34. *See also* Germany; state, the
women, 3, 132, 174, 196n17, 212n9
Woolf, Virginia, 84, 196n12, 202n8
World's Fair (Paris), 78, 200n3
World War I, 10–11, 23, 29, 40, 217n12
World War II, 11

Yiddish, 123, 207n9, 211n1, 218n16; and identity, 128, 138–39, 143, 147, 157–58, 161–62; stereotypes of, 136

Zionism, 125, 147–48, 163–65, 207n9, 218n16, 219n21; criticism of, 221n32; satirizing of, 220n28, 220n30

Joela Jacobs is Assistant Professor of German Studies at the University of Arizona. Her research engages with plants, animals, the environment, Jewish identity, science, gender, and sexuality in Germanophone literature and culture since the nineteenth century. She cofounded and maintains the Literary and Cultural Plant Studies Network.

For Indiana University Press

Tony Brewer, Artist and Book Designer
Dan Crissman, Editorial Director and Acquisitions Editor
Anna Francis, Assistant Acquisitions Editor
Anna Garnai, Editorial Assistant
Brenna Hosman, Production Coordinator
Katie Huggins, Production Manager
David Miller, Lead Project Manager/Editor
Dan Pyle, Online Publishing Manager
Pamela Rude, Senior Artist and Book Designer
Stephen Williams, Assistant Director of Marketing